# the espn effect

PETER LANG
New York • Bern • Frankfurt • Berlin
Brussels • Vienna • Oxford • Warsaw

# the espn effect

## Exploring the Worldwide Leader in Sports

EDITED BY
**John McGuire
Greg G. Armfield
Adam Earnheardt**

PETER LANG
New York • Bern • Frankfurt • Berlin
Brussels • Vienna • Oxford • Warsaw

Library of Congress Cataloging-in-Publication Data

The ESPN effect: exploring the worldwide leader in sports /
edited by John McGuire, Greg G. Armfield, Adam Earnheardt.
pages cm
Includes bibliographical references and index.
1. ESPN (Television network)—History. 2. Television broadcasting of sports—History.
I. McGuire, John.
GV742.3.E75    070.4'49796—dc23    2014048991
ISBN 978-1-4331-2601-7 (hardcover)
ISBN 978-1-4331-2600-0 (paperback)
ISBN 978-1-4539-1500-4 (e-book)


Bibliographic information published by **Die Deutsche Nationalbibliothek.**
**Die Deutsche Nationalbibliothek** lists this publication in the "Deutsche
Nationalbibliografie"; detailed bibliographic data are available
on the Internet at http://dnb.d-nb.de/.

The paper in this book meets the guidelines for permanence and durability
of the Committee on Production Guidelines for Book Longevity
of the Council of Library Resources.

© 2015 Peter Lang Publishing, Inc., New York
29 Broadway, 18th floor, New York, NY 10006
www.peterlang.com

Printed in the United States of America

Dr. McGuire would like to thank his mentors in the higher education ranks, Dr. Jeff McCall of DePauw University and Dr. Michael Porter, for their support over the years. Dr. McGuire also dedicates this work to his mother Jane, who put up with a son who was forever talking to himself doing practice play-by-play.

Dr. Armfield would like to thank Dr. Debbie Dougherty, Dr. Michael Kramer, Dr. Michael Porter, and Dr. Michael Stephenson for their continued mentorship and guidance. Dr. Armfield dedicates this project to his parents who have always cheered from the stands and supported his academic and nonacademic pursuits. He also dedicates this to his wife and her ESPN T-shirt that reads "HUSBAND FOR SALE (remote not included)."

Dr. Earnheardt thanks Dr. Andrew Billings (University of Alabama) for early advisement on this project, and Dr. Paul Haridakis (Kent State University) for his guidance. Dr. Earnheardt dedicates this project to fellow sports junkie, and his biggest fan, his mother—Grace—who encouraged his love of all-things sports and media, and taught him the responsibilities of a sports fan.

# Table of Contents

## Section Two: Race, Gender, and the ESPN Effect

## Section Three: Journalism and the ESPN Effect

**Section Four: The ESPN Effect and Its Audience**

**Section Five: The Future of the ESPN Effect**

# Acknowledgments

The editors extend their thanks and gratitude to the many authors in this text for their work and patience during the production of this text. We would also like to thank Mary Savigar and Sophie Appel at Peter Lang for their efforts in bringing this project to reality.

The editors would like to thank Associate Professor Ray Murray of Oklahoma State University for his assistance in reviewing chapters for this text.

# Preface

## You've Come a Long Way, Baby

GREG G. ARMFIELD AND JOHN MCGUIRE

August 1980. A college student moves back into his dorm room for a new semester. Hooking the cable up to his 13-inch black-and-white television, the aspiring sportscaster is about to have a life-changing moment. When he turns on the set and starts spinning around the cable-box dial, he realizes there is a new channel on the system: the sports network with the funny name he had heard and read about for months. There was Canadian football, with 12 guys running around on a field that seemed a mile long. There were replays of college football games morning, noon, and night. Then there was that *SportsCenter* show, with a bunch of guys who seemed to be just out of college. Guys named Mees and Ley and Berman (he was the one who had all the crazy nicknames like "John Mayberry RFD"). There they were, on his television at 1:30 in the morning, talking about nothing but sports. And that college student was absorbing every word. He was not alone. All across the United States, as quickly as cable companies could string or lay cable, children, teenagers, and adults of all ages were getting their first glimpse of this new world of sports programming.

During its first 35 years, ESPN (and its sister networks) has been the preeminent source for sports for millions around the globe. Its never-ending, 24-hour barrage of sports news and programming has cultivated generations of sports consumers, using multiple ESPN platforms for news and entertainment. From having once relied on Australian Rules Football and tractor pulls to attract audiences, ESPN has held the programming rights to every major U.S. professional and collegiate sports league at one time or another during its history. The network went from being a blip in the media universe to a multibillion-dollar enterprise whose reach extended across nearly every continent.

The people on ESPN also became part of U.S. pop culture. In the 1990s, Dick Vitale and Jimmy Valvano showed up on an episode of *The Cosby Show*. Chris Berman played a big part in a Hootie and the Blowfish sports-themed music video. In the 2000s, John Anderson took his *SportsCenter* humor and brought it to the ABC competition show *Wipeout*. ESPN's anchors and personalities are seemingly everywhere in commercials, pitching everything from fast food to diet products. When there is a sports-themed movie made, ESPN seems to be the network covering the fictitious event, from *Kingpin* to *Dodgeball*. ESPN even reimagined itself through its "This is *SportsCenter*" spots, portraying the network's Bristol, Connecticut headquarters as a storybook place where ESPN anchors spend all day working with athletes and team mascots.

ESPN has become a destination for movie stars promoting their latest projects across all of the network's different platforms. In turn, ESPN created an event called "The ESPYS," trying to capitalize on the synergy of bringing celebrities, musicians, and athletes together for a gala awards show that would fill programming slots during the dog days of summer (before National Football League training camps opened).

But there are far more important economic, social, cultural, and mass communication impacts of ESPN that must be studied and debated. That is what this book is about.

## CONCEPTUALIZING THE ESPN EFFECT

If there is one chapter in ESPN's history that perhaps crystalizes the theme of this text, it is the story of *Playmakers*. The fictional episodic series that aired from August to November of 2003 was seen as another step in ESPN's efforts to attract and build viewership beyond its traditional sports events and information programming. The series, in the tradition of prime-time soap operas, proclaimed itself as a realistic look at life in and out of the locker room for members of a professional football team called the Cougars. Fogel (2012) noted the series used many hot-button social issues (e.g., homosexuality, illicit drug use, domestic violence) as plot lines away from the playing field while also discussing on-field controversies (e.g., use of performance-enhancing substances, violent plays resulting in life-threatening injuries). Critics at the time of the series premier noted *Playmakers* bore some resemblance to Oliver Stone's *Any Given Sunday*, examining the darker side of America's most popular sport. Reviews of the series were generally positive from those who critiqued entertainment fare. Tom Shales (2003) of the

*Washington Post* noted, "It's well enough acted and written to sustain interest as a story of professional people under almost preposterous pressure" (p. C1). Ratings (at least for a cable television network) were also seen at exceeding the network's expectations (Peyser, 2004).

One entity saw *Playmakers* as neither positive nor realistic. The National Football League (NFL) viewed the program as an attack on the league (even though the Cougars were never portrayed as being part of the NFL) and those who ran the game. League officials and the league's players' union offered criticism of the show after its debut. Commissioner Paul Tagliabue argued the salacious storylines were a poor reflection on the game and the people who actually play it (Romano, 2003). One NFL team owner, Philadelphia Eagles' Jeffrey Lurie, was especially outspoken in his criticism of the series. Lurie cited one episode that depicted a Cougars' player using cocaine during halftime of a game. Lurie suggested such depictions (even in a fictional story) would end up damaging the reputation of the NFL and its players. Lurie then suggested the following about the corporation that owned ESPN: "Disney's brand is Mickey Mouse, Magic Kingdom. How would they like it if Minnie Mouse was portrayed as Pablo Escobar and the Magic Kingdom as a drug cartel?" (Brookover, 2003, para. 7). Others associated with the sport, most notably former player Deion Sanders, praised the series for its realism.

The portrayal of players was just one of many issues raised about *Playmakers*. The treatment of women was another. While the series offered up gratuitous sex scenes just like other prime-time shows in the soap opera genre, critics attacked *Playmakers* because of the frequent objectification of women in the series, depicting many female characters as one-dimensional, powerless characters that lived only through their athlete husbands or boyfriends.

*Playmakers* even managed to stir up trouble for ESPN with journalistic colleagues. Thea Andrews, who co-hosted an ESPN2 program at the time called *Cold Pizza*, appeared in the series as reporter Samantha Lovett. From a journalistic standpoint, Andrews's participation in the ESPN series while working as a host on an ESPN news program suggested an obvious ethical problem to some in the journalism industry. The Association for Women in Sports Media also complained that the character of Samantha Lovett (and other female reporters depicted in the series) was stereotyped in a way that denigrated those women actually working in the field. ESPN's response justified its stance by arguing other journalists had played fictional roles in entertainment without jeopardizing their credibility and that Andrews was not portraying herself in the show (Overman, 2003).

Despite obtaining the ratings and critical reviews desired for *Playmakers*, ESPN punted the show from its schedule in February 2004 after only one season (Peyser, 2004). Ironically, the decision came only days after the infamous Janet Jackson wardrobe malfunction at Super Bowl XXXVIII, in which one of Ms. Jackson's breasts was exposed during the halftime show. Media observers immediately seized upon this news, suggesting that the NFL had actually forced ESPN to pull the plug on the series (a charge that ESPN denied). One could not help but make that assumption. While *Playmakers* represented experimental programming for ESPN, the network's association with the NFL was its bread and butter. From the network's early days and televising the league's annual draft to ESPN's telecast of its first NFL game in 1987, the network had worked to associate itself with the country's most popular sports league. By 2003, ESPN's financial commitment to the NFL was $600 million a year for rights to nearly 20 games a year plus ancillary programming (Fatsis & Pope, 1998).

Just this one piece of ESPN's 35-year history is instructional on many levels about what we believe is the ESPN effect. First, we note that ESPN is a business, focused on generating revenues for its parent company (Disney). ESPN also sits at the confluence of what McChesney (2004) called the media-sport complex: where media companies such as ESPN are critical business partners with sports leagues such as the NFL, and where the financial success of each entity is highly reliant upon the other. This is true of any sports media entity that partners with professional or collegiate sports leagues for game telecasts. ESPN's actions in the case of *Playmakers* represented the network's true bottom line as a business entity focused on business. As discussed in the early chapters of the text, ESPN's effect on the sports media business has been extraordinary. Yet we also believe ESPN wields influence beyond the bottom line. This is another aspect of the ESPN effect: The pervasiveness of ESPN's branded content across multiple media platforms, delivering programs and information 24 hours a day, 365 days a year, to influence how sports fans think and feel about the people who play and control these games. *Playmakers* generated plenty of controversy (and attention) for ESPN, from the show's portrayal of professional athletes to the ethics of sports journalism. ESPN's approach to sports coverage, from Jeremy Lin and LeBron James to Tim Tebow and Johnny Manziel, has often morphed beyond the discussion of athletic performances to broader societal debates. As ESPN continues expanding through new and social media, the effect will only expand in coming years.

## ABOUT THE VOLUME

The editors have shaped the present volume under five sections exploring the business of sports media, gender and race, journalism, audience, and the future of ESPN. The first part tackles ESPN's impact on the sports media business and the economics of sports. Chapters by McGuire and Armfield and Stein examine ESPN's corporate status, from its earliest days to its eventual takeover by Disney. Fortunato and Corrigan provide background about the economic strategies that vaulted ESPN into a place of economic prominence among all cable networks.

Finally, the section concludes with Puente examining ESPN's struggles with its Spanish-language network, ESPN Deportes.

The second section of the text focuses on ESPN's role in culture with regards to how society may think about sports in terms of race and gender. Daniels begins the discussion by exploring the role ESPN has taken covering race, and Sipocz furthers the discussion while analyzing ESPN's coverage of two of the most popular and controversial issues the network covered where race became a central theme. The ESPN effect is also covered with regards to gender. Hartman analyzes the coverage of the 40th anniversary of Title IX. Wolter explores how female athletes are portrayed on espnW, and Lavelle analyzes the representation of women in ESPNs *30 for 30* film series, which also covered the 40th anniversary of Title IX. Moving on to other ESPN outlets, Kian, Smith, Lee, and Sweeney examine marketing and branding of *ESPN the Magazine*'s "Body Issue" through ESPN's various multimedia platforms while analyzing how ESPN frames athletes in these issues.

The third section focuses on the journalistic efforts of ESPN. Returning to ESPNs *30 for 30* series, Billings and Blackistone analyze five *30 for 30* episodes and how such programming shapes our memories. Lambert explores the effect of ESPN's coverage of college basketball and how the framing of ESPN's coverage influences viewer perceptions of the NCAA Tournament bubble and what schools are selected. Staton then examines ESPN's relationship with PBS's respected public affairs series *Frontline* while investigating the issue of concussions in football. Jay gives insight into the multimedia presence of ESPN. The section wraps up with an examination by Naraine and Abeza of ESPN's impact on Canada's TSN (The Sports Network).

The fourth section considers ESPN's impact on the participation of its audience with network content. Ruihley, Hardin, and Billings demonstrate one of the ways ESPN has expanded its empire into society through the world of fantasy sports. Gentry and Castleberry offer a critical examination of ESPN's coverage of certain sporting events over others and how the authors believe it has contributed to the decline in physical fitness in the United States.

The final section of the text considers the future of ESPN, beginning with an interview conducted by Billings with Chris LaPlaca, ESPN senior vice president. In the last chapter, Earnheardt provides an overview of the book and discusses future directions for research about ESPN.

For those in sports media research, the 2000s and 2010s have been a time of significant growth, both in the quantity and quality of scholarship being produced and published. As the first academic text dedicated to the self-proclaimed "Worldwide Leader in Sports," the editors hope this scholarship will contribute to this growth and provide a starting point for scholars examining present and future impacts of ESPN.

Let the games begin.

# Business and the ESPN Effect

# CHAPTER ONE

# In the Beginning

## The Rasmussens and the Launch of ESPN

JOHN MCGUIRE AND GREG G. ARMFIELD

The omnipresent nature of the Entertainment and Sports Programming Network (ESPN) on today's media landscape stands in stark contrast to the company's start-up in 1979. What began as an idea for a cable sports network that would serve the state of Connecticut became one of the world's biggest media companies. This chapter offers a case study of the entrepreneurial aspects of ESPN's start-up covering 1978 through 1981. Particular attention is given to the roles Bill Rasmussen and his son Scott played as nascent entrepreneurs. Through the use of published first-person accounts and media reports during that period, this case study considers how events in ESPN's start-up years contributed to what became a $50 billion business (Badenhausen, 2014).

## NASCENT ENTREPRENEURSHIP

Research examining nascent entrepreneurs has expanded during the 2000s. Although there are multiple definitions for the concept, this research uses Parker and Belghitar's (2006) definition of "individuals who are actively involved in starting a new business" (p. 81). Parker and Belghitar surveyed nascent entrepreneurs to learn what factors influenced outcomes of these start-up ventures. The researchers' findings confirmed a general truth about all forms of entrepreneurism: Having deep financial pockets made a significant difference between success and failure.

Their research showed that the availability of financial resources (i.e., adequate amount of start-up capital) allowed these new ventures time to sustain through early struggles. Parker and Belghitar (2006) also found many of these nascent entrepreneurs had experience in the fields they were trying to get their venture started in.

Other studies of nascent entrepreneurs have considered the issue of self-efficacy (i.e., level of belief individuals have that they can successfully reach their goals) among nascent entrepreneurs. Hechavarria, Renko, and Matthews (2012) examined responses from more than 800 nascent entrepreneurs in a longitudinal study. Through regression analysis, researchers identified self-efficacy and business planning as significant factors and that "entrepreneurial self-efficacy and business plan formality were dependent constructs" (p. 696). Although the researchers suggested these factors contributed to maintaining a start-up effort rather than abandoning it, the researchers also found entrepreneurs with detailed plans would be more likely to bail out if financial projections could not be met.

Timmons (in Legge & Hindle, 1997) identified what he called four key ingredients to entrepreneurial ventures: (a) appropriate financing (equity and debt); (b) having both a technically feasible and marketable product and/or service; (c) achieving a complete analysis leading to an effective business plan; and (d) having talented lead entrepreneurs while assembling a strong team (p. 80). Of these ingredients, Timmons identified the financial aspect as most critical. These four factors will be used as a framework for this case study to analyze Bill Rasmussen's and Scott Rasmussen's efforts as nascent entrepreneurs.

## THE RASMUSSENS AND THEIR "ESP"

Had the New England Whalers made the World Hockey Association playoffs in 1978, media history might have been different. Because New England did not, Bill Rasmussen was among a group of Whaler employees released following the season (Schawbel, 2012). With a background in sports broadcasting and public relations, Rasmussen, his son Scott, and others pursued an idea that had been on Rasmussen's mind: creating a cable television network in Connecticut with a focus on the state's sports teams. Within 16 months, that idea blossomed from a statewide venture originally called ESP Network to a national network that became ESPN. In analyzing the events that unfolded from 1978 to 1981, the Rasmussens' great idea met up with good timing at several crucial junctures. But factors relating to lack of experience and financial resources would mean an early departure for both Rasmussens from the network they helped start.

## Appropriate Financing

What early financing there was for the Rasmussens' proposed venture came from investments from friends and relatives and maxing out credit cards. Bill Rasmussen became a traveling salesman in 1978 and early 1979, pitching the vision of an all-sports network to potential financial saviors (Rasmussen, 1983). It would take several meetings before Rasmussen found an interested party. Getty Oil representative Stuart Evey had limited knowledge of the cable television business and doubts about Rasmussen's business projections. However, as a sports fan, Evey saw promise in the concept (Evey, 2004). With the go-ahead from Getty's board, the company acquired an option to purchase an 85% stake in ESPN, making an initial $10 million investment in the Rasmussens' venture in February 1979 ("In Brief," 1979; Rasmussen, 1983; Smith, 2009). Getty formally followed through on its purchase option a few months later (Rasmussen, 1983). The ESPN deal would later appear to be part of Getty's overall strategy to invest in media. In 1980, the company announced a venture with several movie studios for an entertainment-based cable network, but the idea was abandoned a year later ("Getty's Dry Hole," 1981; "Pay-Cable World," 1980).

Getty's financial involvement had proved crucial to sustaining ESPN through the network's early years of operation. Unfortunately for Getty, the investment never paid off. The company's financial loss on ESPN was estimated at more than $100 million by the mid-1980s (Heller, 1987). Texaco, which had acquired Getty Oil, sold its majority stake in ESPN to ABC (which already owned a minority stake in the network) in 1984 (Smith, 2009).

## Technically Feasible and Marketable Product

The need to demonstrate they had a marketable product was probably the easiest task in the Rasmussens' quest. Televised sports had proven to be a valuable commodity for the commercial television networks over the decades. The challenge would be obtaining the quantity of content required for a 24-hour sports network—and content of sufficient quality to attract an audience. The Rasmussens targeted college sports in particular in their initial planning. Over the months leading up to ESPN's debut, the Rasmussens engaged in a back-and-forth exchange with the National Collegiate Athletic Association (NCAA) leadership and members of its television committee. Limitations were in place about what programming could be seen and when. The biggest restriction regarded Division I football games, as the existing commercial network contract prohibited live telecasts on other networks. The Rasmussens proposed tape-delayed coverage of college football games for its start-up network as well as coverage of other NCAA events, including opening round games of the Division I men's basketball tournament. The NCAA deal was secured only months before the network's launch (Rasmussen, 1983). Although the first week of ESPN programming did feature top-flight college football games on delay (e.g., Oregon-Colorado), it also included slow-pitch softball and Munster hurling from Ireland (Rasmussen, 1983).

The technical feasibility of delivering ESPN around the country was a matter of emerging technology meeting up with good timing. It was in the process of learning about the technical requirements for delivering a statewide cable service that the Rasmussens came upon a crucial part of their venture's development and eventual success. They found that they could acquire a transponder on the Satcom 1 satellite and affordably deliver their proposed network across the country (see Corrigan's discussion of satellite delivery in Chapter 4). The Rasmussens' ability to assure national distribution of their network to cable systems was essential in recruiting investors. K. S. Sweet, the company assisting the Rasmussens in that effort, lent the father and son $75,000 during those early months using the transponder, for all practical purposes, as collateral (Evey, 2004; Miller & Shales, 2011).

Another technical challenge was building the ESPN production and studio facilities from scratch. Plainville, Connecticut, had been the proposed headquarters for the network, but community zoning regulations blocking satellite dishes forced Bill Rasmussen to identify another site, this one in Bristol, Connecticut (Rasmussen, 1983). Part of the challenge with facilities was self-imposed, as the Rasmussens had publicly identified September 7, 1979, as the night of the first telecast (about the same time traditional television networks launched their fall seasons). In Rasmussen's recounting of the chaotic days leading to ESPN's launch, he recalled that equipment was still being installed in the hours leading up to the September 7 launch. Evey, who had the title of ESPN's Chief Executive Officer, and other new executives such as Network President Chet Simmons were upset with this public pronouncement, particularly while so much work remained to be done in the summer of 1979 (Rasmussen, 1983).

Building ESPN's audience was hampered in those early years by technical circumstances beyond the Rasmussens' control. In 1979, cable television's infrastructure was limited. Even by 1981, industry data showed the nation's biggest media markets had only a fraction of television households passed by cable (i.e., having the capacity to receive cable television signals). New York City's designated market area (DMA) had only 28% of all television households passed by cable while the Los Angeles DMA had 23%. These numbers were even worse in other top-ten markets, with only 6% of the households in the Chicago DMA and just 1% in the Dallas-Fort Worth DMA passed by cable ("Championing the Cause," 1981). The lack of infrastructure would curtail ESPN's early efforts to build an audience, but the eventual acceleration in cable construction during the 1980s (created in part by ESPN's popularity) would factor into the network's eventual financial success.

## Developing an Effective Business Plan

It is ironic that for everything Bill and Scott Rasmussen were successful in accomplishing while bringing ESPN to reality, their efforts began without any formal research or business plan. Bill Rasmussen recalled that in the summer of 1978, while on a trip to his daughter's birthday party with his son Scott, they sketched out the initial business strategies for a national cable sports network (Rasmussen, 1983). It was only after the Rasmussens started working with K. S. Sweet that a more formal business proposal was created for potential investors.

As the Rasmussens and their partners were up against mounting financial deadlines at the end of 1978, they found themselves trying to keep conversations going, sometimes saying one thing to one party and something completely different to another. Smith (2009) suggested Bill Rasmussen "bluffed business partners and cynical journalists, bringing skeptics along until the next deal arrived just in time" (p. 7). Bill Rasmussen also acknowledged the use of this verbal jui-jitsu:

> We didn't recognize it at the time, but the strategy that emerged from that whirlwind time was really simple: tell the investor (Getty) of the NCAA and MSO [multiple cable system operators] enthusiasm; tell the NCAA of the investor (never mentioning Getty) and MSO enthusiasm; and tell the MSOs of the NCAA and (no name) investor enthusiasm. (p. 139)

It would not be until 1980 that Evey hired a consulting company to analyze ESPN's potential and establish a traditional business plan for the company (Evey, 2004).

ESPN executives did execute several strategies for gaining awareness with advertisers and cable systems in the network's first years. An examination of *Broadcasting* magazine from 1979 to 1981 found ESPN was aggressive in paid print pieces targeting cable system operators and potential clients. In the week ESPN first went on the air, the network purchased a two-page advertisement in *Broadcasting* that touted the opportunity for advertisers to reach one of ESPN's key target demographics (men ages 18–34) and the availability of sponsorships for NCAA championship events ("Seven Ways," 1979). Starting in 1980, ESPN ran advertisements highlighting individual national sponsors, including Timex and Hilton hotels ("Timex Makes," 1980; "Why Does Hilton," 1980).

ESPN, as the Rasmussens once envisioned, was starting to sell itself. After having only 12 national advertisers when the network premiered in 1979, the number reached 82 by the end of 1980 ("Cable Advertising, 1981"). Anheuser-Busch was the most important of these advertisers. Even before ESPN went on-air in 1979, the St. Louis–based brewery bought $1.3 million of advertising time on the fledgling network (Consoli, 2004). As one Anheuser-Busch executive noted, the network had the promise of delivering the audience they wanted: young males who had a taste for Budweiser products (Consoli). Anheuser-Busch increased its commitment to ESPN in 1980 with a $25 million deal that would run through the mid-1980s. Many industry analysts (and ESPN executives, in hindsight) thought the deal was crucial in helping ESPN earn credibility with advertisers and cable system operators alike (Consoli, 2004).

After its initial focus on advertisers and cable systems, ESPN shifted advertising to promote itself to consumers. ESPN would spend more than $6 million in advertising in the final quarter of 1981 and all of 1982 ("From Trade to Consumer," 1981). This aggressive approach was deemed necessary to achieve a 15% penetration rate for cable households so that ESPN's audience could be measured by Nielsen—something critical to advertisers ("ESPN's Simmons," 1981; "From Trade to Consumer," 1981). That goal was achieved during 1982 (Consoli, 2004).

## Having Talented Lead Entrepreneurs and a Strong Team

That Bill and Scott Rasmussen had the idea of a 24-hour sports network did not mean the pair had the professional background to get it to air. Bill Rasmussen acknowledged in his book about the network's early days that he knew little about the cable television business and even less about the technology required to achieve what he and his son envisioned. When Evey was arranging for Getty to buy a majority stake in the fledgling network, he said he recognized that Bill Rasmussen lacked the professional expertise to bring a national cable sports network to reality (Evey, 2004). That job fell to a network television sports veteran Chet Simmons, who had worked 15 years with NBC's sports division.

The level of mistrust between the different ESPN leadership figures was high, with issues stemming from both professional and personal differences. In the first few months leading up to and past the network's launch, Evey was serving as chief executive officer, Simmons was president, and Rasmussen was ESPN chairman, though the position carried little authority (Evey, 2004). Professionally, Simmons and Evey had issues with Bill Rasmussen speaking on behalf of the network in the months leading up to the September 1979 launch. Evey was also frustrated that some of the deals Bill Rasmussen had made with cable system operators provided no income for the operation (Evey, 2004). Although Evey, in a sense, was Simmons's ally in the battles with the Rasmussens, there was a level of animosity between Evey and Simmons over who had ultimate power of the cable network (Freeman, 2000). The power struggles resulted in Scott Rasmussen's forced departure from ESPN days after the network first went on the air. His father, Bill, left the company about one year later (Rasmussen, 1983). Simmons and Evey also proved to be short-timers: Simmons left ESPN in 1982 to become the first commissioner of the United States Football League. Evey left the CEO position to become ESPN's chairman until 1985 (Evey, 2004). Simmons's successor as network president in 1982 was an internal hire, Bill Grimes, who would become the figure who would provide stability in the network's executive level (Smith, 2009).

Although the internal discord at the executive level created tensions within ESPN's highest levels, the hiring of Simmons created stability within the network's day-to-day operations. Scotty Connal, another longtime NBC Sports veteran, was one of Simmons's first hires. Although there was only a window of a few months before ESPN's launch in September 1979, Simmons and Connal quickly assembled key personnel in front of and behind the camera, relying in large part on NBC employees who had worked for them before. Jim Simpson, ESPN'S first lead play-by-play announcer and its most prominent on-air personality at the time of the launch, was among them. The multiple NBC hires caused some in the business to brand ESPN as "NBC North" (Evey, 2004; Smith, 2009). Bill Rasmussen also credited Connal as providing the managerial expertise necessary to meet the September 1979 launch date: "In my opinion, he was and is the most important employee ever hired by ESPN" (p. 213). That Simmons and Connal were able to quickly bring together a production team with organizational experience proved significant not only in helping get ESPN on the air but also giving it immediate credibility within the industry.

## ASSESSING ESPN'S ENTREPRENEURIAL START-UP

It would be foolish to consider the efforts of Bill and Scott Rasmussen to bring their all-sports network to reality as nothing less than one of the most successful start-up media ventures in history. But to borrow from a branded ESPN segment, one needs to go "Inside the Numbers" prior to rendering a final judgment about their effort. Using research concerning nascent entrepreneurs and entrepreneurial start-ups, one can argue the Rasmussens failed in addressing or achieving basic steps in such start-ups. For instance, the Rasmussens were successful in getting ESPN on the air, despite lacking detailed research or a specific business plan in the initial months of the effort, contrary to the findings of Hechavarria et al. (2012). But the Rasmussens' inability to self-bankroll the development of ESPN (and the eventual sale of control to Getty) eliminated their ability to guide the network for any sustained period of time. As Parker and Belghitar (2006) discussed in their research about nascent entrepreneurs, financial resources are critical to the outcome of such start-ups. The Rasmussens were forced to seek funding elsewhere as the future of their start-up appeared doomed. Parker and Belghitar also noted that extensive experience on the part of the entrepreneur was typically an important factor in successful start-ups. Although Bill Rasmussen had sports industry experience, he and his son lacked the expertise in cable television and national sports programming that paved the way for their early departure from their venture.

So what went right? In the case of ESPN, it was the technological component. That Bill and Scott Rasmussen secured the Satcom 1 transponder in 1978 for distributing ESPN's signal at a time before many in the media industry understood its value was a seminal moment in the network's start-up. Securing the technology for distributing ESPN's signal helped land Getty, which provided the network with needed capital. Getty's involvement in turn helped land the programming deal with the NCAA and in hiring key personnel such as Simmons and Connal who could get the network on the air and look professional.

Another factor from ESPN's start-up that merits attention is the short amount of time it took for the Rasmussens' idea for an all-sports network to become reality. There had been frustration with the Rasmussens' push to get ESPN on the air in 1979, 16 months after they had the original idea. It is argued, however, that as this era saw the start-up of what are now heritage cable networks (e.g., USA Network, CNN), this self-imposed time pressure may have been another critical factor in ESPN's success. Rasmussen told Evey as much in their first face-to-face meeting in December 1978:

> If we move quickly, we'll preempt others who may be considering the same thing. Half a dozen people have already tried our idea, but their timing was wrong. What makes us different is our RCA transponder on Satcom [1] and a proposed arrangement with the NCAA. (Rasmussen, 1983, p. 123)

That Bill and Scott Rasmussen understood the competitive pressures at hand and were motivated and successful in pushing to get ESPN on the air when they did may have closed the door on other potential start-ups.

Perhaps most important for ESPN's start-up success was that the people who came up with the idea knew it could work and had the urgency and self-efficacy to see the idea through to its launch. Despite their many doubters in the media field, Bill and Scott Rasmussen believed their concept of an all-sports network had the potential to attract an audience that advertisers wanted to reach.

More than three decades after seeing his all-sports network launched, Bill Rasmussen described ESPN's continued success as stemming from the network's underlying organizational culture, created in those hectic first years: "To serve sports fans. Anytime. Anywhere" (Schawbel, 2012, para. 19). Although the Rasmussens' time with ESPN was short, these nascent entrepreneurs managed to secure their place in sports and media history.

# CHAPTER TWO

# The Mouse that Scored

## Disney's Reconfiguration of ESPN and ABC Sports

ANDI STEIN

In 1996, under the direction of then CEO Michael Eisner, the Walt Disney Company purchased Capital Cities/ABC for $19 billion. The sale included ABC sports programming such as *Monday Night Football* and *Wide World of Sports*. Disney's acquisition of an 80% interest in ESPN, which ABC had purchased from Texaco in 1984, also was part of the deal.

The timing of the sale dovetailed with Disney's efforts to develop a presence in the sports arena. A few years before the Capital Cities/ABC acquisition, Disney had initiated a venture into professional sports with the creation of a hockey expansion team called the Mighty Ducks in 1993 and an investment in the California Angels baseball team in 1995.

In the decade following the Capital Cities/ABC purchase, Disney attempted to integrate ABC's sports offerings with the powerhouse that was ESPN. Disney's intention for the reconfiguration was to shore up ABC's longstanding sports programming while leveraging the well-known brand identity of ESPN to do so. The company's ultimate goal was to transform ESPN into the "overarching brand for all sports programming carried on the ABC Television Network" (Deitsch, 2006, para. 1). By 2006, the retooling effort was complete, and ABC Sports was rebranded as "ESPN on ABC."

This chapter uses a case study approach to trace the development and reconfiguration of ESPN and ABC Sports under the umbrella of the Walt Disney Company. Using brand identity theory as its grounding, the chapter examines the integration of ESPN and ABC Sports, the changes that were made to accomplish this, and the result of these changes. This chapter will also consider what turned out to be Disney's ill-fated venture into professional sports and contrast Disney's experience in trying to integrate entertainment and sports with the integration of ESPN and ABC Sports.

## BRAND IDENTITY

According to Kapferer (1997), a company's value had traditionally been determined by its tangible assets, such as its land, buildings, or equipment. In the 1980s, however, an increase in corporate mergers and acquisitions spawned a new concept of value based on public recognition of an organization's brand.

A company's brand can be described as something that characterizes the products or services of an organization in a way that makes them instantly recognizable and differentiates them from their competitors. Companies use a variety of techniques to establish what a specific product or service should represent and how this representation should be communicated to the public. This may be accomplished through the use of a name, logo, symbol, package design, or other means of presentation (Ghodeswar, 2008).

The practice of brand identity development has become commonplace within the realm of corporate marketing activities. Margulies (1977) defined the concept of identity as "the sum of all the ways a company chooses to identify itself to all its publics—the community, customers, employees, the press, present and potential stockholders, security analysts, and investment bankers" (p. 66). How a company portrays this identity can ultimately influence the public's perception or image of the organization.

De Chernatony (2010) explained brand identity as "the distinctive or central idea of a brand and how the brand communicates this idea to its stakeholders" (p. 53). Petek and Ruzzier (2013) characterized the brand identity process as a series of building blocks that weave together the different branding-related concepts proposed by various authors over the years. They outlined these components as a combination of "vision, mission, values, personality and core competencies, which are evident in most reviewed brand identity models" (p. 63).

Vision can encompass a number of elements, such as goals, motivating forces, and reason for existence (Collins & Porras, 1996). The corporate mission represents the philosophy of an organization, which is closely linked to the purpose of the company's existence and is reflected in its brand. In many ways this makes it the most important aspect of the brand's identity (Melewar & Karaosmanoglu, 2006).

Values communicate the "functional, emotional, and self-expressive benefits delivered by the brand that provide value to the customer" (Aaker, 1996, p. 95).

The strongest brand identities are those that possess both functional and emotional benefits (Aaker, 1996).

Personality attributes human characteristics to a company's brand. Aaker (1996) referenced five traits that can be used to describe a brand in terms that give it human appeal: sincerity, excitement, competence, sophistication, and ruggedness. He noted that a brand's personality essentially encourages consumers to develop the same kind of affinity toward that brand as they might feel about their personal relationships.

Petek and Ruzzier (2013) described the core competencies of a brand as "strong, favourable and unique brand attributes or associations" (p. 65). Ideally, these should stem from the vision and values associated with that brand.

The way a company positions a brand can have an impact on consumer awareness. According to Kapferer (1997), "Positioning a brand means emphasizing the distinctive characteristics that make it different from its competitors and appealing to the public" (p. 96).

Part of the challenge of solidifying a brand's identity lies in determining how to communicate this identity to potential customers. Ghodeswar (2008) observed, "successful brands are built through creative repetition of themes in various types of media" (p. 7). Channels of communication such as advertising, promotion, direct marketing, and online communication can help generate awareness of the brand.

Increased consumer awareness of a company's brand contributes to its value in the case of a merger or acquisition. Instead of simply buying a shoe manufacturer or a brewery, for example, the purchaser is instead acquiring the recognition factor of a brand name such as Nike or Heineken. As Kapferer (1997) noted, "The strength of a company like Heineken is not solely in knowing how to brew beer; it is that people all over the world want to drink Heineken. The same logic applies for IBM, Sony, McDonald's, Barclays Bank or Dior" (p. 16).

## DISNEY AS SPORTS ENTERTAINMENT BRAND

For Disney, the acquisition of both ESPN and ABC Sports came at a time when the company was also trying to establish itself as a player in professional sports. The attainment of two well-known sports brands meshed nicely with plans the company had begun setting in motion a few years earlier.

In 1993, Disney made inroads into the sports arena when it was granted a franchise to establish a National Hockey League (NHL) expansion team, the Mighty Ducks, to be based in Anaheim, California. The franchise acquisition came a year after Disney had released a movie called *The Mighty Ducks*, the story of a youth hockey team overcoming the odds and winning a championship. Although the movie was only a moderate hit at the box office ($50 million in box office sales), the profits were enough for Disney to produce two *Mighty Ducks* sequels. The Ducks logo created for the fictional team in fact became the basis of the first official logo for Disney's NHL team (Dodds, 2014).

Disney proceeded to launch an all-out marketing blitz to build a following for the real Mighty Ducks team and show the public the potential of hockey as entertainment. The effort involved the creation of a team logo, a mascot called "Wild Wing," and a dazzling display of music and laser shows featured at each Ducks game. Initial public response to the marketing effort resulted in steady ticket sales and a cadre of devoted fans (Horn, 1993).

Disney's initial success with the Ducks led to the company's next move—an investment in Major League Baseball's (MLB) California Angels. Entertainer Gene Autry, known to millions as the "Singing Cowboy," had purchased the Los Angeles Angels in 1961, renamed the team the California Angels, and moved it to Anaheim in 1965. By the 1990s, after a 30-year run, Autry and his wife, Jackie, were ready to relinquish control of the team and began looking for an investment partner. In 1995, Disney CEO Michael Eisner negotiated his company's 25% investment in the Angels with the option to purchase the remaining 75% upon Autry's death. After Autry died in 1998, the Angels officially became Disney's second professional sports team (Stein, 2011).

Disney had used the California franchise as the basis for a family-oriented sports movie (1994's *Angels in the Outfield*). Disney attempted to use the same marketing approach with the Angels that had initially been so successful with the Mighty Ducks. One reporter dubbed the endeavor a "total Disney makeover: a bigger marketing budget, more community relations, new uniforms, new mascots, pregame shows, bands, videos and other entertainment designed to attract youngsters and families to the ballpark" (Hesketh, 1996, p. 1). The company also changed the name of the team to the Anaheim Angels to give it more of a local focus.

Disney's final attempt to expand its brand identity into the world of sports encompassed a foray onto the turf of youth sports. In 1997, the company unveiled a sports complex on the grounds of its Walt Disney World property in central Florida. The complex housed facilities for a wide assortment of sports and included playing fields, a baseball stadium, tennis courts, and a basketball arena (Stein, 2011).

Disney partnered with the Amateur Athletic Union, a nonprofit organization that sponsors and promotes competitive athletic events. The intention was to attract young athletes from all over the world to come to Orlando, Florida, to compete and train at the sports complex. While in Orlando, they and their families also had the opportunity to enjoy the four Disney theme parks and other attractions in the vicinity. Because the sports complex made its debut soon after Disney's acquisition of Capital Cities/ABC, it was aptly named "Disney's Wide World of Sports" (Stein, 2011).

## TROUBLING TIMES FOR DISNEY SPORTS

By the early 2000s, change was in the air at Disney, which was to have an impact on both of its professional sports offerings. Although initial response to both of the company's professional sports teams, the Mighty Ducks and Anaheim Angels, had been positive, the momentum did not last long. Once the novelty of entertainment-infused hockey wore off, Ducks fans quickly became disenchanted when the team wasn't able to win the majority of its games. Although Disney had invested big bucks in the presentation of Ducks hockey games, the company had not put a lot of money into acquiring top-notch athletes. By 2002, Mighty Ducks games had the lowest attendance record in the NHL (Fatsis & Orwall, 2002).

As for the Anaheim Angels, the razzle-dazzle approach to baseball Disney took did not sit well with the team's serious baseball fans, especially when the company began raising ticket prices to cover the cost of some of the cosmetic changes. As Fatsis and Orwall (2002) noted, "Attendance tumbled 21%... as the team finished last in its division in 1999 and next to last in 2000 and 2001" (p. A6). It was becoming increasingly clear that Disney's venture into the world of professional sports teams was not following the company's originally anticipated course to success.

Disney began actively seeking buyers for both teams in 2002. Ironically, that turned out to be the year the Angels won the World Series, but it was not enough to make a difference in the company's plans. In 2003, Disney sold the Angels to businessman Arturo "Arte" Moreno for $184 million. In 2005, Henry Samueli purchased the Mighty Ducks for $75 million (Stein, 2011). The only piece of the sports portfolio Disney retained was its youth facility in Florida.

## HISTORY AND BACKGROUND OF ABC/ESPN PURCHASE

While Disney's venture into professional sports was struggling, the company's investment in Capital Cities/ABC appeared to show greater promise. With the purchase, in many ways the Walt Disney Company returned to its television roots. ABC had been instrumental in introducing Disney to television audiences when the network launched a weekly variety series, *Disneyland*, and a children's program, *The Mickey Mouse Club*, in the mid-1950s, making Walt Disney's name a household word in the process (Stein, 2011).

By the 1990s, Disney was well-established as an entertainment powerhouse with its film and theme park divisions, but its acquisition moved the company back into television's big leagues. At the time, Disney's purchase of Capital Cities/ABC was the second-largest corporate takeover in U.S. history (Telotte, 2004).

Disney gained access to ABC's entertainment programming as well as to the company's news division, which included programs such as *20/20* and *World News with Charles Gibson*. Disney also took possession of the network's ABC Sports division, which Roone Arledge had spearheaded from the 1960s until the mid-1980s, and had become known under his leadership for its inventory of sports programming such as *Monday Night Football* and *ABC Wide World of Sports* (Stein, 2011).

The acquisition of the Entertainment and Sports Programming Network—better known as ESPN—as part of the package was an added benefit for Disney. Entrepreneurs Bill and Scott Rasmussen helped launch the network but sold a majority stake in the company to Getty Oil in 1979. After Texaco took over Getty, the company also acquired majority ownership in ESPN, which it sold to Capital Cities/ABC in 1984. A few years later, ABC sold 20% of its stake in ESPN to Nabisco, which later sold the share to the Hearst Corporation (Stein, 2011). By the time of Disney's Capital Cities/ABC purchase in 1996, ESPN had become to sports programming what Disney was to family entertainment, or what Shea (2000) later referred to as "the king of sports television" (p. 45).

At the time of the acquisition, there was a great deal of speculation on the part of the media about what impact this combination of forces would have on both sports and entertainment in the long run. In a tongue-in-cheek assessment of the acquisition, Lefton (1996) predicted a world where a future Olympic Village would be "marked by a pair of 30-foot statues honoring the city's most important icons, Mickey Mouse and Shaquille O'Neal," and "cast members wearing lab coats with Mickey on their lapels had discovered how to grow grass in a domed stadium" (p. 30).

In many ways, however, the blending of the world's most prominent entertainment company with the leader of the pack in sports programming made good sense. The concept of sports as entertainment had been gaining hold with both the media and the public for a number of years:

> Six, seven years ago, we used to say that "sports is entertainment," and it raised a lot of eyebrows. Now, it's become increasingly clear that the two can no longer be separated as entertainment companies enter the sports business and sports companies start thinking like entertainment companies. (Bernstein, 1997, p. 41)

Bernstein noted that in addition to Disney's newly assumed stewardship of ESPN, Time Warner's inheritance of Turner Broadcasting had resulted in discussion of the development of a competing all-sports cable channel and a sports apparel brand called WB Sport.

Reporters also speculated on the brand-building potential of the two entities. Disney had spent decades building its brand, first under the guidance of founder Walt Disney and later under the tutelage of Eisner. In the process, Disney had become synonymous with the concept of corporate synergy. The company was a master of integrating its various enterprises to promote and sustain its brand identity (Stein, 2011).

According to Vagnoni (1996), ESPN had come a long way in developing its brand with help from in-house talent and advertising agency Wieden & Kennedy.

> ESPN has since managed to create for itself a hip, sophisticated and utterly cool brand identity. That they've done it in the fast-paced, voracious-appetite, retail-oriented context of on-air promotion, with its endless demands for tune-in information, is an impressive achievement, kind of like a wild card team making it to the Super Bowl. (p. 26)

The challenge for Disney was to assess how to manage both of these well-known brands and to determine whether to maintain their separate brand identities or ultimately merge them into one.

## ABC AND ESPN: BLENDING BRANDS

As noted above, the timing of the Capital Cities/ABC acquisition and the resulting assimilation of ESPN and ABC Sports into the Disney empire worked well to foster Disney's interest in becoming a leader in sports entertainment. It was then up to the company to determine how to make the best use of these two entities to expand its own brand identity in sports.

Even before the acquisition became official in February 1996, there were rumblings in the media of how Disney would deal with the two sports giants—whether the company would keep them as separate brands or attempt to blend them. It did not take long to find out.

At the time of the acquisition, ABC Sports operated under the leadership of president Dennis Swanson, who had succeeded Arledge in 1986. Swanson was a 20-year veteran of ABC whose credits included launching *The Oprah Winfrey Show* while general manager of WLS-TV in Chicago in 1983 (McConnville, 1996).

Steve Bornstein was ESPN's leader at the time. He started his career in programming at the cable sports channel in 1980, eventually becoming president and CEO in 1990 at 38 (Hiestand, 1997).

In the spring of 1996, Disney announced plans to merge the operations of ABC Sports and ESPN under the supervision of Bornstein, who would assume the title of president. Bornstein was quoted as saying that despite the merger, the two units would continue to operate as "separate and distinct businesses" (McConnville, 1996, p. 18). Swanson left ABC Sports in May 1996.

At the time, some saw the move as a logical one. Although ABC Sports had long been a dominant force in sports, in the years preceding the acquisition, ESPN had been quietly catching up. As Dupree (1996) explained:

> As ESPN's status in the sports world has grown, ABC Sports' clout in the sports marketplace has shrunk. In recent years, ABC has lost the rights to baseball and the Olympics and its anthology series, Wide World of Sports, has suffered in the ratings from the added competition of cable TV and regional networks. (p. 6)

Although the two units initially remained separate as Bornstein had indicated, as time progressed, they began inching closer to one another. In 1998, rumors began circulating in the media that Disney was contemplating combining the advertising sales units for ABC Sports and ESPN into a single division. One reporter suggested Disney was also considering forging a stronger connection between the entities by "possibly replacing the ABC Sports moniker in some programming.... The linkage might give ABC sports programming stronger brand recognition, while providing extra exposure for the ESPN brand" (Stroud, 1998, p. 14).

The same article (Stroud, 1998) included a quote from analyst Harold Vogel who characterized the developments as "an interesting example of the cable network sports tail wagging the broadcast network dog" (p. 14).

By the fall of 1999, the advertising sales divisions had been combined, and Ed Erhardt was brought in as president of advertising sales and customer marketing, overseeing the blended departments (Ross, 1999). This move surprised a number of people in the industry, for Erhardt's background was in print media, not broadcast. He came to ESPN/ABC Sports after a stint as vice president and group publisher of *Advertising Age* magazine ("ESPN, ABC Sports," 1999).

## EXPANDING THE ESPN BRAND

While adjustments were being made to align ABC Sports with ESPN, those running ESPN had been slowly developing and expanding the products and services specifically associated with the cable channel's brand. The creation of *ESPN The Magazine* was one of the first steps in the process.

Launched as a direct competitor to Time, Inc.'s *Sports Illustrated,* the publication made its debut in March 1998. It premiered as a biweekly containing sports news and entertainment features in a format modeled after ESPN's *SportsCenter* news show (Ito & Mallory, 1997). Distribution of the magazine was handled by the Hearst Corporation, which held a 20% stake in ESPN (Gremillion, 1997). The initial magazine circulation base was 350,000 in 1998 (Granatstein & Schwirtz, 1998); by 2006, that number had grown to 2 million subscribers (Lemke, 2006).

The magazine added another dimension to the sports channel by enabling ESPN to extend its brand to a wider audience of sports fans using a new medium.

The expansion of ESPN Radio followed soon after the magazine launch when Disney's ABC Radio acquired Chicago-based WMVP-AM and began airing 24-hour sports programming (Schwirtz, 1998). A year later, the company's website, ESPN.com, reconfigured its subscription-based content area called ESPN Insider using Disney's Internet portal, Go.com. The intent was "to strengthen ESPN's cross-branding efforts with other Walt Disney Co. properties" (Shaw, 1999, p. 13). ESPN Insider was cross-promoted to customers on the cable channel, on ESPN Radio, and through *ESPN The Magazine* (Shaw, 1999).

ESPN Deportes, a 24-hour Spanish-language sports channel, went live in early 2004, with an aim to reach Latino/a sports fans (Burt, 2004). Within the next two years, the company also introduced a broadband Internet service called ESPN 360, and Mobile ESPN, which gave sports fans access to ESPN products on their smartphones (Lemke, 2006).

## PRAISE FOR ESPN LEADERSHIP

While ESPN's brand identity continued to grow, the ABC Sports brand remained stagnant. It was becoming increasingly evident that Disney was gradually moving toward a full assimilation of ABC Sports into what had become the more widely recognized ESPN brand. George Bodenheimer, then ESPN president, noted, "Our brand is bigger than any one sport. The continued success will come from a hat-trick of brand, franchises and technology" (Burt, 2004, p. 11).

ESPN was beginning to look like the one bright spot when it came to sports entertainment for its parent company. In subsequent years, the process of blending the ABC Sports brand into ESPN became even more pronounced. By 2005, ESPN had taken over the programming activities of ABC Sports, and the network's financial, legal, and communications divisions were folded into ESPN ("Stand by," 2006).

Five years after the two sports programmers merged their sales and marketing forces, another change was unveiled. In 2005, the company revamped the sales and marketing division to "charge its representatives with managing all activity across the spectrum of ESPN and ABC Sports media assets, including TV, Web site, radio, print, wireless, broadband, video games and other businesses" (Thomaselli, 2005, p. 8).

The idea for the change was credited to Ed Erhardt, who had proven to be a winner in his role of ESPN/ABC Sports president of sports customer marketing and sales. Although a number of media critics had initially been skeptical of the choice of Erhardt to lead the sales and marketing division, within a few years, they were singing his praises in successfully blending the sales forces of the two sports media giants. As one reporter explained, "Erhardt has accomplished what many thought an impossible task—to successfully integrate two very different cultures in ABC Sports and ESPN—and he did it in part because he was an outsider" (Consoli, 2003, p. 24).

Reporters also repeatedly praised George Bodenheimer, who had been president of ESPN since 1998 and of ABC Sports since 2003, for his contribution in consolidating the two entities. Karrfalt (2005) noted:

> ESPN has become the most profitable and the most highly valued cable network in America under Mr. Bodenheimer's watch. He has orchestrated an incredible expansion of the brand on the Internet, at newsstands, on cellphones and, of course, on television, presiding over an empire that prompted the Sporting News to name him the most powerful person in sports in 2003. (p. S6)

Bodenheimer was also recognized for developing the ESPN brand as a "model for a wide range of companies, media and others, struggling to make their brands work in new markets" (Lowry, 2005, p. 66).

## END OF AN ERA

Eventually, it became evident that the powers that be at Disney were ready to make the consolidation of ABC Sports and ESPN a permanent one. In August 2006, Disney announced that all sports coverage airing on ABC would hereafter be branded as "ESPN on ABC," starting with ABC's kickoff coverage of the college football season the following month. The intention was to complete the integration of the ABC Sports and ESPN brands, which had been steadily evolving during the past decade ("Disney brings ESPN," 2006). The *Orlando Sentinel* reported ("Stand by," 2006), "The new approach covers all production efforts, including on-air, graphics and branding. Promotional efforts—including those on ESPN—will direct viewers to ABC, but viewers will see ESPN's graphics, ESPN microphones and sets and ESPN signs in stadiums when they tune in on ABC" (p. D7). Columnist Barry Horn (2006) summed up the change: "For ABC Sports, 'the thrill of victory' has given way to 'the agony of defeat'" (p. 1). Horn was not alone in his reaction to the announcement. *New York Times* reporter Richard Sandomir (2006) delivered the news as though he were writing an obituary.

> ABC Sports, which once defined sports television and was the home of Roone Arledge, Jim McKay, "Wide World of Sports," Howard Cosell, 10 Olympics and Mexican cliff diving, died yesterday after one final big gulp by ESPN.... ABC Sports was only 45. (p. 11)

ESPN executives were quick to acknowledge ABC's longstanding history and contributions in paving the way for a new era in sports programming. Both ESPN president George Bodenheimer and vice president John Skipper emphasized the move "was about ESPN's strength in the marketplace as opposed to the devaluing of the ABC Sports brand" (Deitsch, 2006, para. 7).

A few years later, the Walt Disney Company renamed its youth sports complex in Orlando the "ESPN Wide World of Sports Complex." It was the company's way of firmly cementing the relationship between the moniker attached to its homegrown sports property and the power of the ESPN brand (Garcia, 2009).

For in the end, it was, indeed, all about the brand. Over the years the brand identity of ESPN had far eclipsed that of ABC Sports. As Horn (2006) explained, "ESPN has evolved into one of the most powerful brands in sports. ABC is just another network" (p. 1).

ESPN successfully transformed itself from a small cable operation into a brand that today is recognized all over the globe. Under the umbrella of the Walt Disney Company, ESPN executives positioned their company's brand to represent all things sports and communicated this message across multiple platforms. This enabled ESPN to far surpass ABC Sports in the way of consumer awareness.

For Disney, the success of ESPN also allowed the company to establish a presence in the world of sports that was in line with its core mission and its well-entrenched brand as an entertainment provider. Although Disney had tried to make a splash in the world of sports through ownership of professional sports teams, this venture was just a bit too far out of the company's comfort zone and, as a result, was short-lived.

Ownership of ESPN/ABC Sports, however, provided Disney the perfect opportunity to mesh its expertise as a producer of entertainment with the public's interest in sports. Although Disney's initial investment in the Mighty Ducks and the Anaheim Angels may have been a costly lesson, in the end the company was able to focus its efforts on its brand strengths and profit from the popularity of the ESPN brand.

Positioning, communication, and consumer awareness are crucial to the successful development of brand identity. In the case of ESPN and the Walt Disney Company, they proved to be a winning combination.

# CHAPTER THREE

# Changing the Competitive Environment for Sports Broadcast Rights

JOHN A. FORTUNATO

The numerous ways in which ESPN has forever altered the sports media landscape are documented throughout this book. The emergence of ESPN in acquiring the broadcast rights to sports leagues and events is one of the most significant economic developments affecting the entire sports industry. Documenting how ESPN has changed the competitive bidding and acquisition environment for sports broadcast rights is the objective of this chapter. By implementing a successful business model of monthly subscriber fees and traditional advertising revenue, ESPN is a major competitor for almost every sports league and event. As of 2014, ESPN had acquired the broadcast rights to the National Football League (NFL), National Basketball Association (NBA), Major League Baseball, several collegiate conferences for football and basketball, the college football playoff that began after the 2014 regular season, every bowl game except one, all four major tennis tournaments, and early round coverage of the Masters golf tournament. The significant impact of ESPN in terms of the business model it implemented is that many professional leagues, collegiate conferences, individual teams, and media companies have created sports cable television networks as a way to replicate and capitalize on this revenue stream.

## THE BROADCAST RIGHTS BIDDING PROCESS

Sports leagues and television networks sign a broadcast rights contract where the network agrees to pay the league a certain dollar amount for a certain number of years for the rights to televise that league's games (e.g., Fortunato, 2001; Wenner, 1989). In the 1950s and early 1960s, the system of sports leagues selling broadcast rights to television networks was legally challenged in court by the Justice Department for violation of antitrust laws designed to ensure free-market competition. Following a contract between the NFL and CBS in 1961, Judge Allan K. Grim ruled that by pooling television rights, NFL franchises eliminated competition among themselves in the sale of these rights, thus voiding the contract between the NFL and CBS. Having failed in court, the leagues and networks petitioned the U.S. Congress for permission to pool and sell the broadcast rights. The result of hearings before Congress was the Sports Broadcasting Act President John F. Kennedy signed into law in September 1961. The Sports Broadcasting Act provided leagues with an antitrust exemption that allowed them to collectively pool the broadcast rights to all of their teams' games and sell them to the highest bidding television network (e.g., Fortunato, 2001; Scully, 2004).

The money from television networks for broadcast rights is the foundation of the economic sports business model and one of the largest revenue sources for a sports league or event. As for the television networks, sports programming is desirable because it delivers a hard-to-reach audience demographic of males 18–49 (e.g., Wenner, 1989). It offers networks the ability to work with their league partners and create schedules that can attract the widest possible audience. It allows networks to promote their other programming during the context of the game when people are more apt to be watching, instead of only during commercials. Sports generally produce consistent audience viewership, whereas a new entertainment program might last only a few episodes before being canceled (e.g., Fortunato, 2013). Finally, sports programming is DVR-proof with fans wanting to watch sporting events live. One estimate is that only 2% or 3% of live sports events in the United States are viewed using a DVR (Ourand, 2014b). Watching sports live is extremely attractive to advertisers because their promotional communication messages will be seen at their desired time (e.g., Fortunato, 2013).

An important variable for a sports league to maximize its revenue from television broadcasts is to have multiple networks bidding for the rights to its games. Any time a sports league can get multiple networks competing against one another for its broadcast rights, there will surely be an increase in the rights fee paid to the league (e.g., Fortunato, 2013). Ourand (2011) provided an example in his description of negotiations for the broadcast rights to the Wimbledon tennis tournament. NBC had been the over-the-air rights holder since 1968, featuring live coverage of the Men's and Women's Championships. At the time of this negotiation for

Wimbledon's broadcast rights, ESPN was the secondary rights holder, providing coverage during the week. NBC was paying $13 million per year and ESPN was paying $10 million. The NBC contract expired after the 2011 Wimbledon tournament, with ESPN's contract scheduled to run through 2014.

After preliminary meetings were held with various network officials in early 2011, the All England Lawn Tennis and Croquet Club that hosts the Wimbledon championships set up a schedule for presentations by the interested networks. Fox made a presentation for why it should be the rights holder on Monday, June 27, followed by NBC and ESPN on June 28. Fox indicated that it would use its soon to be re-branded sports cable channels to televise matches. At the end of its meeting Fox informed the All England Club that it was prepared to sign a 10-year, $350 million contract. NBC pledged to show all matches live by also using its cable properties once it acquired all Wimbledon television rights in 2014. NBC did not make a monetary offer in its presentation meeting. ESPN stressed in its meeting that its networks had a larger audience reach than the other television networks' cable properties. ESPN made a similar monetary bid to that of Fox.

On Wednesday, June 29, the All England Club would contact all the networks. Fox would be informed that it would have to increase its bid to acquire the rights at which time Fox declined and took itself out of contention. NBC would make an offer for an average annual payment in the mid-$30 million range while ESPN increased its bid to $40 million per year. On Saturday, July 2, NBC made a final bid for a 12-year contract with an average annual payment in the high-$30 million range. The All England Club would return to ESPN for a final offer, explaining that if the network increased its $40 million per year bid from 10 years to 12 years it would acquire the rights. ESPN agreed, and beginning in 2012 for the first time the entire Wimbledon tennis tournament was televised on a cable network (Ourand, 2011).

## THE CREATION OF MORE BIDDERS

The key to launching a network is acquiring content that will attract viewers. The growth of cable and satellite technology allowed for the creation of many diverse television networks, especially sports-oriented networks. This meant more networks bidding for sports league and event broadcast rights, providing the necessary competition to increase rights fee payments to leagues.

In the infancy of cable television ESPN, USA Network, and WTBS (which Ted Turner owned) were competitors for sports broadcast rights. Turner used satellite technology to create the first Superstation in 1976, with WTBS televising Atlanta Braves and Hawks games to the entire country. In the network's early days, ESPN provided exposure to seldom seen sports (e.g., Australian Rules Football and the America's Cup). In their need for programming, the influence of ESPN and Turner in inflating rights fees was evident in bidding for even less popular sports properties. Desperate for live programming, Turner and ESPN put in a bid for Division II football. ESPN offered $7 million for a two-year package, only to be outbid by Turner's $17 million offer (Miller & Shales, 2011).

In 1982, with ESPN in 15 million homes, representing only 18% of all television households, Chet Simmons, the first president of ESPN, predicted that the network's bigger impact on the sports industry would be as another major bidder for broadcast rights to prominent sports leagues and events. Simmons stated, "I don't think all of a sport will be on pay cable. Not all of the NFL will be on pay cable (by 1988), but I think some of it will be. The revenue-generating potential is so overwhelming, it's just going to demand it" (Taaffe, 1982, p. D2). In 1983, Neal Pilson, CBS Sports president, countered, "ESPN provides supplemental sports, but it's not a business force. We reach 83 million homes. How many do they? Twenty million? They can't charge the advertising rates. They are a zero factor" (Alfano,1983, p. B12).

Early round games of the NCAA men's basketball tournament provided ESPN with an opportunity event that was more than a supplemental sport and gave ESPN its first programming where it was the relevant network to which people turned to watch live games. Simmons claimed, "We created college basketball. The attention we gave to the early rounds changed the tournament. Nobody else was televising the early rounds, and nobody else had the time to do what we did" (Miller & Shales, 2011, p. 62).

In 1982, the NBA signed broadcast contracts with cable networks, illustrating the role these networks had in increasing rights fees payments. The NBA reached two-year agreements with ESPN and USA Network, with each network carrying 40 regular season games and 10 playoff games. Larry O'Brien, NBA commissioner, commented, "It was our hope that we could increase our current revenue from cable five times, but we even exceeded that. I would say we've increased sevenfold. It's the best cable payment in the history of sports and far beyond any TV package we've had in the past" (Hershey, 1982, p. M2).

## THE DUAL REVENUE STREAM MODEL

The biggest change in the financial future of ESPN and the network's influence on the broadcast rights process and the overall sports industry occurred when ESPN moved from a solely advertising-based revenue system it had been using through 1982 to a business model started in 1983 that included the substantial second revenue stream of monthly subscriber fees. In the early days, ESPN had paid cable operators to carry the network; now, ESPN would follow the business model CNN established of asking cable operators to pay the network to carry it on their cable systems (Eskenazi, 1989). By acquiring content that viewers desired ESPN would be able to convince cable providers to pay the per-subscriber fee by threatening to turn off the network. By 1984, ESPN was earning $.13 per subscriber, per month (Chad, 1987). After losing money from 1979 to 1984, ESPN finally broke even in 1985 before becoming profitable (Eskenazi, 1989). Roger Werner, ESPN CEO, explained, "the cable-programming business wouldn't be what it is without the development of a two-revenue-stream business model. Because of it ESPN has fueled the growth of sports overall, the inflation of player salaries, the cost of 30-second spots, and the cost of tickets to games. It's all interlinked" (Miller & Shales, 2011, p. 114).

As of 2014, ESPN was the most expensive cable network. Cable and satellite providers paid more than an estimated $5.54 per subscriber, per month to have ESPN as part of the package of channels that they offer to customers (Deitsch, 2013; Miller, Eder, & Sandomir, 2013). By being in nearly 100 million households, ESPN generated more than $6 billion in subscriber fees in 2013 (Miller et al., 2013).

## ESPN AND THE NFL

The dual revenue stream economic business model and the impact of ESPN on the broadcast rights bidding process reached its initial apex in 1987 when ESPN acquired the rights to some NFL games. One strategy that leagues employ to get more networks involved in the bidding process is to take a portion of their games and create another television package that they could sell to the networks (e.g., Fortunato, 2013). In 1987, when ABC, CBS, and NBC were not going to increase their rights fees paid to the NFL, the NFL developed a package of Sunday night games that ESPN would acquire. By 1987, ESPN was in 42 million homes, approximately 47% of all television households (Eskenazi, 1989; Fabrikant, 1987). ESPN became the first cable network to broadcast the NFL, paying $153 million in a three-year contract to televise eight regular season games on Sunday nights during the second half of the season, the Pro Bowl, and four preseason games (Chad, 1987; Fabrikant, 1987). J. William Grimes, ESPN president and chief executive officer, described the broadcast rights deal with the NFL at the time as "the most significant sports agreement in cable television history" (Janofsky, 1987, p. A1). Art Modell, owner of the Cleveland Browns at that time and chairperson of the league's broadcasting committee, explained, "the reason we're in cable at all is that there was a shortfall in dealing with the networks. They are coming off a soft television market, with increasing costs. So we turned to cable to help fill that shortfall for our member clubs" (Janofsky, 1987, p. A1).

On November 8, 1987, the New York Giants and the New England Patriots played in the first regular-season NFL game broadcast on cable television.

Longtime ESPN host Chris Berman commented, "Next to coming on the air, getting the NFL is the biggest thing to happen to ESPN" (Fortunato, 2006, p. 97). The NFL did stipulate that the games on ESPN would also have to be televised on an over-the-air network in the visiting team's city and the home team's city so long as the game was sold out 72 hours prior to kickoff (Fortunato, 2006; Goodwin, 1987).

Upon acquiring the NFL, ESPN set a subscriber rate of about $.27, an increase of about eight to nine cents (Chad, 1987; Miller & Shales, 2011). In commenting about ESPN's request to increase its monthly subscriber fee, Charles Dolan, chairperson of Cablevision, stated, "It seems likely that we will pass along the rights costs to our subscribers" (Fabrikant, 1987, p. 1).

In 1990, the NFL started having games on Sunday night for the entire season, with Turner Sports showing games on TNT for the first half of the season and ESPN showing games for the second half of the season. After sharing the Sunday night package with Turner from 1990 through 1997, ESPN won the rights to the entire season in January 1998. When ESPN acquired the full season of the NFL, the network was able to convince cable operators to pay a 20% increase in subscriber fees compounded annually over the length of a seven-year contract. In 1998, the increased subscriber fee pushed the monthly rate for ESPN to over $1 for the first time (Donohue, 1998). By 2003, the monthly subscriber fee for ESPN was $1.93, well above the industry average of $.13 for other cable networks (Lowry & Grover, 2003). Steve Bornstein, ESPN executive, explained, "that 20 percent compounded interest is the most important thing that ever happened to ESPN financially and still probably the most significant contributor to ESPN's success today" (Miller & Shales, 2011, p. 396).

The business model has led to great prosperity for the both the NFL and ESPN. Some reports estimate that the NFL earned $10 billion in the 2013 season, with television money being its largest revenue source (Futterman & Clark, 2013; Kaplan, 2013). In 2011, ESPN revenues were estimated at more than $8 billion (Miller & Shales, 2011, p. 727). In September 2011, the NFL reached an extension with ESPN that would run through the 2022 season, with ESPN paying an estimated $1.9 billion per year, a 63% increase over the network's previous deal with the NFL ("The Season That Was," 2012). ESPN paid an additional $100 million in 2014 for the rights to an NFL wild card playoff game that season, the first time that an NFL playoff game was televised on cable (Ourand & Karp, 2014).

## ESPN GROWTH

Even after acquiring the NFL and earning an annual profit in the 1980s, there were disagreements about the impact that ESPN and other cable television networks were having on the sports broadcasting industry. In 1988, Seth Abraham, HBO senior vice president, stated, "I think that cable has become part of the fabric of American sports. There's going to be a real blurring of the line in people's minds—there won't be so much of a distinction anymore of whether something's on cable or free broadcast" (Chad, 1988, p. F3). Neal Pilson of CBS, however, continued to be skeptical of cable's impact, contending, "I think it's part of the general marketplace, but I can't anticipate any situation in which (the networks) don't have product that we want to have. The networks are not going to be forced out of the sports business. Cable growth is going to level out. Even at its maximum penetration, the biggest projection I've ever seen for cable is 60 to 65 million homes in five to eight years. At that time, the networks will still be in every home, over 100 million" (Chad, 1988, p. F3). By 1989, ESPN was in 53 million homes, representing 58% of all television households. ESPN had annual profits estimated at $100 million (Eskenazi, 1989).

With its business model proving lucrative, the growth of ESPN was then fueled by the acquisition of more broadcast rights and the creation of other branded networks. For example, ESPN acquired the broadcast rights to Major League Baseball starting in 1990 with a four-year, $400 million package that had the network televising six baseball games per week.

In 1993, concerned that other media companies might try to implement the business model of monthly subscriber fees along with advertising revenue and challenge ESPN by starting an all-sports network, ESPN decided to launch ESPN2. Designed initially to reach a younger demographic, ESPN2 went on the air on November 2, 1993. Bornstein believed the ESPN brand name would persuade cable providers to add ESPN2 to their channel lineup. He stated, "the programming will be powerful enough. This is what affiliates want" (Sandomir, 1993, p. 35).

To generate interest in ESPN2 and get fans to call their cable providers and encourage the addition of ESPN2 as part of their channel offerings, games that fans wanted to see were strategically placed on ESPN2. Four months after its launch, ESPN2 aired a basketball game between highly ranked Duke and North Carolina. Bornstein explained the strategy: "I always planned it for ESPN2, but I wanted to cause a consumer outcry so the cable operators had to televise ESPN2. There was great political pressure. Governors, everybody else, calling and saying, 'Why don't you just put it on ESPN? My cable system doesn't carry ESPN2.' Every citizen in North Carolina and every college basketball fan thought we did a bait-and-switch on them. But it truly established ESPN2 as must-have cable" (Miller & Shales, 2011, p. 271). ESPN2 was followed by the creation of ESPNU, ESPNNews, and ESPN Classic. These networks provide additional content space to carry games, such as ESPNU's coverage of college sports. As of November 2013, ESPN2 was in 97 million homes earning $.73 per subscriber, per month, and ESPNNews and ESPNU were both in 75 million homes with each earning $.20 per subscriber, per month ("Nielsen-Rated," 2013).

As ESPN was able to create and brand more networks, its broadcast rights offers became more comprehensive. The first part of what would become this strategic opportunity was when ABC acquired majority ownership of ESPN. Although being run as separate sports divisions initially, the divisions would be consolidated, allowing for not only monetary resources but also creativity in the bidding process. When ESPN returned to televising the NBA for the 2002–2003 season, it offered a multi-network platform in which regular-season games, some playoff games, and the Finals would be on ABC, regular season and playoff games on ESPN and ESPN2, and historic games on ESPN classic. Ancillary NBA-themed programming would also be televised across many ESPN networks. In winning the rights away from NBC, Mark Shapiro, ESPN executive, commented that NBC "simply couldn't compete with the dual revenue stream we had, which gave us the ability to pay more. I'd like to think that our multiplatform strategy also had something to do with it. It was the right time for the league to make such a move to cable. And it did bring us happy days on the ratings front. It was a big game changer" (Miller & Shales, 2011, p. 483).

The availability of collegiate conference broadcast rights was another major development in the growth of ESPN. Following the 1984 U.S. Supreme Court decision that stripped the NCAA of singularly negotiating all college football television contracts, collegiate conferences obtained the ability to negotiate their own television deals with the networks. These collegiate conferences would begin selling packages of games for networks to bid similar to professional sports leagues. The Big Ten, Pac-Ten, Atlantic Coast Conference (ACC), and independent University of Miami reached agreements with CBS in January 1985. The universities in the SEC, Big Eight, Southwest Conference, and independents such as Notre Dame and Penn State were part of the College Football Association and collectively negotiated contracts with ABC and ESPN in March 1985. In the two-year agreement, ABC paid $31 million to broadcast a minimum of 21 games each season. ESPN paid $24 million to televise 17 games each season ("ABC, ESPN," 1985). For the 1987 season, ABC reached four-year agreements with the Big Ten and Pac Ten conferences for an estimated $50 million, with CBS agreeing to a four-year, $60 million contract with the College Football Association (Goodwin, 1986). The College Football Association would begin dissolving in 1991 when Notre Dame agreed to sell the broadcast rights to all of its home games to NBC. In subsequent years, all major football conferences negotiated their broadcast rights contracts with the networks.

ESPN and ABC have become prominent in acquiring these collegiate conference broadcast rights. In some instances, ABC and ESPN alone have the broadcast rights to the conference, such as the ACC. In other instances ESPN is the secondary, cable rights holder. In football, for example, the SEC has an exclusive contract with CBS as its over-the-air rights holder where the network only shows that league's games every Saturday afternoon. The SEC contract with ESPN is for prime-time games so that once CBS selects the game it will air on its network, ESPN will then select the next two SEC games each week that it will air on ESPN and ESPN2 on Saturday night.

In 2013, ESPN had broadcast rights agreements with eight collegiate conferences, accounting for more than 450 college football games to be televised on the networks of ESPN (Miller et al., 2013, p. A1). University of Florida president Bernie Machen stated, "The growth of the exposure to college football is directly related to ESPN's increased involvement in it" (Miller et al., 2013). ESPN has also acquired the broadcast rights to the college football playoff that began following the 2014 regular season. In a 12-year agreement ESPN will pay an estimated total of $715 million per year (Ourand & Smith, 2012).

Television money has been a major factor in universities joining other conferences. The addition of universities has allowed conferences the opportunity to re-open their broadcast rights agreements. The addition of Pittsburgh and Syracuse to the ACC led the ACC to renegotiate its agreement with ESPN, increasing each school's annual payment from $13 million to more than $17 million (Hiestand, 2012).

ESPN has even created college football games for the purposes of television broadcast. ESPN was instrumental in developing the Chick-fil-A Kickoff Classic, Cowboys Classic, and Texas Kickoff Classic, with all games televised on the ESPN family of networks. In 2012, Alabama played Michigan in the Cowboys Classic in a game televised on ABC with each university earning approximately $4.7 million (Miller et al., 2013). As of 2014, ESPN not only televised every Division I bowl game except one (CBS televises the Sun Bowl), it owned several of the games outright (e.g., Hawaii Bowl).

## FOLLOWING THE ESPN BUSINESS MODEL

The significant impact of ESPN in terms of the business model it implemented is that many professional leagues, collegiate conferences, individual teams, and media companies have created cable television networks as a way to replicate and capitalize on this revenue stream. This has allowed for these networks to have a role in the sports broadcast rights bidding and acquisition process. The so-called Big Four professional sports leagues have networks. As of November 2013, the NFL Network was in 72 million homes earning $1.13 per subscriber, per month; the MLB Network was in 70 million homes earning $.27 per subscriber, per month; and the NBA Network was in 59 million homes earning $.19 per subscriber, per month ("Nielsen-Rated," 2013). The National Hockey League's NHL Network was seen in 43 million homes as of July 2013, earning $.29 per subscriber, per month (Ourand & Botta, 2013).

The concept of a league-owned network emerged as early as 1988 when Major League Baseball Commissioner Peter Ueberroth thought of the idea as a way to mitigate against any potential downturn in the money paid by the television networks for baseball's broadcast rights. Bryan Burns, Major League Baseball senior vice president for broadcasting, simply explained the benefit of a league-owned network, "when you eliminate the middleman, you usually can make more money" (Chad, 1988, p. F3).

These league-owned networks have in essence created another potential bidder for broadcast rights in that if the league is not satisfied with any offers from the networks, the league could simply put games on its own network (e.g., Fortunato, 2013). Having games on these networks could also boost the monthly subscriber fees that can be charged to cable and satellite providers. In the NFL, every game is televised by one of its national broadcast partners. For baseball, basketball, and hockey, games not televised on the national networks revert to the teams to sell to a local or regional channel. These local broadcast contracts continue to be a major source of revenue for these teams. For example, the Los Angeles Lakers reached a 20-year, $3 billion deal with Time Warner Cable (Pucin, 2011). More recently, the Los Angeles Dodgers contracted with Time Warner Cable receiving $8 billion in a 25-year deal that lasts through 2038. Some teams have opted to create a network (Fisher & Ourand, 2013). For example, in 2001, the New York Yankees announced the formation of the Yankees Entertainment and Sports (YES) Network. The primary programming of the regional 24-hour all-sports network has been Yankees baseball since March 2002. One estimate is that the YES Network earned more than $435 million in 2010 (Sandomir, 2011).

Collegiate conferences have followed the same path. The Big Ten Network, launched in 2007, earned $1 per subscriber, per month in the geographic footprint of the universities in the Big Ten, and an average of $.37 in other geographic regions (Ourand & Smith, 2014). In August 2011, ESPN and the University of Texas launched the Longhorn Network, which pays the school $15 million a year over 20 years (Vascellaro & Everson, 2011). The Longhorn Network has, however, struggled to receive wide-scale distribution, including a failure to reach agreements with DirecTV and Comcast. In 2014, ESPN and the SEC Network reached agreements with enough cable operators to be available in 87 million homes upon its launch in August of that year (Quinlan, 2014). The SEC Network received an estimated $1.40 monthly subscriber fee in that conference's 11-state footprint and $.25 in other geographic regions (Ourand & Smith, 2014).

To try to compete with ESPN, traditional over-the-air broadcast networks have developed branded cable channels to support their efforts to acquire sports broadcast rights. NBC Sports re-branded the Versus channel in January 2012, creating the NBC Sports Network. This cable channel was instrumental in Comcast/NBC extending its broadcast rights agreement with the NHL with the majority of the package, including some Stanley Cup Finals games, airing on the cable channel. In February 2014, the NBC Sports Network was in 85 million homes, earning approximately $.35 per subscriber, per month (Ourand, 2014b). The Golf Channel, also part of the NBC family of networks, televises early-round coverage of PGA tournaments and is in 82 million homes earning $.29 per subscriber, per month ("Nielsen-Rated," 2013).

In 2013, News Corporation rebranded two of its cable networks (Speed Channel and Fuel TV), creating Fox Sports 1 and Fox Sports 2. As of November 2013, Fox Sports 1 was in 89 million homes, earning $.23 per subscriber, per month. Fox Sports 2 was in 36 million homes, earning $.15 per subscriber, per month ("Nielsen-Rated," 2013). Acquiring programming for Fox Sports 1 was a reason that Fox extended its national television contract with Major League Baseball. In a contract extending through 2021, Fox will televise only 12 regular season games on its over-the-air network with another 40 games to be televised on its Fox Sports 1 cable channel. Fox will continue to air on free television the World Series, the All-Star Game, with one of the League Championship Series and two of the Division Series having games possibly on both its over-the-air channel and its cable channel (Fox will also sell two Division Series games to the MLB Network). Fox will pay Major League Baseball an annual average of $525 million for these broadcast rights (Ourand, 2012).

The launching of Fox Sports 1 was also pivotal in Fox's acquiring United States Golf Association (USGA) tournaments starting in 2015, including the U.S. Men's Open. The U.S. Open in 2014 received early-round coverage on ESPN with third- and final-round coverage on NBC. The day after a 60-day exclusive negotiating window between the USGA and then rights-holders NBC and ESPN expired, Fox began negotiating to acquire the broadcast rights. Fox's eventual bid of $85 million per year more than doubled the $38 million the USGA was earning from NBC and ESPN combined (Smith, 2013). The acquisition of the U.S. Open gives Fox some days where in all probability its cable network will be more relevant than ESPN. Randy Freer, Fox Sports executive, explained the impact of its cable channel in the bidding process, stating, "having FS1 was a huge help. For the number of hours committed to this, the only way that would have been possible is due to the addition of FS1. We're here to compete for rights and you need to have fully distributed outlets to do that with" (Smith, 2013, p. 33).

## DISCUSSION

ESPN implemented a dual revenue business model of monthly subscription fees and advertising income that has altered the media landscape and the entire sports industry. Because of this lucrative business model, ESPN is a major competitor for the broadcast rights to almost every sport. The competition that ESPN has helped create for broadcast rights has greatly increased the rights fee payments to all of these leagues and events. For example, each NFL team in 2014 earned $158 million in national television money with an estimate that the payment to each team will reach at least $181 million by 2016 (Kaplan, 2014).

The process remains cyclical in that as ESPN acquires more desirable programming it can continue to raise its monthly rate, which in turn allows the network to acquire more league and event rights. Duplicating this business model by creating more channels, such as ESPN2, ESPNU, and the SEC Network, further provides the ability for ESPN to acquire and televise more sports leagues and events.

A more significant impact of ESPN in the sports broadcast rights bidding and acquisition process is that others are trying to replicate its success. Professional sports leagues, professional teams, collegiate conferences, and other media companies have launched cable television networks using the same business model. For example, News Corporation's re-branding and launching of Fox Sports 1 was instrumental in the network's acquisition of broadcast rights for Major League Baseball and the U.S. Open golf tournament. Cable television networks need quality content to attract viewers and start the process of increasing their monthly subscriber fees. Fox is doing what ESPN did three decades earlier.

Finally, because of ESPN and other cable networks having this dual revenue stream allowing for the ability to acquire broadcast rights, prominent sports events appearing on cable television is a standard practice. For example, ESPN televised the first NFL playoff game on cable after the 2014 season as well as the first College Football Playoff to determine a national champion. The success of this business model indicates that this trend of prominent sports events being televised on cable will continue for the foreseeable future.

A more debatable question regarding the future of this sports programming business model is if cable providers will continue to pay a monthly rate for sports networks and pass these costs along to their customers. One estimate is that sports networks make up 37% of an average customer's cable bill (Lazarus, 2014). This carriage dispute came into focus in 2014 when Time Warner was not able to convince cable providers to pay $4 per subscriber, per month for its new SportsNet LA channel, whose primary programming is Dodgers' games. The dispute has meant that 70% of Los Angeles homes do not have access to Dodgers' games

(Plaschke, 2014). Similar disputes have occurred in Houston and Philadelphia with Comcast-owned regional sports networks not being able to reach an agreement with DirecTV to carry the channel. Continued stalemates between networks and cable providers could lead to changes in distribution models, such as sports channels being bundled in a tier package that subscribers could choose to purchase or even complete a la carte channel selection by customers (e.g., Lazarus, 2014). Because ESPN has the most prominent sports events, it has largely avoided some of these carriage disputes that have affected other networks.

# CHAPTER FOUR

# Digging the Moat

## The Political Economy of ESPN's Cable Carriage Fees

THOMAS F. CORRIGAN

ESPN is the most profitable brand in media and a cash cow for its owner, the Walt Disney Company. Two cable networks—ESPN and the Disney Channel—generate more than half of Disney's annual operating revenue (Badenhausen, 2013). In 2013, advertisers paid $3.5 billion to reach ESPN's large male audience; however, an astounding $6.5 billion of ESPN's revenue came from carriage fees—the fees cable and satellite providers pay to Disney to include ESPN on their channel lineups (Thompson, 2013). At $5.54 per subscriber annually, ESPN's 2013 carriage fees were 20 times more expensive than the average cable channel ($0.28 per subscriber) and 4 times that of the nearest nationally distributed cable channel, TNT[1] ($1.33 per subscriber) (Bui, 2013).

For the most profitable brand in media, there is a surprising dearth of scholarly attention to ESPN as a business. Much of what we know about ESPN's history and strategy comes from reporting in the trade press (e.g., *Advertising Age*, *SportsBusiness Journal*) and the business press (e.g., *Forbes*, *New York Times*), as well as accounts in popular histories (Freeman, 2001; Miller & Shales, 2011), executive memoirs (Evey & Broughton, 2004; Rasmussen, 2010), and management guides (Smith & Hollihan, 2009). This work is valuable, and this chapter leans on it extensively; however, it is limited by each genre's reporting and narrative conventions. The trade and business press tend to report on mergers, hirings, product launches, and other business events as discrete happenings rather than contextualizing those events in relation to broader political, economic, and sociocultural trends (Bettig, 1996). Contextualization requires explanatory frameworks, and professional journalists are supposed to report—not explain. Popular histories and executive memoirs tend to focus on ESPN's key personalities—especially corporate executives and creative talent—and the choices they made in pursuit of power and profit. Surely, those at ESPN's "helm" have shaped its fortunes; however, focusing on power struggles can divert attention from the broader structural pressures and constraints within which those power struggles occur.

Two works do stand out in their attention to the business of ESPN. One is Anthony F. Smith and Keith Hollihan's (2009) management guide, *ESPN The Company*. A longtime consultant for ESPN, Smith provides an insider's look at executive decision-making and ESPN's corporate culture. Smith argued ESPN has had the right executives at its helm during each phase in the company's development; however, he places a particular emphasis on the ESPN's fan-friendly corporate culture. For Smith, the company's success with sports fans is attributable in large part to the fanaticism encouraged among those that produce its content. Gamache's (2014) study of "the ESPN assemblage" connects ESPN to the broader political economy of Late Capitalism (p. 72). Like others (e.g., Bellamy Jr., 2006; Rader, 1984), Gamache highlights Americans' "insatiable appetite" for sports and corporate advertisers' demand for young male audiences' attention (p. 75). He attributes ESPN's success to its ability to continuously whet fans' appetites for sports, corporate brands, and itself through its expansive and compelling "assemblage" of texts and properties. In the end, then, Smith and Gamache both lean on frameworks of supply, demand, and promotion to explain ESPN's ascendancy.

This chapter does not write off these considerations; instead, it aims to explain ESPN's rise and dominance by situating the company within a broader set of law and policy developments that have affected the sports, cable, and satellite television industries since the early 1960s. Although ESPN benefited from savvy executives, charismatic talent, and seemingly insatiable demand from audiences and advertisers, this chapter argues that these political and legal developments created the context for ESPN's market dominance and spectacular profitability.

## THE RASMUSSENS' SATELLITE EPIPHANY

In 1978, ESPN cofounders Bill and Scott Rasmussen conceived of a network focused on Connecticut sports and some movies that they planned to market to Connecticut cable providers. National distribution was, at the time, cost prohibitive; programmers paid by the mile to transmit content over AT&T's leased lines, restricting national distribution to the major broadcast networks (Rasmussen, 2010). Plans changed after a meeting with RCA salesman Al Parinello, though. RCA had tasked Parinello with persuading cable programmers, such as ESPN, to relay their programming to providers using RCA's Satcom 1 satellite rather than AT&T's landline network. In his pitch, Parinello tapped one of satellite communications' key economic advantages—its economies of scale (Miller & Shales, 2011). RCA's satellite could reach every cable provider in the country with an RCA Earth station. Further, it was no more expensive for ESPN to reach 1,000 cable providers than it was to reach one (Hudson, 1990; Parsons, 2008). Scott Rasmussen crunched RCA's rates and concluded that it would be less expensive to distribute a national satellite signal than to send the same programming to only Connecticut providers via landline. Seeing an opportunity, the Rasmussens signed a 5-year, $34,167 per month lease for a 24-hour transponder on RCA's Satcom 1. It would become the ESPN's "most prized possession" (Miller & Shales, 2011, p. 14).

Although satellite television may fall from the sky, cable and satellite systems— like that the Rasmussens were evaluating—do not. According to McChesney (2004), media pose a "problem" for contemporary societies. Choices must be made—many at the level of public policy—between alternative structures for producing and distributing media. And these structural choices affect the resulting content, which is evident in any comparison of public and commercial media. Media policy is bound to benefit some groups and stymie others. A brief history of cable and satellite industry deregulation during the 1970s and 1980s illustrates that key policy choices created a fortuitous context for ESPN's emergence and ascendancy.

## "Open Skies"

Prior to satellite communications, cable television was little more than a system for extending broadcast television to communities underserved by free-to-air stations. Cable providers erected large, powerful antennas on hilltops, and they distributed the broadcast signals available at those locations—via coaxial cable—to homes in nearby communities: hence, cable's original name, Community Antenna Television (CATV). As CATV grew, providers began using microwave relay to pipe distant signals into larger communities—many with existing broadcast stations. Broadcasters argued that CATV violated copyright protections and threatened the viability of local stations. Although CATV forced few stations off the air (if any), in the 1960s the FCC asserted its regulatory authority over cable and its public interest mandate to preserve broadcast localism. The FCC's 1966 Second Report and Order required that all cable providers carry local broadcast stations and that any imported signals not duplicate that local programming. More important, the FCC restricted importation of signals into the top-100 markets, effectively freezing cable's urban expansion (Parsons, 2008; Parsons & Frieden, 1998); why pay for a service that offered no more programming than that available for free from local broadcasters?

Meanwhile, Russia's 1957 launch of Sputnik touched off massive U.S. investments in space exploration, including the creation of NASA. In 1965, the public-private satellite corporation COMSAT launched Intelsat-1—the first commercial communications satellite, built by Hughes Aircraft Corporation. ABC applied to the FCC for permission to distribute its programming via the Hughes satellite; however, the FCC returned the application, saying it needed to weigh the implications of privately owned and operated satellites. The nascent technology raised various fears, including its potential use for Soviet propaganda and American cultural imperialism. The FCC opened a Notice of Inquiry in 1966, but the matter of private corporations' involvement in satellite communications would not be resolved until 1972 (Hudson, 1990; Parsons, 2008).

Proposals submitted in response to the FCC's 1966 Notice of Inquiry illustrate the range of directions commercial satellite communications could have taken. Seeking to extend its terrestrial monopoly to satellites, AT&T proposed a single, multipurpose satellite that would operate as a common carrier for its telephone, data, and television relays. In a bid to cut costs and break AT&T's distribution monopoly, CBS proposed a network-financed satellite that would also distribute public television at no cost. A Ford Foundation proposal recommended taking $30 million of broadcasters' projected $44 million in savings and putting those savings toward educational programming—a "people's dividend" for taxpayers' space investments. And in 1969, the National Cable and Telecommunications Association (NCTA) cable lobby also developed plans for a cable programming network consisting of only broadcast reruns and "nonentertainment" channels—no original entertainment programming (Hudson, 1990; Parsons, 2008).

Two aspects of these proposals are worth considering. First is their evolutionary (rather than revolutionary) thinking about broadcasters' role in the future of satellite communications. The incumbent networks occupied key roles in each proposal's programming and/or subsidy structures (even if that subsidy was reinvested as a "people's dividend"). Second, when revolutionary programming was proposed, it was noncommercial or educational in nature (although the NCTA proposal included sports as cultural fare). In 1961, FCC chairman Newton Minow had famously described broadcast television as a "vast wasteland"—hardly a regulatory environment amenable to the expansion of entertainment fare (Minow, 2003, p. 398). To come to fruition, non-network entertainment programmers, such as ESPN, would need a more competitive programming market and a more laissez-faire regulatory environment.

A combination of utopian thinking about cable's democratic potential and the appointment of regulators amenable to "free market" solutions made the 1970s ripe for the commercial expansion of cable and satellite television. In 1970, the Nixon Administration's new Office of Telecommunications Policy recommended to the FCC an "Open Skies" policy permitting private ownership and operation of communication satellites by "qualified" parties. The policy was adopted in 1972, and a flurry of private applications was approved; however, a recession, limited non-network programming, and cable's urban freeze all retarded cable-satellite interconnection (Parsons, 2008; Parsons & Frieden, 1998).

In 1976 and 1977, though, measures to protect broadcast localism gave way to deregulatory efforts purporting to expand competition and consumer choice. The FCC relaxed (among other rules) its restrictions on importing distant signals into urban areas, paving the way for superstations, such as Ted Turner's WTBS. In 1977, the D.C. Court of Appeals also struck down restrictions on HBO's "siphoning" of content away from broadcasters (Parsons, 2008; Parsons & Frieden, 1998). HBO could now run more recent movies, and cable programmers could compete with broadcasters for sports events. Urban market penetration and expanding programming options mutually reinforced one another and drove cable industry adoption of satellite relay. An entirely novel cable programming industry emerged, including USA, CNN, MTV, and ESPN.

When the Rasmussens signed their 5-year transponder contract with RCA in 1978, they found themselves at the lead edge of this demand for cable programming. Over the next year, ESPN used its transponder's national reach to put together $10 million[2] in financing from Getty Oil, a contract with the NCAA for early rounds of the men's basketball tournament, and a $1.4 million advertising contract with Anheuser-Busch—the largest in cable history. Indeed, six weeks after ESPN locked in its transponder lease, a *Wall Street Journal* article characterized satellites as the future of communications, and RCA's transponder prices quickly shot into the millions annually (Miller & Shales, 2011; Smith & Hollihan, 2009).

It is fair to attribute cable's subscriber and revenue growth during the late 1970s and 1980s to Americans' demand for new programming options, including ESPN; however, this section illustrates that policy choices shaped cable and satellite communications in ways that made a network such as ESPN viable in the first place. The FCC's 1972 "Open Skies" policy ensured that private, commercial considerations would drive satellite communications going forward, rather than real educational and non-commercial alternatives. Further, late 1970s deregulation saw consumer choice trump existing measures to protect local broadcasters from cable competition, particularly in urban markets. These were policy decisions with real winners and losers, and ESPN could not have better timed its transponder acquisition and entry into the emerging cable programming industry.

## THE DUAL REVENUE MODEL

ESPN scored some contractual coups in 1979 and the early 1980s, including NCAA basketball and hockey, the NFL draft, and the new USFL football league; however, it was unable to match competitors' bids for even Division II NCAA football, much less premiere professional sports and major college football. ESPN's programming revolved around mostly non-revenue NCAA sports and cheap, relatively obscure, prerecorded events, such as slow-pitch softball and Australian Rules Football—anything to make good on the network's promise to cable providers of 24-hour sports (Miller & Shales, 2011).

Despite ESPN's cheap sports contracts and cable industry–leading advertising revenues, the network did not come close to covering its costs. Following broadcast industry conventions, ESPN management had structured contracts with providers that promised ESPN's signal for free or for just a few cents per subscriber, monthly; however, cable's market penetration and ad rates did not stack up to its broadcast predecessors. A McKinsey and Company consultant, Roger Werner, painted two options for ESPN—liquidate the company or ask cable providers to pay for the channel. In January 1983, ESPN went hat-in-hand to cable providers, seeking four cents per subscriber in the first year, then six and eight cents in subsequent years. Negotiations were heated, but ESPN ultimately settled with every major cable provider for between 5 and 10 cents per subscriber over the next year-and-a-half (Miller & Shales, 2011; Parsons, 2008; Smith & Hollihan, 2009).

Like its acquisition of the RCA transponder, 1983 and 1984 proved an opportune time for ESPN's shift to a dual revenue model. CBS Cable had failed in 1982, and providers feared the loss of more programmers; if cable was to continue penetrating urban markets, providers needed stable, attractive programming—even if it meant paying for it. More important, though, 1984 saw two major developments that would greatly augment ESPN's ability to extract revenue from cable providers: the Supreme Court's *NCAA v. Board of Regents* decision and the Cable Communications Policy Act (the 1984 Cable Act). The following sections outline the implications of each.

## NCAA v. Board of Regents

Since 1953, the NCAA had exercised tight control over its member schools' television appearances on grounds that television exposure undermined gate receipts. The NCAA also equally distributed broadcast revenue among member schools in the name of fairness and competition. In 1977, though, 62 football powerhouses formed the College Football Association (CFA) in a bid to wrest control over their television appearances and revenue from the NCAA. When NBC offered the CFA a television contract in 1981, the NCAA threatened to ban CFA schools from championship events in every sport.

In 1984, the Boards of Regents for the Universities of Oklahoma and Georgia brought a successful antitrust suit against the NCAA for control over their respective broadcast rights. The NCAA appealed the case to the Supreme Court, arguing that its television policy was necessary to protect gate receipts and to facilitate competition among member institutions. The Court considered the NCAA's arguments since competition is, indeed, a necessary prerequisite for staging college football; however, it upheld the rulings of lower courts. A 7–2 majority found that the NCAA's television policy amounted to price-fixing and a restriction of output, and it found no sufficient evidence of pro-competitive benefits (Scully, 1985; Suggs, 2010).

The 1984 *NCAA v. Board of Regents* ruling meant schools could individually negotiate their broadcast contracts. College football's powerhouses initially opted for the CFA or their conference to negotiate broadcast contracts. In the shift from a single seller (the NCAA) to multiple sellers, football telecasts flooded the market and broadcast rights fees dropped precipitously. In 1983, the NCAA's centrally negotiated contract fetched $69.7 million. In 1984, the sum of all independently negotiated contracts amounted to just $43.6 million, despite many more games being broadcast (Staples, 2012). With its ample airtime and a new revenue stream (albeit nascent), ESPN set its sights on this flood of competitively priced football programming. In 1984, ABC also bought Getty's remaining stake in ESPN, further strengthening ESPN's bargaining position and access to rights. Just before the 1984 season, ABC signed a four-year contract with the CFA, which included ESPN's rights to a full season of major college football—48 live games (Gregory & Busey, 1985; Miller & Shales, 2011).

## The 1984 Cable Act

ESPN had now signed up cable providers to pay for its programming, and it had programming that consumers wanted. It would take one final deregulatory act to fully open subscribers' wallets to cable providers and programmers, though. While the FCC and the courts were busy deregulating cable at the federal level during the 1970s and early 1980s, a complex patchwork of franchising, programming, and rate regulations had developed on a local, municipality-by-municipality basis. By the early 1980s, the NCTA and the National League of Cities (NLC) were both looking for a more streamlined process, but they differed in their desired level of municipal regulatory control—the cities seeking to maintain their regulatory authority, cable interests seeking to roll it back. After several failed negotiations and legislative efforts, the two groups and legislators arrived at a compromise in 1984. Under the 1984 Cable Act, cities received official, statutory authority to license cable franchises, and they could require providers to reserve some channel space for public access (or PEG) channels. For cable providers, the law prohibited municipalities' tinkering with programming and authorized rate regulation only in localities without "effective competition"; however, "effective competition" was defined broadly enough to prohibit rate regulation for roughly 97% of U.S. cable systems (Parsons, 2008; Prager, 1992).

By standardizing cable's relationship with municipalities and removing rate regulations, the 1984 Cable Act ushered in an era of Wall Street investment and rapid industry expansion. In their local markets nearly all providers now operated as largely unregulated monopolies, and rosy industry prospects contributed to "merger mania" at the cable system level (Parsons, 2008). Rate regulations were completely phased out by December 1986, and subscription rates rose precipitously. According to the U.S. General Accounting Office (U.S. GAO, 1990), by December 1986, average monthly rates had risen 43% for providers' lowest priced basic cable packages and 39% for the most popular basic packages. Economists disagree about whether these rising cable rates reflected providers' monopoly pricing power or subscribers' willingness to pay for more and better programming (e.g., Anstine, 2004; Prager, 1992). Indeed, GAO data show that providers added an average of seven channels to both their lowest cost and most popular basic packages (U.S. GAO, 1990). In either case, rate deregulation meant that programming cost increases could be passed along to subscribers as rate increases.

At ESPN, the network could now pursue more expensive and attractive sports rights, increase its carriage rates, and expect providers to pay those increases—so long as subscribers were willing to foot the bill. ESPN's acquisition of college football (via the *Regents* decision) helped the network expand its subscriber base and advertising revenue, and it provided leverage in ESPN's carriage negotiations; providers dare not pull the plug on someone's alma mater (Staples, 2012). Thirty years later, ESPN has become synonymous with college football. With current broadcast contracts that include the ACC, Big 12, Big Ten, Pac-12, SEC, and the new College Football Playoffs, the network has made itself indispensable to both football fans and the cable providers that want to keep them as subscribers.

In the mid- to late 1980s, though, college football also served as a stepping-stone to other lucrative broadcast contracts. In what proved a virtuous cycle, ESPN used its expanding advertising and carriage fee revenues to acquire contracts for the America's Cup, NHL, Formula One, NASCAR, horse racing, and—most important—a full season of Major League Baseball and a half-season of NFL *Sunday Night Football*. The latter allowed ESPN to tack an 8–9 cent NFL surcharge on top of its 27 cents per subscriber carriage fee (Miller & Shales, 2011; Nagle, n.d.). Larger revenues begot premiere programming, which begot greater leverage vis-à-vis providers, which begot even greater revenue, and so on.

## Re-Tiering and Retransmission Consent

Defenders of Congress' 1984 cable rate deregulation argued that emerging multi-channel video systems, including videocassette recorders, videotape rentals, wireless cable, and direct broadcast satellites, would provide a check on cable subscription rates. Meaningful cross-industry competition never materialized, though (Parsons & Frieden, 1998). Amid growing consumer frustrations, Congress passed the 1992 Cable Television Consumer Protection and Competition Act (the 1992 Cable Act). The act included minimum customer service requirements and tasked the FCC with regulating basic cable rates. Using rates in competitive markets as its benchmark, the FCC mandated that uncompetitive systems roll back their basic cable rates by up to 10%—a figure it increased to 17% in 1994. Cable companies responded to this re-regulation with re-tiering. They hollowed out basic cable, pushing their most desirable programming, such as ESPN, to expanded tiers that were not subject to the same rate regulations. This re-tiering helped providers and programmers continue to pass along costs to consumers, and it gave those rate increases the façade of consumer choice—these packages remain providers' most popular, after all. Ultimately, though, the 1996 Telecommunications Act wiped away what limited rate regulations existed for these expanded tiers (Parsons, 2008; Parsons & Frieden, 1998).

The 1992 Cable Act's "Must Carry" and "Retransmission Consent" rules were just as important for ESPN as the re-tiering loophole, though. The Must Carry provision codified cable's long-standing industry requirement to include even small broadcast stations on their channel lineups; however, large, popular broadcast stations benefited from the act's Retransmission Consent provision. Under this provision, broadcasters could waive their Must Carry privilege and, instead, demand payment from a cable provider for carrying its signal. The provider could turn down the broadcaster's offer, of course, but retransmission consent nonetheless opened the door for cable's compensation of broadcasters for their programming (Mullen, 2008; Parsons, 2008; Parsons & Frieden, 1998). Although seemingly tangential, ESPN had its connections—through its broadcast owners—to this Retransmission Consent provision. In 1985, Capital Cities Communications' acquisition of ABC/ESPN had created a broadcasting behemoth. Then, ABC's largest affiliate owner, Hearst, purchased a 20% share in ESPN in 1990 (Miller & Shales, 2011). These connections to broadcast stations meant that CapCities/ABC and Hearst could use retransmission of their broadcast stations to improve ESPN's leverage with cable providers. As explained shortly, this leverage proved crucial in the 1993 launch of ESPN2.

The year 1990 also saw Steve Bornstein take the helm at ESPN. Bornstein aimed to transform ESPN from a single network to a multimedia brand synonymous with sports. Longtime ESPN consultant Anthony F. Smith uses the phrase "digging the moat" to describe the company's multiplatform brand expansion under Bornstein. The metaphor refers to "serv[ing] fans in every possible way, while taking up all the open space in a market" (Smith & Hollihan, 2009, p. 29). Bornstein started by launching ESPN Radio in 1992—a significant reach into every nook and cranny of the sports fan's life. In Bornstein's assessment, though, a single 24-hour sports network was not enough to keep attractive sports rights from a competitor such as Liberty Media's regional sports network affiliates—Prime Sports Network. ESPN needed a second network to dig the "moat" (Miller & Shales, 2011).

Bornstein approached the CapCities/ABC brass with a problem and a proposition. In the wake of the 1992 act, cable providers had organized a united front against paying for broadcast signals under the Retransmission Consent provision. Cable leaders threatened to take large broadcast stations off the air before they would ever pay for those signals (Parsons, 2008; Parsons & Frieden, 1998). Facing an impending standoff, Bornstein argued that CapCities/ABC should pass on cash for retransmission of its broadcast stations' signals, and negotiate, instead, for channel space for its new network—ESPN2 (Miller & Shales, 2011). Fox struck the first such arrangement for its fX cable network (Parsons, 2008), and CapCities/ABC, on Bornstein's recommendation, followed suit. With both the CapCities/ABC- and Hearst-owned signals as leverage, in October 1993, ESPN2 launched in 10 million homes—at the time, the largest launch in cable television history (Miller & Shales, 2011).

Following MTV's model, ESPN2 aimed to lure young males with action sports, highlights set to rock music, and brash, irreverent hosts. This Gen-X branding ultimately went by the wayside, but the channel proved a valuable delivery vehicle for ESPN's spillover programming, generating $0.68 per subscriber by 2013 (Bui, 2013; Miller & Shales, 2011). In subsequent years, ESPN would launch more channels, including ESPN Classic (1995), ESPNews (1996), ESPN Deportes (2004), ESPNU (2005), and HD versions of each. In negotiating for these channels' carriage and fees, Disney continued using ABC-owned broadcast stations as leverage. This strategy has sometimes resulted in bitter carriage disputes (Salop, Chipty, DeStefano, Moresi, & Woodbury, 2010; Stelter, 2012); however, Disney executives have bluntly underscored the importance of retransmission consent in growing and monetizing the ESPN family of networks. As Disney chair Michael Eisner told investors in 2004:

> Without ABC in our own stations, we would not have been able to achieve the major growth we have realized at ESPN and our other cable holdings; because ABC offers the highly valued programming that cable operators need, i.e., retransmission consent. (Rogerson, 2005, p. 36)

All this is to say that the wide availability and high carriage fees for the ESPN family of networks are not solely a function of consumer demand for these networks. They are also a function of broadcasters' ability to demand in-kind compensation from cable providers (i.e., carriage of new cable networks) in exchange for retransmission of local broadcast signals. This opportunity would not have been possible had Congress not included the Retransmission Consent provision in the 1992 Cable Act. In this, demand for ABC content is built into carriage fees of

ESPN2 and ESPN's wider family of networks. Indeed, it is part of the reason these and many other cable networks exist in the first place. They emerged as an alternative to cable providers paying to carry network broadcast stations on their channel lineups.

## Compounding Rate Increases

From 1987 to 1997, ESPN broadcast *Sunday Night Football* during the second half of the NFL season (TNT broadcast the first half from 1990 to 1997). With its NFL contract up for renegotiation in 1998, Steve Bornstein wanted a full season for ESPN, yet he had new bosses to answer to. The Walt Disney Company had purchased CapCities/ABC for $19 billion in 1995, and convincing Disney to spring for more football would be tough. ABC was—at least on paper—losing plenty of money on *Monday Night Football*. If Disney was to invest in both ABC's *Monday Night Football* and ESPN's *Sunday Night Football*, ESPN would need to show that its carriage fees could close the gap between advertising revenues and the NFL's enormous broadcast rights fees. Eisner tasked ESPN's longtime affiliate sales representative George Bodenheimer with determining what kind of premium cable providers would pay for a full NFL season on ESPN. After consulting with providers, Bodenheimer reported that ESPN could secure 20% yearly carriage fee increases, compounded annually. And, indeed, after ESPN won its full season of *Sunday Night Football* in 1998, the network inked those increases for seven full years (Miller & Shales, 2011).

It is from 1998 on, then, that ESPN's carriage fees soared. By securing not only annual rate increases but also compounding increases, ESPN ensured itself exponential carriage fee growth. Indeed, during ESPN's 1998–2005 NFL contract, the network's average carriage fee jumped from 40 cents per subscriber to more than $3.00 (Cruppi & Bachmann, 2010; Miller & Shales, 2011). How could ESPN command those sorts of rate increases? Americans have demonstrated an insatiable appetite for sports (Rader, 1984), but demand alone cannot explain rate hikes like this. One must also look at the market structure for U.S. professional sports broadcast rights—the supply side—to make sense of ESPN's market power. And, like the cable, satellite, and college football marketplaces already discussed, there is nothing natural about the professional sports broadcast rights marketplace; it is the product of antitrust law dating to the early 1960s.

## The Sports Broadcasting Act of 1961

Prior to 1962, NFL teams negotiated their broadcast contracts on a franchise-by-franchise basis, and contract values varied widely by market size. In 1960, though, the upstart American Football League (AFL) tried a new strategy—pooling their broadcast rights for centralized sale and equal distribution of the revenue. In June 1960—before playing a game—the AFL contracted with ABC for five years at $2.1 million annually. The NFL followed suit, pooling its broadcast rights in two giant 1961 deals; however, a federal court voided the NFL's regular season contract with CBS on antitrust grounds.

In 1961, NFL Commissioner Alvin "Pete" Rozelle went to Capitol Hill to lobby for an antitrust exemption for the sale of professional sports rights. Rozelle argued that centralized broadcast rights sale and revenue distribution was necessary to ensure competitive parity between small- and large-market franchises (an argument much the same as the NCAA's in the 1984 *Regents* case). Rozelle faced limited opposition, and in September President John F. Kennedy signed the Sports Broadcasting Act of 1961 (SBA). The SBA has been called "one of the most important pieces of sports law ever promulgated" (Walker & Bellamy, 2008, p. 229). It granted professional baseball, basketball, hockey, and football leagues an antitrust exemption for the pooled sale of "sponsored telecast" rights. In this, the SBA replaced a reasonably competitive (if unbalanced) market of franchise-by-franchise rights sale with a monopolistic market where broadcasters bid for a single NFL rights package (Corrigan, 2011; Corrigan & Formentin, 2011).

In the United States, the major professional sports leagues all use the SBA's antitrust exemption to pool their national broadcast rights for sale as exclusive packages. And unlike the NBA or MLB, which sell their local broadcast rights on a franchise-by-franchise basis, the NFL only sells its rights as exclusive national packages. Thus, if ESPN wants rights to any NFL games, it can only purchase those rights from the NFL (not individual franchises), and only ESPN can broadcast those particular games (not another network). For ESPN, the central, monopolized sale of exclusive national broadcast rights meant that the company could "dig the moat" around itself as *the* source for NFL football on cable. Yes, consumer demand for NFL football was strong, and cable providers were willing to pay ESPN's carriage fee increases to attract and keep their subscribers; however, without the SBA's antitrust exemption, ESPN would have found it much more difficult to foreclose other cable networks from acquiring NFL programming.

## THE DIGITAL ERA

Digital media have proved something of a mixed bag for ESPN and its lucrative dual revenue model. On the one hand, 500-channel cable lineups, the Web, and mobile applications have all created new avenues for ESPN to further dig the moat and ingrain itself in sports fans' lives. ESPN.com has carved out a spot as one of the top U.S. sports Web properties in both traffic and consumption (Fisher, 2014).

And while the ESPN Mobile phone proved a bust, ESPN's mobile apps deliver a stunning 70% of all sports content consumed on mobile devices (Greenfeld, 2012).

This success in online and mobile spaces has created opportunities for ESPN to translate its dual revenue model to the Web. With ESPN3 and WatchESPN streaming video services, consumers can watch thousands of live sports events and ESPN studio programming on their laptops, mobile devices, and "smart TVs." ESPN bundles these "TV Everywhere" offerings as part of its negotiations with cable companies and other Internet service providers (Ourand, 2011). Consumers who authenticate as a subscriber with a participating provider can watch ESPN's streaming video. Others are prompted to call their provider and ask for ESPN3 or WatchESPN (i.e., complain). Although authentication systems have stymied these services, ESPN is committed to the system; it completes only deals that include mobile and broadband rights for TV Everywhere (Ourand, 2011).

New media have ushered in new competition for audiences and broadcast rights, though. The NFL, MLB, Big Ten Conference, and New York Yankees (among others) have created cable networks that essentially compete with ESPN for their broadcast rights (Ourand, 2010). Further, 21st Century Fox, Comcast-NBCU, and CBS Corporation have started (or repurposed) cable sports networks geared to national audiences—Fox Sports 1 (2013), Fox Sports 2 (2013), NBC Sports Network (2012), and CBS Sports Network (2011). With their conglomerate backing, these networks could challenge ESPN for premiere broadcast rights packages. Still, ESPN's carriage fees are 17 to 34 times that of these networks, meaning that ESPN can better absorb the costs of any potential bidding war ("What You Pay for Sports," n.d.).

As audiences fragment across the media landscape, live sports remain one of the few remaining tools for consistently aggregating mass audiences, ensuring their attention to ads, and keeping them subscribed to cable. Thus, rights fees, carriage fees, and cable subscription rates continue to rise (Garfield, 2012; Ourand, 2011). For more than a decade, Senator John McCain (R-Arizona) has tapped into consumer frustration with cable rates, railing against Disney and other cable programmers' practice of "bundling" together multiple cable channels in their negotiations with cable providers. Instead, McCain advocates for an a la carte structure where consumers pay for only those channels they watch (Sandomir, Miller, & Eder, 2013).

No company is a bigger opponent of a la carte proposals than Disney/ESPN, which generates the bulk of its revenue from its cable bundle. Aside from traditional lobbying, Disney uses its assets in creative ways. Just before the FCC released a 2004 study on cable economics, Disney invited FCC chair Michael Powell to be a guest on ABC's *Monday Night Football* and pitch the FCC's digital television transition to consumers. Weeks later, the FCC's cable study said debundling would raise consumer rates and reduce the diversity of programming—a coup for Disney. House Energy and Commerce Committee Chairman Joe Barton (R-Texas) would also play an important role in any potential bundling legislation. In 2005, Disney donated tens of thousands to Barton's political action committee, and it paid for a lavish Disney World trip for Barton to do some fact finding. When McCain eventually proposed de-bundling legislation, Disney's lobbying paid off. The vote failed in committee, 20 to 2 (Sandomir et al., 2013).

Bundles or no, some consumers are taking things into their own hands by cutting the cord and going without cable TV. Through a combination of cable alternatives, such as Netflix, Roku, and free-to-air stations, industrious cord-cutters can watch plenty of quality television without paying for cable. Ironically, this may *increase* the value of live sports and the networks that carry them. Because live sports are not readily available on the Web, cable providers know it is one of the few programming genres keeping some consumers from cutting the cord (Garfield, 2012). Even this is changing, though. Peer-to-peer screen-sharing technologies have advanced to a point where consumers can acquire unauthorized, high-quality feeds of sporting events from around the globe from websites, such as wiziwig.com (Corrigan, 2014). Because this piracy undermines rights holders' lucrative exclusivity, sports leagues and media firms (including Disney) came together in 2008 to form The Sports Coalition—a group dedicated to lobbying against sports piracy (Fisher, 2009). Whether it is bundles or piracy, Disney knows that law and policy outcomes will continue to shape ESPN's digital fortunes. The key difference now is that ESPN is powerful enough to meaningfully influence the law and policy that affects it.

## CONCLUSION

The existing literature on ESPN tends to explain the network's phenomenal success as a function of savvy executives, charismatic talent, and Americans' insatiable appetite for sports. Each of these factors has certainly been important; however, ESPN did not achieve its dominance in a vacuum. This chapter identified several key law and policy developments that since the 1960s have shaped the sports, cable, and satellite television industries in ways that were fortuitous for ESPN. Yes, ESPN's executives recognized Americans' demand for live sports and witty banter; however, there is nothing natural or inevitable about the markets for sports or media. They are products of struggle over law and policy, and ESPN has been a clear beneficiary of those struggles.

One theme illustrated in this chapter is ESPN's fortuitous timing. Network executives consistently embarked on major business endeavors at just the moments when law and policy developments helped ensure the success of those endeavors. First, the Rasmussens didn't just see the value in RCA's satellite transponder in

1978; they did so at just the moment when "Open Skies" satellite policy and dereg-ulation of urban cable markets produced a budding cable programming industry, making that transponder's reach extraordinarily valuable. Second, ESPN pursued its dual revenue model as a matter of survival in 1983 and 1984. Before the ink could dry on those contacts, though, the *NCAA vs. Board of Regents* case made col-lege football available to ESPN and the 1984 Cable Act removed rate regulations. With fans footing the bill for premiere sports and the increased carriage fees that accompanied them, ESPN's dual revenue model helped it not only survive but also thrive. Third, the launch of ESPN2 in 1993 helped ESPN expand its carriage fee business, as well as its moat within the sports broadcast marketplace. ESPN2's historic launch got a boost, though, from the 1992 Cable Act's Retransmission Consent provision, which allowed ESPN to use ABC broadcast stations as lever-age in securing broad carriage for the new network. All of these developments occurred, though, in the larger context of the 1961 Sports Broadcasting Act's an-titrust exemption. Its impact is seen most clearly in ESPN's ability to translate its NFL contract into annually compounding rate increases; however, this law also inflates the value of all other national broadcast rights contracts, of which ESPN owns many and passes their costs along to providers and subscribers.

Digital media are a mixed bag of threats and opportunities for ESPN, allow-ing the network to expand its "moat" and monetize new platforms; new media also bring new competition, calls for debundling, and threats from piracy. Although any projections about ESPN's digital future are speculative at best, what is certain is that law and policy outcomes will continue to shape ESPN's fortunes—they always have. The key difference now is that ESPN is powerful enough to mean-ingfully influence the law and policy outcomes that affect it. Indeed, to the extent that Disney's success hinges on ESPN's, the network has a powerful backer in advancing its policy agenda.

## NOTES

1. Some regional sports networks also command high carriage fees, but they reach a fraction of ESPN's and TNT's audiences.
2. Smith and Hollihan (2009) and others peg Getty's 1979 investment at $10 million, and Miller and Shales (2011) put the figure closer to $15 million.

# CHAPTER FIVE

# ESPN Deportes

## Numero Uno?

HENRY PUENTE

The Pew Research Center revealed that the number of people who spoke Spanish at home in the United States is expected to swell from about 25 million in 2000 to about 40 million by 2020 (Lopez & Gonzalez-Barrera, 2013). The growing number of Spanish-speakers caught some mainstream cable networks such as ESPN off guard. ESPN ironically had successfully begun to multiplex sister channels such as ESPN2 in 1993 to attract additional sports fans (Smith & Hollihan, 2009, p. 16). ESPN, however, failed to develop a 24-hour Spanish-language channel in the 1990s. When ESPN Deportes (Spanish for *sports*) debuted on a part-time basis in 2001, it represented ESPN's initial venture in acquiring content, simulcasting its current content in Spanish and producing programming that specifically targeted these sports fans. The launch of ESPN Deportes lagged far behind FOX Deportes (formerly Fox Sports en Español) that had begun to target Spanish-speaking sports fans as early as 1996 (Guthrie, 2012).

This chapter examines whether ESPN Deportes will be able to keep up with strong competitors, such as FOX Deportes and Univision Deportes, and fend off emerging competitors such as beIN Sports. It initially chronicles ESPN Deportes' emergence to becoming Nielsen's most watched Spanish-language sports cable network for four consecutive years (Nunez, 2013). The chapter also pinpoints why FOX Deportes overtook ESPN Deportes; current and future challenges for ESPN Deportes; and why, despite being one of the current Spanish-speaking sports cable network leaders, ESPN Deportes' future is clouded with uncertainty.

## SPANISH-LANGUAGE MARKET

ESPN Deportes' debut illustrated that its owners, Disney/ABC, could no longer ignore the Spanish-speaking market that had swelled to $650 million in buying power (Wilbert, 2003). ESPN wanted to use ESPN Deportes as a vehicle to build brand awareness within this increasingly lucrative market. But Spanish-speaking sports fans were accustomed to watching their sports on other networks such as Univision. While ESPN Deportes clearly was the leading Spanish-language sports network until 2012 (Consoli, 2013), Nielsen ratings indicated that FOX Deportes had attracted 25% more daily primetime viewers than ESPN Deportes (78,000 vs. 59,000) by May 2013 (Consoli).

ESPN Deportes and some Spanish-language sports cable networks have identified this market with more than 50 million people and more than $1 trillion of buying power as an important demographic to target (Bercovici, 2012; Kissell, 2013). More than 36% of U.S. Latinos/as older than 12 were considered serious sports fans, which exceeded serious sports fans across other ethnic and racial groups (Gonzalez, 2002). Latinos/as also had become more valuable to these relatively new Spanish-language sports networks because they are significantly younger than the mainstream population (27 versus 41), watched more television than Caucasians, and primarily consumed television in both English and Spanish (Morello, 2011; Piñón & Rojas, 2011). FOX Deportes lastly has illustrated that these viewers can be quite loyal if a sports cable network could secure the right type of sports content (Piñón & Rojas, 2011).

Along with an increasing number of Spanish-language sports cable networks, ESPN Deportes also needs to be concerned with a potential subscription limit as the demographics of the U.S. Latino/a market change. The growth within the U.S. Latino/a market is coming from births and not immigration ("Lights, Camera," 2012). Assimilated Latinos/as prefer watching mainstream cable or television networks programming instead of Spanish-language programming ("Lights, Camera"). Although second-generation Latinos/as may prefer mainstream programming, they retain a high level of bilingualism and continue to watch Spanish-language television (Piñón & Rojas, 2011; Tran, 2010). As a result, ESPN Deportes has the ability to retain this growing number of bilingual viewers with its Spanish-language programming.

## ESPN DEPORTES' EMERGENCE AND SUCCESS

ESPN Deportes was ESPN's second attempt to develop a Spanish-language network. ESPN initially wanted to start a cable network named ESPN en Español (Dempsey, 2001). The ESPN en Español venture was not feasible because many

Multiple System Operators (MSOs) could not place the network on their line-ups due to limited channel space (Dempsey). ESPN en Español would have had large production costs because it produced a lot of live programming. These high expenses could not be offset by the MSOs' limited carriage space. As a result, ESPN stopped pursing the ESPN en Español plan. MSOs eventually made technological improvements to their systems, which finally enabled ESPN to launch a Spanish-language network several years later (Dempsey).

ESPN Deportes entered a much different marketplace from its mainstream predecessor, ESPN. When ESPN entered the sports cable television world in 1979 with coverage of a slo-pitch softball game, the network had little to no competition from any other English-language sports cable network ("ESPN Becoming," 2004). ESPN Deportes initially debuted in April 2001 as a part-time network that aired five hours of programming on Sunday nights, featuring *Sunday Night Baseball* in Spanish (Dempsey, 2001; Sutter, 2003a). By the time ESPN Deportes finally debuted as a 24-hour cable channel with its first program, *Somos ESPN Deportes* on January 7, 2004, the company—perhaps for the first time—was entering a marketplace in which it was not starting out as the clear-cut leader.

ESPN's initial goal was to use ESPN Deportes to target the growing number of Spanish-speaking and bilingual U.S. Latinos/as by simulcasting its current content. The network initially had about eight million subscribers (Prentis, 2001). ESPN Deportes quickly grew to about 11 million subscribers in about three months (Prentis). Candy Maldonado, an ESPN Deportes analyst, contended that viewership had grown because baseball had many Latino superstars and Spanish-speaking fans enjoyed watching baseball games in their native language (Prentis).

ESPN Deportes managed to grow quickly by not charging MSOs a carriage fee ("ESPN's Spanish Network," 2004). It essentially provided subscribers with an extended free preview. ESPN Deportes reached about 13 million subscribers by 2003 through this strategy (Sutter, 2003). ESPN Deportes planned to keep its current subscription base and attract more subscribers by televising 200 live events, including MLB, UEFA Champions League, National Basketball Association (NBA), and boxing (Silvestrini, 2004).

When ESPN Deportes went to a full-time network in 2004, it decided to discontinue its free preview and begin charging cable system a carriage fee ("ESPN's Spanish Network," 2004). Many MSOs and satellite carriers responded by pulling ESPN Deportes off their lineups. Although some cable systems in heavily populated Latino/a markets, such as Los Angeles and Miami, continued to carry ESPN Deportes, this plan backfired as the number of subscribers plummeted to about a million ("ESPN Increases," 2005; Silvestrini, 2004; Sutter, 2003b).

The owners of ESPN (Disney/ABC) stepped in and helped ESPN Deportes in securing carriage on more MSOs by lowering its retransmission consent fees in

2004. MSOs could not afford to pay ESPN and its sister channels the skyrocketing retransmission consent fees along with ESPN Deportes' fee. ESPN, in turn, agreed to reduce carriage fee increases to large MSOs, such as Charter and Cox cable systems, from a 20% down to a 7% annual increase (Dempsey, 2004). ESPN simultaneously leveraged lower retransmission consent fees to secure carriage for ESPN Deportes on cable systems like Charter (Dempsey). Had ESPN not lowered its retransmission consent fees, MSOs and satellite carriers might not have placed ESPN Deportes back on their respective lineups.

ESPN Deportes lacked a strong presence with Spanish-speaking sports fans in 2005. For example, the network did not receive adequate human resources from its parent company to cover vital Los Angeles events, one of the most important Spanish-speaking cities in the United States (Stewart, 2007). ESPN began to address this problem in 2005 when it agreed to build a five-story building in the LA Live Sports and Entertainment District, now adjacent to the Staples Center (Johnson & Stewart, 2005). George Bodenheimer, president of ESPN and ABC Sports, said, "the Southern California center would play a significant role in producing content produced for ESPN Deportes" (Johnson & Stewart, 2005, para. 14). ESPN and ABC additionally launched ESPN Deportes Radio in Los Angeles on KWKW-AM (Stewart, 2005a). ESPN then developed a partnership between *ESPN The Magazine* and Mexico's *Editoriales Televisa* to produce a magazine entitled *ESPN Deportes* ("ESPN Increases," 2005). ESPN's increasing focus on Spanish-speaking fans in 2005 certainly played a major role in helping ESPN Deportes become a more recognizable brand with younger Spanish-speaking sports fans.

In 2005, ESPN Deportes also began airing more original programming and secured some significant sports licenses that would appeal to Spanish-speaking fans. For example, after securing the television rights to Major League Soccer (MLS), ESPN Deportes produced programs such as *Futbol Picante*, centered on Mexican soccer, and *Cronomento*, a Spanish version of *Pardon the Interruption* (Gutierrez, 2005). A Spanish-language network had never produced so much original content from a MLS site on game day in its short history (Gutierrez).

ESPN Deportes focused much of its coverage on Los Angeles–based MLS teams, including Chivas USA, to attract viewers from the largest Spanish-speaking market in the United States (Gutierrez, 2005). ESPN Deportes began to cover the X-Games in Spanglish (Spanish that includes use of English words), including Latino street skateboarding star Paul Rodriguez (Arritt, Thomas, & Abrams, 2005). The X-Games also had an ESPN Deportes Day (Stewart, 2005b). While its ratings continued to lag behind Fox Sports en Español, ESPN Deportes' increasing focus on Spanish-speaking fans certainly began to close the gap (Stewart, 2007).

In 2008, ESPN Deportes grew rapidly into new markets by taking advantage of MSOs' improved technology and their heightened focus on Spanish-speaking subscribers. As MSOs expanded their bandwidth to accommodate more content, they targeted a growing number of Latino/a households in their local affiliate markets by adding Latino/a-oriented channels to their lineups (Winslow, 2008). Time Warner, Comcast, Cox, and Dish Network developed special Latino/a-oriented bundles or added more Latino/a cable networks to their current lineups (Gibbons, 2009; Winslow, 2008). ESPN Deportes subsequently secured carriage with large MSOs such as Time Warner and was able to expand its subscription base in 2008 (Stewart, 2007). Although ESPN Deportes certainly benefited from the MSOs' improved technology, it also made it easier for more Spanish-language sports cable networks such as Univision Deportes to enter the market as the number of Latino/a-oriented cable networks grew from 88 in 2008 to 131 in 2013 (Winslow, 2008, 2013).

That year, ESPN Deportes benefited from being added to Nielsen Homevideo Index Hispanic (NHIH) service. ESPN Deportes became the sixth cable network this service rated (Ibarra, 2008). Shortly thereafter, NHIH reported that ESPN Deportes had become the number-one rated sports and most watched cable channel for Spanish-speaking fans ("ESPN Deportes Reloads," 2008). It went on to report that ESPN Deportes had the top five Spanish-language cable sports news and commentary programs over the two weeks from April 28 to May 11, 2008 ("ESPN Deportes Reloads"). NHIH's initial ratings illustrated to advertisers that ESPN Deportes had overtaken FOX Sports en Español as the Spanish-language sports leader. ESPN Deportes' programming decision to televise more soccer games and tournaments, including the popular 2008 UEFA European Football Championship, was working (Cakirozer, 2008; Stewart, 2007).

ESPN Deportes bolstered its soccer programming in 2009 by adding Jorge Ramos, a popular FOX Sports en Español sportscaster, to its lineup, creating more synergy between ESPN Deportes radio and television programming. Ramos produced and co-hosted *Jorge Ramos en Vivo* with Hernan Pereyra ("ESPN Deportes Enters," 2009). They previously had FOX Sports en Espanol's highest-rated studio show ("ESPN Deportes Enters").

Ramos has enjoyed a long and illustrious career as a soccer sportscaster who, by that time, had covered four World Cups. His audience knew him as "El Relator de las Americas" (Commentator of the Americas) ("ESPN Deportes Debuts," 2009). ESPN Deportes radio listeners were already familiar with his soccer program, *Jorge Ramos y Su Banda,* a popular three-hour radio program he began in 2005. The program often offered its listeners exclusive interviews with some of the best-known soccer personalities ("ESPN Deportes Debuts"). The simulcast of Ramos's program certainly could attract his FOX Sports en Español viewers to ESPN Deportes, which could increase the network's ratings or subscription base. Perhaps more important, ESPN Deportes had acquired a popular sportscaster and simultaneously took away one of its competitor's best assets.

ESPN Deportes continued to produce soccer programming that appealed to Spanish-language sports fans. ESPN Deportes televised a documentary, *Frente al Reto* (Facing the Challenge), featuring goalkeeper Guillermo Ochoa and midfielder Giovanni Dos Santos, both members of the popular Mexican team (Baxter, 2010). The documentary focused on the various players' triumphs and setbacks prior to Mexico's final selection of its 2010 FIFA World Cup roster (Baxter). The film appealed to soccer-crazed Mexican sports fans living in the United States.

ESPN Deportes continued acquiring important soccer programming, providing Spanish-language coverage of the 2010 FIFA World Cup. By 2012, ESPN Deportes began televising a daily soccer match that included the Barclays Premiere League and international soccer friendlies ("ESPN Deportes Unveils," 2012). In 2014, ESPN Deportes acquired the rights to more than 120 Liga MX and Copa MX games and produced several documentaries around the 2014 FIFA World Cup (Nunez, 2013). ESPN Deportes had done an excellent job of acquiring soccer content in an effort to increase its subscription base and keep its target audience happy.

ESPN Deportes continued improving its facilities outside of the network's headquarters in Bristol, Connecticut, which enabled it to produce more Spanish-language content for its viewers. For instance, ESPN Deportes used its various international and U.S. bureaus in Miami and Los Angeles to produce *E:60 en Español* episodes (Nunez, 2012). Patterned after the English-language version of *E:60,* the investigative sports program focused on stories that would be of interest to the Spanish-speaking audience (Huff, 2011). ESPN Deportes also debuted *Nación ESPN* (ESPN Nation), which Adriana Monsalve and David Faitelson co-hosted. Modeled after ESPN's *SportsNation,* this was the first studio show to be produced in Los Angeles (Nunez, 2011). The program utilized studio technology to access different platforms, such as various social media sites, to engage Latino sport fans and weave their comments into the program (Nunez, 2011). ESPN Deportes added state-of-the-art technology into its Miami studios to improve the viewing and listening experience of *Jorge Ramos y Su Banda* fans ("ESPN Deportes Unveils," 2012). With state of the art studios, ESPN Deportes could now easily produce more original Spanish-language content out of its Miami and Los Angeles studios.

Besides its good ratings and significantly bolstering its programming, ESPN Deportes had managed to keep its low carriage fees, enabling it to secure carriage of many MSOs and satellite operators. Dish Network, for example, had once paid ESPN Deportes about $.47 per subscriber in 2005 (Gardner, 2013). In 2008, Verizon only paid $.03 per subscriber (Gardner, 2013; Raymond & Baker, 2013). These low carriage fees, however, will eventually create an enormous challenge to remain profitable in an era of increasing sports licensing costs.

ESPN Deportes could continue leveraging its various platforms, such as ESPN Deportes *La Revista* (Spanish-language version of *ESPN the Magazine*), espndeportes.com, ESPN Sync, and ESPN Deportes Wireless to make media buys more attractive to advertisers (Nunez, 2013; Stewart, 2007). Its NHIH figures along with its various platforms certainly would be useful tools for ESPN Deportes to attract more advertisers.

## ESPN DEPORTES' COMPETITORS

ESPN Deportes' long delay in getting into the Spanish-language market meant that it would have to overcome several competitors. With better cable technology to carry more channels, the Spanish-language sports market has been saturated with several new cable networks such as Latin American Sports. ESPN Deportes consequently finds itself in a heated battle with FOX Deportes and other well-financed cable networks along with sport-specific cable networks, such as beIN Sports. Some of their competitors, Univision Deportes among them, have been able to leverage their well-known over-the-air television networks to secure carriage on most large MSOs and satellite carriers.

Univision Deportes, which debuted in 2012, is ESPN Deportes' primary competitor (Kissell, 2013). Univision Deportes has secured carriage deals with several large cable systems, including Time Warner Cable, and reaches 35 million viewers, which doubles ESPN Deportes in subscribers (Reynolds, 2013). Univision Deportes covered more Liga MX soccer than any other U.S. network ("Hispanic Upfront," 2013). Its coverage of Liga MX attracted more viewers than NBC's English Premier League and had 14 of the top 15 rated soccer telecasts in the first quarter of 2014 (Kondolojy, 2014). It also had the rights to the Mexican and U.S. national soccer team games, MLS, and Formula 1 racing as of 2013 (Reynolds, 2013). In 2014, Univision Deportes signed an eight-year deal with MLS and U.S. soccer that will include coverage of the MLS Cup, AT&T MLS All-Star Game, and retain the rights to four U.S. national men and women's matches until 2022 ("MLS, U.S. Soccer," 2014). Univision Deportes seems intent on backing up its claim to being the leading network for Spanish-speaking sport fans (Reynolds). Univision Deportes could also benefit from Univision's alliance with the powerful Televisa, a large Mexican mass media conglomerate. Televisa owns a couple of Mexican soccer teams, including the popular Club America. Televisa could easily grant Univision exclusive television rights to its two soccer teams because Liga MX teams negotiate individual television deals within Mexico and abroad (Parrish & Nauright, 2014, p. 189). Univision possesses the U.S. television rights to most of the Liga MX teams (Guthrie, 2012). This well-financed sports network has illustrated the ability to match, even exceed, the amount that ESPN Deportes can pay for sports content.

FOX Deportes was the trendsetter in the Spanish-language sports network and unseated ESPN Deportes to become the current Nielsen leader in ratings (Maglio, 2013). As of 2013, it has about 21 million subscribers, which is more than ESPN Deportes (Reynolds, 2013). The cable network is a joint venture between 20th Century Fox and Fox Pan American Sports LLC. FOX Deportes initially had some strong soccer programming that included Euro 2004 and MLS and featured several Latino stars ("Fox Sports World," 2004; Jones, 2003). FOX Deportes expanded outside of soccer by beginning to broadcast NASCAR in Spanish in 2006 (Ginn, 2006). The cable network possesses the rights to the popular UEFA Champions League and Copa Libertadores (South American soccer tournament) (Maglio, 2013). It also televises non-soccer U.S. sports content such as the American and National League Championship Series, MLB games, college football, and UFC fights (Maglio). FOX Deportes also telecast the 2014 Super Bowl in Spanish for the first time (Prieto, 2014).

Fox's change in programming has resulted in higher ratings and an increase in advertising revenue (Maglio, 2013). FOX Deportes claims it averages more viewers in the key 18–49 demographic and primetime viewers than ESPN Deportes (Maglio). Although FOX Deportes did not earn the Spanish-language rights for the 2018 World Cup and 2022 World Cup, its mainstream partner acquired the English-language rights to cover the next two World Cups (Longman, 2011). FOX Deportes certainly will use this synergy to produce original Spanish-language programming around this popular sporting event. This network affiliation with a media conglomerate like Fox also gives it the financial support necessary to compete with ESPN Deportes for sports content such as future World Cups.

Deportes Telemundo, which Comcast/NBC owns, has entered the chase for Spanish-speaking sports fans. Telemundo acquired the network television rights to the 2018 and 2022 World Cups for $600 million (Guthrie, 2012; "Lights, Camera," 2012). It also purchased the rights to the 2015 and 2019 Women's World Cup and the rights to other FIFA soccer tournaments, including the Confederation Cups (Longman, 2011; Rosenblatt, 2011). Telemundo's successful World Cup bid is significantly more money than ESPN and Univision paid for either the 2010 or the 2014 World Cup (Longman). The bid also represents Telemundo's increasing effort to attract more Spanish-speaking sports fans to its network. Deportes Telemundo also secured the Spanish-language television rights to games from the Barclays Premier League, one of the most popular soccer leagues in the world, when its corporate owner NBC/Universal paid $80 million a year for broadcast rights (Prindiville, 2013). Backed by its media conglomerate's assets, Telemundo will be a significant ESPN Deportes' competitor in the future.

beIN Sports is a looming competitor. Al Jazeera owns it and the Qataran government finances it (Flint, 2013). Its wealthy investors have enabled beIN Sports to reverse the standard business model between a cable network and a cable system. It secured carriage by paying Comcast and other large satellite systems instead of receiving a carriage fee from MSOs (Belson, 2012). It has secured the rights to Spain's La Liga, which features some of world's biggest stars, such as Lionel Messi, and popular global sports teams, such as Real Madrid C.F. and FC Barcelona, by paying twice as much as former license holder Gol TV (Belson, 2012). beIN Sports also has the rights to Ligue 1 (French First Division), Serie A (Italy's First Division), and the South American World Cup Qualifying. Backed with more resources, beIN Sports clearly is in position to overtake Gol TV and challenge ESPN Deportes. beIN Sports will be a serious ESPN Deportes rival with their specific focus on soccer, which appeals to many Latino/a sports fans.

Gol TV, another of ESPN Deportes' competitors, launched in 2003. Gol TV was the first bilingual soccer channel. The network lags behind ESPN Deportes and other Spanish-language sports networks in subscribers. After losing Spain's La Liga to beIN Sports, Gol TV has been dropped by some MSOs such as Comcast and satellite operators such as DirecTV (Pierce, 2013). Gol TV suffered another blow in 2014 when it lost rights to future German Bundesliga games to the networks of 21st Century Fox (including Fox Sports Deportes). Gol TV has the rights to popular soccer leagues such as Argentina's Primera Division, but the network appears to have been severely crippled by losing La Liga and does not appear to have the resources to compete with more well-financed sports channels such as ESPN Deportes in the long term.

Perhaps ESPN Deportes' biggest challengers in the future will be professional sports leagues' cable networks (e.g., MLB Network) that could simulcast in Spanish or create a Spanish-language channel. The MLB Network possesses content that is quite popular with Spanish-speaking sports fans. Networks that professional sports leagues own will want to control more of their content to fill their future programming needs. In turn, that may limit sports programming inventory in the future and most likely will elevate their prices immensely. These increasing prices to secure sports content will hurt ESPN Deportes and other niche cable networks that cannot easily offset their higher licensing costs through retransmission consent fees or advertising revenue. These looming scenarios could result in ESPN Deportes' struggle to meet the future programming needs of its target audience.

## ESPN DEPORTES' BATTLE FOR PROGRAMMING

The acquisition of more Liga MX soccer games is one potential strategy that could increase advertising revenue and combat the potential subscription limit. Spanish-language sports fans prefer Mexican soccer by a large margin (E. Gonzalez, 2013). Univision Deportes possessed the U.S. television rights to 12 of the 18 Liga MX teams and has Major League Soccer games as of 2014 (Guthrie, 2012; "MLS, U.S. Soccer," 2014). Univision Deportes currently also has the television rights to the Mexican national team games through 2014 (Hiestand, 2013). ESPN Deportes will need to outbid Univision Deportes to acquire more sports programming like Liga MX and future Mexican national team games, especially during World Cup years. ESPN Deportes has been making an effort to televise more Mexican soccer games. It has successfully secured the rights to some Liga MX games (Nunez, 2013).

Second, ESPN Deportes must figure out how to include more programming that appeals to its target audience without alienating the relationship between ESPN and the National Football League. ESPN has strong relationship with the National Football League (NFL). The NFL has televised games on ESPN Deportes in an effort to attract more Spanish-language fans. ESPN Deportes has attracted more Spanish-speaking Latinos/as to NFL games by using a separate broadcast (Baysinger, 2011). The NFL, however, does not appeal to as many Spanish-speaking or bilingual fans as Mexican soccer (E. Gonzalez, 2013). ESPN Deportes consequently cannot televise too many NFL games or NFL-oriented programming. This programming decision, however, could hurt ESPN's relationship with the NFL.

Third, ESPN Deportes must retain some of its current programming and acquire new sports programming that will appeal to a younger and more bilingual demographic. It must be willing to pay more money to secure its existing licenses with MLB and NBA that are popular with many Latino/a viewers. It also will need to continue to televise boxing matches that feature current U.S. Latino/a and Latin American champions or contenders. ESPN Deportes ultimately will need to acquire more content like the UFC in the future. The UFC has a long-term deal with FOX Deportes until 2018 (Gross, 2011). ESPN Deportes will need to acquire content like MMA that is popular with Latino/a viewers. As an alternative, it has begun to televise Jungle Fights, a Brazilian mixed martial arts competition (J. Gonzalez, 2013). More boxing and MMA matches along with its old stalwarts like the MLB could somewhat offset critical losses in soccer content (e.g., World Cup).

## ESPN DEPORTES' IMPLICATIONS

Despite being a sister channel to the most powerful cable network in the marketplace, ESPN Deportes faces an uncertain future. ESPN Deportes will have to overcome a dwindling number of cable subscribers as well as subscribers who are downgrading their bundles. Individuals known as *cord cutters* are rebelling against escalating cable rates (Lazarus, 2013). The cable industry lost more than 300,000 subscribers from 2012 to 2013 (Lazarus). Other cable subscribers are downgrading their cable subscriptions because of high prices. These subscribers are known as *cable shavers*. According to Park Associates, up to 20% of cable subscribers in 2013 have or will downgrade their cable subscriptions ("Multi-Screen TV Motivators," 2012). A huge percentage of these cable shavers are Spanish speakers. A GfK study cited that a large number of Spanish-speaking households do not pay for cable (Grotticelli, 2013). These households use a traditional antenna to receive their programming (Grotticelli). ESPN Deportes will have to figure out how to attract this growing number of price-sensitive viewers.

Attracting enough advertising revenue to remain profitable in a growing Spanish-language or U.S. Latino/a television industry will be another of ESPN Deportes' challenges. The number of cable networks that are pursuing bilingual or Spanish-language Latinos/as has grown to more than 100 networks (Winslow, 2013). These networks are fighting harder to secure advertising revenue. Because advertisers do not perceive this audience to be affluent, they do not spend as much money to attract this audience. Latinos/as make up 22% of all people 18–49 (Flamm, 2011). Advertisers, however, spend about only 9% of their budget on Spanish-language television (Flamm). The limited advertising budgets that companies have allocated for this market are not large enough to support the growing number of Spanish-language cable networks.

ESPN Deportes continues to struggle with its distribution. It initially lingered behind Fox Sports en Español and Gol TV (King, 2014). The cable network has since grown to approximately 17 million subscribers (Reynolds, 2013). However, ESPN Deportes remains in a distant third behind Univision Deportes and FOX Deportes in Spanish-language households (King, 2014). Lino Garcia, the general manager for ESPN Deportes, points out its distribution struggles.

> My expectation was [distribution] was going to be a whole lot more, a lot faster, but it didn't turn out that way for various reasons. I'll tell you something: There is a blessing and a curse to being part of a large media company and a large group of networks. It really affects [distribution] negotiations. It can affect them in a good way, but also a not so good way. Sometimes it takes longer because you're negotiating for a whole lot more than just one network. (King, 2014, p. 3)

ESPN Deportes needs to secure additional carriage from the other larger cable system operators and to increase its subscription base significantly.

Critical to ESPN Deportes' long-term success will be its ability to secure new and rather inexpensive sports programming that will attract a broader base of Latino/a viewers. This programming would also supplement its expensive sports programming such as the NBA. Jai alai or rugby are examples of sports that are played in many parts of Latin America that could become popular with Latino/a viewers. The discovery of another emerging sport that attracts Latino/a fans that can be licensed at relatively inexpensive price will be vital to its offset stagnant carriage fees, a limited advertising pool, and distribution issues.

## ESPN DEPORTES' FUTURE

Without a doubt, ESPN has been a trendsetting network for mainstream sports fans, though ESPN Deportes has not been able to find similar results with the Spanish-speaking audience. A large part of ESPN Deportes' initial success has come from ESPN leveraging its brand name and lowering its carriage fees to cable system operators. ESPN Deportes' current content, however, has failed to increase its subscription base significantly. ESPN Deportes' reliance on soccer, baseball, basketball, and football does not appear to be creating strong brand recognition with Spanish-speaking or bilingual fans because stronger traditional brands for this specific audience, such as Univision, have developed similar cable networks. With the emergence of strong competitors like beIN Sports, ESPN Deportes clearly is failing to achieve its original goal of becoming the clear leader within the Spanish-language cable network market.

With more sports cable networks vying for Spanish-speaking and a growing number of bilingual fans, ESPN Deportes finds itself in an increasingly heated competition with FOX Deportes and other cable networks to emerge as the leading sports network for these brand-loyal sport fanatics. ESPN Deportes certainly can improve its chances of overtaking Univision Deportes by acquiring the television rights to the Mexican national team and more Liga MX teams. Surpassing FOX Deportes will be more difficult in the short term because it has secured the rights to sports content popular with assimilated Latino viewers like UFC, college football, and Golden Boy boxing (Maglio, 2013). ESPN Deportes has improved its chances of keeping up with its two primary competitors by keeping its carriage fees low and by acquiring some sports content such as soccer that Latino/a fans enjoy.

In addition to acquiring additional television rights, ESPN Deportes needs to alter its current programming to attract all types of Latino/a viewers. A programming strategy that crosses over to more assimilated Latino/a viewers could be critical for the long-term viability for most Spanish-language sports cable networks. With the escalating costs of licensing sports content and little to no growth among Spanish-speaking Latinos/as, several current sports cable networks will not survive over a prolonged period if it does not adapt to the changing U.S. Latino/a market.

Unlike ESPN, ESPN Deportes did not enter this marketplace first. Although ESPN clearly stands out with English-language sports fans, other sports cable networks such as Univision Deportes have stronger brand recognition with

Spanish-speaking and bilingual viewers. A number of Spanish-language television networks and cable networks appear to be willing to pay more than ESPN Deportes for the television rights to the World Cup and other important sporting events for their Spanish-language or bilingual fans. Univision Deportes, FOX Deportes, beIN Sports, and even Telemundo consequently have better positioned themselves by securing vital programming to either overtake or remain ahead of ESPN Deportes in the Spanish-language sports cable marketplace.

# Race, Gender, and the ESPN Effect

# CHAPTER SIX

# "The Worldwide Leader in Sports" as Race Relations Reporter

## Reconsidering the Role of ESPN

GEORGE L. DANIELS

More than a half-century has passed since a series of events changed how our nation deals with matters of race. It took the presence of armed federal troops forcing the integration of two flagship institutions in the Deep South, the killings of four little girls attending Sunday school in a Birmingham church, the assassinations of a Mississippi NAACP leader and a U.S. president for that change to happen. The mass media played a huge role in forcing the nation to look back on those events. This chapter is about the intersection of race and sports and how the two played out on ESPN. One can examine race through many lenses. For this study, the research has primarily chosen to look through the lens of two programs ESPN developed and aired in 2012.

In September 2012, through its investigative reporting program *Outside the Lines*, ESPN examined the historic hire of the first White coach in the history of Alcorn State University, which is one of the 105 schools designated as a historically Black college and university (HBCU) and its significance not only for the future of HBCUs, but also the status of African American football coaches. In October 2012, ESPN Films resurrected a groundbreaking investigation *ESPN The Magazine* first published in 2010. *Ghosts of Ole Miss* was the story of an all-White football team whose perfect season, the best in the history of the institution in Oxford, Mississippi, was overshadowed by violence that claimed the lives of two people as James Meredith enrolled as the first African American student in 1962. The premiere of the *Ghosts at Ole Miss* documentary added a dimension to ESPN's investigation, for those in the 2010 magazine story were on camera.

Employing textual analysis technique, this chapter spotlights ESPN's handling of two historic events in one of the last states to desegregate its institutions of higher learning and to do what some journalism historians have termed "socially responsible journalism" (Smith, 2006, p. 49). Like their predecessors on *The Race Beat* (Roberts & Klibanoff, 2007) during the Civil Rights Movement a half-century before, the cross-platform journalists at ESPN in 2012 sparked a new dialogue about race.

## MODELS AND A FRAMEWORK

For this study, the author identified two professional models of journalism and a conceptual framework from journalism studies that were useful for analyzing the organization of the ESPN media texts. Nearly four decades ago, University of Chicago sociologist Morris Janowitz sought to conceive professional models under which most journalists were operating. He contrasted the traditional journalism with technical expertise and a sense of professional responsibility who applied the canons of the scientific method to increase his objectivity and his performance with the journalist as critic and interpreter who participated in the advocacy process (Janowitz, 1975). The former, more traditional type of journalist, which Janowitz termed the gatekeeper model, dated to World War I, and the latter emerged during the 1960s as what was known as the advocate journalist.

Going a step further than Janowitz, Zelizer (1993) suggested rather than a profession, journalists operate in what she called an interpretive community united through this shared discourse and collective interpretations of key public events. Under this view, journalistic discourse around key events in history becomes a means of understanding the shared past (collective memory) through which journalists make their professional lives meaningful and unite themselves. Zelizer (1993) has applied this frame of interpretive community to two events central to American journalism—McCarthyism and Watergate.

In 2007, Zelizer argued that three dimensions have helped establish eyewitnessing as a way to understand journalism: the eyewitness as report, witness as role, and eyewitness as technology. All three function as different carriers of meaning about journalism over time. Zelizer (2007) presented them as having developed chronologically alongside technological innovations in journalism. In so-called first-stage eyewitnessing, or the establishment of report, the eyewitness accounts provided legitimacy to news from afar such as Christopher Columbus's report of what he saw in 1492. Centuries later, newspapers sent individuals to events to collect eyewitness accounts in this form. The mid-1800s saw the second-stage eyewitnessing or the expansion of reporting and role to a less overtly subjective (and presumably more reliable) mode that included images as potential carriers of truth-value. The key for this eyewitnessing stage was realism. During the twentieth century, Zelizer suggested a third stage of eyewitnessing accommodated an increasingly wide range of technological alternatives available for delivering including sound (and eventually moving pictures). In this stage, the newsreel offered an important mode of relaying eyewitness reports.

According to Zelizer (2007), contemporary eyewitnesses, who she argued could be construed as a fourth stage, add nonconventional journalists (i.e., citizen journalists, bloggers) to the combination of technology that was a part of the third stage. Because of their reliance on technology and eyewitness accounts, both ESPN Films' *Ghosts of Ole Miss* and the *Outside the Lines* investigation into the hiring of Alcorn State's first White head football coach can be interpreted and understood using Zelizer's framework of the eyewitness, especially given the different positions of the leading journalists in each of these 2012 news products. Furthermore, if we accept the idea of journalists as members of an interpretive community (Zelizer, 1993) or the notion of the advocate-journalist (Janowitz, 1975), it becomes easier to understand the role of ESPN in 2012 as a race relations reporter. Before we unpack the media texts that allow us to make this argument, it is important to contextualize this research within the literature in race and sports, race and college, and football and the role of the sport documentary.

## CONTEXT

Textual analysis highlights the cultural assumptions, ideologies, and possible readings of a text. It also situates the text within the conditions of production. As Kellner (2003) explained, if we want to understand the role that media play in our lives and our view of the world, we have to understand what messages participate in the culture construction of our view of the world, then what meanings audiences are making of the television programs, films, or newspapers they consume.

There are a number of studies situated at the intersection of race and sports. Focusing primarily on how athletes of color are or have historically been represented in the media, Grainger, Newman, and Andrews (2006) found that the vast majority of scholarship on race, sport, and media has focused on the encoded and encoding of meanings and the politics of representation with the sports media. They suggested, among other things, there was a need for further analysis of the politics and practices of the production of sports media texts and how these serve to reinforce, reproduce, or even challenge the dominant discourses of Black athletes within media culture (p. 462). Siegel (1994) studied the plight of the Black male athlete in higher education. Even in studies of a fictional professional football team, traditional stereotypes of African American athletes as deviant, animal-like, and physically gifted were the focus (Strudler & Schnurer, 2006). In another study, Oates (2007) focused specifically on Black men who are participating in the National Football League (NFL) draft. Providing a critical reading of the draft as a cultural text, he considered the process of the NFL draft as an erotic problem, as a cultural site where the admiration of male bodies by men reflects an example of a type of homoerotic subtext of American football (Oates, 2007).

A team of researchers analyzed articles addressing athletes associated with criminal activity that appeared in the *Los Angeles Times*, the *New York Times*, and *USA Today* during a three-year period (Mastro, Blecha, & Seate, 2011). Even when high-profile stories on steroid use, the Duke University men's lacrosse rape case, and the Michael Vick dog-fighting case were removed from the group of articles for analysis, Black athletes were overrepresented as criminal compared to White athletes in terms of their proportion of athletes in professional sports. Mastron, Blecha, and Seate (2011) found no differences in terms of how Black and White athletes were discussed in crime stories, but the crimes Black athletes committed were addressed in more explicit detail and were associated with more negative consequences (p. 539).

The research on race also extends beyond Blacks. Butterworth (2007) analyzed 50 news media accounts from a larger pool of 300 articles on Lexis-Nexus focused on the 1998 home run race between Mark McGwire, a White man, and Sammy Sosa, a Latino originally from the Dominican Republic. He found in coverage of Sosa, the focus was often on his heritage. Consistent references to Sosa as Dominican reinforced the distinction between him and McGwire, whose race was never mentioned. McGwire was situated in the media as the predetermined front-runner. Sosa was the intruder or runner-up in the race (Butterworth, 2007).

This chapter is not the first academic examination of a media text that falls in the genre known as documentary. Though they represent the aspect of the documentary tradition, sports documentaries remain an under-researched area of critique both in documentary studies and sports studies (McDonald, 2007). *Hoop Dreams*, a 1994 film that has become a well-known example of sport documentary, was not only about basketball, but also basketball as a form of cultural expression and resistance that simultaneously reinforces and subverts the ideology of the American Dream. The producer of *Hoop Dreams*, Steve James, has since received some attention in film studies for one of his more recent projects, *The Interrupters*, which was about a nongovernmental organization trying to stop gang violence in Chicago's South Side neighborhoods (Tyree, 2011).

## Research Questions

Given the claims outlined in the previous research, this project sought to answer the following:

RQ1: How does *Ghosts of Ole Miss* reflect ESPN's overall strategic goals on the cutting edge of sports filmmaking?

RQ2: What stage of Zelizer's eyewitnessing framework is reflected in the ESPN *Outside the Lines* investigative report and *Ghosts of Ole Miss* documentary?

RQ3: Which of Janowitz's (1975) models of the journalist is displayed in the reporting?

## Method

Textual analysis is a way of gathering and analyzing information. It allows the researcher to discern latent meaning of a media text. With the exception of McKee's (2001) guide to textual analysis, there are few texts that explicitly state step-by-step strategies for employing the method. That's because each textual analysis is different and not meant to be replicated in the way a scientist would employing the scientific method. Many media studies have employed textual analysis to unpack journalistic content (Fursich, 2002; Fursich & Lester, 1996; Lester, 1994). The method has also been employed to analyze other media texts such as cartoons (Ryan, 2010), Latin American TV dramas (Acosta-Alzuru, 2003), corporate mission statements (Williams, 2008), and fortune cookie sayings (Yin & Miike, 2008). As Lester (1994) explained, the principal work of textual analysis is to reveal not how a version of the news compares with what really happened (though knowledge of what happened is important), but the constructed nature of reporting and what some of the dimensions of that construction are. Knowing that news is a social construction of reality (i.e., news is what the journalist says it is), a textual analysis is aimed at deconstructing and understanding that media text.

To conduct this textual analysis, the author gathered the elements of the media text. For the *Outside the Lines* investigation, there were four elements to consider: a prepackaged news report, a Web version of the story with photos, a debriefing interview with the principal on-air journalist, and an in-depth interview with three newsmakers. A full transcript was generated from the debriefing interview and in-depth newsmaker interview that aired on *Outside the Lines*. Where books or other articles the newsmakers produced in the in-depth interview were referenced, copies of those resources (which represented contextual items) were also obtained. The websites for each of the newsmakers were reviewed for background information on each of the newsmakers in the in-depth interview. Finally, background reading on other media reports of the main breaking story were located for context, and a history of Alcorn State University was obtained for background on the school at the center of the investigation.

The second phase of the analysis focused on *Ghosts of Ole Miss*. The author purchased a DVD copy of the documentary, which included subtitles for ease of note taking and analysis. Multiple viewings of the 51-minute documentary enabled a close reading of the text. Careful notes were taken from the principal speakers in the documentary. Statements from the director and excluded scenes, while available on the DVD version of *Ghosts of Ole Miss*, were excluded from the analysis because they were not part of the original airing in October 2012. Because the text was based on an original 2010 story, a copy of the original story was downloaded from the *ESPN The Magazine* Web archive. Designed to promote the premiere of *Ghosts of Ole Miss* across ESPN's various platforms, two interviews with the principal on-air journalist, one on ESPN Radio and the other on *Outside the Lines*, were also viewed and fully transcribed. Three historical references (including two books by the leading historian on Ole Miss integration) noted in the documentary were also examined.

## Texts

### Outside the Lines

Four months after Jay Hopson was hired as the first White head football coach at Alcorn State University, the nation's oldest historically Black land grant university, *Outside the Lines* featured the story in its September 19, 2012, edition. With the Web headline "Alcorn State's White Shadow," the seven-minute video story included footage of summer practices; file video of the May 28, 2012, hiring from Jackson, Mississippi, television station WAPT-TV; interviews with Dr. Chris Brown, Alcorn State University president, Duer Sharp, Southwestern Athletic Conference (SWAC) commissioner, and Heish Northern, an African American head football coach at Prairie View A&M University, and Monte Coleman, an African American head football coach at University of Arkansas-Pine Bluff (both SWAC schools). It aired along with a three-minute debriefing of the principal on-air journalist, Jemele Hill.

Following that debriefing interview, anchor Bob Ley conducted a 10-minute interview with three key newsmakers in the story—Dr. Derek Greenfield, director of equity and inclusion at Alcorn State University and a member of the search committee; Dr. Fitzgerald Hill, president of Arkansas Baptist College, a historically Black college in Little Rock and the coauthor of the 2012 book, *Crackback: How College Football Blindsides the Hopes of Black Coaches*; and Floyd Keith, who at the time was executive director of Black Coaches and Administrators, a

25-year-old nonprofit advocacy organization for ethnic minorities at all levels of sports (Keith stepped down in March 2013).

### Ghosts of Ole Miss

*Ghosts of Ole Miss*, based on the story in *ESPN The Magazine*, premiered as a 50-minute documentary on October 30, 2012, which the author of the original magazine story, Wright Thompson, a native Mississippian, wrote. Thompson is a senior writer for ESPN.com and *ESPN The Magazine*. This was the second documentary in the *30 for 30* series in which he was involved. He also narrated *Roll Tide/War Eagle*, a documentary about the rivalry between the University of Alabama and Auburn University.

Ghosts of Ole Miss opens with a cross-burning reenactment as Thompson recalled the incident happening in his front lawn, an indication that as a child, he knew that some in his hometown did not approve of his parents' political activism in the Mississippi Delta. The entire documentary is built around his journey to understand what happened in 1962 when James Meredith, following a violent clash between federal marshals and rioters on the Oxford campus, helped integrate the University of Mississippi. Thompson's quest was to also tell the story of the Ole Miss football team, which had a 9–0 season but managed to rank only third in the country, some say because of the national notoriety brought on by the deadly clash on campus that year. The film featured several members of that Ole Miss football team reflecting on their season, as well as William Doyle, author of *An American Insurrection*, a history of the University's integration (Doyle, 2001), and James Meredith, who was the first Negro student at Ole Miss and who went on to receive his law degree and has written two books about his experience (Meredith, 1966; Meredith & Doyle, 2012). The film was organized in similar fashion to the *ESPN The Magazine* story in 2010 with chapters on the battle on the eve of Meredith's October 1, 1962, enrollment; the reconstruction of the campus; the progress of the university, including recent clashes over the use of the Confederate flag; and a look at the reunion held for the 1962 football team, which included Meredith.

## Analyses

### Outside the Lines

Like any good news report, the *Outside the Lines* investigation was conducted in part to draw an audience, and one can immediately sense the controversy by the clips included in the preview video or cold open (video used to begin the 30-minute show). Along with video of the White head coach leading his football team to practice, there is the Black coach (at a competing SWAC school) asking whether he could have been considered for the position. In the audio track, Ley lays out the two primary issues of the investigation: the challenges facing Black coaches and the 2012 mission of historically Black colleges. It is noted that the reporter, Hill, an African American woman, is included in this preview as she queries Alcorn State University's Chris Brown about what she perceived to be an effort to distance Mississippi's oldest Black school from the HBCU label, an admission that Brown affirms. Ley listed the three area of focus for the program: questions of race, opportunity, and history.

Along with explaining the history and significance of Alcorn State as a school where former National Football League players Donald Driver and Steve McNair got their start, Ley introduced the main investigative news report with a note about former Redskins quarterback Doug Williams, who returned to Grambling State University, for he was unable to secure a coaching position after wining three Black national championships in his previous stint at Grambling.

In her opening track of the seven-minute news package, Hill posed the question of what was awkward about the picture of a Black football team from Alcorn State with its White football coach, Jay Hopson, slightly blurred out in the foreground. The video then cuts to Hopson talking about how much his coaching experience is like he's coaching at Louisiana State University, University of Florida, or Marshall University. What is implied there is the norm for a White coach is not to be at an all-Black school at what is for most schools their highest profile position in the athletic department—the head football coach. Hill's video report does not provide the context included in the Web version of the story, which was published on ESPN.com. There she explained other sports at Alcorn (tennis and golf) and at other HBCUs where there are White coaches.

The video report cuts to the obligatory new coach introduction video where the new coach dons the paraphernalia of the school. In this case, the WAPT-TV video of Hopson being introduced is inserted into the story. Instead of full sound bites from the news conference, Hill cuts to her question of Brown about why he thought the SWAC was ready for a White football coach. Brown responded he was not sure whether the SWAC was ready, but Alcorn was ready. Brown's argument for why Hopson was the best coach for the job lies in part with Hopson's deep local roots in Southwest Mississippi.

As file video of the confederate flag flying and civil rights demonstrators being pelted with firehoses rolled, Brown drew sharp generational contrast between the older alumni who went through the period of integration and younger students who did not want the history and baggage of the past to drive the institutional direction for the future. Then, two SWAC head football coaches are shown, with Heish Northern of Prairie View A&M questioning Hopson's credentials, and Monte Coleman, University of Arkansas-Pine Bluff, arguing for why HBCUs have to diversify. After the discussion of the mission of HBCUs, Hill's video version of her report shifted back on the field, noting that Hopson's goal was for Alcorn State to have its first winning season in six years. Hopson received a Gatorade bath as Hill reported that Alcorn defeated the defending SWAC champion, Grambling State, on September 1, 2012, in Alcorn State's season opener. Hopson reached his goal, for the Alcorn Indians had a 9–3 season in 2013. Entering his third season in August 2014, he received a three-year contract extension (Blevins, 2014).

The matter of Hopson's hire was further discussed in Ley's debriefing of Hill. Here we see the role of journalist that Janowitz (1975) explored in his research. In response to RQ3, Hill reflected the traditional "gatekeeper" role both in her reporting of the story and in her discussion of the issue. The closest she came in even hinting at her opinion was in a question from Ley about the likelihood that Hopson's hiring represented a trend. Rather than weighing in with her opinion as an African American as Janowitz (1975) would advocate, Hill suggested people were looking to see how successful Hopson would be and what resources he could bring to the university. With the Alcorn State president describing the scene in the room as older, Black alumni on the search committee considered Hopson to be football coach and WAPT-TV's video of the announcement, the *Outside the Lines* news report exhibited Zelizer's Stage 3 of the eyewitnessing framework in its use of multiple technologies for eyewitness accounts.

There were at least two airings of the report and Ley's debriefing with Hill. In one airing of the broadcast, the *Outside the Lines* news report and debriefing were followed by a newsmaker panel that focused primarily on the plight of Black coaches. Dr. Fitz Hill, a former coach himself and now HBCU president, was perhaps the most outspoken of the panelists. While respecting Alcorn President Chris Brown's decision, he called attention to the lack of role models for African American males. Only speaking once during the 10-minute panel, Floyd said that his organization, Black Coaches and Administrators, never said it wanted an African American for the coaching job, but the best candidate. He noted that there were African American candidates in the pool. The third panelist, Derek Greenfield, educational equity and inclusion director for Alcorn State and member of the search committee, reiterated a point made in the video report—Hopson being a known quantity and a local guy.

### Ghosts of Ole Miss

More than a month after ESPN aired its *Outside the Lines* investigative report on Hopson's historic hire at Alcorn State, the *30 for 30* documentary *Ghosts of Ole Miss* premiered on the main network Tuesday, October 30, 2012. As racially charged as the mission of historically Black colleges and universities and the challenges facing Black football coaches are, the efforts of those at Mississippi's oldest institution of higher learning to deal with the scars of a deadly riot more than 50 years ago during its integration were equally as challenging. This was evident by Thompson's comments about the documentary even before it aired.

In an interview with Ivan Maizel on the *ESPNU College Football* podcast, Thompson recounted his strong resistance and reluctance to be involved in a remake of his original 2010 *Ghosts of Ole Miss* story for *ESPN The Magazine*. His hesitation is quite clear when one sees his internal struggle characterized in the documentary, which shows Thompson, a White man, coming face-to-face twice with the real possibility that members of his family participated in some of the violent opposition with which Meredith was met a half-century ago.

In the first five minutes of the documentary, Thompson is shown going through old yearbooks and artifacts in the Department of Archives and Special Collections at J. D. Williams Library at Ole Miss. He finds a notebook used by one of the soldiers guarding Meredith that included the name of one of Thompson's deceased great uncles and saw what he thought was another relative in a crowd that was photographed shouting at Meredith.

*Ghosts of Ole Miss* is perhaps most noted for the questions that it posed through the experience of Thompson: What is the cost of knowing our past? What is the cost of not knowing our past? How many people in the mob (on the eve of Meredith's October 1, 1962, enrollment) do I know? What ghosts remain, after all the people slipped away, most denying that they had ever been there at all? Along with the chronological accounting of what happened with integration, which the documentary showed with full-screen date prompts, interviews with students provided a level of credibility to the story. Zelizer's (1993) second stage eyewitnessing was reflected in the *Ghosts of Ole Miss*. But, unlike Hill in *Outside the Lines*, Thompson exhibited traits of what Janowitz (1975) labeled an advocate-journalist. Despite his methodological use of research methods to understand the past, Thompson, as a White, native Mississippian, had a personal stake in seeing the story of the 1962 Ole Miss Rebels told. He illustrates perfectly how journalists can operate in what Zelizer (1993) called the interpretive community. Thus, in answering RQ2, it is suggested Zelizer's work is demonstrated in Thompson's *Ghosts of Ole Miss* more so than in Hill's reporting for *Outside the Lines*. Although Thompson was not alive for those events in 1962, they became the events through which he saw his work for this story and through which he talks to other journalists in this interpretive community.

As Vogan (2012) noted, documentaries have traditionally served as markers of prestige within the context of television—both for the outlets that produce and exhibit them and the companies that use them to advertise. Although an analysis of the advertisers for *Ghosts of Ole Miss* was beyond the scope of this study, there was clear evidence in *Ghosts of Ole Miss* of serving educational and civic functions, often ignored by television. In reporting on the 1962 Ole Miss football team and its followers, the ESPN film *30 for 30* crew treated sports in a more authentic, detailed, and artful manner than regular sports programs (Vogan, 2012).

## Reconsidering ESPN as Race Relations Reporter

Besides the fact that Alcorn State University and the University of Mississippi were situated in what is called the most segregated state in the nation, which at one time had the highest percentage of African Americans of any state (Doyle, 2001), *Outside the Lines* and *Ghosts of Ole Miss* were tied together because they both either focused on or used as a context the 50th anniversary of the 1962 desegregation of the flagship university at Oxford. Since they both aired on ESPN and involved journalists from the Worldwide Leader in Sports, this chapter sought to unpack whether, in fact, the texts represented a role for the cross-platform network as a key reporter of race relations.

On its website, the September 2012 *Outside the Lines* investigative video report carried the headline *Alcorn State's White Shadow*—presumably a reference to the 1970s television series featuring a retired White Chicago Bulls player, Ken Reeves, who took a job at predominantly Black Carver High School in South Central Los Angeles—the headline could also speak to the shadow that hangs over the football program in Lorman, Mississippi, the only one in the SWAC with a White head football coach who broke a racial barrier, ironically put there by Whites who barred African Americans from attending its kind in the Southwestern Athletic Conference. Elsewhere online, if one looks for this September 2012 video, he or she will find the headline *Alcorn State and a New Race Debate*.

Sometimes journalists do little more than report and reflect a debate that is underway. By constructing the news around a controversial issue, they pretend to be making the news when they are just restating what's known. Reflecting Janowitz's (1975) traditional gatekeeper model of journalism, Hill interviewed sources on both sides of the debate. Her report, the product of a multi-month effort to get insights from those around the SWAC and show some impact of the new coach, was mostly a run-of-the-mill news report on a known problem. There is a plethora of research about the status of HBCUs, even one about the situation in Mississippi. These studies did more to advance what is known than the *Outside the Lines* investigation. The story of the selection of a White coach made national news, but was not a major story of national importance. ESPN's program was used as a broad platform to raise the issue. But outside of a discussion involving key figures on the national scene of Black coaches and administrators, the *Outside the Lines* team did not truly uncover or unearth anything not known to most who have known about the tenuous position of historically Black colleges and universities.

Vogan (2012) has noted that despite ESPN's pervasiveness, popularity, and value, it has not been known for artful products and lacks journalistic integrity, in part because it privileges sensationalized speculation and amplifies scandals surrounding the sports world (p. 138). In answering RQ1, however, ESPN did in fact accomplish its goal of telling what sports meant during a particular era through Thompson's documentary. Thompson showed the role that emotion was intended to play in the way *Ghosts of Ole Miss* was told. Because of the difficulty in finding sources to talk on-camera, this effort to uncover and display for all to see an uncomfortable period in history represented a groundbreaking effort in what the sports documentary can do to help a community heal. Two of the Old Miss football players on the 1962 team interviewed for the documentary likened the events on the Ole Miss campus that year to an old wound that won't heal. While Whites such as Thompson might find the documentary brings them to tears, others in the audience, especially African Americans whose descendants were treated as second-class citizens, may experience different emotions. The admission that some White man had to make after 50 years to reflect truthfulness in the 2010 "Ghosts of Ole Miss" *ESPN The Magazine* story or to be seen on national television in the *Ghosts of Ole Miss* documentary was astounding.

*Ghosts of Ole Miss* was not only for those in Mississippi but also those outside of the state to see where we are as a nation in dealing with our race problem. Just as *Sports Illustrated*'s 1968 series "The Black Athlete: A Shameful Story," did with its controversial investigative analysis (Smith, 2006), ESPN Films provided an example of socially responsible journalism. Maybe it was because of the time allotted, the cinematography that the filmmaker had at his disposal, the strength of a key event in American history, and not only a well-known racial incident or the passion of the journalist who had a personal stake in the project. *Ghosts of Ole Miss* did position the ESPN brand in a way that separated it from the sensation and scandal that are products of the daily news (and sports) reporting cycle in a 24-hour cable news environment.

For those interested in the study of minorities and communication, the analyses of these two texts by subsidiaries of the same media operation provided an ideal opportunity to see a contrast in the way the news media handle the issue of race. It was a chance to unpack the way in which two journalists with different circumstances in the same state can approach the ever-timely issue of race. The rather superficial way that the team behind this particular *Outside the Lines* project handled the issue of status of HBCUs and a historic coaching hire is far more common among news operations than we would like to imagine. Terms such as *investigation* or *enterprise* don't always mean that the work is going to result in high-quality, impactful journalism. Bringing public attention or highlighting both sides of a debate does not constitute the same kind of journalism as a product that has the potential to change hearts and minds of an entire community or nation.

In the scholarship of minorities and communication, more studies such as the one presented in this chapter are certainly warranted to spotlight this difference.

Some might ask whether this difference between the *Ghosts of Ole Miss* and *Outside the Lines* is a matter of only the format—news show versus documentary. In this chapter, an effort has been made to show the content of the program is what matters the most, not necessarily format. The sources that are featured, the juxtaposition of various viewpoints, and the angles that are chosen all exemplify important aspects of the content. It is certainly likely that one could find sensationalism in some of the *30 for 30* documentaries just like it is possible to identify an impactful investigation by the *Outside the Lines* producers. This is less a matter of format and more one of content. Perhaps this is a call for more so-called point-of-view sports reporting when it comes to discussion and debate on issues of race. What is most important here is to acknowledge or recognize ESPN as a player in moving forward the discussion of race. Even if sensationalistic, ESPN is a reporter of race relations. Fortunately, with *Ghosts of Ole Miss*, ESPN's production of documentaries has the potential to make a difference.

# CHAPTER SEVEN

# Race in the Kingdom

DANIEL SIPOCZ

ESPN is more than a 24-hour cable channel dedicated to sports programming. The self-proclaimed "Worldwide Leader in Sports" is a cultural and social institution with a global reach (Farred, 2000). Content broadcast by the network extends beyond sports and entertainment, as on-air talent narrate highlights from games and debate each other about topics of the day. With 115 million viewers on average watching *SportsCenter* each week ("ESPN Fact Sheet," n.d.), ESPN has the opportunity to affect culture like other television outlets and programs influence American culture (Fiske, 1985) through the expression of a dominant discourse about race as race intersects with sports and society. Media scholar Stuart Hall (1981) argued, "the media construct for us a definition of what race is, what meaning the imagery of race carries and what the 'problem of race' is understood to be" (p. 35). ESPN's coverage of race is often complicated, controversial, and sometimes offensive, but the network remains a powerful player in assisting society to make sense of race (Bloom & Willard, 2002).

ESPN sportscaster Chris Berman idealistically wrote that sports can help break down societal divisions, such as those formed by race, by leveling the playing field in competition (Berman, 1999). Yet minority athletes are represented differently from their White counterparts (Eastman & Billings, 2001; McCarthy & Jones, 1997; Rainville & McCormick, 1977). This chapter will critically examine two of the more recent, high-profile controversies in ESPN's coverage of race. The purpose of this chapter is to illustrate, through critical race theory, ESPN's role in the commodification of race as a packaged sports product for financial benefit as well as the company's influence on society by perpetuating stereotypes. This chapter will analyze ESPN's coverage of Jeremy Lin and "Linsanity" as well as the fallout from LeBron James's one-hour special *The Decision*, including the Nike commercial "Rise." This chapter not only considers the role of race in ESPN's coverage of these two controversial news events but also how the power of ESPN as a cultural institution marginalized racial minorities in James's and Lin's instances.

## CRITICAL RACE THEORY

In much of his work, Hall (1981) explained that race is part of a "cultural map" (p. 31). These cultural maps "provide the frameworks through which we represent, interpret, understand and 'make sense' of some aspect of social existence" (p. 31). In other words, people create constructs, such as race, in a social manner to understand the world surrounding them (Brooks & Rada, 2002; Bruce, 2004). Although placing people into categories can help make sense of the world, the action has consequences. Consequences are divisive, allowing those in a majority group to take control and suppress minority groups. According to Pease (1989), "Minorities seem to have made little progress since 1965 in terms of having their voices and concerns heard, their problems discussed, their triumphs and sorrows reported and their opinions considered" (p. 34). How minority success is measured and described by the media is altered as a consequence of their underrepresentation. Croteau and Hoynes (2000) described this reality as one in which racial minority groups are measured against the White norm. Consequently, the playing field is not level.

Critical race theory (CRT) began as a way to challenge White hegemony by analyzing and critiquing laws that kept the dominant class, Whites, in the dominant social position (Crenshaw, 1995). Developed by Bell to address the limited progress made toward racial equality in society, CRT was a necessary development to move discussions of race and racism to the forefront in culture. Parker and Lynn (2002) described CRT as having three goals: to present storytelling and narratives as valid approaches for someone to examine race and racism, to argue for the elimination of racial suppression while recognizing that race plays a role in society, and to illuminate nuances in the relationship between race and society. All three of these goals can be used in this chapter's examination of coverage surrounding Lin and James. ESPN could have used their storytelling and narratives to explore the racial boundaries in sports and society and argue that the type of coverage presented should have been altered to challenge the stereotypes that were being reinforced.

Largely because of ESPN's coverage, professional basketball, in particular, the National Basketball Association (NBA), is one of the United States' most popular sports (Rovell, 2014). The league consists of nearly an entirely White ownership but a majority of the players are African American (Koch & Vander Hill, 1988; Peterson, 2009). Consequently, the dramatic racial divide that exists between the league owners and the players who are the product sold to the masses reinforces a White hegemony. This hegemony is only furthered by ESPN, owned and run by mostly White executives. The network's coverage, consequently, supports the racial divide, even if unintentionally. Griffin (2011) described the problem with the racial divide in the NBA:

> When applied to the NBA, CRT offers a means to reveal the oppressive labor of interest convergence, Whiteness, and racism in particular by high-lighting the sharp contradictions between the NBA's public image of racial transcendence and the actual representation of Blacks in the league, the commodification of Black male players by the league, and the racialized maintenance of unequal power relationships within the league. (p. 4)

The racial divide that Griffin brings to light in the NBA when applying CRT to the league's product offers a stark contrast between the players, who are the commodity, and the owners who package players and the game they play as products. It is not only the owners and NBA executives who are a part of this racial divide, however. ESPN also packages the NBA and the players, commodifying them as a sports product sold for the network's financial benefit. According to Hogarth (2008), "Because the NBA is a league that markets the hip, highly visible blackness of its star players, the racism which is foundational to its media representations is often overlooked" (p. 68). Racial representation is often overlooked because fans do not think about the meanings behind the messages and promotions being run. CRT, as applied by Griffin, helps to reveal that the images ESPN and the NBA present to the fans do not match reality. Gardiner (2003) noted that the media (re)constructs and objectifies minorities and their representation through everyday myth and fantasy. The media use these myths and fantasies to reinforce stereotypes about minorities while CRT challenges these racialized stereotypes. By challenging the stereotypes, CRT addresses inequalities and racism in sport (Hylton, 2010).

ESPN's coverage appears to promote diversity and minority athletes; however, how the athletes are packaged does not challenge stereotypes or further racial equality and diversity. Instead, athletes are packaged by ESPN to protect revenue as well as maintain the status quo. ESPN has the power to package athletes however they wish and can do so without permission from those athletes. The athletes do not have any say in how they are covered and represented. Whannel (2002) noted that "Sport is now so conscious of its status as show business that image and charisma are central concerns for any sport promoter or agent" (p. 191). Consequently, ESPN is able to package athletes and present coverage in ways that ensure profits without regard for the implications of the power it holds over the athletes and society. To protect its revenue, ESPN uses its sports programming to package athletes such as Lin and James in an objectified, stereotyped manner. Hype and style best generate profits for the network rather than substance. The packages promote the athletes through slogans, catch phrases, puns, and tabloid style news and highlight reels. The network's coverage of Lin and James serves as high-profile examples of packaging for profits and neglecting to use the narratives to examine race in sports and society. All of this has an impact on the representation of athletes and the sports they play.

## ESPN, the Cultural Institution

Before the catchphrases, flashy sets, and tabloid style news reports, ESPN's coverage was much more modest and the sports were the center attraction. Media executives doubted a network dedicated to sports would be successful when ESPN was born in 1979. Lee Leonard explained ESPN's mission then in the opening of the first broadcast of *SportsCenter* on September 7, 1979—a mission that remains 35 years later: "If you're a fan, *if* you're a fan, what you will see in the next few minutes, hours, and days to follow may convince you that you've gone to sports heaven" ("Everything You Always Wanted to Know," 1999). As the network found its voice and presentation style, its popularity and ratings began to grow. Consequently, ESPN was able to expand its presence from covering slo-pitch softball games to having the broadcasting rights of the most popular sports in the United States, such as the NBA, National Football League (NFL), college football and basketball, and more, to make ESPN "the most powerful and prominent name in sports media" (Smith, 2009, p. xiv). According to Smith (2009), ESPN reaches people in more than 200 countries worldwide, providing more than 30,000 hours of coverage each year ("ESPN Fact Sheet," n.d.). ESPN's reach and influence is significant, putting the network and its on-air personalities in a powerful position to influence society because they can create and redefine meanings relating to race (Bruce, 2004).

ESPN can influence and redefine meanings related to race based on how coverage of sports and athletes are presented to those watching the network's programming, but also in the representation of the athletes. Quite often, minority athletes are not portrayed in the same ways as White athletes are in sports media. Former NFL player Ahmad Rashad recalled his experience with sports media using racial stereotypes to describe African American athleticism while covering games:

> If you close your eyes and listen, you can tell whether a commentator is discussing a white or a black athlete. When he says that somebody is a "natural," so fluid and graceful, you know he's talking about a black performer. When you hear that this other guy's a hard worker, or

that he comes to play every day on the strength of guts and intelligence, you know that the player in question is white. Just open your eyes. (Rashad & Bodo, 1988, p. 83)

Although Eastman and Billings (2001) found there has been some improvement in the descriptors of athletes used by sports media, the representation of race was still problematic. The coverage still described White athletes and minority athletes in different ways. The differences in how ESPN covered Lin and James also serve as evidence in how the network covers race holds significant power in how people view race. Instead of focusing on challenging stereotypes, ESPN's coverage of Lin and James capitalizes on race, using it as a means of commodifying the athletes and sports the network covers for financial benefit with little concern for the racial stereotypes that are reinforced and cultural implications that result. This becomes a concern, as Delgado and Stefancic (2001) noted: "Most people in their daily lives do not come into contact with many persons of radically different race or social station. We converse with, and read materials written by, persons in our own culture" (p. 28). Consequently, racial stereotypes are reinforced as fact in media portrayals of minorities, undermining discussions of race and equality.

## "LINSANITY" SURROUNDS JEREMY LIN

Before February 2012, Asian American NBA player Jeremy Lin had little media attention while being seldomly used on an 8–15 New York Knicks team that was struggling to be competitive. With its two biggest stars, Carmelo Anthony and Amare Stoudamire, out of the lineup, the Knicks turned to Lin for help. Receiving the first significant playing time in his career, Lin set records, becoming only the second player in NBA history to average more than 20 points and 7 assists per game in his first 8 starts in the NBA (Brown, 2012). The individual success helped spark team success as two weeks later Lin had led the Knicks to a 15–15 record (Mahoney, 2012). The success sparked intense media coverage, dubbed "Linsanity," that passionate fan reaction fueled.

The majority of the media coverage of Lin focused on racially based content rather than Lin's skill or backstory. Many media organizations, including ESPN, used puns emphasizing Lin's Asian roots in headlines that attempted to generate ratings, revenue, and clicks. The media frenzy that surrounded Lin was unique, not only for the racial elements involved. Lin was everywhere on ESPN and other media outlets, much like NFL quarterback Tim Tebow had been the months before Lin's emergence. Lin's 181 mentions on *SportsCenter* from February 17 to February 23, 2012, were 113 more than fellow NBA star Kevin Durant, who received the second most mentions, 68, that week (Burns, 2012a).

The intense media attention was a breakthrough moment for minorities such as Asian Americans who are far less visible in the media. According to Molden (2013), "Asian Americans like Lin exist at neither extreme of the Black-White ethnic poles, they can become invisible on the one hand or absorbed into the opposite pole" (p. 25). In other words, Asian Americans often get "othered" and ignored. Asian Americans are, consequently, underrepresented in the media (Mok, 1998; NAPALC, 2005; Texeira, 2005). Lin's breakthrough was such a rare moment of visibility that even NBA Commissioner David Stern commented on the media coverage. Stern admitted that "no player has created the interest and frenzy in this short period of time, in any sport, that I'm aware of like Jeremy Lin has" ("David Stern," 2012, para. 3). Reporter Jeff Yang from the *Wall Street Journal* explained that the Lin phenomenon was particularly interesting because there had not been an Asian American like him in sports before ("Video: The Jeremy," 2012). Yang further described that there was something "infectious" about Lin that contributed to the frenzy of media coverage surrounding him. Consequently, the focus on packaging "Linsanity" with puns and racially based headlines demonstrated ESPN's commitment to creating revenue instead of advancing a national conversation regarding race.

The subject of race bubbled over in coverage at every turn, however. "Linsanity" at its peak had ESPN mentioning Lin 350 times in a week on *SportsCenter* (Burns, 2012b). The heavy coverage equated to Lin being mentioned once every minute *SportsCenter* was on air (Burns, 2012b). The media coverage of Lin in general lacked challenges to inequality and demonstrated the commodification through reinforcement of stereotypes for financial gain. Relatively few media organizations attempted to discuss important issues regarding Lin's race, such as why it was significant that an Asian American was a success in the NBA. The narratives ignored important questions and goals of CRT outlined by Lynn and Parker (2002) that would have challenged stereotypes the media was reinforcing. Instead the coverage emphasized catchphrases and headlines. Yahoo! took note of coverage surrounding Lin, compiling a list of 949 puns media organizations published (Stableford, 2012). These puns ranged from "Lincitement" and "Lincome tax" to "Lincorrect," "Lindestructable," "Amasian," and "Lin-your-face" (Stableford, 2012). Instead of the media focusing on Lin's background or why so few Asian Americans play professional basketball, it seemed there was a competition to see who could come up with the most puns. ESPN helped to further the "Linsanity" narrative so many other media organizations focused their attention on, rather than challenging the Asian stereotypes and creating meaningful coverage that discussed race in a different way. The coverage of Lin's race that did exist played on Asian stereotypes in describing Lin as a humble, intelligent, well-educated model citizen.

With so much attention focused on Lin, it was only a matter of time before controversy surrounding race and Lin would strike ESPN. Following a Knicks loss on February 18, 2012, the espn.com website ran the phrase "Chink in the Armor" as a headline with a photo of Lin alongside it. The phrase, usually a cliché in sports coverage, in this case was an inflammatory racial slur. Further, it was part of the packaging of ESPN's coverage of Lin—commodifying his race for financial benefit. The headline remained on the ESPN mobile front page for 35 minutes, garnering much attention (McNeal, 2012). However, the controversy did not end with the headline being removed. The controversy regarding the headline continued later in the day as an on-air personality repeated the headline on air multiple times (McNeal, 2012). ESPN fired the headline writer, and the on-air personality who repeated the headline was suspended for 30 days (McNeal, 2012). ESPN executives issued multiple statements offering apologies for the incidents and calling for a change in coverage:

> At ESPN we are aware of three offensive and inappropriate comments made on ESPN outlets during our coverage of Jeremy Lin…. We again apologize, especially to Mr. Lin. His accomplishments are a source of great pride to the Asian American community, including the Asian American employees at ESPN. Through self-examination, improved editorial practices and controls, and response to constructive criticism, we will be better in the future. ("ESPN Statement," 2012, para.1)

On the surface ESPN's response to headline controversy sounded as if the network would change the way it would cover Lin. The statement appeared to embrace a philosophy that Hylton (2010) described as a means to fulfill the goals of CRT: Challenge the stereotypes in the coverage, and address both inequality and racism in sports (Parker & Lynn, 2002). However, ESPN's coverage changed little. The popular debate show *Around the Horn*, known for the panelists talking over one another or being muted by the show's host, held a segment in which four panelists discussed race in sports. The viewpoints expressed in that segment did not reflect ESPN but, rather, the journalists participating in the discussion. The journalists did not repeat ESPN's apology; they seriously discussed race in sports and how important it was to talk about it despite the topic making many uncomfortable. The segment, as well as *Pardon the Interruption*'s segment on race and Lin, were honest attempts to respectfully illuminate the impact sports can have on culture. Despite the discussion on *Around the Horn* and *Pardon the Interruption*, ESPN's coverage of Lin and the slur was more commodification than responsible journalism. The controversy and ensuing segments further promoted ESPN, helping the network attract viewers to its programming.

The coverage of Lin remained so intense following the panelists remarks on *Around the Horn* that anchors on an episode of *SportsCenter* said Lin more often than using the words "If," "but," "are," "be," and "what" (Burns, 2012b). In doing so, ESPN continued to commodify Lin in stereotypical and at times offensive ways for their financial benefit despite pleas by its journalists to address race in ways that Parker and Lynn (2002) described as productive. Consequently, the network failed to reconstruct Lin, or his race, to reflect the diversity of the country. The package of "Linsanity," puns and all, in actuality reinforced blatant racism by avoiding a discussion that would have added significant understanding of how rare Lin's sudden success was. As Gardiner (2003) argued, the media objectifies minorities through myth, fantasy, and stereotypes. Linsanity was rooted in Asian stereotypes and myth that failed to create an educated narrative and understanding of Asian Americans in society and why Lin's success and the media coverage surrounding him were important.

## PACKAGING LEBRON JAMES, *THE DECISION,* AND THE AFTERMATH

Two years before Lin became the target of intense media coverage, LeBron James, one of the most prominent NBA stars, became a free agent. In becoming a free agent on July 1, 2010, James set off a frantic frenzy of courtship from seven teams as well as heavy media coverage. Speculation of James's landing spot was consistently the top sports story across the country. Interest in where James would play increased each day as he met with different teams. Media coverage of such an event normally concludes when a free agent signs with a team. However, James's announcement of his choice only began a firestorm of controversy and, remarkably, even heavier media coverage. A vast majority of the coverage was hype and ESPN took their place in the lead in the intense publicizing of James. In packaging James and his free agency as an attraction, ESPN commodified James rather than shifting some focus of the coverage toward race's role in how James reached such a high point in his life.

James revealed his intention to play for the Miami Heat on July 8, 2010, during a much-hyped ESPN special, *The Decision.* The program was a ratings bonanza for ESPN and allowed the network to brag about having the announcement exclusively on their programming. Don Ohlmeyer, ESPN's ombudsman in 2010, noted that network executives saw *The Decision* as a means to further enhance its reputation as the Worldwide Leader in Sports because it would have mass audience appeal that would motivate fans to view hours of network programming (Ohlmeyer, 2010a). In addition, executives felt the program would further cement ESPN as the sports media organization to turn to for big events and news (Ohlmeyer, 2010a). ESPN benefited in the ratings, drawing the third-highest rated cable television event of 2010 with 9.95 million viewers ("Decision," 2010). By surrendering the advertising revenue to charity as a fundraiser for the Boys and Girls Club, ESPN also was able to leverage the program into a display of good citizenship and corporate responsibility even though it was James selling and donating the money to charity.

The announcement immediately drew overwhelming amount of criticism of both James and ESPN from other media organizations and fans alike for arrogance (Arnovitz, 2010; Ohlmeyer, 2010a). James and Nike turned to an advertising company, Wieden & Kennedy (Boland, 2010), to create a commercial in response to the backlash of *The Decision*. Directed by Stacy Wall (Georgiadis, 2010), the advertisement titled "Rise" initially aired on TNT as James's first NBA season with the Heat tipped off. The commercial was supposed to make a peace offering to all those who criticized ESPN and James but instead rekindled the images and words that inflamed so many NBA fans. The commercial focused on James sitting on the set of *The Decision*. In the next 90 seconds, with the setting changing, James asked his critics many questions: "What should I do?" "Should I really believe I've ruined my legacy?" "Do you want to see my shiny new shoes?" Or should he admit he is not a role model? "Maybe I should just disappear." The advertisement ends with James asking: "Should I be who you want me to be [the bad guy]?" before cutting to the trademark black screen and Nike logo.

The reaction to the commercial as well as *The Decision* focused on James and arrogance for making his announcement about him (Gregory, 2010; McCarthy, 2010; Ohlmeyer, 2010b; "Stern," 2010; Wallace, 2010; Young, 2010). Panelists on the ESPN show debate program *Around the Horn* summed up the media coverage of James, pointing out that it was about paying attention to James and nothing more. The only way ESPN or James could benefit from any of the coverage was if people were paying attention to it. In that regard, both ESPN and James succeeded. Both the network and James received a large quantity of attention, but the focus was not on the most concerning elements of *The Decision* and ensuing Nike commercial. ESPN and James both commodified James, but together they had commodified the underprivileged children of the Boys and Girls Club without ever discussing the racial implications.

James and the kids became a product to ESPN. The network could have sold a narrative about James overcoming a tough childhood and that basketball was his way out and then detailing the children's stories. Instead, there was only hype and a focus on James as ESPN again attempted to prove its dominance in the sports media world. Had race played a factor in the coverage, ESPN not only could have used James's story as evidence of an African American success story, rising from inequality and disadvantage, but also it could have argued sports were an equalizer, just as ESPN personality Chris Berman had suggested (Berman, 1999). ESPN's coverage of James and *The Decision* may have had good intentions behind it, particularly in raising money for charity, but it played upon the idealistic notion that sports is an equalizer without ever discussing race. Perhaps ESPN thought James transcended race at this point, but neglecting to acknowledge the racial elements suppressed the notion of equality in contemporary society. Campbell (1995) described contemporary racism as "being fostered by the news media's 'commonsense' myths despite even the best intentions of journalists caught up in a system dominated by majority culture values and sensibilities" (p. 13). In other words, James was announcing that he was signing a contract worth more than $100 million so race was no longer a factor. Race hardly registered on the radar following comments from James in which he said that race was a factor in the reception to *The Decision*, the "Rise" commercial, and subsequently how he was represented in the media (Gregory, 2010; McCarthy, 2010; Young, 2010). James was not incorrect in his assessment.

Race had played a factor in how James was represented in ESPN's coverage before the decision. The commodification of James was slightly more subtle than of Lin because sports help to make African American athletes more visible, putting them under a microscope for constant surveillance and scrutiny (Yancy, 2005). This was particularly true of James, who had built an image through ESPN coverage dating all the way back to high school. Journalist Bob Boland (2010) summed this up best when he wrote, "His [James] entire career has always had hype but it has been largely contrived hype, like his trademark pregame chalk explosions that *SportsCenter* has made famous." The spectacle of James in high school, being one of the youngest NBA players, and then the most heavily covered free agency history outshined the significance of James's race in sports.

## RESONATING BEYOND SPORTS

Sports have a pervasive existence in millions of people's lives around the world. As such, ESPN has the opportunity to expose different cultures, ideas, and social perspectives to their audience regarding the identity of those in the network's coverage. Television is one of the strongest platforms that influences American culture (Fiske, 1985). By covering elements of identity such as race, gender, ethnicity, and nationality, TV can teach the audience something about its culture, society, or even its identity. However, what lacked from the network's coverage is also significant. Sabo and Jansen (1992) noted that often, "What is *not said* in sports media reveals as much about how hegemonic processes work within the US sports industry as what *is said*." Although ESPN helps Lin and James promote themselves, their team and brand, the network remains the entity in control of the coverage. ESPN determines who is allowed to speak, when, and what is said. Consequently, ESPN is determining meaning behind the words and images used in its coverage of Lin and James. Hall (1981) described this power as a means to determine what the problems are associated with race. The coverage of Lin and James on ESPN reinforced the hegemonic power the network holds over the athletes. The use of stereotypes and puns serve as a subtle reminder to society where the power lies. Whannel (2002) wrote, "Star performers are not in control of their own images, which are a product of the social construction of stardom, the routine production practices of the media, the discursive fields within which they are produced, and the specific social and historical conjunctures out of which they emerge" (p. 184). Therefore, Lin and James have relatively little power in how they are covered and the resulting response to them. They become characters in ESPN programming, used to create controversy and drama to draw viewers and generate review. Turning Lin and James into characters furthers ESPN's position of power in sports. ESPN has significant power in circulating representations of identity to mass audiences; that power resonates far beyond sports regardless of whether ESPN realizes it. When that power is used for the company's financial well-being over providing meaningful discussion of issues, such as race, everyone loses. Hughes (2004) noted that the NBA is the primary circulator of African American image and culture to mass audiences, meaning the NBA and its television partners (ESPN) are responsible for how the athletes appear on and off the court. Sabo and Jansen (1992) noted the media's role in the construction of specific images used to cover African American athletes that produced stereotypes and that "It would therefore appear that sport media are complicit in... the larger institutional and cultural processes that reproduce and exonerate white men's domination over black men" (p. 182). ESPN maintains the status quo and power by telling the athletes and society what is valued. When applied to ESPN, CRT illuminates the network's coverage of Lin and James as racially oppressive. If Lin or James were White, the network would cover them differently. The use of stereotypes, puns, racial slurs, or packaging athletes as products to promote its coverage help ESPN financially but more importantly, it imprints specific meanings regarding Lin, James, and race in the societal fabric of America. The coverage tells Lin, James, and society that ESPN has tremendous power. ESPN can use its power however it chooses and its bottom line is its primary concern; whatever most effectively generates the most revenue and ratings is what will be broadcast. Consequently, much of the time ESPN will air hype, puns, and stereotypes that do not offer any deeper understanding of what is covered. Although revenue must be considered, as ESPN must make a profit to stay in business, it must balance financial benefit with contributing to society in a positive way. The network can do so by challenging stereotypes that objectify and commodify identities, such as Lin and James, and attempt to (re)define race relations simultaneously. CRT offers ESPN a means of, at the least, identifying the differences between stereotypes and highlighting the significance of stereotypes when necessary.

ESPN may have had the best of intentions in mind promoting and covering Lin and James so heavily, but in doing so the network reinforced stereotypes and marginalized them. In the case of James, ESPN took advantage of James for financial gain with *The Decision* and then tried to appear generous by allowing James to donate a portion of the proceeds to charity. The network's ombudsman in 2010, Ohlmeyer, eloquently described how the coverage of James—which can also be applied to the coverage of Lin—resonated beyond sports:

> Beyond James, it's a cautionary tale for ESPN. If the network wants to be considered the true worldwide leader in sports, it must accept the responsibility that comes with it. As the biggest player in the space, ESPN can establish and give credibility to a story. (Ohlmeyer, 2010a, para. 13)

Although in general ESPN's coverage of race lacked a significant discussion of race or a challenge to racial stereotypes, at least one of the network's journalists called for a careful examination of content. In a column for ESPN's website, J. A. Adande (2012) wrote about the racially charged coverage used to commodify Lin that failed to advance a serious discussion of race in sports or society:

> The rules have changed. The lesson is to exercise greater caution, to consider all the ramifications of what we say. It's not too much to ask. It will lead to smarter conversations. And if that's the place to which Jeremy Lin has brought us, it's another way his impact resonates far beyond Madison Square Garden.

The coverage of Lin and James should resonate far beyond what they do on the court. Their success and popularity help to shine a light on the media's failings, especially ESPN's as the network is the world's leader in sports coverage, to challenge the racially based content that reinforces stereotypes of minorities and inequality that many around the world still face in their everyday lives. ESPN has the power to create and redefine the meanings regarding race that it disseminates to society as a product of its coverage.

It is impossible to expect that ESPN can or should discuss race and inequality any time the network covers a minority. However, when important moments in sports coverage surrounding a minority such as James or Lin come around, ESPN must act and challenge the stereotypes being reinforced. This expectation may be difficult to uphold, however; according to Delgado and Stefancic (2001), "The idea that a better, fairer script can readily substitute for the older, prejudiced one is attractive, but falsified by history" (pp. 28–29). The network must make money but maintain a semblance of the style that helped make ESPN into the global media powerhouse it is. Yet, as Adande (2012) wrote in his ESPN column, ESPN must encourage smarter discussions regarding social issues such as race. This will take hard work and commitment from executives to on-air talent. Meeting Adande's goal is possible. To ESPN's credit, it provided the airtime to *Around the Horn* and *Pardon the Interruption* to challenge the problematic racial representations of Lin and James. ESPN is one of the most powerful and influential media entities in the world and that platform it provided to Adande and other journalists can make a difference in challenging stereotypes in sports coverage. That platform to challenge and discuss what is wrong with coverage and the significance of race in stories to, as the main tenets of CRT suggest, advance discussions of race and equality in places where the topics are often ignored, is significant.

# CHAPTER EIGHT

# ESPN's Mythological Rhetoric of Title IX

KAREN L. HARTMAN

The passing of Title IX as part of the Education Amendments Act in 1972 significantly altered the treatment and protection of women and girls within educational institutions receiving federal funds. Although commonly understood in terms of athletics, Title IX served as a response to gender discrimination in which women were denied entry into universities and medical schools, refused employment over men, and received unequal pay. Today the law is recognized for its impact and success but also its controversy as application of the law has been unevenly practiced.

The 40th anniversary of Title IX, however, generated an increase in media attention specifically surrounding the history of women's athletics. ESPN was arguably leading the celebration with the most public platform. For the anniversary espnW, a segment of ESPN focused on women athletes and sports, launched a microsite titled *The Power of IX* that served as the "digital destination for ESPN's examination and recognition of the 40th anniversary of Title IX" ("Multi-faceted," 2012, para. 1). The site, and overall media coverage from the network, provided an in-depth look analyzing what the law means for women athletes and society. The content plan included several elements: feature stories; a countdown of the top 40 athletes of past 40 years; *Title IX is Mine!* video vignettes; *The Lineup* (a series of lists looking at 9 heroes, 9 sibling rivalries, 9 women's dynasties, etc.); social media (including a collection of women athlete user-submitted photos to make the largest collection of women and girls' sporting images, along with Twitter and Facebook postings); a week of television content from June 17–23 on ESPN, ESPN2,

ESPNU, and ESPN Classic; stories in *ESPN The Magazine* (including the magazine's first "Women in Sports" issue); and the ESPN Film series, *9 for IX*. This multifaceted celebration crossing various ESPN platforms arguably reached more potential people than any other celebration or discussion of the law.

ESPN serves as the leading broadcaster of sport to millions of people globally, thereby indicating its ability to influence and frame sport for its viewers. The network's capability to reach households and individuals is unrivaled by other media forms; ESPN's *SportsCenter* averages 115 million viewers a month (ESPN, Inc., n.d.). The coverage of the 40th anniversary of the law, along with the creation of espnW, suggests it is open to covering women athletics, but research shows it lacks a consistent approach. For example, in 1997 ESPN's *SportsCenter* devoted 5% of its coverage to women's athletics and in 2002 the coverage dropped to less than 5% (Adams & Tuggle, 2004). ESPN's 40th anniversary, however, offered a rare opportunity for the network to cover women's athletics in a purposeful and serious manner by delving into the complexities of the law, as well as providing significant coverage of women athletes.

Although such attention is encouraging, ESPN's rhetorical framing of Title IX ultimately mythologizes the law and diminishes the legal and social realities facing women in sport. Three themes emerge from ESPN's coverage: equality, opportunity, and pressure for young women athletes. This study demonstrates how the mythologizing of Title IX is a rhetorical strategy that evades any serious discussion of the law and its implementation. The discourse also serves to delegitimize female athletes by creating a separate, distinct rhetorical space where female athletes can be admired or discussed only as a teleological consequence of the Title IX narrative. The consistent and repetitive messages about the greatness of the law through the opportunities and equality it provides leaves out the critical and accurate voice demonstrating the challenges the law faces. Because this is a significantly diminished part of the rhetoric, a one-sided and inaccurate version of the law is told that threatens real dialogue about where the law stands. The mythological language also frames female athletes as a privileged group rather than athletes who remain underrepresented, ignored in the media, and inaccurately blamed for creating a quota system that leads to the dissolution of men's sport teams.

## SIGNIFICANCE AND LITERATURE REVIEW

Analysis of Title IX comes at a particularly important time as the struggle over maintaining the law is under attack. Title IX is far from being fully integrated into high school and college athletics and past estimates show that 80% of all educational institutions are not in compliance with the law (Priest, 2003). No institution has had its federal funding pulled for noncompliance, and research on the media framing of Title IX shows patriarchal reporting that threatens to perpetuate misunderstandings of the law (e.g., Hardin, Simpson, Whiteside, & Garris, 2007). In 2000, the Republican Party made Title IX reform part of its platform and in 2002 the Bush administration formed a commission to review the law. The commission favored changing the law and gave the Department of Education (DoE) unilateral control to suggest other ways of achieving equity (Hardin et al., 2007). Beyond the federal government, the law generates controversy on academic campuses as coaches, fans, and administrators approach and perceive the law differently.

Incorrect interpretations of the law suggest there is a "quota" that must be fulfilled. However, rather than one approach that all schools must follow, the law offers three options for compliance: (1) The number of participation opportunities for male and women athletes is substantially proportionate to their respective enrollments; (2) The institution has a history and continuing practice of expanding participation opportunities responsive to the developing interests and abilities of the underrepresented sex; or (3) The institution is fully and effectively accommodating the interests and abilities of the underrepresented sex. Although schools must demonstrate compliance with at least one of the elements, schools are not required to adhere to all three ("Title IX Information," n.d.). Ultimately schools have flexibility dependent on the specifics of their student body and athletic program makeup. Regardless, the controversy remains. For example, Hardin, Whiteside, and Ash (2014) assessed a group of sports information directors (SIDs) responsible for distributing information about college sports and found the following:

> A majority agreed that it is a "contentious" issue, pointedly reminding women's sports advocates that Title IX is still not a settled law, but rather continues to generate controversy almost 40 years after its signing. The data also showed a possible trend indicating that younger SIDs may be less supportive of Title IX initiatives compared with their older colleagues. (p. 58)

Forty years after its passage, dialogue is needed to truly address where the law is, how it is implemented, and how it affects athletics.

Regardless of how people feel about Title IX, the law greatly influenced women's sports. In the early 1970s, before Title IX became law, approximately 294,000 girls competed in high school athletics. In 2012, almost 3.2 million girls competed—a 980% increase ("A Title IX Primer," n.d.). At the college level, approximately 16,000 women played sports in 1970, while in 2012 there were approximately 200,000 female athletes participating—the highest in history (Acosta & Carpenter, 2012). Furthermore, in 2012 there were 13,792 female professionals employed within intercollegiate athletics, 9,274 women's intercollegiate teams, and 8.73 women's teams per school (Acosta & Carpenter, 2012). Title IX clearly empowers women to participate in sport and the number of women participating and benefiting from the law grows every year.

The opportunities have not come at the expense of men—an often-used narrative to discredit and undermine the law's implementation (Hardin & Whiteside, 2009). High school boys' participation reached an all-time high in 2010–2011 with approximately 4.5 million boys participating ("High School Sports," n.d.), equating to 1.4 boys for every girl playing (Acosta & Carpenter, 2012). In administrative positions, 57.1% of women's teams had male coaches, approximately 98% of men's teams had male coaches, and 69.3% of head athletic trainers and 90.2% of sports information directors were men (Acosta & Carpenter, 2012). Title IX serves to empower women and increase participation rates, and research shows that men continue to play, coach, and administer at higher rates. The misperceptions, however, continue.

Misperceptions often come through media's framing of the law. Framing "is to select some aspects of a perceived reality and make them salient in a communicating text, in such a way as to promote a particular problem definition, causal interpretation, moral evaluation and/or treatment recommendation of the item described" (Entman, 1993, p. 52). Media portrayals can be positive, neutral, or negative and in sport, research shows that media are powerful and persuasive producers and senders of messages about culture and gender ideology (Weber & Carini, 2013).

Female athletes are a marginalized group whose athletic achievements are minimalized and athletes are often sexualized (Weber & Carini, 2013). Sport is one of the biggest perpetuators of male (and heterosexual) hegemony: "[M]ediated sports are central to the reinforcement of a class-bound social hierarchy that privileges whites and (heterosexual) men and creates a social landscape that is decidedly *not* an 'equal playing field' for groups that are not either (white or heterosexual men)" (Hardin et al., 2014, p. 43). Female athletes and sports become negatively skewed and marginalized through media framing and this is no different with media portrayals of Title IX.

Research analyzing media narratives from 1972 through the mid-2000s suggests that the complexities of Title IX legislation and enforcement are often simplified and provide a male hegemonic frame. For example, Walton (2003) found that from 1972 to 2002 the media provided a "simplistic analysis" that misled and negatively framed the law. The debate, as it played out in the media, was portrayed as an "either/or" division of resources between women's athletics and men's minor sports with Title IX sitting at the center of the argument. Regional and national newspaper coverage from 2002 to 2005 found that paper size, placement of stories, and the reporter's gender affected the ways stories framed the law (Hardin et al., 2007). Although articles during this time framed the law neutrally, when stories discussed controversial aspects of the law, the tone changed:

> [I]n stories that involve controversy or coverage of discourse about the law's impact, reporters oftentimes resort to framing similar to that found by Walton (2003) and others: "simplistic

analysis" and use of patriarchal frames that assume gains for women are losses for men even in the face of facts that say otherwise. (p. 231)

Similarly, rhetorical messages within the media framing of the law demonstrate conflicting and antagonistic media narratives. Staurowsky (1998) analyzed trade publications from 1994 to 1997 and found that the rhetoric of the Title IX debate used an adversarial model by using war metaphors such as "battle of the sexes," "dispute," "fight," and "tug-of-war." This model framed Title IX and gender equity discourse as polarizing and minimized genuine problem solving by stakeholders in the debate. The use of this violent rhetoric fostered a competitive rather than problem-solving approach between the two sides. Framing in this manner turns women—the underrepresented group Title IX aims to protect—into the privileged, advantaged group (Staurowsky, 1996). Such framing thwarts change because it finds fault with the groups with the least power while deflecting attention from the central issues.

Rhetorical approaches to media framing suggest that the media's language can create and perpetuate myths by creating larger ideological systems of thought. Barthes (1972) argues that myths are not simply stories but are larger ideological systems that become naturalized. The naturalization allows myth to be experienced as natural speech: "[M]yth is experienced as innocent speech: not because its intentions are hidden—if they were hidden, they could not be efficacious—but because they are naturalized" (p. 131). Myths are not about being "true" or "false," but are about the power they hold. Burke (2001) defines *mythos* as the name for some particular action or the choosing of one story over another and views myth as a part of cultural coherence and a force for identification. Media frames include verbal frames that encompass myths, narratives, and metaphors that are understood and are often unquestioned by society (Hertog & McLeod, 2003). The language surrounding Title IX creates a mythic frame that ultimately shapes how people view the law.

Sport is ripe with mythology and Suggs (2005) identifies a common myth associated with Title IX. He states that although American men's sports are viewed as beginning in the mid-nineteenth century and evolving to their current state, women's athletic history begins in 1972 with the passage of Title IX. ESPN's celebration, though situated as a recognition of women athletes and the power of the law, instead perpetuated this myth through its framing of the law as ushering in the "beginning" of sport for American women and communicating that the "fruits" of the law have been realized.

## ANALYSIS

ESPN's 40th celebration provided a public mediated platform for millions to view via various modes—social media, films, print, *SportsCenter* coverage, etc.

This analysis includes all elements of the espnW microsite (http://espn.go.com/espnW/title-ix/), all 54 videos espnW provides in relation to the campaign, the *9 for IX* movie series, and *ESPN The Magazine*'s "Women in Sport" issue. These elements provide the most well-publicized and circulated items of the campaign, offering a strong overview of the campaign and the messages sent. Thematic analysis of the segments reveals predominate themes communicated through the celebration: equality, opportunity, and guilt/pressure for future generations. Analysis also reveals areas of coverage where the law is ignored, as well as areas that present a complex and critical view of the law.

## Equality

The first theme emphasized throughout all facets of the campaign is equality—an inherent element to the law. As communicated through the campaign, Title IX encourages equality on the sports field with the ideal that it will then transcend into society. This is demonstrated a multitude of ways. For example, on a video segment on espnW, "The Word" host Cassidy Hubbarth introduced and framed the law as providing equality for women and helping to level the playing field. In several *Title IX is Mine* videos (:30 to 1:30 minute long video segments of men and women addressing how Title IX affected their lives through the question "What does Title IX mean to you?") equality is the main theme. For example, ESPN analyst Sage Steele stated how Title IX was about equality and going after your dreams. Dick Vitale, an NCAA basketball commentator, stated that the law was about equality and how far the law has come. He stated:

> I hear the word Title IX and you think about equality. It's phenomenal what has transpired over the years. My family surely has benefited from that when my daughters, Terry and Sherry, went to Notre Dame and getting full scholarships, the same kind of scholarship aid that was given to football players and basketball players and that's the way it should be. They felt that, "Heck, if I'm good enough to earn a scholarship equal to the guy that's playing football, well then I want to get that scholarship." (Vitale, 2012)

Similarly, Bruce Bowen, a former NBA player and current ESPN analyst, stated that the law enables the world to see how much women can do and it leads to women becoming leaders in sport and society. Mike Hill, a sportscaster with ESPN from 2004 to 2013 and currently with Fox Sports 1, stated that the law is about equality and it offers a chance for women to do what they want and that the law is necessary in today's social and sporting landscape. One last example is from Tina Thompson (2012), a former WNBA player, who stated, "The true definition of Title IX is being able to aspire to be almost anything you want to be."

The theme of equality continues in *ESPN The Magazine*'s "Women in Sport" issue. The issue was released on June 11, 2012, and had an approximate 2.1 million circulation rate ("The Top 25," 2013). This theme is predominantly articulated through the article, "33 Women Who Changed Sports," which included descriptions of 33 women deemed "game changers." Nancy Hogshead-Makar, a lawyer and senior director of advocacy for the Women's Sports Foundation who fights for gender equality and Title IX, and Judy Sweet, the co-director of the Alliance of Women Coaches and a gender equity and Title IX consultant, were included on the list. The descriptions highlight these two women who are directly involved with Title IX reform and frame them through the equality lens. The remaining women discussed in the article are either recipients of Title IX progress, such as professional basketball player Brittany Griner, or are perceived as "breaking the glass ceiling," such as Sue Falsone, the head athletic trainer of the Los Angeles Dodgers.

This theme as communicated in the campaign suggests the law provides immediate equality to all girls and women who participate in sport. Equality is so deeply ingrained, and even assumed, that athletes barely need to even think about going after one's dreams. Title IX provides a framework where equality is given and inherent to sport participation.

## Opportunity

A second theme the campaign communicates is that Title IX provides opportunities to women that without the law would not be available. Title IX is the reason—and predominantly framed as the reason—for women's rising acceptance and growth in sport. For example, on ESPN's *SportsCenter*, anchor Laurece "Rece" Davis discusses the "Top 40 Athletes of the Past 40 Years" with retired women's soccer player Mia Hamm, who won the top honor. As he introduced the law, he framed it as the landmark legislation that opened doors for women. Hamm's response stated that she would not have had any opportunities to even play high school soccer as playing would have been over after the club level.

The *Title IX is Mine!* vignettes continue the theme of opportunity and how Title IX provided them. Holly Rowe, an ESPN analyst, stated that the law was a huge factor in the growth of women in broadcasting because there is more women's sport on TV. She continued to state that Title IX has provided "the new normal." Jay Wright (2012), an NCAA men's basketball coach, stated:

> When I hear Title IX, I think opportunity for women athletes, opportunity for women coaches, opportunity for officials, opportunity for women fans. For my daughter to look at herself not by her relationship to male sports but by her relationship to her team and her athletic accomplishments, that's something that I've learned is great about Title IX and I think she's learned a lot.

Continuing the theme, NCAA president Mark Emmert stated that the law makes him think of the extraordinary opportunities that he gets to experience and that the law presents a generational shift. He concludes by stating that it is "stunning" to know that there are opportunities Title IX provided exclusively. Other athletes and sports commentators such as ESPN analysts Prim Siripipat, Cassidy Hubbarth, and Rebecca Lobo, professional soccer player Abby Wambach, former professional player Tina Thompson, and professional basketball player Ruth Riley commented that Title IX allowed them to receive university scholarships and served as the opportunity to make their dreams a reality. A final example is from former U.S. women's soccer national team player and current ESPN analyst Julie Foudy during a two-minute segment that aired as a part of the June 23, 2012, *SportsCenter* episode. Similar to other discourse during the celebration, Foudy discussed how Title IX is one of the most profound civil rights and how it provided scholarships for women. She stated that without Title IX as a part of the women's sports landscape, opportunities for women in a variety of industries would be reduced:

> [W]e wouldn't have nearly as many women running corporations, sitting on boards, and that's the really wonderful effect of Title IX besides all the physical benefits of playing, but just who it shapes and what you become after you are an athlete and you know scientists, astronauts, lawyers, and they all look back and say sports did it for me. (Foudy, 2012)

In *ESPN The Magazine*, Michelle Obama emphasized opportunity by discussing how the law affects her daughters and how it shapes the ways young girls see themselves and encourages them to set high goals in the future. She concludes that the law is something we can all be proud of and it provides hope for the future of all young girls and boys.

Title IX, as expressed through the campaign, provides opportunities that would not exist without the law being passed. Being able to participate in the opportunities the law provided allows women to attain certain goals such as getting an education, earning a scholarship, and playing professionally.

## Guilt/Pressure for Future Generations

A third theme that emerged from the rhetoric of the campaign, which differs significantly in tone from the other two, emphasized the need of younger generations to recognize the importance of Title IX. Comments suggested that unlike older generations, young girls were unaware of the law and what it provided them. The commentators, therefore, enthymematically presented a sense of guilt and pressure for future generations to know more about the law, appreciate it, and be thankful for the female athletes who came before them. For example, on *SportsCenter* when Hamm discussed being the recipient of the Top Athlete of the Past 40 Years, she emphasized that younger female athletes need to take advantage of the environment that they are in and be sure they make the most of it, not only for themselves but for future generations. Sheryl Swoopes, on an espnW video segment, stated it is necessary to remind ourselves and educate people, especially young women and girls, about the importance of Title IX. In the *Title IX is Mine!* vignettes, Teresa Edwards (2012), a former professional basketball player and Olympic gold medalist, stated that the law is bigger than a basketball game and young people should serve as ambassadors and promoters of the game:

> When you start to really think about the journey that women have taken, and we still continue to take, it's bigger than just our basketball game. There's always going to be challenges because we're going to always want more so the challenge is going to be to have young women follow suit of being promoters and pushing the game. And we just have to keep working hard, having fun, and making sure that the opportunity exists years to come.

Several elements of the campaign, however, tempered the guilt and pressure with statements highlighting how the law's benefits have been achieved and are not a focus for young women. For example, ESPN broadcaster Chris McKendry discussed what Title IX means for team sports and the growth of team sports but questions admonishing young athletes for not knowing about it. McKendry suggests that not knowing could serve as a sign of success and ultimately the law's benefits could be viewed as a birthright. Hope Solo, a women's professional soccer player, stated she understood how young people might not immediately recognize the importance of the law, and for her it meant more to her the older she became. Finally, Abby Wambach, a professional soccer player, acknowledged that the older generations complain about the younger generations but concluded by saying, "That's the point." For her, the point of Title IX is for younger generations to have opportunities that older generations did not.

This theme communicates that if you are a female athlete, you must know about Title IX. If you do not, or are unaware of its history and what the law means, you are letting down the women before you. This not only creates a layer of guilt to the rhetorical framing of the law and women athletes, it also creates potential divisions within the sporting realm particularly between younger and older generations of women athletes.

## The Law Is Ignored

The campaign produced three main themes framing the law and provided awareness and commentary for the celebration. Beyond these three themes, however, a significant portion of the campaign did not discuss the law at all. The non-discussion arguably presented an unclear connection for viewers who saw elements of the celebration without a direct link to Title IX. For example, the film series *9 for IX*, a series of nine movies about female athletes, which female filmmakers created, does not analyze the law or even reference the law. The films aired on ESPN from July to August 2012 and highlighted individual athletes as well as larger social issues affecting women sport. The films featured professional tennis player Venus Williams, former University of Tennessee women's basketball coach Pat Summit, free diver Audrey Mestre, professional basketball player Sheryl Swoopes, Olympic gold winner Katarina Witt, 1984 Olympic track runner Mary Decker, and the 1999 U.S. women's national soccer team. The films also highlighted female journalists, including Lesley Visser, Jane Gross, and Claire Smith, and their experience breaking barriers in the male locker room and the branding of women in sport that often turns athletes into sex symbols. Although the films provide significant coverage of important women athletes and moments in the history of sport, the films do not mention Title IX at all. Therefore, while the *9 for IX* series was a major component of the 40th celebration, they had no clear connection to the law nor did they provide any discussion of it even though some of the subject matter presented options to do so—such as the case with films analyzing women sport in the United States (e.g., the films on Pat Summit or the 1999 U.S. women's national soccer team).

Besides the *9 for IX* series, *ESPN The Magazine*'s "Women in Sport" issue also largely ignored discussion of the law. Although the magazine offered the first issue devoted to women's sports, something significant in itself, it only contained three articles that directly connected to the law while the rest focused on general women's and men's coverage. Sample feature stories included a cover photo and article, "Defining Danica Patrick," "Future of Women Athletes," a photo series titled "Playing Like a Girl," "Sarah Burke's Legacy," "Victoria Azarenka's Rise to No. 1," "Michelle Wie, 9 Years Later," and the "Tragic Story of Rosalind Ross." Although the three articles that did discuss Title IX provided an in-depth understanding of the law or a relatively unknown historical feature of the law, the majority of the magazine was devoted to female and male athletes without any clear connection to the law.

## Critical Views of the Law

Although the celebration provided themes to suggest women "have made it," or ignored the law in high-profile pieces, there were a few elements that offered a glimpse of a more complex view of Title IX. For example, Julie Foudy, who served as the primary (if not only) critical voice, provided a rationale for the mixed perceptions people have of the law on espnW's *The Word*. She stated that 80% of schools with Division I football programs do not make a profit, but other sports such as men's minor teams are cut to provide funding to football. In responding to what she believes needs to be done, Foudy identified a significant issue: scholarship funding. She stated that women have about $150 million less in scholarship funding than men. Foudy further responded to a question regarding misconceptions about the law particularly among young women:

> It's actually shocking. I ask girls every summer we do camps, "How many of you guys know what Title IX is," and now these are high school and junior high girls who have largely benefited from what I think is one of the most profound civil rights laws we've had in the country, and literally 5–10% raise their hand. I've even had one girl say, "Isn't that a golf company?" And if they do know what it is, the sad thing about it is they have a negative perception about it and so there are a lot of misconceptions, which saddens me because it has been a wonderful law. (*Kristine Lilly*, 2012)

On the same segment, Kristine Lilly, a former professional soccer player and Foudy's teammate, also responded to misperceptions and stated that people need to be reeducated to help both male and female sports. She stated that in the future she does not want to have conversations such as these, and she hopes the law will be so ingrained people will not have to consider one's sex in sport.

*ESPN The Magazine* published two articles that offered a realistic view of the law. An article titled "Thanks but No Thanks" discussed how since 1972, the percentage of female coaches for women's teams have dropped (from 90% to 42.9% in 2012) and how female coaches rarely get second chances. A second article, "Yale's Pioneers," discussed the 1976 Yale women's crew team that protested the unfair treatment it received. The women had no access to showers after their cold, early morning practices while the men did. In protest, they went to the director of women's athletics and physical education. They stripped naked in her office with the words "Title IX" or "IX" written on their bodies and read a statement describing the unfair things they were subjected to and how they were treated inhumanely. The article effectively presented a more complex version of the events. Rather than reciting how the group succeeded in voicing its protest, the article illustrated how some women refused to participate, felt guilty, or were looked down upon by family members.

Finally, some segments included brief mentions of race and class within the celebration. For example, Foudy's (2012) *SportsCenter* segment provided critical feedback to the host's question: "Where do you see that women's sports needs improvement right now? Where else can it grow?" Foudy responded:

> The big area that we don't talk about is… one in three girls are playing today but most of those strides have been made in white, affluent neighborhoods. So when you look at lower income communities, you're just not seeing the girls, or the boys for that matter, playing

in those communities. So I think when you look at that we need to get into underserved communities at a greater rate and introduce them to sports and physical activity because we can see the benefits.

She also discussed how the law has received a bad reputation in connection with the drop of men's sports, and that its purpose of equality and the true value of the law needs to be emphasized. Finally, on the espnW microsite the article "Too High a Price to Pay" (Farrey, 2012) details how Title IX does not reach low-income communities and how this needs to be a priority for the future of the law.

## DISCUSSION

Although ESPN's coverage of the 40th anniversary of Title IX was unprecedented, the celebration ultimately failed to accurately frame the law. Analysis of the celebration reveals that it might not accomplish the positive celebration it meant to achieve. The celebration overwhelmingly ignores a critical discussion of the law, and when discussion does occur, the law is presented primarily by describing what it has done for women and girls as a teleological consequence. Also the equality and opportunities discussed in the themes are not necessarily true. Approximately 80% of schools are in noncompliance, men receive millions of dollars more in scholarship offerings, and no school has ever had its funding revoked for noncompliance. Furthermore, Rowe discussed how TV is filled with women's sports and how Title IX provides the new normal, but research shows that women's televised sport coverage currently receives the lowest amount of coverage ever (Cooky, Messner, & Hextrum, 2013).

ESPN relies on language and frames to present the law overwhelmingly as established, non-controversial, and fully implemented—a mythologized understanding of the law. Although the celebration had opportunities to effectively advance the conversation of where the law is and how educational institutions fall short of its full implementation, they did this rarely in the campaign. The campaign, through the themes of equality, opportunity, and pressure for future generations, suggests that equality has been reached when the whole point of the law is to serve as an ongoing campaign for equality. Furthermore, women athletes are viewed as a consequence of the law—that they are not necessarily successful because they are outstanding athletes, but they are only successful because the law provided them the tools and means to do so. In other words, women have made it and there is little else to do.

ESPN's 40th celebration of Title IX has some strong elements to it as it provides a huge public platform for the American audience to hear about the law, understand its impact, and see how it changed people's lives. Foudy's comments and the handful of critical articles discussing the law and socioeconomics offer some hope for a more accurate view of the law. Ultimately, however, these positive elements are overshadowed by the overwhelming lack of critical Title IX analysis. Looking forward, it is vital for Title IX educators and sports media to provide accurate information about the law so audiences can better understand how far the law has come and how far it has to go.

# espnW

## Catering to a New Audience

SARAH WOLTER

espnW, whose motto is "One letter says a lot," is ESPN, Inc.'s first business unit specifically targeted to female fans and female athletes (Glass, 2013). Founded in 2010, the mission of espnW is to "serve women as fans and athletes. espnW.com provides an engaging environment that offers total access to female athletes and the sports they play, takes fans inside the biggest events, and shares a unique point of view on the sports stories that matter most to women" (espnW, n.d., para 1). espnW content appears on television, in films, during events such as the Women's World Cup, and on digital and social platforms (espnW, n.d.). The business unit has also hosted a "espnW: Women + Sport Summit" for the past four years where attendees "focus on driving change and opportunity for women in sports... an overarching goal of developing actionable outcomes each year, thought-provoking and differentiated content, and the integration of invigorating sports activities in a beautiful setting" (espnW Women + Sports Summit, n.d., para 2).

The espnW.com website offers readers three sections of content: "News & Commentary," "Athlete's Life," and "W in Action." Seven contributors (six women and one man) provide content for the site and a 24-member advisory panel of 18 women and 6 men from the ranks of professional athletes to doctors, academics, and coaches provide guidance on content for the site (espnW, n.d.). espnW secures 2.5 million users per month on espnW.com and has increased female viewership of ESPN.com to 10 million unique users per month (ESPN, 2013). Users spend an average of 9.73 minutes on espnW.com, which is an increase of 73% from

2011 (ESPN, 2013). espnW has a combined 150,000 Facebook fans and Twitter followers (ESPN, 2013).

espnW vice president Laura Gentile said the website was created as a dedicated platform for women after two years of research on girls, women, the ESPN brand, the female marketplace, and information from "athletes, coaches, moms, industry insiders, [and] journalists" (Gentile, 2010, para 11). Gentile said the research showed that "women see us [ESPN] as an admirable brand that has authority. But they see us as their father's brand, or husband's brand, or boyfriend's brand. They recognize it's not theirs" (Gentile, in Hiestand, 2010, para 3). Gentile used her opening remarks at the 2010 espnW Women + Sports Summit to claim, "There is no one sports media outlet for us 'W's' that speaks to our many roles as athletes, fans, organizers, dreamers, doers, leaders, matriarchs. There is no one global commons" (Gentile, 2010, para 7). Thus, espnW is meant to be additive to ESPN, serving needs of female consumers outside of the needs that are met through ESPN (Dosh, 2010).

This analysis shows that espnW challenges hegemonic constructions of sport because female athletes are portrayed often and as competent sportswomen on the site. Situating espnW in past media coverage of female athletes and specifically media coverage of athletes online sets up analysis of how athletes are covered on the site.

## REVIEW OF LITERATURE

### Media Coverage of Female Athletes

Two trends characterize representations of female athletes in media, regardless of level of play (high school, college, professional, Olympic) or medium (television, print, online): (1) girls and women make up over 40% of total athletes yet receive 2–4% of media coverage; and (2) girls and women are more likely to be portrayed off the court, out of uniform, and in sexualized positions compared to male athletes (Tucker Center for Girls & Women in Sport, 2013). For example, Messner and Cooky (2010) analyzed six weeks of early evening and late night sport news on three California-network affiliates and ESPN's *SportsCenter* and found that men's sports were covered 96.3% of the time, women's sports were covered 1.6% of the time, and gender-neutral topics were covered for 2.1% of the broadcasts. Additionally, ESPN's *SportsCenter* dedicated 1.4% of its airtime to women's sports (Messner & Cooky, 2010).

Second, media coverage of female athletes consistently emphasizes femininity and heterosexuality over athletic prowess (Daniels, 2009; Kaester & Xu, 2010; Kane, 2011; Martin & McDonald, 2012). This could be in response to what

Knight and Giuliano (2003) call an *image problem* for women's sports, which is the assumption that all female athletes are lesbian. Female athletes often portray femininity and heterosexuality in media accounts to counter this assumption (Knight & Giuliano, 2003). For example, in an analysis of female athletes in *Sports Illustrated* swimsuit issues from 1997 to 2009, Kim, Sagas, and Walker (2011) found that gender stereotypes still permeate representation and that sexuality rather than athleticism was emphasized in the portrayals. At the collegiate level, analysis of Division I media guides showed that male athletes were consistently portrayed as more competent athletes than female athletes because they are portrayed more often than female athletes in action and on the court (Buysse & Wolter, 2013).

Media coverage of the 2014 Winter Olympic Games may offer a change toward parity. Two weeks into the Games, a preliminary tally of coverage by sports studies scholar Andy Billings showed NBC's primetime coverage of men at 45.4% of coverage, women at 41.4%, and pairs sports at 13.2% (Laskow, 2014). This does not mean, however, that coverage is equal. Historically, women Olympians have been covered in more "feminine," less-respected sports such as ice dancing and have been described in demeaning ways, using descriptors like *girls* instead of *women* (Laskow, 2014).

Research on online depictions of female athletes is relatively new: "the production and consumption of media sport is in flux, constituting an unstable, unpredictable synthesis of the old and the new, the familiar and the strange, the predictable and the unanticipated" (Rowe & Hutchins, 2013, p. 1). Online digital platforms offer an opportunity for female athletes to be presented in more positive ways than traditional media because many online forums bypass traditional gatekeepers who control what appears in shows and in print (Hardin, Zhong, & Corrigan, 2012; Rowe, 2004; Sanderson & Kassing, 2011). Fans and athletes can post content themselves, which seems a lucrative way to present female athletes in a more positive light than in traditional media (Hardin & Whiteside, 2012; Hardin et al., 2012).

Most coverage of female athletes online, however, shows that representations mirror depictions of female athletes in traditional media (Hardin, 2011; Leonard, 2013) or continue to privilege a narrative that favors White, male, heterosexual athletes (Dart, 2009; Meân, 2011; Oates, 2009). For example, in an analysis of the discursive, representational, and textual utterances related to U.S. athletes Serena Williams, Brittney Griner, Allison Stokke, Alex Morgan, and Hope Solo, Leonard (2013) found "the relative 'openness' of the Internet has not diversified the representations of female athletes or the discourses that surround them" (p. 112). Another analysis of the 10 most popular sports blogs reveals that male athletes garner more photographic coverage than female athletes and that female athletes are much more likely to be sexualized (Clavio & Eagleman, 2011).

These problems with media representations of female athletes indicate the threat that women pose to traditional gender ideals of masculinity defined by physical strength, competence, and action (Media Education Foundation, 2005). Femininity defined as sex appeal and marriage/mothering threaten the historically masculine institution of sport, which favors male exclusivity, male entitlement, and homophobia (Media Education Foundation, 2005). Media portrayals of athletes are important because sport is one of the key places where norms of gender are defined, circulated, and maintained (Media Education Foundation, 2005) and so to determine how athletes on espnW, ESPN's first dedicated platform for female athletes, are covered, the following research questions were posed for this study:

RQ1: How are athletes presented in photographs on the main page of espnW according to sex, sport, level of sport, and team/individual sport?

RQ2: Do photographs on the main page of espnW feature athletes in uniform, on the playing surface, and in action of their respective sports?

RQ3: How are athletes presented in articles on the main page of espnW according to sex, sport, level of sport, and team/individual sport?

RQ4: In feature articles on the main page of espnW, how are athletes portrayed in terms of game/nongame reporting, reference to athleticism, and references to psychological/emotional strengths/weaknesses?

RQ5: In feature articles on the main page of espnW, are athletes' nonsporting lives, specifically references to physical appearance, family roles, or personal relationships, referenced?

## METHOD

The methodological approach for this study is quantitative content analysis, which is "the systematic assignment of communication content to categories according to rules, and the analysis of relationships involving those categories using statistical methods" (Riffe, Lacy, & Fico, 2014, pp. 3–4). Quantitative content analysis involves choosing representative samples of data, training coders according to a coding schema, and analyzing data to see if patterns or characteristics or relationships exist among variables (Riffe et al., 2014). The researcher used SnagIt, screen capturing software, to capture photographs and feature articles on the homepage of espnW between 10 p.m. and 11 p.m. each day from December 20, 2013, to March 15, 2014. This time period encompasses partial or entire seasons for the NFL, NBA, NCAA college basketball, LPGA Tour, PGA Tour, MLS, NHL, WTA, and significant events such as the NFL playoffs and Super Bowl, the College Football Bowl games, the WTA Australian Open, the X-Games, the Sochi Winter Olympics, the NBA All-Star game, and the NASCAR Subway Fresh Fit

500. It also represents a time period during the year that has not been analyzed in previous research.

The coding procedure for this study was derived from past studies on mediated representations of female athletes. Articles and photographs that appear on the main page of espnW.com were coded because they were set off by a box design and represent the feature photographs and the feature articles of the website. To code photographs, the principal researcher adapted variables from Buysse and Embers-Humbert's (2004) and Kane and Buysse's (2005) analyses of intercollegiate media guides. For each photograph, date, position of photograph (lead photograph or side photograph), sport, team versus individual sport, level of sport (recreational, high school, college, professional, Olympics), sex of athlete featured in photograph, focus of the photograph (athlete[s], head coach, combination of athlete[s] and head coach, N/A), uniform presence, pose presentation (in action or passive), court/field/pitch location, presence of femininity/masculinity, and presence of sexual suggestiveness were coded. Sample size for photographs was 368.

Article coding variables were adapted from Kian, Mondello, and Vincent's (2009) analysis of Internet coverage of NCAA March Madness. For each article, date, position of article (lead article or side article), article/video (whether or not the article includes a video), sport, team versus individual sport, level of sport, sex of athlete featured, focus of the article, game/non-game reporting, mention of physical appearance/sexuality/attire; mention of athletic prowess/strength; mention of athletic weakness/limitations; mention of positive skill level/accomplishments; mention of negative skill level/failures; mention of family role/personal relationships; mention of psychological strengths/emotional strengths; and mention of psychological weakness/emotional weakness were coded. Sample size for articles was 362.

To ensure reliability, two coders were trained and coded every photograph and article. The process started with the principal researcher holding an extensive training session with both coders. Both coders then coded 20% of the sample, and then the principal researcher assessed reliability using Cohen's Kappa. Intercoder reliability for the first 20% of photographs was 0.657 to 1.000 and for the first 20% of articles was 0.596 to 1.000. Coders then met with the principal researcher to clarify definitions of variables and to go through each of the discrepancies until consensus was reached. Coders then coded the remaining 80% of the data and intercoder reliability for the last 80% of photographs was 0.726 to 0.990 and articles was 0.710 to 1.00. The principal researcher then went through any remaining discrepancies with the coders until consensus was reached.

Frequency statistics were generated for both photographs and articles using SPSS 17.0. Cross-tabulation, the "process of creating a contingency table from the multivariate frequency distribution of statistical variables" (Black, 1999, p. 645), was used to analyze combinations of two variables, and chi-square test for two independent samples was used to determine statistical significance of at least .05.

Statistics were calculated using the categories that relate to research questions, and variables that do not relate were left out (e.g., the categories "both female and male athletes" and "photograph is not of an athlete" for "sex of athlete").

## Theoretical Framework

Hegemonic masculinity, a pattern of social practice that is defined as "the configuration of gender practice which embodies the currently accepted answer to the problem of the legitimacy of patriarchy, which guarantees (or is taken to guarantee) the dominant position of men and the subordination of women" (Connell, 2005, p. 77), served as the theoretical framework for this study. Hegemonic masculinity has been applied to numerous sporting contexts to illustrate the dominance of masculinity in sport (e.g., Hundley's [2004] symbolic decoding of language used on golf scorecards reveals hegemonic masculinity upholds everyday practices of golf). The premise of this scholarship is that sport has historically been considered a masculine endeavor due to characteristics needed for successful participation, such as aggressiveness, competitiveness, superiority, mental and physical toughness, initiative, strength, power, and confidence (Duncan, 2006; Mawson, 2006). The idealized sporting body, then, is male, muscular, and aggressive, and comprises the standard against which all sporting bodies are measured. Men are *naturally* built for sport, which makes women *not naturally* built for sport (Hardin & Whiteside, 2010; Media Education Foundation, 2005).

## RESULTS

Results are presented by analysis of photographs and then by analysis of articles. For each section, frequency statistics, cross-tabulations, and chi-square analyses were calculated to determine in what ways female and male athletes are presented on espnW.

### Presentation of Athletes in Photographs on espnW

The first research question for this study asks how athletes are presented in photographs on the main page of espnW according to sex, sport, level of sport, and team versus individual sports. Of photographs that included athletes from December 20, 2013, to March 15, 2014, female athletes were the focus of 87.5% (N = 274/313) of photographs and male athletes were the focus of 12.5% (N = 39/313) of photographs (the remaining 55 photographs either featured male and female athletes together, did not feature athletes, or coders were unsure whether the athletes were male or female). The top five sports portrayed in photographs during that time were basketball at 26.1% (N = 96/368), football at 8.2% (N = 30/368), tennis at 7.6% (N = 28/368), soccer at 5.7% (N = 21/368), and figure skating at 5.2% (N = 19/368). Forty-two other sports made up the remaining 47.2% of photographs.

Results for level of sport reveal that espnW portrayed Olympic sports the most at 31.5% (N = 116/368) and professional sports second at 31.0% (N = 114/368). College sports were featured 23.9% (N = 88/368) of the time, recreational sports were shown 3.8% (N = 14/368) of the time, and high school sports came in at 2.4% (N = 9/368) of the total. Paralympic sports were shown 0.3% (N = 1/368) of the time. Coders were unsure of level of sport for the remaining 7.1% of photographs. Table 9.1 shows distribution of sex of athlete and level of sport from photographs that depict athletes; categories "both male and female athletes" and "unsure" make up 53 of the total photographs and are omitted.

Table 9.1. Sex of athlete by level of sport in photographs on espnW.

| Level of sport | Percentage of photographs by level of sport that depict female athletes | Percentage of photographs by level of sport that depict male athletes |
|---|---|---|
| Recreational | 81.8 (N = 9/11) | 18.2 (N = 2/11) |
| High school | 100.0 (N = 9/9) | 0.0 (N = 0/9) |
| College | 88.4 (N = 76/86) | 11.6 (N = 10/86) |
| Professional* | 76.0 (N = 73/96) | 24.0 (N = 23/96) |
| Olympics* | 97.2 (N = 103/106) | 2.8 (N = 3/106) |
| Paralympics | 100.0 (N = 1/1) | 0.0 (N = 0/1) |

*Note.* $^*p < .05.$ $^{**}p < .01.$ $^{***}p < .001.$

Pearson chi-square test for sex of athlete and level of sport as a whole shows significant differences $\chi^2$ (5) = 22.703, $p$ = .000 between male and female athletes excluding ambiguous sex categories and ambiguous level of sport categories. Significance should be interpreted with the caveat that cell counts for this chi-square analysis are small. After deploying chi-square tests for sex and each individual level of sport variable, significance shows up specifically in the professional and Olympic categories, where $p < .001$ for each.

Coders also coded whether the sport featured in the photograph was a team sport, an individual sport, or multiple sports. If the photograph highlighted individual events in a team sport (e.g., gymnastics or track), co-researchers marked the sport as individual if the article associated with the photograph talks about individual events rather than the team as a whole. Team sports amassed 54.7% (N = 162/296) of the total and individual sports amassed 45.3% (N = 134/296) of the total. The remaining 72 photographs for this variable were either "both individual and team sports" or coders were unsure if the sport was team or individual;

these 72 are not included in chi-square or crosstab calculations. Of the photographs that portray athletes, female athletes appear in 78.4% (N = 127/162) of team sport photographs and male athletes appear in 21.6% (N = 35/162) of team sport photographs. Female athletes appear in 97.8% (N = 131/134) of individual sport photographs and male athletes appear in 2.2% (N = 3/134) of individual sport photographs. Pearson chi-square test of sex and team/individual sport shows significant differences, $\chi^2$ (1) = 22.88, $p$ < .001, excluding ambiguous sex categories and ambiguous team versus individual sport categories.

## Uniform, Court, and Pose Presentation in Photographs on espnW

The second research question for this study addresses to what extent espnW portrays athletes in uniform, on the playing surface of their respective sports, and in action for photographs. For the uniform variable, co-researchers coded the athlete as "in uniform" if the athlete was wearing a game uniform, including warm-ups, in the photograph. Athletes were in uniform for 83.0% (N = 254/306) of the photographs (the remaining 62 photographs were either not of athletes or the athletes were not in uniform; these 62 are not included in chi-square or crosstab calculations). Female athletes comprised 90.9% (N = 231/254) of the sample and male athletes comprised 9.1% (N = 23/254) of the sample. Pearson chi-square test of sex and uniform presence shows significant differences, $\chi^2$ (1) = 11.338, $p$ = .000, excluding ambiguous sex categories and ambiguous uniform presence categories.

Second, coders identified whether or not athlete(s) were presented on the court/field/pitch where the game she or he plays is played. Results show athletes on the court/field/pitch 74.4% (N = 227/305) of the time (the remaining 63 photographs were either not of athletes, the athletes were shown off the court/field/pitch, or coders were unsure of the location of the photograph; these 63 are not included in chi-square or crosstab calculations), 89.0% (N = 202/227) of which were female athletes and 11.0% (N = 25/227) of which were male athletes. Pearson chi-square test of sex and court location does not show significant differences, $\chi^2$ (1) = 0.671, $p$ = .413, excluding ambiguous sex categories and ambiguous court location categories.

Third, coders identified whether the athlete in the photograph was in an active pose, which was defined as exhibiting a skill that the athlete might exhibit during her or his sport game or practice (e.g., shooting, passing, running). Athletes were active in 47.9% (N = 146/305) of the photographs (the remaining 63 photographs were either not of athletes, athletes were passive, or coders were unsure of pose; these 63 are not included in chi-square or crosstab calculations). Of the photographs that included athletes, female athletes comprise 90.4% (N = 132/146) of the active photographs and male athletes comprise 9.6% (N = 14/146) of the active photographs. Pearson chi-square test of sex and pose does not show significant differences, $\chi^2$ (1) = 1.271, $p$ = .260, excluding ambiguous sex categories and ambiguous pose presentation categories.

## Presentation of Athletes in Articles on espnW

The third research question for this study asks how athletes are presented in articles on espnW according to sex, sport, level of sport, and team versus individual sport. Female athletes are the focus of 89.9% (N = 266/296) of articles and male athletes are the focus of 10.1% (N = 30/296) of articles (the remaining 66 articles are either not of athletes, articles that feature both individual and team sports, or articles where coders were unsure if the sport was team or individual; these 66 are not included in chi-square or crosstab calculations). The top five sports portrayed in photographs are basketball at 25.4% (N = 92/362), tennis at 8.3% (N = 30/362), football at 7.7% (N = 28/362), soccer at 5.5% (N = 20/362), and a tie between ice hockey and figure skating at 4.7% (N = 17/362). Thirty-seven sports make up the remaining 43.7% of sports represented in articles.

Level of sport in articles was coded with the same variables as level of sport in photographs. Results show that in articles, espnW portrayed Olympic sports the most at 35.4% (N = 128/362) and professional sports second at 31.5% (N = 114/362). College sports were featured 22.9% (N = 83/362) of the time, high school sports were shown 3.0% (N = 11/362) of the time, and recreational sports came in at 2.5% (N = 9/362) of the total. Paralympic sports were shown 0.28% (N = 1/362) of the time. The remaining 4.7% of articles either did not portray a sport or coders were unsure what level of sport was portrayed. Table 9.2 shows distribution of sex of athlete and level of sport for articles about athletes.

Table 9.2. Sex of athlete by level of sport in articles on espnW.

| Level of sport | Percentage of articles by level of sport that depict female athletes | Percentage of articles by level of sport that depict male athletes |
| --- | --- | --- |
| Recreational | 100.0 (N = 7/7) | 0.0 (N = 0/7) |
| High school | 100.0 (N = 10/10) | 0.0 (N = 0/10) |
| College | 93.8 (N = 76/81) | 6.2(N = 5/81) |
| Professional* | 76.8 (N = 73/95) | 23.2 (N = 22/95) |
| Olympics* | 97.0 (N = 98/101) | 3.0 (N = 3/101) |
| Paralympics | 100.0 (N = 1/1) | 0.0 (N = 0/1) |

*Note.* $^*p$ < .05. $^{**}p$ < .01. $^{***}p$ < .001.

Pearson chi-square test shows significant differences $\chi^2$ (5) = 26.726, $p$ < .001 overall between male and female athletes and level of sport excluding ambiguous sex categories and ambiguous level of sport categories. Specifically, chi-square tests for male/female and each level of sport shows significant differences for professional sports $p$ < .001 and Olympic sports $p$ = .006.

Coders also coded whether the sport featured in the photograph was a team sport, an individual sport, or multiple sports according to the same criteria as photographs. Team sports made up 54.4% (N = 174/320) of the total articles and individual sports made up 45.6% (N = 146/320) of the total articles (the remaining 42 articles either featured both male and female athletes, were not about athletes, or coders were unsure; these 42 are not included in chi-square or crosstab calculations). Of the articles about athletes, female athletes appear in 83.2% (N = 129/155) of team sport articles and male athletes appear in 16.8% (N = 26/155) of team sport articles. Again, of the articles that feature athletes, female athletes appear in 97.7% (N = 128/131) of individual sport articles and male athletes appear in 2.3% (N = 3/131) of individual sport articles. Pearson chi-square test of sex and team/individual sport shows significant differences, $\chi^2$ (1) = 16.313, $p$ = .000, between male and female athletes for individual versus team sports excluding ambiguous sex categories and ambiguous team versus individual sport categories.

## Seriousness of Athletes in Articles

Results relating to the third research question for this study are presented in terms of the following variables: whether articles on espnW cover game reporting or non-game reporting and/or reference athleticism of athletes in terms of athletic prowess/strength, athletic weakness/limitations, positive skill level/ accomplishments, negative skill level/failures; and/or reference psychological/ emotional strengths/weakness of athletes.

### Game/Non-Game Reporting

The variable game/non-game reporting has to do with whether the focus of the article was on events that occurred during a game or non-game topics such as coaching contracts or suspensions. Game reporting occurred in 59.4% (N = 215/362) of articles. Of these articles that were about athletes, 92.6% (N = 189/204) are about female athletes and 7.4% (N = 15/204) are about male athletes. Pearson chi-square test of sex and game/non-game reporting shows significant differences, $\chi^2$ (1) = 4.88, $p$ = .027, between male and female athletes excluding ambiguous sex categories and ambiguous game/non-game reporting categories.

## Athletic Prowess/Strength

Athletic prowess/strength measures whether articles reference the athletic prowess/ strength of an athlete in a general sense, not according to specific accolades or statistics. An example of athletic prowess/strength is, "nobody hits as hard as her. Nobody. Not even her sister" (article 289). Athletic prowess/strength is mentioned in 58.0% (N = 210/362) of articles. Of these articles that are about athletes, 94.0% (N = 189/201) are about female athletes and 6.0% (N = 12/201) are about male athletes. Pearson chi-square test of sex and athletic prowess/strength shows significant differences, $\chi^2$ (1) = 10.10, $p$ = .001, between male and female athletes excluding ambiguous sex categories and ambiguous athletic prowess/strength categories.

## Athletic Weakness/Limitations

Athletic weakness/limitations measures whether articles reference general athletic weakness or limitations of athletes not according to specific accolades or statistics. An example of athletic weakness/limitations is, "Yesterday the Prince showed that he did not have the strength to play at the NFL level" (article 304). Athletic weakness/limitations are mentioned in 27.9% (N = 101/362) of articles. Of these articles, 91.4% (N = 85/93) are about female athletes and 8.6% (N = 8/93) are about male athletes (the remaining eight articles are either about both female and male athletes, not about athletes, or coders were unsure; these eight are not included in chi-square or crosstab calculations). Pearson chi-square test does not show significant differences, $\chi^2$ (1) = 0.052, $p$ = .819, between male and female athletes excluding ambiguous sex categories and ambiguous athletic weakness/ limitations categories.

## Positive Skill Level/Accomplishments

Positive skill level/accomplishments measures whether articles mention specific statistics or accolades of an athlete rather than general athletic prowess. An example of positive skill level/accomplishments is, "Yani Tseng, 22, came from two shots back to win the RICOH Women's British Open and make news as the youngest player—male or female—to capture five major titles" (article 218). Positive skill level/accomplishments are mentioned in 56.9% (N = 206/362) of articles. Of these articles, 94.9% (N = 186/196) are about female athletes and 5.1% (N = 10/196) are about male athletes (the remaining 10 articles either were about both male and female athletes, not about athletes, or coders were unsure; these 10 are not included in chi-square or crosstab calculations). Pearson chi-square test shows significant differences, $\chi^2$ (1) = 14.37, $p$ < .001, between male and female athletes excluding ambiguous sex categories and ambiguous positive skill level/ accomplishments categories.

## Negative Skill Level/Failures

Negative skill level/failures measures whether articles reference specific statistics related to negative sport performance rather than more general athletic performance. An example of negative skill level/failures is "Pavlyuchenkova had reached the quarterfinals of the French, to lose to Sciavone after leading, 6–1, 4–1" (article 301). Negative skill level/failures are mentioned in 27.3% (N = 99/362) of articles. Of these articles, 92.3% (N = 84/91) are about female athletes and 7.7% (N = 7/91) are about male athletes (the remaining eight articles are either about both female and male athletes, not about athletes, or coders were unsure; these eight are not included in chi-square or crosstab calculations). Pearson chi-square test does not show significant differences, $\chi^2$ (1) = 0.336, $p$ = .564, between male and female athletes excluding ambiguous sex categories and ambiguous negative skill level/failure categories.

## Psychological Strengths/Emotional Strengths

Psychological strengths/emotional strengths measure whether articles reference information about psychological or emotional strengths of an athlete. An example of psychological strengths/emotional strengths is, "Even when your quivering legs tell you otherwise, chances are you've got one more rep in you. Imagine that. Literally…. 'When you visualize an action, your brain develops a model of how it will go in the real world. This allows you to recruit the muscles you need and perform more effectively and efficiently when you actually do it… it's a testimony to the power of the mind-muscle connection'" (article 14). Psychological strengths/emotional strengths are mentioned in 45.9% (N = 166/362) of articles. Of these articles, 93.6% (N = 147/157) are about female athletes and 6.4% (N = 10/157) are about male athletes (the remaining nine articles are either about both female and male athletes, not about athletes, or coders were unsure; these nine are not included in chi-square or crosstab calculations). Pearson chi-square test does not show significant differences, $\chi^2$ (1) = 3.76, $p$ = .052, between male and female athletes excluding ambiguous sex categories and ambiguous psychological strengths/emotional strengths categories.

## Psychological Weaknesses/Emotional Weaknesses

Psychological weaknesses/emotional weaknesses measure whether articles reference any information about psychological or emotional weaknesses of the athlete(s) in the article. An example of psychological weaknesses/emotional weaknesses is, "If the thought of freestyling through open, unlined, even murky water with 800 other athletes makes you queasy, rest assured: You're not alone" (article 19). Psychological weaknesses/emotional weaknesses are mentioned in 17.4% (N = 63/362) of articles. Of these articles, 96.7% (N = 58/60) are about female athletes and 3.3% (N = 2/60) are about male athletes (the remaining three articles are either about both female and male athletes, not about athletes, or coders were unsure; these three are not included in chi-square or crosstab calculations). Pearson chi-square test does not show significant differences, $\chi^2$ (1) = 2.683, $p$ = .101, between male and female athletes excluding ambiguous sex categories and ambiguous psychological weaknesses/emotional weaknesses categories.

## Non-Sporting Lives in Articles

Results relating to the fourth research question are presented according to references to physical appearance, family roles, and/or personal relationships.

### Physical Appearance/Sexuality/Attire

The physical appearance/sexuality/attire variable measures whether any of these elements are referenced in articles on espnW. An example of a reference to physical appearance is, "Ordinarily, Victoria Azarenka's blue eyes sparkle. Sitting on her changeover chair in Arthur Ashe Stadium, they were dead as she stared vacantly into the yawning void" (article 296). An example of reference to sexuality is, "'COME ON!!!!!!' McIlroy tweeted as his girlfriend, Wozniacki, labored to avoid the upset. Six exclamation points—so you know the relationship between the two must be getting serious" (article 306). An example of reference to attire is "from Tracy Austin's pinafores to Serena Williams' catsuit, they can help define who the player is. In this era of big money, ratings and stadiums, clothes can establish a connection with the crowd" (article 311). Physical appearance/sexuality/attire is mentioned in 15.5% (N = 56/362) of articles. Of these articles, 89.3% (N = 50/56) are about female athletes and 10.7% (N = 6/56) are about male athletes. Pearson chi-square test does not show significant differences, $\chi^2$ (1) = 0.002, $p$ = .968, between male and female athletes excluding ambiguous sex categories and ambiguous physical appearance/sexuality/attire categories.

### Family Role/Personal Relationships

The family role/personal relationships variable measures whether the article references any family members or personal relationships of the athlete(s) or if the athlete(s)' role as a family member or as a part of a personal relationship is referenced. An example of family role/personal relationships is, "For many of these boys-turned-men overnight, their moms may become increasingly important sources of guidance and stability" (article 13). Family role/personal relationships are mentioned in 31.2% (N = 113/362) of articles. Of these articles, 86.1% (N = 87/101) are about female athletes and 13.9% (N = 14/101) are about male athletes (the remaining three articles are either about both female and male athletes, not about athletes, or coders were unsure; these three are not included in chi-square or crosstab calculations). Pearson chi-square test does not show significant differences, $\chi^2$ (1) = 2.416, $p$ = .120, between male and female athletes excluding ambiguous sex categories and ambiguous family role/personal relationship categories.

## DISCUSSION

espnW vice president Laura Gentile advanced a bold challenge in an interview immediately after espnW's launch: "We thought long and hard about these five letters, espnW, and what they need to represent and what they need to stand for.... They need to be action oriented and forward looking, consistently progressive, innovative and also of the highest quality" (Glass, 2013, para 9). Based on this analysis, her charge is being fulfilled.

Hegemonic masculinity frames the institution of sport; however, the institution embodies multiple, complex meanings that are inconsistent with one another when women challenge existing ideology in myriad ways (Coakley, 2009). espnW is a challenge to the hegemonic masculinity that defines the institution of sport. Female athletes are featured more frequently in espnW photographs and in articles than in traditional mediums, at 87.5% and 89.9%, respectively. Additionally, female athletes appear as competent sportswomen, appearing in uniform 90.9% of the time, on the court 89.0% of the time, and in action 90.4% of the time in photographs. Statistical significance appears for level of sport and team/individual sport for both photographs and articles, uniform for photographs specifically, and game/non-game, athletic prowess/strength, and positive skill level/accomplishments for articles specifically. The only variable that marred presentation of female athletes as competent sportswomen was team versus individual sport. Because team sports are typically more revered in terms of popularity and financial support, female athletes could be losing important visibility by being sidelined and covered more in individual sports.

Comparing the results of this study to the results in Wolter's (2013) analysis of espnW from April–October 2011 shows that the site has continued a trend of elevating female athletes and that percentages for photograph variables changed less than 10% in all categories except for level of sport, where portrayals of college athletes increased from 9.4% to 23.9% and portrayals of professional athletes decreased from 73.5% to 31.0% in favor of portraying more Olympic athletes at 31.5% versus 4.6% in 2011. Portrayals of female athletes in photographs also increased from 68.0% in 2011 (Wolter, 2013) to 87.5% in 2013.

Change from 2011 to 2013 also appeared in article representation, with female athletes increasing from 68.2% to 89.9% and representations of college athletes increasing from 8.3% to 22.9% while representation of professional athletes went from 74.7% to 31.5% and Olympic athletes went from 4.3% to 35.4%. Additionally, game reporting increased from 24.4% to 59.4% of articles, but athletic prowess/strength and positive skill level/accomplishments went down, from 79.4% to 58.0% and 75.2% to 56.9%, respectively. To counter this, psychological strengths/emotional strengths increased by 20% and references to physical appearance/sexuality/attire decreased by 14.8%. Minimal differences reflect espnW's on one line initial commitment to highlight female athletes and to be an additional outlet for information not found on ESPN's main site. The bigger differences in numbers are mostly due to the timing of the data collection, which occurred during the 2014 Sochi Olympics.

Although positive representations of female athletes are promising, statistics on visits to espnW temper results. ESPN Customer Marketing and Sales (2013) reports 2.5 million users go to espnW.com every month compared to espn.com's 40.4 million unique visitors per month. Female athletes are represented in positive ways according to the variables from this study, but few individuals are experiencing content on the site.

## CONCLUSION

Limitations of this study include the time period from which the sample was drawn and the variables chosen to measure portrayal of athletes. The most popular sports and the levels of sport featured the most were likely because of the athletic seasons from which the sample was drawn. December to March represents the midst of the NBA and college basketball seasons, including NCAA March Madness, and the 2014 Sochi Olympics were in February. The variables chosen to measure portrayal of athletes shaped the way results turned out because investigators focused on some aspects of photographs and articles at the expense of others. Quantitative research also does not present a complete picture of what is going on in articles on espnW, as content is not deeply analyzed.

Undertaking an analysis of espnW is important for many reasons, but two stand out. First, espnW is a website dedicated to women as fans and as athletes produced by one of the largest sports media organizations in the world. Importantly, it was ESPN's *first* attempt at a site dedicated to female athletes and fans. ESPN has a history of denying female athletes television coverage (Messner & Cooky, 2010) and of sexual harassment of female employees, especially in the 1990s (Freeman, 2000), so analyzing espnW to see that the site transcends this history to offer more positive portrayals of female athletes than they have in the past is important to gauge its future.

Second, examining the ways female athletes are portrayed is important because of the potential for images to influence generations of girls. Growing up in a post–Title IX era undoubtedly positively shapes the sporting opportunities for young women, but images of female athletic bodies are also shown to be more powerful than other discourses surrounding sport related to success, health, and personal responsibility (Heywood, 2007). Portrayals of strong female athletes have the potential to empower girls to view their bodies for what they can *do* rather than how they *look* as billboards for beauty (Daniels, 2009). More broadly, sport is a social construction that affects gender roles in our entire culture, not just on the field (Coakley, 2009; Riebock & Bae, 2013). Based on the variables in this analysis, espnW is a step in the right direction.

# CHAPTER TEN

# The ESPN Effect

## Representation of Women in
## *30 for 30* Films

KATHERINE L. LAVELLE

"ESPN is truly a widespread media giant, offering content in virtually every conceivable domain" (Billings, 2011, p. 5). A number of scholars have examined ESPN's global reach and found the company upholds normative views about female athletes (Adams & Tuggle, 2004; Cooky, Messner, & Hextrum, 2013; Turner, 2013). Meân (2011) has described ESPN as having "a powerful, authoritative position given that identities are prominently linked to... the consumption of sport" (p. 163). Despite achievements by female athletes, ESPN continually underrepresents them in its coverage; a longitudinal study found that "women's sports received only 1.3% of the coverage on ESPN's SportsCenter" (Cooky, Messner, & Hextrum, 2013, p. 19). When they are covered, female athletes have been featured through the lens of emphasized femininity, which "accommodate(s) the interests and desires of men, and often characterized by a display of sociability, receptiveness, and passivity" (Kristiansen & Broch, 2013, p. 98). It is critical to examine ESPN's role perpetuating these stereotypes because "mediasport is not an innocent player in society—the ideologies, attitudes, and values that are present in mediasport production powerfully shape our understandings of ourselves and of others" (Bruce, 2012, p. 133). Sports coverage is an intimate part of our everyday lives and evaluating how underrepresented groups are presented is critical.

This chapter examines how emphasized femininity is used in ESPN's *30 for 30* series. This acclaimed film series has featured only three female athletes in its first set of films (Hale, 2013), so these films provide a text to analyze how *30 for 30* films represent women. Working from Vogan's (2012) contention that *30 for 30* films function as "useful objects through which to investigate the cultural value attached to sports television" (p. 139), this chapter will evaluate two films from the first volume of *30 for 30* films (*Marion Jones: Press Pause* and *Unmatched*) to examine how female athletes are represented. After reviewing the scholarly literature and analyzing these two films, this chapter will draw some implications for the role of *30 for 30* films.

## LITERATURE REVIEW

Sport media is a growing form of media content (Meân, 2011) that upholds a "masculine-dominant culture" in the United States (Bernstein & Kian, 2013, p. 324). Sports media, which often includes television commentary and news coverage, simultaneously upholds masculinity while trivializing femininity (Kane, LaVoi, & Fink, 2013; Meân & Halone, 2010; Poniatowski & Hardin, 2012). A number of factors are present in coverage of female athletes: (a) they are minimized as compared to male athletes (Poniatowski & Hardin, 2012), (b) they are ignored (Kane, LaVoi, & Fink, 2013), and most importantly, (c) women's sports are "filtered through a male gaze that struggles to reconcile discourses of sport and discourses of femininity" (Bruce, 2012, pp. 132–133). Despite the increasing numbers of female athletes, stereotypes have frequently been used to make meaning for the audience.

Sports media reinforces an ideology that privileges masculine values while giving little agency to female athletes (Hardin, 2011; Hardin & LaVoi, 2013; Rowe, 2011). When women have been represented, often the coverage reproduces stereotypical representations of women that transcend all media coverage (Cooky, Messner, & Hextrum, 2013). As part of their longitudinal analysis of *SportsCenter*'s coverage of female athletes, Cooky, Messner, and Hextrum (2013) have found that "a foundational assumption of those who create programming for men on programs like *SportsCenter* seem to be that the mostly male viewers want to think of women as sexual objects of desire, or perhaps as mothers, but not as powerful, competent, competitive athletes" (p. 21). Although these studies focus on news broadcasts, this research applies to ESPN programming as well. As Meân (2011) has framed it, ESPN viewers are part of an "interpretive community" where audience members read texts in a similar way "despite the availability of multiple readings" (p. 165). In other words, if *SportsCenter* is using stereotypical depictions of female athletes, it is possible that other ESPN programming uses a similar approach.

Given these conditions, understanding how *30 for 30* films uphold emphasized femininity is critical. Unlike the previous ESPN film series, *SportsCentury*, *30 for 30* films function not only as biographies but also as collections of fragments of a sports event. For example, the film *June 17, 1994*, uses archival news coverage to show the connections in sports on the day of the infamous O. J. Simpson Bronco chase (Morgan, 2010). Many fans remember this incident in isolation, but a number of other sports events took place that day, including the opening of the men's soccer World Cup in Chicago and an NBA Final game (Morgan, 2010).

Because the producers of *30 for 30* films want these films to operate as cultural texts, they can be evaluated in conjunction with larger cultural issues (McDonald, 2007). The narratives in these films can function as "intertexual projects" (Birrell & McDonald, 2012, p. 344), meaning that they explain how elements within a biography create a specific reading about the subject. The presences and absences within a narrative explain "what sort of cultural work the narrative accomplishes" (p. 345). Bruce (2012) has argued that narratives used by sports media emphasize artificial differences between men and women. Because the narratives are stories, they can seem more truthful than the news. Often the subject is an active participant and the story focuses on their life, so their participation can function as an endorsement of their story. *30 for 30* films are not only biographies. *30 for 30* films were developed to expand ESPN's artistic credentials and create interpretations of sports history using ESPN's archival footage (Vogan, 2012, 2013). Despite public comments to the contrary, the producers determine the artistic direction of *30 for 30* films, not the individual directors (Vogan, 2013). Consequently, these films can be examined together as a rhetorical/critical text.

This chapter conducts a close textual analysis of *Marion Jones: Press Pause* and *Unmatched. Marion Jones: Press Pause* (2010) is a documentary about the journey from track and field star, to prisoner, to her attempts at an athletic comeback. Marion Jones was one of the most decorated American athletes in a single Olympic Games—she won five track and field medals at the 2000 Sydney Olympics—but she had to return the medals after she tested positive for performance-enhancing drugs (Hall, Dhar, & Singleton, 2010). The 51-minute film includes interviews with Jones and her husband as well as reporters and narrator/director John Singleton. *Unmatched* (2010) chronicles Chris Evert and Martina Navratilova's relationship as competitors and friends. Chris Evert and Martina Navratilova are two of the most successful tennis players of all time, dominating the 1970s and 1980s professional circuit (Lax & Stern Winters, 2010). They act as interviewees and interviewers in this 51-minute documentary, set at an elegant beach house. To evaluate how ESPN *30 for 30* films represent femininity, these films are analyzed for how they uphold femininity, portray family relations, and present displays of emotions.

## *MARION JONES: PRESS PAUSE*

### Upholding Femininity

*Marion Jones: Press Pause* emphasizes Marion Jones's femininity through visual images. Unlike traditional documentaries, where the subject might be sitting in a staged room, Jones's interviews take place in her real life. In interviews in the park, and while sitting on the floor of her house with her children nearby, Jones is dressed in feminine clothing, wearing V-neck tops and noticeable makeup. John Singleton, while acting as the film's narrator, calls Jones "easy to love" because she is "smart, funny, and sexy" (Hall, Dhar, & Singleton, 2010, p. 2). There are archival images of Jones on the cover of fashion magazines and participating in modeling shoots. The opening credits of the film look like a made-for-TV movie; they are constructed of photographs that document Jones's rise as a promising athlete to her federal court appearance. The film opens with childhood photographs of Jones wearing ballerina costumes. These overt references use camera positioning to re-enforce femininity in the film (Duncan & Messner, 1998). Jones is presented as not only a track and field athlete but also a woman who can appropriately project her femininity.

Throughout the film, there are a number of male authority figures who play prominent roles in Jones's story. In the film's opening, Jones's legal problems are discussed by Rich Nichols, her attorney who was present at her interrogation by federal investigators. The editing of this sequence involves back and forth between Jones and Nichols, where the speed of the edits gets faster, creating tension. Nichols recalls advising Jones to be truthful. "We made it clear to Marion that you cannot lie to federal investigators. Period, end of story" (Hall, Dhar, & Singleton, 2010, p. 3). Nichols looks directly at the camera and appears to be on a balcony in an urban setting, while Jones is in a park, looking away from the camera. While Nichols speaks calmly, Jones appears increasingly agitated while recounting her interrogation. Jones recalls feeling intimidated by the investigator because of his size and approach to questioning. Edwin Moses, a track and field coach and gold medalist, argues that Jones was powerless against investigators. "The federal pros-ecutors have almost an unlimited budget, so they can prosecute, they will find out what they want to find out. Or ruin you in the process" (Hall, Dhar, & Singleton, 2010, p. 5). Finally, John Singleton acts as an authority figure in the beginning of the film, where he speaks as a narrator. He talks directly to the camera while walk-ing past bleachers in a park. Singleton tells the audience, "I want to remind you that Marion was a global superstar" (Hall, Dhar, & Singleton, 2010, p. 1). Here, he shapes the audience's interpretation of the magnitude of Marion Jones's fall. The presence of these men explaining Jones's downfall helps reinforce hegemonic masculinity because they are speaking for her (Smith & Bissell, 2012). By helping

Jones remember the context of her legal problems, it suggests to the audience that Jones does not have the capacity to remember what happened.

## Family Relations

Jones used her family as the reason that she lied to federal investigators. Jones claims that she lied because "I am not going to risk my family's future" (Hall, Dhar, & Singleton, 2010, p. 3). It is unclear in that statement if she is discussing her children or her family in general. In a frequently used archival video of her on the courthouse steps, Jones cries when she talks about letting down her family. On October 7, 2007, Jones admitted publicly that she had lied about using performance-enhancing drugs. This footage is frequently referenced in the film and serves as a turning point for Jones, which functions to cement the reality of her legal situation.

After getting out of prison, Jones describes her family as "priority" (Hall, Dhar, & Singleton, 2010, p. 10). In the post-conviction part of the film, there are a number of images of videos of her children. Her husband, Obadele Thompson, is featured throughout the film. Thompson and Jones co-narrate the struggle that they felt while she was in prison. Jones recalls her drive to federal prison when she wanted to hold her husband's hand. Thompson describes Jones's prison term as "a joint effort" and Jones identifies Thompson as the only person who supported her when she was in prison. Jones spent nearly 50 days in solitary confinement during her prison term, where she missed her sons' birthdays and was unable to talk to them on these days. While discussing her separation, there are images of her sons celebrating birthdays without her.

As presented in the film, the family life that Jones has with Thompson seems different from her previous family life. Jones was previously married to C. J. Hunter (Kreidler, 2007) and dated Tim Montgomery (Axon, 2013), both of whom have been cited for performance-enhancing drug use. They are not named or seen in the film. However, Melissa Johnson and Sylvia Hatchell (from Jones's alma mater, University of North Carolina) indirectly blame them for Jones's legal problems. Edwin Moses references her inner circle as "on the gravy train." But journalist Ron Rapaport characterized this theory as "the bad man theory" (Hall, Dhar, & Singleton, 2010, p. 5) and rejects it because "she was in control of her surroundings" and argues that there could have been a "private part that was out of control" (p. 5). However, he hypothesizes that she was in control. To support his point, he tells a story early in the film about how Jones dealt with the press as a high school athlete. Although her coach feared how she would handle experienced reporters, his fear didn't last long; as Rapaport describes it, "she would wrap them [the press] around her finger" (Hall, Dhar, & Singleton, 2010, p. 2). Rapaport has credibility in the film because he had covered Jones since high school. Moses, Hatchell, and Johnson are positioned separately from Jones's professional track career. This theme about her as controlled by the men in her life creates a double bind for Jones. If she was under the influence of these men, she is not an independent, strong woman. But if she is not, she is not ethical and her contention that her associates caused her downfall is not true.

Jones's journey to redemption is reflected through her children in the film, specifically her role as a mother. Jones is depicted mothering her three children, giving her infant a bath and playing with all of them. When her trial is discussed, there is a map showing the journey that her sons took from Texas to Barbados to be out of the country when the media attention was intense. Later in the film, she narrates her life in 2010, where she is running errands with her children in a minivan. The side of the screen shows a speedometer counting the number of miles that Jones travels in a typical day as she attempts to make her athletic comeback in the WNBA. Jones negotiates her practice schedule around her children's school schedule. These attempts to show Jones as a working mom suggest that her children limit her athletic success schedule, a condition not often present for male athletes.

The film even documents the birth of her daughter. This event is intimately presented; the film includes footage of her having contractions in a parking lot, in labor in the hospital, and holding her baby shortly after birth. Jones is visibly pregnant in the film and these scenes remind the audience that she is biologically different from male competitors. Jones reinforces her emphasized femininity when describing her children. She calls her daughter "the princess" and calls herself "the queen" of the house (Hall, Dhar, & Singleton, 2010, p. 10). Jones is excited that there are so many "kisses and hugs" (p. 10) with the introduction of the new baby. Jones's childbirth even becomes a lens to evaluate her return to professional sports. She discusses her baby weight and her changed body as an obstacle to her athletic training. A *SportsCenter* anchor suggested that Jones getting the call from the WNBA while she was pregnant was incredible, implying that pregnancy is an obstacle to athleticism. When Jones gets a WNBA contract, one of her former UNC teammates asked, "are you actually bionic, Marion?" (Hall, Dhar, & Singleton, 2010, p. 15), suggesting that most women would not be able to recover their athletic strength after childbirth. These types of comments and representations suggest that the film reinforces "specific gender norms" (Kristiansen & Broch, 2013) by emphasizing how motherhood limits athletic success.

## Display of Emotions

Duncan and Messner (1998) have argued that when female athletes are shown in tears, it conveys weakness to the audience. There are a number of times where

Jones's emotional moments are emphasized in the film. For instance, there is repeated reference to her confession on the courthouse steps in 2007. Jones cries throughout the press conference, having difficulty publicly admitting her guilt. In prison, she says she was too emotional to watch the Beijing Games in 2008, even though she can hear the results from her cell. While in prison, Jones is placed in solitary confinement because of an emotional outburst. She hits a cellmate with a cooler and makes her bleed. Jones's emotions prevent her from staying out of trouble while in prison.

Most important, Jones's description of and experience with federal investigators is shown to be driven by emotions. As Jones describes her emotional state while being questioned, she puts up her finger to her head and spins it around, at one point, suggesting that she is out of control. She is inarticulate when recalling the experience, suggesting that she doesn't quite remember it. In contrast, attorney Rich Nichols says, "She could have said, I wanted to take a break, I want to talk to my attorney. And, had she done that, had she done that, her life would be different" (Hall, Dhar, & Singleton, 2010, p. 4). His quote is immediately followed by Jones stating, "But I didn't do that. And it really wouldn't have taken more than five minutes. It could have taken less than two. But I kept on with the questioning, and really, it's that moment that really changed so much." So much of this recollection of the interrogation scene is based on editing. And by juxtaposing Jones's comments after Nichols's argument, it suggests to the audience that Jones's inability to control herself during questioning meant that she was unable to take control of her life. This editing is an example of Duncan and Messner's (1998) contention that direction and editing are critical to creating judgments about female athletes. At no point is Jones's legal case discussed, in terms of detailing the actual charges against her, so the viewers rely on the film presentation to understand Jones's situation. From watching the film, it is clear that Jones did not understand the magnitude of her charges.

In summary, throughout *Marion Jones: Press Pause*, Jones is presented as a woman with little control of her destiny. She is led into legal trouble by boyfriends, she makes rash decisions, and she is ultimately the happiest in the domestic sphere. In the last third of the film, through discussion by her husband and footage with her children, the film concludes that Jones is only complete as a person when she embraces her role as wife and mother. Even though she finds some success in the WNBA, her success is limited by her role as a mother. Jones drives from Austin, Texas, to San Antonio every day, working around the schedule of her children. Even though being a mother and a wife is compatible with her role as a successful athlete, the film spends considerable time framing her motherhood as determining her success as an athlete, not the other way around.

## *UNMATCHED*

## Upholding Femininity

The visual style and structure of *Unmatched* upholds normative views on femininity. Smith and Bissell (2012) have noted that "power balance" is upheld by presenting female athletes in a way that "highlights femininity" (p. 3). Much of *Unmatched* upholds femininity. Outside of brief archival pieces, Chris Evert and Martina Navratilova do all of the talking—they ask each other questions, they speak in monologue, they are the film. They are alone at the house and surrounded by a gentle beach. They drive a classic car on an empty wooded road. Evert tells Navratilova, "We always said that we would have a glass of wine and talk about everything that has happened and have a few laughs about it" (Lax & Stern Winters, 2010, p. 1). This focus on the leisure time that they have suggests that these former players have some degree of privilege because they have the time to chat.

In some ways, the film feels like a Nancy Meyers[1] production. It takes place in a beautiful beachfront home with expensive white furniture and a spacious, well-stocked kitchen. Their clothing suggests wealth and similarity. At one point, there is footage of Evert and Navratilova walking next to each other on the beach at dawn. From a distance, it looks like they are twins, wearing expensive jeans, white long-sleeved shirts, colorful scarves, and similar-length blonde hair. The song "Kind and Generous" by Natalie Merchant plays repeatedly in the background. This song has a particular cultural reference that suggests female empowerment and is associated with the female-centered Lilith Fair. This emphasis on wealth and privilege is an example of what Carty (2005) has discussed as "legitimizing the power and privilege of appropriate white heterosexuality" (p. 146). Even though Navratilova is a lesbian, the film emphasizes the similarity and symbiotic relationship between these two that creates a privileged form of femininity.

The film emphasizes the relationship between Evert and Navratilova. Director Lisa Lax frames the film as an examination of their relationship as "they are real best friends, and isn't that amazing?" (Lax & Stern Winters, 2010, p. 1). At the end of the film, Navratilova explains, "there is a closeness that Chris and I share that I'll never have with anyone else" (Lax & Stern Winters, 2010, p. 15) and speaks directly to the camera and says, "Chris, I am so happy that I was one half of a whole" (Lax & Stern Winters, 2010, p. 19). Evert talks about how they can call each other whenever they need to talk to each other. They hug and laugh together. They recall hugging each other at the net when Navratilova finally beat Evert at Wimbledon, "the nicest moment I had with anyone" (Lax & Stern Winters, 2010, p. 5). They share stories of prepping together before Grand Slam matches in the days before they had coaches. Toward the end of the film, they reminisce about a Federation Cup trip to Prague, which marked Navratilova's first trip back since defecting 10 years earlier. Both talk about the significance of them going to Prague together. Navratilova describes it as "to come back to Czechoslovakia without you was just unthinkable. You know, we were just so intertwined at that point" (Lax & Stern Winters, 2010, p. 14). The film includes so many anecdotes and examples of their friendship, while downplaying their rivalry.

While Navratilova and Evert discuss their closeness, they criticize the media for framing them as rivals. Evert was known as an all-American girl, an image reinforced in the film with a montage of magazine covers and archival footage emphasizing this image, and Navratilova was known, as she calls it, as "this muscular lesbian." Lenskyj (2013) has identified how sports media operates as a level of "social control" by how it promotes emphasized femininity. Although Evert and Navratilova discuss this difference in treatment together, Navratilova later revisits this issue by talking about her belief that some fans resented her for being an open lesbian. Spencer (2003) has found that previous ESPN documentaries about Evert and Navratilova reinforced their differences based on national origin and sexuality. Although *Unmatched* addresses the problems with this representation, the use of black-and-white photos (as opposed to color video of Evert) emphasize the differences in upbringing between Navratilova and Evert, by suggesting that Evert was more relatable because she was American. This "othering" of Navratilova creates distance between her and the audience.

## Family Relations

The discussion of family relations is often used to demote female athletes (Duncan & Messner, 1998). In *Unmatched,* both fathers are critical to Evert's and Navratilova's careers. Evert's father, a local tennis pro, ended her childhood fun of BBQs and pool parties with a friend. There is archival footage of Mr. Evert walking to the park, pushing a cart of tennis balls. Evert didn't fight her dad because "I didn't say boo to my parents" (Lax & Stern Winters, 2010, p. 4). The description Evert provided suggests that her father was strict and not compromising. Evert's mom was influential as well; Evert claimed that her inability to criticize other players was based on her mom's advice, which she felt would "sort of compromise my honesty" (Lax & Stern Winters, 2010, p. 7). This expectation for women is in line with traditional notions of femininity, where women don't want to offend anyone (Bernstein & Kian, 2013).

Navratilova's father was influential as well. She talks about her tennis family and having to "hit against the wall for two years" (Lax & Stern Winters, 2010, p. 3). Her dad "whacked me on the butt" (Lax & Stern Winters, 2010, p. 3) when she tried to showboat after a junior circuit win. Her dad was part of her decision to defect to the United States, and he told her to not tell her mom because she couldn't handle it. Navratilova's decision to defect to the United States at 18 was "stupid" because when you are 18 "you make the big decisions with a much lighter heart" (Lax & Stern Winters, 2010, p. 7). When returning to Czechoslovakia in 1986, one of Navratilova's dreams was to take Evert to meet her mom and have her "cook dumplings" for them (Lax & Stern Winters, 2010, p. 14). Evert and Navratilova frame their families as fitting in with conventional notions of masculinity and femininity, by having dominant father figures and mothers who encouraged more passive roles.

Evert's romantic relationships are highlighted over Navratilova's. They discuss a double date they had with the sons of Dean Martin and Desi Arnez. They conclude that if a date with Dean Martin's son can't make Navratilova straight, no one would. Evert and Navratilova talk about Evert meeting her second husband, Andy Mill, who rescued Evert as she was downhill skiing. Evert and Mill had sex for the first time together in Navratilova's bed. In contrast, the discussion of Navratilova's brief relationship with Nancy Lieberman focuses on Lieberman's negative behavior: "friends were not in her vocabulary" (Lax & Stern Winters, 2010, p. 8). During a confessional, Navratilova thanks Evert for being "gay friendly" (Lax & Stern Winters, 2010, p. 10) when it wasn't expected. Otherwise, there is no discussion of Navratilova's current romantic partners or long-term relationships. As has been discussed by Spencer (2003) in her previous analysis of Evert and Navratilova, Evert's heterosexuality is preferred over Navratilova's homosexuality, and preference is evident in *Unmatched*.

## Display of Emotions

Emotions help frame the film. There are frequent laughs during the interviews and photographs of hugs. They talk about their emotional states as young tennis players. Navratilova tells Evert, "You were like the marshmallow with the steel ball. I'm like the hard ball with the little mush inside" (Lax & Stern Winters, 2010, p. 2). They talk about Navratilova's emotional reactions on the court. Evert asks, "Why can't she control herself? We're in front of 60 million people!" (Lax & Stern Winters, 2010, p. 2). Evert discusses how emotions drove some of her off-court decisions, such as the decision to stop playing doubles with Navratilova and her motivation to play better. Navratilova has tears when she goes back to Czechoslovakia. "I still cry when I hear the Czech National Anthem" (Lax & Stern Winters, 2010, p. 10). It is shown on screen in archival footage where she zooms in on Navratilova crying during the ceremony. Given the individual nature of tennis, a female player who cries gets attention because she is the main focus in a story. Although Navratilova had other emotional reactions as a player, her negative emotions are highlighted.

Evert and Navratilova seem connected to each other during the interviews. They listen to each other's answers and use positive nonverbal behaviors and set up discussions together. Their seating/positioning toward each other suggests that they are close. They are facing each other or at an angle, and there are shots including both of them. They are sitting close to each other on couches and kitchen chairs, not only at a table or an interview panel. By focusing so much on the emotional connection between these competitors, the film downplays their competitive drive during their career. This approach is different from other *30 for 30* films documenting tennis rivals. *This Is What They Want* (2013) chronicled American tennis player Jimmy Connors's 1991 U.S. Open comeback. This film celebrated Connors's competitive approach, which was often rude and selfish. In the film, Connors expresses joy in crushing his opponent (Aaron Krickstein) in a way, which ended their friendship and Krickstein's professional career (Rosen, 2013). Even though Navratilova and Evert were intense rivals, the film argues that their friendship is more important than winning. Within the *30 for 30* world, male athletes are given more latitude in their behavior, whereas female players are praised for being friends.

## IMPLICATIONS

These two *30 for 30* films about female athletes are critical to evaluate because of the reach of ESPN films. The opening volume of *30 for 30* films was designed to make a statement about historically significant sports events using ESPN archival footage (Vogan, 2012). The audience seeks a culturally and/or socially significant approach to sports, and these films are readily available on streaming video and ESPN rebroadcasts (Vogan, 2012).

Despite the inclusion of stories about female athletes, these films reinforce emphasized femininity. Jones, Evert, and Navratilova are some of the most accomplished athletes in their respective sports, yet these films focus on their femininity in terms of dress, social relations, and emotional life. By focusing on how these accomplished female athletes conform to conventional notions of femininity, it suggests that successful female athletes must uphold these norms to be accepted. Navratilova, who during her playing career rejected many notions of femininity with her muscular body and status as an open lesbian (two issues that are prominently discussed in the film), seems to have accepted conventional notions of femininity in *Unmatched*. Throughout the film, she and Evert (who is coded as conventionally feminine) look and dress similarly. The filmmakers take great care to use visual imagery to remind the audience, even though Navratilova is a lesbian, she "looks" like a conventionally feminine woman. Consequently, looking at this collection of emphasized images and actions that uphold conventional norms of femininity, it means that they don't function as transformative representations of female athletes; they reinforce cultural expectations of women.

The representation of women in these films is critical to explore because *30 for 30* films are discussed as historical documents as opposed to only films (Vogan, 2012, 2013). There is much for sports fans to admire about the *30 for 30* film series and its attempts to contextualize critical events in sports history. But by failing to provide more inclusive and diverse representations of women, these films support the argument that female athletes' accomplishments are understood only through the lens of emphasized femininity and, consequently, are less important than men's. If these films are truly to operate as groundbreaking cultural texts, they must better interrogate how they represent women.

## NOTE

1. Nancy Meyers is the director of films that often focus on wealthy, older women, such as *Something's Gotta Give* and *It's Complicated* (Fleming, 2013).

# CHAPTER ELEVEN

# ESPN *The Magazine* "Body Issue"

## Challenging Yet Reinforcing Traditional Images of Masculinity and Femininity in Sport

EDWARD M. KIAN, LAUREN REICHART SMITH,
JASON W. LEE, AND KRISTI SWEENEY

Launched in 1979, ESPN dominates the global sport media landscape (Miller & Shales, 2011). The extent of ESPN's supremacy can be seen through the self-proclaimed "Worldwide Leader in Sports" televising 13 channels in a variety of countries and contracting to broadcast nearly every major sporting league/association in the Western world.

However, *Sports Illustrated* (*SI*) has long been and remains both the most circulated and influential sporting magazine in the United States (Bishop, 2003; Lulofs, 2013; Lumpkin & Williams, 1991). Much of *SI*'s commercial success, however, can be attributed to selling sexualized images through its much-publicized annual "Swimsuit Issue," which celebrated its 50th edition with a 252-page, 2014 issue that included 112 pages of advertising, much of that also featuring women in bikinis (Fisher, 2014).

After first appearing in a regular issue alongside regular sports articles in 1964, *SI*'s Swimsuit Issue became a stand-alone issue in 1997, meaning no sport content (e.g., articles, photographs, statistical graphics, etc.) accompanied numerous photographs of female models. Moreover, with each passing year, those models seemingly appear in more scantily clad clothing; some wear no clothes and are instead adorned in body paint (Kim, Sagas, & Walker, 2011).

A few sports figures do appear in the *SI* Swimsuit Issue in a short section devoted to current athletes. However, those athletes are mostly framed in similar poses as the models. For example, the 2014 Swimsuit Issue published a combined

18 photos of only three athletes, all of whom were attractive, young women whose appearance offered sex appeal to most heterosexual men (i.e., soccer star Alex Morgan, basketball player Syklar Diggins, and surfer Anastasia Ashley). All 18 shots featured the three athletes wearing swimsuits and showed no indication of their respective sports, or even featured these women in athletic poses.

Launched in 1998 and published biweekly, *ESPN The Magazine* quickly ascended to become the second most popular sport magazine in the United States behind only *SI* (Eagleman, Pedersen, & Wharton, 2009). However, at least some of its rapid success can be attributed to ESPN including free subscriptions to *ESPN The Magazine* with the purchase of subscriptions to ESPN insider (Lee, Sweeney, Gregg, Kane, & Kian, 2012).

First published in 2009 and immediately attaining commercial success (Rovell, 2009), *ESPN The Magazine*'s annual "Body Issue" has sparked widespread attention and debate (Dusenbery, 2012; Smith & Smith, 2011). The Body Issue is primarily noted for revealing naked photographs of athlete models in celebration of the human body in various forms. Like the *SI* Swimsuit Issue, *ESPN The Magazine*'s Body Issue offers plenty of sex appeal. However, the Body Issue features athletes instead of the full-time models who adorn *SI*'s Swimsuit Issues.

Male athletes also appear in the Body Issue, including on the multiple Body Issue regional covers *ESPN The Magazine* publishes annually. Further, unlike *SI*'s Swimsuit edition, the majority of pages in each of *ESPN The Magazine* Body Issues feature regular sports articles and photographs that are unrelated to the Body Issue and similar to the type of content that appears in *ESPN The Magazine*'s regular issues. Whereas the *SI* Swimsuit Issue has been the subject of much academic inquiry dating to the 1980s (e.g., Davis, 1997; Duncan, 1990; Fink & Kensicki, 2002; Kane, 1988; Lumpkin & Williams, 1991; Weber & Carini, 2013), scholarship on *ESPN The Magazine*'s Body Issue is minimal (Cranmer, Brann, & Bowman, 2014; Eagleman, 2011; Eagleman et al., 2009; Smallwood, Brown, & Billings, 2014; Smith, Hull, & Schmittel, 2014).

Considering its position in the overall global sport media complex, there needs to be more scholarship on ESPN, especially because most of the existing academic literature focused on ESPN television, with a few studies on ESPN.com (e.g., Adams & Tuggle, 2004; Billings, 2000; Bissell & Zhou, 2004; Coche, 2013; Eastman & Billings, 2000; Kian & Clavio, 2011; Kian, Fink, & Hardin, 2011; Kian, Mondello, & Vincent, 2009; Martin & McDonald, 2012; Tuggle, 1997; Turner, 2013; Wolter, 2013).

In particular, the use of provocative and often unusual imagery enabled *ESPN The Magazine* Body Issue to distinguish itself in a cluttered marketplace, which warrants scholarly examination. This chapter attempts to help fill that void by examining how the Body Issue is marketed and branded through multimedia platforms, followed by a brief review of literature on gender framing by sport media and body image in sport media content. Finally, content and thematic analyses of all photographs published in the history of the Body Issue are critiqued in relation to theories on masculinities and femininities.

## ESPN'S MARKETING OF THE BODY ISSUE BRAND

*ESPN The Magazine* attempts to draw a younger readership advertisers desire through graphics, eye-catching artwork, shorter articles, humor, and content focusing on topics such as nontraditional sporting events (e.g., X-Games) and youth athletics (Eagleman, 2011). That strategy has been largely successful as nearly half of *ESPN The Magazine* subscribers fall within the 18–34-year-old age range that is most coveted by potential advertisers (Eagleman, 2011).

Echoing this theme, Gary Belsky, former editor-in-chief of both *ESPN The Magazine* and ESPN insider, stated the primary goal behind the launch of the Body Issue was to appeal to 18–34-year-old readers (Ohlmeyer, 2010C).

> We know that some fans may find the contents inappropriate or otherwise objectionable," Belsky said. "That's why we spend considerable time weighing the purpose, relevance and ramifications of every image and story in the issue, among a diverse group of senior staff members that includes people of various backgrounds, faiths, ethnicities and sexual orientations, as well as parents with young children. More importantly, though, we see the body issue as conforming to our broader mission of providing readers a unique perspective on sports, in this case a celebration and exploration of the athletic form. (Ohlmeyer, 2010c, para. 5)

The Body Issue provided broader media coverage for a variety of well-known sport personalities and household names that have reached celebrity crossover status. More obscure athletes with limited visibility due to their niche sport involvement and/or nationalities (e.g., Paralympic athletes, foreign sumo wrestlers) have also been afforded greater exposure to broader audiences through their appearances in the Body Issue. "It's such good exposure for roller derby," USA Roller Derby co-captain Suzy Hotrod told espnW when asked why she agreed to pose nude for the Body Issue. "It's the best opportunity to show that our sport is genuinely athletic. I want people to know that we are athletes, and we live our lives like athletes. We train hard, like anyone else posing for this magazine" (espnW, 2011a, para. 2).

More popular and well-known athletes, such as controversial U.S. soccer goalkeeper Hope Solo, who was subject to much Internet criticism for her muscular physique while appearing on the popular American television show *Dancing*

*With the Stars*, offered personal reasons for agreeing to appear semi-nude in the Body Issue:

> Growing up, I felt insecure about my build," Solo responded when asked why she posed nude. "I didn't feel very feminine. But as time went on, I learned to completely embrace my body. It's helped me attain all my dreams and goals. I didn't have an issue posing nude, because now I see my body as empowering.... In 2008, I was maybe the fittest I had ever been, and we won the gold medal. I started to see the connection between my body and my accomplishments. I couldn't have been a great goalkeeper without power, agility and quickness. (espnW, 2011b, para. 2–3)

Women portrayed in the pages of the five Body Issues published through 2013 included muscular tennis star Serena Williams, Ironman triathlete and amputee Sarah Reinersten, a then-eight-month-pregnant USA softball player Jessica Mendoza, and robust USA Track & Field hammer thrower Amber Campbell. Male athletes gracing the pages have been just as diverse a collection, including 73-year-old swimming champion Jeff Farrell, muscular and tattooed American football stalwart Patrick Willis, 7-foot basketball superstar Dwight Howard, and 340-pound sumo wrestler Byambajav Ulambayar.

The Body Issue's reputation has been strengthened through its association with athletes—both those appearing in the issue and their teammates—to generate awareness for the magazine, having the "Worldwide Leader in Sports" as its parent company, and the athletes themselves promoted within the publication, many of whom view appearing in the publication as a marketing opportunity. The Body Issue receives regular coverage throughout ESPN's many mediums including television networks, ESPN.com, the ESPN investigative reporting show *Outside the Lines*, and such sub-brand sites as espnW.

Such "buzz worthy" exposure has enabled the Body Issue to build brand awareness to differentiate itself in a crowded marketplace. In addition to the magazine, ESPN.com offers consumers opportunities to watch videos, see interviews with featured athletes, and additional content associated with the Body Issue, including extra photos of the athletes—all of which help to publicize and further develop branding efforts of the publication.

## HEGEMONIC MASCULINITY AND EMPHASIZED FEMININITY

A common finding in hundreds of published scholarly works over the past 30 years is that male athletes and men's sports generally receive the vast majority of sport media content throughout the world regardless of the medium, age of athletes, or level of competition (e.g., Bernstein & Kian, 2013; Bruce, Hovden, & Markula, 2010; Smith & Bissell, 2014; Urquhart & Crossman, 1999).

Men's sports receiving the majority of media coverage emphasize traditional masculine qualities such as strength and speed, although which sports are construed as masculine vary by country (Vincent, Imwold, Masemman, & Johnson, 2002). For example, in the United States, American football is considered the most masculine of the popular team sports and thus receives the most media coverage (Anderson & Kian, 2012; Eastman & Billings, 2000). The majority of the limited media coverage allotted to female athletes mostly goes to those who participate in individual sports offering sex appeal for heterosexual males and construed as more gender-appropriate for women, such as gymnastics and figure skating; women in sports perceived as more masculine (e.g., rugby, softball) receive little media coverage (Bissell & Duke, 2007; Cooky, Messner, & Hextrum, 2013; Yu, 2009).

Furthermore, researchers found qualitative differences in how media frame men's and women's sports (Kian & Vincent, 2014; Knight & Giuliano, 2001). *Framing* is a term used to describe how journalists make sense of the world and determine what is newsworthy by selecting which storylines to include (Gitlin, 1980; Tuchman, 1978). In general, media frame the most popular men's sports as culturally and historically significant events, whereas female athletes often have their skills and athleticism compared to male athletes, which media typically frame as the standard basis for comparison in sport (Jones, 2006; Kian, 2008).

Moreover, media tend to focus on female athletes' physical appearances, family relationships, and perceived psychological vulnerabilities far more than they do for men's sports and male athletes (e.g., Billings, Halone, & Denham, 2002; Kane, 2013). Female athletes have historically been photographed by most media outlets in ways that attempt to appeal to a heterosexual male audience through overtly sexualized portrayals that have little/nothing to do with sport (Bissell & Smith, 2013; Duncan, 2006).

Male athletes are more likely than female athletes to be framed in action shots, whereas female athletes are more likely to be photographed in portrait shots in non-sport settings (Hardin, Chance, Dodd, & Hardin, 2002; Kane, Lavoi, & Fink, 2013). Duncan (1990) went so far as to contend that female athletes are occasionally photographed in poses similar to those that are commonplace in softcore pornography.

Not surprisingly, much of the research on photographs in sport media focused on *Sports Illustrated*, particularly its influential Swimsuit Issue (e.g., Hardin, Lynn, & Walsdorf, 2005; Kim et al., 2011; Lumpkin & Williams, 1991). Female athletes accounted for only 10% of the published photographs in *SI* from 1997 to 1999 (including the Swimsuit Issue in that total) and most of these women participated in what have been socially constructed as traditionally feminine sports such as gymnastics and figure skating (Fink & Kensicki, 2002).

Moreover, there has little been change in *SI*'s photographs of women over the years. Weber and Carini (2013) found women appeared in less than 5% of *SI* covers from 2000 to 2011, which was less than the percentage of *SI* covers women appeared on from its inaugural issue in 1954 through 1965. Further, "women's participation in sport was often minimized by sharing covers with male counterparts, featuring anonymous women not related directly to sports participation, sexually objectifying female athletes, and promoting women in more socially acceptable gender-neutral or feminine sports" (Weber & Carini, 2013, p. 196). Ideal female body types for each American generation are largely portrayed through *SI*'s Swimsuit Issue, which affects individual body images.

Body image refers to one's personal body image being parallel to one's perception of his or her ideal body image (Tigman, 2003). The media-driven ideal body image can directly influence a person's satisfaction with his or her body. The ideal body image therein varies from those seeking to emulate an elite athlete, fitness professional, celebrity, or other such role model. Historically, female athletes struggled to balance their femininity with their muscularity (Adams, Schmitke, & Franklin, 2005).

In recent years, the ideal body image framed by media tends to be thin or ultrathin for women and lean and muscular for men (Bell & Dittmar, 2011). This presents a paradox for female athletes that seek not only to excel on the athletic field but also to maintain an acceptable mainstream feminine physique. Whereas body image issues have historically been limited to women, research indicates that both men and women find it undesirable to be overweight; men also find it undesirable to be seen as too lean and less muscular (Labre, 2002; Neumark-Sztainer, Story, Hannon, Perry, & Irving, 2002).

The limited research on images and content in *ESPN The Magazine*'s Body Issue offered similar findings. In the most extensive study, Eagleman et al. (2009) found that men's sports accounted for 94.7% of *ESPN The Magazine* photos published from 1998 to 2007 specifically focused on a men's or women's sport, and/or a female or male athlete. That was a lower percentage than the 96.6% of feature articles on men's sports from 1998 to 2007 (Eagelman et al., 2009). Furthermore, men's sports accounted for 97.5% of *ESPN The Magazine* covers in that span. It should be noted, however, this longitudinal study analyzed *ESPN The Magazine* before publication of its first Body Issue in 2009.

Cranmer et al. (2014) examined 157 images featured in various *ESPN The Magazine*'s Body Issue, finding that the most recent issues of the series have become more sexualized and removed from the sporting context. Smallwood et al. (2014) compared media consumers' perceptions of images published in *SI*'s Swimsuit Issue versus those in *ESPN The Magazine*'s Body Issue. Not surprisingly, *SI*'s model-based Swimsuit Issue received higher ratings for femininity and sexuality, and *ESPN The Magazine*'s Body Issue earned higher scores for muscularity and athleticism (Smallwood et al., 2014).

Most of these research findings on *ESPN The Magazine* (Cranmer et al., 2014; Eagelman et al., 2009) mirrored previous studies on media framing of women's sports and female athletes that examined articles, images, narratives, photographs, and storylines in magazine, newspaper, radio, and television, and online coverage throughout the world (Billings & Eastman, 2003; Crolley & Teso, 2007; Kian, 2014; Nylund, 2007).

Many of these scholars and others concluded that sport and mass media are two of the main cultural institutions helping to preserve hegemonic masculinity in the democratized world, often working in conjunction to uphold the status quo (e.g., Connell, 1990; Lenskyj, 1998; Wenner & Jackson, 2009). Gramsci (1971) used the term *hegemony* to describe ways in which a dominant social class uses ideology to create consent for its dominance over others throughout society. Connell (1987) defined hegemonic masculinity as the configuration of gender practices that strengthen the dominance of men who conform to and exhibit desirable masculinities. The two most ostracized groups in hegemonic masculine societies or cultures are women and openly gay men (Anderson, 2005; Connell, 2005).

Sport media content assists in the formation and upholding of hegemonic masculinity through three primary ways. First, the vast majority of media content focuses on men's sports and male athletes (Vincent, Kian, Pedersen, Kuntz, & Hill, 2010; Whannel, 2002). The near or complete absence of coverage often provided to female athletes serves to "symbolically annihilate" their existence to many sport media consumers (Tuchman, 1978).

Second, sport media content often includes descriptors and images that highlight the physical differences between men and women in sport, while also minimizing, trivializing, and/or injecting humor in relation to the accomplishments and skill level of female athletes and women's sports (Billings, Angelini, & Duke, 2010; Vincent, 2004).

Finally, sport media content sexualizes female athletes, whose dating lives and personal relationships are examined more in-depth than male athletes (Harris & Clayton, 2002; Whiteside & Hardin, 2011). This overt sexualization of female athletes is most prevalent in photographs and televised images (Kane, 2013; Messner, Duncan, & Cooky, 2003).

Connell (1987) also wrote about emphasized femininity, which means that women must conform to gender ideals and desires of heterosexual men in how they dress and act, with looks serving the primary basis for valuing women in hegemonic masculine societies. Likely due in part to women's sport participation having long been perceived as a threat to hegemonic masculinity (Rader, 2008), media covering female athletes have emphasized athletes' femininity, particularly through "girl-next-door" poses in photographs and sexualized images in telecasts (Greer, Hardin, & Homan, 2009).

Hegemonic masculinity's dominance in sport media is not limited to content. Men significantly outnumber women in all mediums of sport journalism in all countries where sport media gender representation has been examined (e.g., Capranica & Aversa, 2002; Claringbould, Knoppers, & Elling, 2004; Kian & Hardin, 2009; Sheffer & Schultz, 2007). For example, a survey of North American sport journalists employed at prominent Internet sites and newspapers revealed men accounted for 94% of sports editors, 90% of sports columnists, and 89% of reporters (Lapchick, Moss, Russell, & Scearce, 2011). Further, women in sport media rarely advance into the "gatekeeper" positions (e.g., editors, producers, directors, etc.), most of whom determine which sports are worthy of coverage and the level of emphasis placed on events (Hardin, 2005).

Moreover, several studies showed that a hegemonic masculine and often chauvinistic culture exists within the sport media workforce (Hardin & Shain, 2005; Kian, 2007; Kian, Anderson, Vincent, & Murray, 2013). This led Pedersen, Whisenant, and Schneider (2003) to conclude, "hegemonic masculinity is entrenched in the sports media regardless of the gender of the persons making the decisions, writing the stories, or taking the photographs" (p. 388).

The Body Issue, however, provides a platform for various perspectives pertaining to body image issues by featuring pictures of athletes from a multitude of sports and of varied body types and abilities from both sexes, some of which seemingly do not conform with hegemonic masculinity and emphasized femininity (Connell, 2005).

## EXAMINING THE BODY ISSUE

This examination builds on two previous studies that specifically analyzed photographs appearing in *ESPN The Magazine* Body Issues published from 2009 to 2013 (Smith et al., 2014; Smith & Smith, 2011). Smith and Smith (2011) examined all 2010 photos and text published in the printed 2010 *ESPN The Magazine* Body Issue, including multiple photos of some athletes appearing in the Body Issue portion of the magazine.

When counting all other sport articles and photos published in the 2010 issue that were separate from the Body Issue section, images and words on men's sports accounted for roughly 80% of all content. However, those differences were less pronounced in the 34 pages of that issue (excluding advertising) dedicated to the Body Issue portion, where women were exclusively shown in 15 of the 24 photos on individual athletes. However, men in the Body Issue section were twice as likely to appear in active, athletic poses than the female athletes in that same section (Smith & Smith, 2011).

In a longitudinal and more detailed study, Smith et al. (2014) examined 139 of the photographs published over the first five years of the newsstand edition of the Body Issue, finding 55% of the Body Issue sections' photos focused on female athletes. Moreover, there were no significant differences in the likelihood of female and male athletes to appear in active or passive poses, nor were there any significant differences in the likelihood of sports historically construed as masculine or feminine to appear in active or passive poses, regardless of the sex of the athletes (Smith et al., 2014).

Those two studies (see Smith & Smith, 2011; Smith et al., 2014) provided important data needed to examine *ESPN The Magazine*'s Body Issues. Accordingly, this chapter is the first-known attempt to list all female and male athletes who appeared nude or semi-nude in the first five years (2009–2013) of the Body Issues' magazine and/or online releases on ESPN.com, excluding the individual names of those who appeared in group portraits (e.g., 12 members of the U.S. national women's water polo team appeared together in a 2010 underwater photo). Accordingly, Tables 11.1 and 11.2 show the variety of female and male athletes who appeared in the first five *ESPN The Magazine* Body Issues from 2009–2013.

Table 11.1. Female Athletes Appearing in *ESPN The Magazine* Body Issue, 2009–2013.

| Athlete | Sport | Year | Nationality |
|---|---|---|---|
| Allison Baver | Speedskating | 2009 | U.S. |
| Claire Bevilacqua | Surfing | 2009 | Australia |
| Gretchen Bleiler | Snowboarding | 2011 | U.S. |
| Carly Booth | Golf | 2013 | Scotland |
| Gina Carano | Mixed Martial Arts | 2009 | U.S. |
| Michelle Carter | Shot Put | 2009 | U.S. |
| Swin Cash | Basketball | 2013 | U.S. |
| Julie Chu | Ice Hockey | 2012 | U.S. |
| Steph Davis | Rock Climbing | 2009 | U.S. |
| Marlen Esparza | Boxing | 2013 | U.S. |
| Courtney Force | Auto Racing | 2013 | U.S. |
| Sylvia Fowles | Basketball | 2011 | U.S. |
| Susan Francia | Rowing | 2009 | U.S. |
| Sandra Gal | Golf | 2009 | Germany |
| Maya Gaberia | Surfing | 2012 | Brazil |
| Marcia Garcia | Speedskating | 2009 | U.S. |
| Tarah Gieger | Motocross | 2013 | Puerto Rico |
| Stephanie Gilmore | Surfing | 2011 | Australia |
| Kim Glass | Volleyball | 2010 | U.S. |
| Biba Golic | Table Tennis | 2009 | Serbia |
| Anna Grezbien | Golf | 2009 | U.S. |
| Daniela Hantuchova | Tennis | 2012 | Slovakia |
| Natasha Hastings | Track | 2011 | U.S. |

| Athlete | Sport | Year | Nationality |
| --- | --- | --- | --- |
| Cheryl Haworth | Weightlifting | 2009 | U.S. |
| Elena High | Snowboarding | 2013 | U.S. |
| Suzy Hotrod | Roller Derby | 2011 | U.S. |
| Kerri Walsh Jennings | Volleyball | 2013 | U.S. |
| Carmelita Jeter | Track | 2012 | U.S. |
| Shawn Johnson | Gymnastics | 2009 | U.S. |
| Erika Jones | Archery | 2010 | U.S |
| Lolo Jones | Track | 2009 | U.S. |
| Natasha Kai | Soccer | 2009 | U.S. |
| Christina Kim | Golf | 2009 | U.S. |
| Kelly Kulick | Bowling | 2011 | U.S. |
| Jeanette Lee | Billiards | 2010 | U.S. |
| Sydney Leroux | Soccer | 2013 | Canada/U.S. |
| Kristi Leskinen | Skiing | 2009 | U.S. |
| LPGA (group shot, 3 athletes) | Golf | 2009 | U.S. |
| Julia Mancuso | Skiing | 2009/10 | U.S. |
| Oskana Masters | Paralympics Rowing/ Skiing | 2012 | U.S. |
| Jessica Mendoza | Softball | 2009 | U.S. |
| Belen Mozo | Golf | 2011 | Spain |
| Dalia Ojeda | Rock Climbing | 2013 | Canary Islands |
| Candace Parker | Basketball | 2012 | U.S. |
| Suzann Pettersen | Golf | 2012 | Norway |
| Cappie Pondexter | Basketball | 2009 | U.S. |
| Agnieszka Radwanska | Tennis | 2013 | Poland |
| Phillipa Raschker | Track | 2010 | Germany |
| Sarah Reinersten | Triathlon/Paralympics | 2009 | U.S. |
| Ronda Rousey | Mixed Martial Arts | 2012 | U.S. |
| Alicia Sacramonen | Gymnastics | 2011 | U.S. |
| Cristiane Santos | Mixed Martial Arts | 2010 | Brazil |
| Hope Solo | Soccer | 2011 | U.S. |
| Jenn Stuczynski | Pole Vault | 2009 | U.S. |
| Meisha Tate | Mixed Martial Arts | 2013 | U.S. |
| Diana Taurasi | Basketball | 2010 | U.S. |
| Anna Tunnicliffe | Sailing | 2012 | U.S. |
| Rachel Yurkovich | Javelin | 2010 | U.S. |
| Esther Vergeer | Wheelchair Tennis | 2010 | Netherlands |

| Athlete | Sport | Year | Nationality |
|---------|-------|------|-------------|
| USA National Team (team shot, 10 athletes) | Hockey | 2009 | U.S. |
| USA National Team (team shot, 4 athletes) | Softball | 2009 | U.S. |
| USA National Team (team shot, 7 athletes) | Volleyball | 2012 | U.S. |
| USA National Team (team shot, 12 athletes) | Water Polo | 2010 | U.S. |
| Abby Wambach | Soccer | 2012 | U.S. |
| Serena Williams | Tennis | 2009 | U.S. |
| Venus Williams | Tennis | 2010 | U.S. |
| Vera Zvoareva | Tennis | 2011 | Russia |

Table 11.2. Male Athletes Appearing in *ESPN The Magazine* Body Issue, 2009–2013.

| Athlete | Sport | Year | Nationality |
|---------|-------|------|-------------|
| Jose Bautista | Baseball | 2012 | Dominican Republic |
| James Blake | Tennis | 2009 | U.S. |
| Carlos Bocanegra | Soccer | 2012 | U.S. |
| Jeremy Campbell | Paralympics Pentathlon | 2011 | U.S. |
| Joba Chamberlain | Baseball | 2009 | U.S. |
| Tyson Chandler | Basketball | 2012 | U.S. |
| Zdeno Chara | Hockey | 2009 | Slovakia |
| Helio Castroneves | Auto Racing | 2011 | Brazil |
| Bryan Clay | Decathlon | 2009 | U.S. |
| Randy Couture | Mixed Martial Arts | 2009 | U.S. |
| Nelson Cruz | Baseball | 2009 | Dominican Republic |
| Vernon Davis | Football | 2013 | U.S. |
| D.C. United (team shot, 6 athletes) | Soccer | 2009 | U.S. |
| Walter Dix | Track | 2012 | U.S. |
| Ashton Eaton | Decathlon | 2012 | U.S. |
| Edmonton Oilers (team shot, 3 athletes) | Hockey | 2009 | Canada |
| Carl Edwards | Auto Racing | 2009 | U.S. |

| Athlete | Sport | Year | Nationality |
| --- | --- | --- | --- |
| Kenneth Faried | Basketball | 2013 | U.S. |
| Jeff Farrell | Swimming | 2010 | U.S. |
| Malliciah Goodman | Football | 2009 | U.S. |
| Blake Griffin | Basketball | 2011 | U.S. |
| Rob Gronkowski | Football | 2012 | U.S. |
| Bill Guerin | Hockey | 2009 | U.S. |
| Ryan Guettler | BMX | 2009 | Australia |
| Ryan Hall | Running | 2011 | U.S. |
| Laird Hamilton | Surfing | 2009 | U.S. |
| Casey Hampton | Football | 2009 | U.S. |
| Matt Harvey | Baseball | 2013 | U.S. |
| Chris Higgins | Hockey | 2009 | U.S. |
| Steven Holcomb | Bobsled | 2010 | U.S. |
| Torry Holt | Football | 2009 | U.S. |
| Dwight Howard | Basketball | 2009 | U.S. |
| Tim Howard | Soccer | 2011 | U.S. |
| John Isner | Tennis | 2013 | U.S. |
| Steven Jackson | Football | 2011 | U.S. |
| Jon Jones | Mixed Martial Arts | 2011 | U.S. |
| Maurice Jones-Drew | Football | 2012 | U.S. |
| Scott Jurek | Ultramarathoner | 2009 | U.S. |
| Colin Kaepernick | Football | 2013 | U.S. |
| Dean Karnazes | Ultramarathoner | 2009 | U.S. |
| Patrick Kerney | Football | 2009 | U.S. |
| Ryan Kesler | Hockey | 2011 | U.S. |
| Mike Komisarek | Hockey | 2009 | U.S. |
| Dannell Leyva | Gymnastics | 2012 | Cuba/U.S. |
| Phil Loadholt | Football | 2009 | U.S. |
| Ryan Lochte | Swimming | 2009 | U.S. |
| Joffrey Lupul | Hockey | 2013 | Canada |
| Evan Lysacek | Figure Skating | 2010 | U.S. |
| Mark Martin | Auto Racing | 2009 | U.S. |
| Sergio Martinez | Boxing | 2011 | Argentina |
| Tim Morehouse | Fencing | 2012 | U.S. |
| Motocross (group shot, 6 athletes) | Motocross | 2009 | U.S. |
| NHL (group shot, 4 athletes) | Hockey | 2009 | U.S. |
| Bryan Namoff | Soccer | 2009 | U.S. |

| Athlete | Sport | Year | Nationality |
|---|---|---|---|
| Adam Nelson | Shotput | 2009 | U.S. |
| Apolo Ohno | Speed Skating | 2011 | U.S. |
| Oguchi Onyewu | Soccer | 2009 | U.S. |
| Manny Pacquiao | Boxing | 2009 | Philippines |
| Adrian Peterson | Football | 2009 | U.S. |
| Gary Player | Golf | 2013 | South Africa |
| Poker (group shot, 3 men and 1 woman) | Poker | 2009 | U.S. |
| Chris Pontius | Soccer | 2009 | U.S. |
| Shane Proctor | Bull Riding | 2009 | U.S. |
| Hanley Ramirez | Baseball | 2010 | Dominican Republic |
| Red Bull Racing (group shot, 4 pit crew members) | Auto Racing | 2009 | U.S. |
| Josh Reyes | Baseball | 2011 | Dominican Republic |
| Brad Richards | Hockey | 2012 | Canada |
| Stephane Robidas | Hockey | 2009 | Canada |
| Kevin Robinson | BMX | 2009 | U.S. |
| Ivan Rodriguez | Baseball | 2009 | Puerto Rico |
| Evangelista Santos | Mixed Martial Arts | 2010 | Brazil |
| Ken Schrader | Auto Racing | 2009 | U.S. |
| Chris Sharma | Rock Climbing | 2013 | U.S. |
| Clyde Simms | Soccer | 2009 | U.S. |
| Kelly Slater | Surfing | 2010 | U.S. |
| Mike Smith | Horse Racing | 2009 | U.S. |
| Alex Solis | Horse Racing | 2009 | Panama |
| Sheldon Souray | Hockey | 2009 | Canada |
| Gincarlo Santon | Baseball | 2013 | U.S. |
| Amare Stoudamire | Basketball | 2009 | U.S. |
| Byambajav Ulambyar | Sumo Wrestling | 2009 | Mongolia |
| Camillo Villegas | Golf | 2010 | Columbia |
| Louie Vito | Snowboarding | 2011 | U.S. |
| Herschel Walker | Mixed Martial Arts (retired football) | 2010 | U.S. |
| John Wall | Basketball | 2013 | U.S. |
| Johnny Weir | Figure Skating | 2009 | U.S. |
| Patrick Willis | Football | 2010 | U.S. |

Overall, 206 athletes appeared in the first five years of *ESPN The Magazine*'s Body Issue newsstand and accompanying online releases published through a section on ESPN.com specifically devoted to the Body Issue. That figure included 99 (or 48.1%) female athletes, compared to 107 (or 51.9%) male athletes. Women, however, were more likely to appear in portraits with other women. For example, the U.S. women's national teams for hockey, softball, volleyball, and water polo have appeared in the first five Body Issues, compared to no U.S. men's national teams from any sport over that span. However, men appeared in group shots with a few members of their professional teams, such as six teammates of D.C. United from Major League Soccer photographed together, as were three Canadian citizens who were members of the National Hockey League's Edmonton Oilers.

Athletes from most sports appeared in the first five years of the Body Issue. Surprisingly, the sports most represented for women—excluding photographs of entire teams or multiple athletes—were golf and basketball, both of which have been largely framed by mass media as gender-inappropriate sports for women's participation (Crosset, 1995; Kian, Vincent, & Mondello, 2008). Not surprisingly, the five most represented sports for individual pictures of male athletes were American football, baseball, hockey, soccer, and basketball, which are also the five most popular men's professional team sports in the United States (Kian & Anderson, 2009).

There were photos of male athletes that reinforce the most desirable, physical characteristics of Connell's (2005) notion of hegemonic masculinity, such as Argentinian boxer Sergio Martinez flexing his biceps with an angered facial display in the 2011 issue, decathlete Ashton Easton appearing in athletic poses representing three of his sports in all three of his photographs published in the 2012 issue, and a flexed National Football League superstar running back Adrian Peterson showing off his chiseled physique in the inaugural 2009 Body Issue.

However, there have also been plenty of counters to hegemonic masculine images commonly shown in sport media, such as a naked 5-foot-4, 115-pound jockey Mike Smith in a relaxed pose with his bald head being licked by a horse in the 2012 issue. There were also photos of strapping athletes in sports construed by most media as masculine in not-so-rugged poses, such as Florida Marlins baseball player Hanley Ramirez ironing a shirt for the 2010 issue.

Although not as prevalent as within the *SI* Swimsuit Issue, there have been plenty of Body Issue photographs of women in passive and/or sexualized poses. For example, the most popular cover for the inaugural 2009 Body Issue featured a smiling and laughing tennis superstar Serena Williams curled up in a fetal position, while inside portraits included Williams in a swimsuit and attractive American track hurdler Lolo Jones offering a seductive stare while framed in a non-athletic pose. A smiling tennis star Daniela Hantuchova appeared in a passive, girl-next-door type pose that is common in the *Sports Illustrated* Swimsuit

Issue in the 2012 *ESPN The Magazine* Body Issue, and the same issue displayed golfer Suzann Petersen sitting relaxed in a sexual pose by a pier with no indication that she is a golfer or an athlete.

The salacious nature of much of the inaugural Body Issue's most controversial images was met with some polarizing receptions. Northeastern University sociologist Linda Blum said, "Women having opportunities to market their bodies represents their achieving a new role as respected athletes who are in control. But those opportunities can also be seen by some to reinforce old-fashioned, negative ideas of women as sex objects" (Roenigk, 2009, p. 11).

The first five Body Issues, however, featured a plethora of photos of female athletes who—by their physiques alone and/or specific sport participation—clearly do not meet Connell's (2005) most desirable characteristics for emphasized femininity. For example, powerful and muscular African American sprinter Carmelita Jeter appeared in a pair of 2012 photos where she is shown coming out of the blocks into a full sprint motion, boxer Marlen Esparza is shown with an angered look on her face while punching a body bag in the gym in the 2013 issue, and 5-foot-9, 210-pound shot putter Michelle Carter exhibited her not-so-thin stomach in the 2009 issue.

Also included are images unlike any ever published in a national sport magazine and not easily classified under any notion of masculinity or femininity. The Body Issue has featured multiple Paralympians, wheelchair-bound tennis player Esther Vergeer, and bobsledder Steven Holcomb displaying extra girth on his stomach in the 2010 issue.

Age has not kept athletes and former athletes from appearing in the Body Issue. A then-73-year-old swimmer Jeff Farrell swimmer appeared in 2010, retired but chiseled German runner (and then-64-year-old) Philippa Raschker ran naked in the woods for the 2010 issue, and senior golfer Gary Player became the oldest athlete to appear in the Body Issue when the then-77-year-old South African posed nude, holding an oversized golf ball over his head for the 2013 issue.

All of this led Gardner (2012) to conclude that the Body Issue does not sexualize female athletes—at least not to the extent that *SI* and other outlets do:

> The Body Issue also features both men and women giving them equal "exposure." It does not focus on just one gender and show them in scantily clad clothes or showing off their cleavage. Athletes in all types of sports are photographed for the issue. There has been a sumo wrestler, a female shot putter, a 1960 Olympian, and several amputee athletes featured. The focus is on all athletes in sports and not just the "beautiful" ones that could have been models…. Of course ESPN is a business and is trying to sell as many copies of their magazines as possible so they are going to put some eye candy in for both men and women. Even though they do this, they have kept from exposing athlete's intimate areas for the sake of selling copies. They present a product that is even different from *Sports Illustrated's Swimsuit Issue* in that they are not just showing hot women in bikinis to sell

magazines. They are trying to show what a hard working athlete's body looks like from working out and playing their sport for years, whereas other publications show off what plastic surgery and implants can make you look like…. The main aspect of *The Body Issue* that makes it more acceptable than other nude or semi-nude publications is that they do not over sexualize the athletes that are posing in the magazine. The point of the issue is for athletes to be able to show off their body in a way that does not just show it in a compromising manner. (para. 4–6)

And then there are the bizarre images, such as a "Heads, Shoulders, Knees and Toes" photo spread in the inaugural 2009 Body Issue in which rarely seen body parts were emphasized and most athletes unidentifiable. For example, mixed martial arts legend Randy Couture's disfigured ear was featured, as was hockey player Stephane Robidas's broken jaw, football player Torry Holt's mangled fingers, football defensive lineman Casey Hampton's mammoth gut, and 300-pound female weightlifter's Cheryl Hanworth's large but mostly undefined left bicep.

These types of images and the unpredictability of what appears in the annual Body Issue is why former ESPN ombudsman Don Ohlmeyer (2010c) largely dismissed criticisms that the Body Issue overly sexualized female athletes. Ohlmeyer instead emphasized that the nakedness of athletes (both male and female) causes discomfort for some readers:

Conflicting points of view generally surface when the discussion turns to nudity. The photographs did not strike me as salacious or lascivious. But that's just one man's opinion. Many of the poses were reminiscent of the classic Greek sculptures of athletes, but that doesn't guarantee some readers won't find them objectionable…. The photos in the "Body Issue" are a total departure from those that normally accompany stories in this publication. Perhaps ESPN should have sent an advisory to subscribers notifying them that the next issue would contain material some may deem objectionable. Because of similar concerns, for example, *Sports Illustrated* allows reticent subscribers to skip its annual swimsuit issue and extend their subscription by an extra week…. Of course, cultures change. SI created a firestorm when it published its first swimsuit issue in 1964… and that franchise now engages 67 million consumers through a multitude of platforms (swimsuit videos, iPhone apps, etc.), compared to an average circulation of 3.15 million for the magazine…. You'd be hard pressed to say ESPN's edition is as blatant an appeal to sexuality as *Sports Illustrated* attempts to do, but there's no question ESPN hopes the athletes-in-motion format can similarly catch fire. In 2009, the "Body Issue" newsstand sales were 73 percent higher than the magazine's average circulation of 2.2 million, and sales for the 2010 edition were up 22 percent over last year. (para. 8–12)

Expect such debate and discussion to be the norm in ensuing years as the Body Issue continues to publish photos unlike those ever revealed in a sport magazines while also continuing to attain the financial success that Ohlmeyer noted above.

# Journalism and the ESPN Effect

# CHAPTER TWELVE

# Sprawling Hagiography

## ESPN's *30 for 30* Series and the Untangling of Sports Memories

ANDREW C. BILLINGS AND KEVIN B. BLACKISTONE

From its onset in 1979, ESPN had always been a sprawling multimedia conglomerate, yet the focus had always been the rendering of live sports, along with continual news, information, and expert advice. That remains the case. Yet, with the advent of *SportsCentury* in 1999, ESPN made a definitive turn toward the memorializing of not only people but also moments. ESPN was a chronicler of history. Billings, Brown, Crout, McKenna, Rice, Timanus, and Zeigler (2008) once argued that "history is not always written by the winners; it is also written by those with the television rights" (p. 229); if so, ESPN—entering its 30-year anniversary in 2009—was the ultimate winner. With interests circling the globe and a presence on virtually any form of traditional and new media platform, ESPN was on its way to a valuation of $66 billion (Wilkerson, 2012).

With that presence came power, and ESPN sought a way to commemorate the ESPN era—while shaping history in the process. *Grantland*'s Bill Simmons noted that "Our 30-year anniversary was coming up and I knew that no company loved celebrating itself more than ESPN. We'll celebrate anything" (Rose, 2010, para. 6). The result was a project clearly intended to "rival HBO" (Rose, 2010, para. 2) by producing the best sports documentaries ever to air. It began as 30 films encapsulating 30 years of ESPN programming, yet *30 for 30* quickly garnered critical acclaim and excellent ratings. The result was a finite 30 films that evolved into an infinite brand: *ESPN Films Presents: 30 for 30*, embossed with the tagline: "too dramatic not to be real." Ancillary projects included *30 for 30 Shorts* (Sandomir,

2012), described as "stories out there that we loved for four to 12 minutes but maybe not for a full hour" (Simmons, 2012, para. 2) and *Nine for IX*, focusing on women's sports in a series of documentaries in 2013 (Whiteside, 2013).

Arising from *30 for 30* and its ancillary properties, ESPN had branded itself the worldwide leader in sports documentary filmmaking, offering consistently "excellent, insightful television" (Holmes, 2009, para. 2). However, some believed ESPN was walking a fine line, for "many of the series' films explore the same types of scandals and controversies that ESPN's regular coverage is often critiqued for sensationalizing" (Vogan, 2012, p. 142) and that some films made in the name of art actually "serve economic purposes" (p. 150). This chapter explores issues such as authenticity, identity, memory, and counter-memory within the cinematic lens of the *30 for 30* series. It is our contention that the films contribute mightily to important conversations outside wins and losses, yet can, in given circumstances, veer into the creation of saints—a sprawling hagiography. The etymology of the word *hagiography* is Greek in definition, combining the Greek words for *holy* (hagios) and *writing* (graphe). The original millennia-old application of its meaning is Christian in origin, being used specifically to describe the creation of the curricula vitae for those among us to be considered for sainthood, which, we argue, is what is happening within some selections of ESPN's *30 for 30* series regarding not only athletes but also coaches and other people involved within seminal moments of sports history.

## FOCUS AND HISTORICAL AUTHORSHIP

The topics and people explored within ESPN's *30 for 30* have always been intriguing to the masses because they are "not necessarily the most famous things that have ever happened in sports, but instead the most interesting" (Holmes, 2009, para. 3). The topics explored within the series seemingly evolved over the development of the initial 30 films, for what ESPN thought the films were chronicling turned out to be different depending on the topics filmmakers were interested in exploring as well as whether a person or event was too big to the point that most of the elements of the story had been told in other formats or renderings. As creator Bill Simmons told Rose (2010):

> I was shocked by how many ideas from the early part of the process... ended up not making the cut. Like Doc [Gooden] and Darryl [Strawberry]—I thought that was a lock. [Jack] Nicklaus and the '86 Masters, same thing. Hell, Nicklaus and the '86 Masters was the example I used in the initial e-mail with the *30 for 30* proposal talking about all the great ideas that were out there that hadn't been done, and somehow we never ended up doing it. But it ended up being a bad fit. Everyone knew the story, we didn't have a fresh angle on it, and we didn't have a filmmaker who was passionate about it. So it died. (para. 16)

Thus, *30 for 30* started to morph based on lesser-told stories, or alternate angles to predominant storylines or beliefs. The creative side—with a clear orientation to top directors—was privileged over which 30 stories had the highest warrant to be told (Deitsch, 2010). In essence, the criteria became (a) topics quality directors were willing to pursue, (b) unique yet relatively untold angles to stories, and then (c) directors who were "the right guys for this topic" (Schell, quoted in Deitsch, 2013, para. 6). Within that third postulate, such a notion implied that some directors were "wrong" for a given topic. The belief in proper/improper storytellers is particularly pertinent in understanding the contributions of creator Bill Simmons, whose ethos is built on fandom—the "homer" guy in the stands, rather than the counter, such as the emotionally detached ESPN journalist Bob Ley on programming stalwart *Outside the Lines*. Selection based on fandom and overall interest seemingly melded with Simmons's worldview, yet potentially made the films more susceptible to hagiographical portrayals. One could argue whether passion and objectivity are polar opposites, but there is little question that the two concepts are far from identical.

Alternate renderings of history, through a process often referred to as counter-memory (Foucault, 1980), reveal layers of storytelling pertinent to understanding editorial choices within *30 for 30*. Visker (1995) argues that the subject of any story is best eliminated from discussions of authenticity. Rather, the storyteller's ability to recall or retell the story to the best of his or her collective memory should be the primary goal, knowing that the notion of truly chronicling a history in which all agree is a fool's errand. Although cultural memory can be defined as "memory that is shared outside the avenues of formal historical discourse yet is entangled with cultural products and imbued in cultural meaning" (Sturken, 1997, p. 3), many mediated narratives are often built to challenge cultural memory, essentially postulating the argument: "you think you know the story of X, but, in actuality, you don't."

Authenticity, a sibling to accuracy, "remains one of the major issues underlying the critique of contemporary social thought" (Hardt, 1993, p. 49), yet the need for it in mediated narratives is difficult to discern, particularly in racial narratives (see Stansell, 1992), which *30 for 30* often adopts. There is a perceived element of teaching within these stories, offering a glimpse of societal beliefs in which others may not have been aware. Nonetheless, even if accuracy in identity-oriented discussions cannot be attained, having it as an objective is perceived to be paramount. Taylor (1994) concurs, writing that "our moral salvation comes from recovering authentic moral contact with ourselves" (p. 33).

## COMMON THEMES WITHIN *30 FOR 30* FILMS

As previously mentioned, the topics embodied in *30 for 30* films would never be presumed to be a surrogate for the most important stories of the past several decades. This is not to diminish their value, but rather to note that the focus is not on the athlete, championship, or specific event. Instead, the primary aim appears to be providing a wider glimpse of what the narrative indicates about society (with the benefit of hindsight).

Holmes (2009) notes that athletes were rarely subjects of the initial films. Sometimes they were in subsequent offerings, but usually not for superstar athletes. Rather, Holmes found the three primary themes embodied in the first three films (*King's Ransom*, *The Band That Wouldn't Die*, and *Small Potatoes: Who Killed the USFL?*) were (a) hurt feelings, (b) devotion, and (c) greed. The overwhelming majority of the subsequent films fit these macro-level themes as well. Although athletes were obviously central to the stories, "these are not stories about athletes as titans, really, except in the sense that they are done with a keen understanding that being a titan carries personal consequences" and seek to answer "questions about behavior—about people and their choices" (Holmes, 2009, para. 8, 10).

Thus, films became a surrogate for larger assessments of society. A film on South Africa's hosting of the 1995 Rugby World Cup, *The 16th Man*, became a mechanism for explaining the effects of apartheid to uninitiated masses. A film on failed NFL quarterback Todd Marinovich, *The Marinovich Project*, became a contemplation on the role of fathers and sons within sports. A film on the late-1980s Detroit Pistons, *Bad Boys*, became a narrative about how "the way this team went about their business... mirrored the city—the toughness and the blue-collar work ethic" (Cocoros, quoted in Deitsch, 2013, para. 9).

Timing mattered greatly, not only for a prominent sense of kairos but also to reach target audiences more deftly. A film on University of Miami's football dominance, *The U*, premiered after the Heisman trophy presentation in 2009; a film titled *June 17, 1994* (showing how an O. J. Simpson Bronco chase could trump a major sports day) first aired on June 16, 2010. *The Price of Gold*, an inside look at figure skating scandal involving Nancy Kerrigan and Tonya Harding, aired 20 years after the event, "on the cusp of the 2014 Winter Olympics" (Gachman, 2014, para. 1).

These synergistic examples underscored one key postulate to understanding *30 for 30*: these films could be conveyed with a great deal of independence, as long as they did not offer direct conflict with core ESPN interests. Lack of editorial control and the need to promote core ESPN properties has always been an issue for ESPN, which canceled the popular NFL-based fictional series *Playmakers* after a season in 2004 because "ESPN decided it no longer wanted to keep on enraging the league" (Sandomir, 2004, para. 3). Similarly, nine years later, ESPN severed a partnership with PBS to produce an NFL-concussion documentary, *League of Denial*, citing lack of complete editorial control. Although "ESPN's hasty decision made a lot of people aware of *League of Denial*" (Sandomir, 2013, para. 7), such messages underscore the parameters of products such as *30 for 30*: the films could be somewhat critical of events and leagues, but direct assaults on the main ESPN commercial product would not be tolerated.

The more limited sense of scope and synergy seemingly resulted in a heavy dose of sympathetic nostalgia films with an underlying message: it is hard to be an athlete. For instance, the 2012 film *Broke* focused on how many athletes making millions of dollars nonetheless lose it all—sometimes through their own means, but other times painting them as victims of circumstance. As Holmes (2012) noted, *Broke* offered issues that most fans fail to consider. "They gamble. They [have] to start over in new cities if they're traded. They pay high tax rates, and then they pay agents and lawyers" (para. 5). Noting this dual reading of issues within a film like *Broke*, Maurer (2012) notes that "The temptation is to... come to one of two conclusions: 1. These poor athletes!... 2. These stupid athletes!" (emphasis omitted, para. 12–14).

However, in attempts to tell stories with more dimensions, athletes could be seen as more angelic than ever. Some films offered tragic narratives involving athletes who were perceived to be on the brink of stardom, such as *The Best That Never Was*, a 2010 meditation on high school superstar running back Marcus Dupree. Such lamentations of lost greatness are understandable. One film, *Benji*, told the story of a talented basketball player who was shot to death. Hale (2012) wrote of how people wanted to retell this story, describing an "eagerness to recall the magic he dispensed on the basketball court" (para. 5). Still, with other narratives, such eagerness can result in perceived rapid image rehabilitation. In *The Price of Gold*, "the film doesn't lionize [Tonya] Harding or turn her into a victim, but it does humanize her" (Gachman, 2014, para. 1). Meanwhile, stories with more nuanced value-contributions become streamlined into positive, saintly narratives—for the benefit of both time and story. Even in initial critiques of the opening films in the series, many felt the films could do better with "the context before and afterward" as these "are what make the event important" (*Sports Business Daily*, 2009, para. 8).

## SPRAWLING HAGIOGRAPHY

Such tendencies to lionize athletes and potentially skew a story can be inherent in the storytelling process, with the combination sometimes facilitating hagiography. Given its historical roots as biographical propaganda, the modern-day use of the word is to describe a sympathetic, flattering, selective-memory biography that comes close to deifying a subject—if it does not canonize the subject. Appropriately, there are few arenas in which the term can be found to apply so frequently as the religious-like secular happening called sports. As the Catholic philosopher Novak (1993) notes: "Sports is, somehow, a religion" (p. xvi), concluding that "most books about sports are hagiography, 'lives of the saints,' hero worship" (p. xix).

Most film documentaries about sports, a genre that debuted at the end of the twentieth century and has doubled in production since the dawn of the twenty-first century, are no different as "sports documentaries… depict athletic achievement, but… also typically provide some epistephilic pleasure to satisfy our inclinations to know more as sports fans" (Ingle, 2013, p. x). ESPN's *30 for 30* series is the major reason for the proliferation of sports documentaries and often promotes hagiographic narratives.

## CASE #1: *THE U*

An early example of *30 for 30*'s celebratory approach to documentary filmmaking is *The U*, a two-hour excursion through the enhancement of the University of Miami football team from a campus diversion into a national spectacle that all but steals championships before collapsing under the weight of its bumptiousness.

ESPN bills the film as a microcosm for 1980s Miami, a city that ESPN (2009) describes as:

> … being at the center of a racial and cultural shift taking place throughout the country. Overwhelmed by riots and tensions, Miami was a city in flux… [but] the image of the predominantly white [University of Miami] was forever changed when coach Howard Schnellenberger scoured some of the toughest ghettos in Florida to recruit mostly black players for his team. With a newly branded swagger, inspired and fueled by the quickly growing local Miami hip hop culture, these Hurricanes took on larger-than-life personalities.

What the film's director, Billy Corben, a Miami native, does not do is underscore that the players of this era of Miami Hurricanes football were viewed by many as the embodiment, if not the originators, of so much that has become loathsome about major college football—particularly the exploitation of Black athletes— their culture and societal stratification—by White institutions of higher learning for financial gain. Corben presents a celebration of the stereotypical mass media view of Black athletes as self-centered, arrogant, mercenary, violent, menaces to society or, quite simply, "black men misbehaving" (Clarke, 1991, p. 267, 270). For example, he highlights the race-based "Catholics v. Convicts" theme of Notre Dame's game against Miami in 1988, dismissing larcenous activity by players in a lighthearted tone. Corben incorporates a point of view that the players' behavior is an outgrowth of overwhelming contempt from the rest of the sports world for their success.

Indeed, most of the criticisms of 1980s Hurricanes football that would appear a few years later in a 1995 *Sports Illustrated* cover story were either ignored or, at best, glossed in *The U* seemingly to maximize entertainment. Wolff

(1995) offered criticisms including "abuses that beset college sports," specifically noting:

> [A]t least one entry in virtually every category: improper benefits; recruiting violations; boosters run amok; academic cheating; use of steroids and recreational drugs; suppressed or ignored positive tests for drugs; player run-ins with other students as well as with campus and off-campus police; the discharge of weapons and the degradation of women in the football dorm; credit-card fraud and telephone credit-card fraud. (p. 22)

Not once is the ostensible reason for attending college—to get a college education and a degree—explored, let alone mentioned, by the filmmaker.

## CASE #2: *THE HOUSE OF STEINBRENNER*

Like Billy Corben and many other *30 for 30* filmmakers, Barbara Kopple is admittedly a fan of her subject: the late George Steinbrenner and the baseball team he owned for the better part of his life, the New York Yankees. As such, her film, *The House of Steinbrenner*, not unlike *The U*, tends toward celebration and away from criticism, no matter how much material for the latter appeared available. Indeed, Kopple opens the film with her testimony:

> When I was a kid I went to Yankee games with my brother and my parents and how could I not want to make a film about the Yankees? I mean, the Yankees are the biggest sports entity in the world. And I think what really made me want to do it is I was home and watching the All-Star Game. And I saw… Steinbrenner going around in a golf cart. He starts to cry. And I just thought, "This could be an amazing film."

But what she produces is amnesiac nostalgia, a symptom of hagiography. For *The House of Steinbrenner*, covering the bequeathing of the Yankees from George to son Hal, with the razing of old Yankee Stadium and opening of new Yankee Stadium as a backdrop, is a selective time machine. Kopple shadows Babe Ruth's granddaughter's visit to Monument Park, where Yankees greats are memorialized. She finds a 93-year-old man who recalls attending games in old Yankee Stadium's inaugural season.

But Kopple does not recall that George Steinbrenner was a convicted felon. He was suspended from baseball for two years after he was found guilty in the early 1970s of illegally funneling money to a President Nixon reelection committee in exchange for contracts for his family's shipbuilding business, into which he was born to wealth. Steinbrenner pleaded down 13 charges to avoid jail, and President Reagan later pardoned him (Johnson, 1989). The film also excludes that baseball later banned Steinbrenner for life, before reinstating him, after it was discovered he ordered Howie Spira, a gambler in-hock to Mafia-connected bookies, to investigate Yankees' star outfielder Dave Winfield. Steinbrenner was growing weary of paying Winfield millions and hoped Spira could produce unsavory information about Winfield that could jeopardize the contract (Anderson, 2012).

It is mostly for those reasons that Steinbrenner, who led the Yankees to seven World Series titles during his reign, has not been elected to the Baseball Hall of Fame at the time of this writing. Yet, for those watching Kopple's documentary, one could likely conclude the Hall of Fame is committing a grievous oversight. The story of Steinbrenner is heavily wrought with controversy; *The House of Steinbrenner* is far different, offering heavily induced fan nostalgia, and perpetuating hagiography.

## CASE #3: *JORDAN RIDES THE BUS*

A third example of hagiography is offered in *Jordan Rides the Bus*, chronicling basketball superstar Michael Jordan's attempt to play professional baseball during a year-and-a-half hiatus from the sport in which he became an icon. It tracks his departure from Chicago, where he starred for the Bulls of the National Basketball Association, to Birmingham, Alabama, where he joined the Barons of Major League Baseball's second-tier minor league.

There was much speculation about why Jordan walked away from the sport in which he had become a global celebrity—at what appeared to be the zenith of his career and popularity—for a sport he had not competed in since he was a schoolboy and in a city and media market off the Nielsen radar. The most titillating rumor was that NBA executives exiled Jordan because of published reports that he had lost over a million dollars gambling on golf and casino wagers. When Jordan's father was found murdered, it, too, became part of the NBA exile tale as rumormongers suggested it was an organized crime hit in which the league did not want to become entangled. The subject of *Jordan Rides the Bus* dismisses such claims as fanciful, primarily through news and commercial footage from his main corporate sponsor, Nike (the filmmakers did not interview Jordan on camera). And, in what became the theme of *Jordan Rides the Bus*, journalists, coaches, and others in the film dismiss the claim as well.

The result is a film that is not as much documentary as it is rebuttal of any criticisms leveled at Jordan and a re-buttressing of the iconography of Jordan: seemingly the height of hagiography. There is no foreshadowing of the Jordan who can be vindictive (as he bared later in his Hall of Fame speech), beset by relationship troubles, and failing as a detached chairman of the Charlotte Bobcats (now Hornets) of the NBA.

To be sure, Hale (2012) noted: "[Director Ron Shelton] squeezes a host of witnesses into this short film" (p. C3) but the witnesses were more similar in tone than they were different. Bulls coach Phil Jackson speaks of the shock/void of losing his superstar; *Sports Illustrated* writer Steve Wulf, originally critical of what he viewed as dilettantism, provides an apology. Shelton interviewed people ranging from coaches to real estate agents from Jordan's time in Birmingham, with Hale noting that "without exception, they fondly recall Mr. Jordan for his work ethic, his willingness to fit in and the excitement and attention he brought to their town" (p. C3).

In keeping with the paradigm of *30 for 30* constructions, ESPN tapped a perfect collaborator in Shelton to cast Jordan's break from basketball as a minor league baseball player. Shelton spent four years playing minor league baseball before becoming a successful filmmaker who made one of the most popular sports movies of all-time, baseball-themed *Bull Durham*, loosely based on Shelton's experience as a career minor-league player. As a result, he was a sympathetic witness for Jordan's experiment. In the face of outside critiques that Jordan was a sham of a baseball player—as evidenced by a batting average hovering at the demarcation line for failure, .200, Shelton elicited testimony from managers, coaches, and teammates praising Jordan's effort as a successful risk-taker, emphasizing the hits and few home runs he managed to produce. It was a script managing to present Jordan's mediocre-at-best baseball statistics as more proof of his otherworldliness as an athlete.

## CASE #4: *MARION JONES: PRESS PAUSE*

A case can be made that Marion Jones was even more otherworldly than Jordan. Consider that she qualified as an alternate for her first U.S. Olympic Track and Field team while in high school. Consider also that, as a first-year basketball player at the University of North Carolina (where Jordan starred), she helped lead the women's basketball team to a national championship. Jones abandoned her basketball career after that one college season to hone her sprinting and jumping skills for Olympic competition and she became one of the most-decorated track and field athletes, winning world and Olympic gold medals, including three at the Sydney Summer Games in 2000, earning the label of world's fastest woman. She was also rumored and eventually charged with having used performance-enhancing drugs.

After many steadfast denials, Jones, in a teary-eyed 2007 press conference, admitted she lied to federal agents about using steroids prior to the Sydney Olympics—as well as her involvement in a check-fraud scam with her former coach and boyfriend. Jones went to prison for six months and was stripped of all medals and titles from 2000 onward. The track and field world governing body suspended her from competition for two years.

But filmmaker John Singleton showed little interest in Jones's past, never broaching the key questions pertinent to the story: How and why? The focus instead was on her life after incarceration—wrapped around an attempt to revive her athletic career as a basketball player in Women's National Basketball Association.

*Marion Jones: Press Pause* (for which this chapter's coauthor, Kevin Blackistone, appears as an interviewee) measures down to a prop piece rather than up to the definition of documentary. As McNamara (2010) noted:

> Those not familiar with Jones' career or the issue of steroid use will have to do some serious Googling if they hope to appreciate the narrative…. She has written two autobiographies, "Life in the Fast Lane" and the just-released "On the Right Track," so she understands the demands of narrative. That she chooses not to explain what she was thinking during those years of crime and coverup is too bad…. (para. 2)

## CASE #5: *SURVIVE AND ADVANCE*

There are few personalities in sports so reconstructed over time as former college basketball coach Jim Valvano, who died in 1993 at 47 after a yearlong bout with cancer. Hired as an analyst by ESPN after his North Carolina State tenure, he is lauded by college basketball and its broadcast partners at the beginning of every season for the fearless manner in which he publically confronted his illness. Each year, ESPN dedicates Jimmy V Week to raise awareness about The V Foundation for Cancer Research. A rousing, emotional speech Valvano delivered two months before he died at ESPN's ESPY Awards is played repeatedly. The film *Survive and Advance,* about Valvano's 1983 unexpected championship season at North Carolina State, only elevates that narrative.

The film adopts its title from the mantra of the NCAA Tournament (college basketball's wildly popular championship playoff known as March Madness) and Valvano's coaching philosophy—which the film suggests may have come first. It tracks how Valvano's Wolfpack strung together nine victories in a row, including several that capped comebacks in the last minute or final seconds, to win the Atlantic Coast Conference championship and then the NCAA Championship. It was the quintessential Cinderella team.

Mostly overlooked by this film—as it has been by so many who have all but deified Valvano over time—is that Valvano's fairytale coaching career was replete with a fairytale's requisite villainy, ironically his. Specifically, the film fails to mention that most of his star players did not earn degrees under Valvano's tutelage. These stars aid in telling the story of court victories in *Survive and Advance,* but that story was made quite narrow in scope for the purposes of a streamlined, positive narrative. After NC State promoted Valvano to athletic director, an investigation in the late 1980s revealed that the team that produced that magical championship run also produced a four-year cumulative grade point average of 1.67 (D-plus). One player had a semester GPA of 0.23 (Cart, 1989).

Spurred by Peter Golenbock's 1991 book, *Personal Fouls: The Broken Promises and Shattered Dreams of Big Money Basketball at Jim Valvano's North Carolina State,*

NC State conducted an internal investigation. Although many of the charges were unfounded, the school found all manner of academic fraud under Valvano's leadership, including having tutors do classwork for players and assigning passing grades to players despite their being found guilty of academic dishonesty. Overall, the report found Valvano lorded over a basketball program in which 29 of the 43 players he recruited since 1980 were either on academic probation or had been when they left NC State (Cart, 1989). Twenty-one of the 43 transferred or left North Carolina State before earning degrees; only two of the 21 had left the school in good academic standing (Cart, 1989). Such details are not part of *Survive and Advance,* though Valvano did just that professionally. Dismissed by NC State in 1989 because of the findings (with a reported $600,000 buyout), Valvano was hired in 1990 as a sportscaster by ABC, the parent company then to ESPN.

Upon the release of the film, book author Golenbock told Engel (2013):

> Valvano was not about basketball. He was about making money and he made a ton of it. What is so beautiful about this guy is after he is fired, the people at ESPN saw that this is the greatest PR guy in the world and they hired him to be their No. 1 basketball guy. He was fabulous. He could go on press row and talk about how important an education was, and none of his players graduated. (para. 20)

In hagiography, Golenbock's view is fortunate to be footnoted.

## CONCLUSION

The point within this series of case studies is not to speak ill of the dead, nor to advance overly critical narratives to replace more appealing ones. Rather, the aim is to note that some authorial and editorial decisions ESPN made may have thwarted or perhaps inadvertently stifled more balanced approaches. The creation of deities can have indirect implications, particularly on those currently positioned within sport who cannot measure up to such canonical expectations (seemingly even more true in a hypermediated age of social media).

ESPN is often dismissed as providing distraction programming intended for an audience to enjoy without feeling like an audience needs to figuratively eat its vegetables by focusing on the oft-seedy inner-workings of sport. However, with the entry of top-line documentary filmmaking, "pro sports are no longer the equivalent of the toy department" (Strachan, 2013, p. C10), meaning that such standards for journalism necessarily need to shift in the process. *ESPN Presents 30 for 30* typically offers uplifting stories from top filmmakers on frequently worthy subjects. What it sometimes does not offer is comprehensiveness and objectivity, two important ingredients when rendering history to the masses in documentary form.

# CHAPTER THIRTEEN

# Framing the Bubble

## How ESPN Coverage of the NCAA Tournament Bubble Changed from 2010 to 2014

SCOTT LAMBERT

Every year as the National Collegiate Athletic Association's men's basketball tournament approaches, hoops fans start arguing about the NCAA Tournament bubble. Some fans take the stance that average teams from power conferences deserve to take the final bids because they have played good competition all year and have been somewhat successful against that competition (for this research, those six power conferences are the Atlantic Coast Conference, Big East, Big Ten, Big 12, Southeastern Conference, and the Pac-12). Other fans argue that top teams from the remaining or nonpower conferences deserve those spots. Those teams, the argument goes, played at a high level all year without the hype and exposure of teams from the power conferences and have earned their shot at the NCAA Tournament because of the success they have had against the schedule they have played.

ESPN's extensive coverage of college basketball since the network's beginning aided the NCAA men's basketball tournament's rise in popularity in the 1980s (Ceasar, 1989). Many of these college basketball fans often turn to ESPN's *SportsCenter* to garner more information about the teams that might qualify as a tournament team. *SportsCenter* runs daily around the clock with shows either live or recorded, using much of the same information all day. As a powerful indicator of what the national sports agenda will be, *SportsCenter*'s predictions about teams that might make the tournament arm its many viewers with information to take into water cooler arguments. News routine would also suggest that other media may tend to follow main stories from an outlet that sets the agenda (Breed, 1955) and that individual journalists tend to follow these paths as well (Shoemaker, Eichholz, Kim, & Wrigley, 2001).

How *SportsCenter* frames questions about the NCAA Tournament bubble may play an important role in perceptions about what teams are deserving of qualifying for the tournament and what teams are not. Although this perception may not influence the diehard fan of a specific team or conference, it may play a role in how others view what teams are selected for the NCAA Tournament.

This chapter examines how ESPN's *SportsCenter* frames the NCAA men's Division I basketball tournament in terms of power and nonpower conference teams. The chapter also examines whether ESPN's *SportsCenter* gives more salience to these so-called power conferences compared to other non-power conferences and how ESPN's *SportsCenter* frames its narrative about the NCAA Tournament bubble. Selection to the tournament is important for athletic conferences because of how the NCAA distributes money from its $10 billion television contract. Getting more teams into the tournament and advancing makes a big financial difference for conferences.

## FRAMING

Agenda-setting, especially second-level agenda-setting, has a relationship with framing, though the two are different means of examining media artifacts (Scheufele & Tewksbury, 2007). Second-level agenda-setting relies on attribute salience, making certain aspects of a story more prominent and easier for an individual to recall those attributes. Framing, according to Scheufele and Tewksbury, assumes subtle changes in wording may affect how the audience interprets information presented to them. Although agenda-setting uses attributes to make it easier for an audience to recall a certain aspect of a story, framing forces the reader to connect specific patterns of thought (Scheufele & Tewksbury, 2007). Framing is a way journalists shape a story to conform to an existing frame of reference for the reader (Entman, 2004). This is done by making certain aspects of a piece of communication more salient by placing the object in a prominent spot of a broadcast or by repeating it often (Entman, 1993).

Goffman introduced frame analysis theory in 1974. It assumed that audience members cannot fully comprehend all that is happening around them, so they classify and interpret their experiences to make sense of the world (Entman, 1993). Entman (1993) wrote: "Whatever its specific use, the concept of framing consistently offers a way to describe the power of a communicating text" (p. 51). Entman also wrote that to frame is to "select some aspects of a perceived reality and make them more salient in a communicating text" (p. 52) and defined salience as "making a piece of information more noticeable, meaningful or memorable to audiences" (p. 52). The underlying presumption is that media messages affect subsequent thought and action.

The use of signifiers to make certain aspects of a story salient is one way to frame a story, and another comes from omitting aspects of a story. The omission of one piece of information or one aspect of a story can sway how people view an event. Framing helps supply the dominant meaning for the audience (Entman, 1993). Entman (1993) suggested researchers should avoid finding secondary meanings from dominant frames. He wrote: "If the text frame emphasizes in a variety of mutually reinforcing ways that the glass is half full, the evidence of social science suggests that relatively few in the audience will conclude it is half empty" (p. 56).

Scheufele (1999) pointed out that frames occur from two perspectives, the media frame and the individual frame: The media frame serves to organize events in such a way that media members can understand (Gitlin, 1980). The media then pass that organized reality to the audience (Scheufele & Tewksbury, 2007). Media frames also serve as part of a working routine for a journalist, providing a road map for the journalist to easily recognize and organize information in a way that allows audiences to easily understand the message (Gitlin, 1980). Media gather information, synthesize it in a way that is easily recognizable to the journalist and also fits into an acceptable frame for the audience, and then pass this information along to the audience in the most easily recognizable form (Scheufele, 1999). Media frames can serve the purpose of systematically affecting how an audience may perceive the information they are presented with (Scheufele, 1999). This is done through a number of processes, including journalistic routines (Zhongdang & Kosicki, 1993). Media frames also establish who is an authority on a situation and who is excluded (Eastman & Billings, 2000).

Examining how *SportsCenter* frames schools from the power conferences compared to other NCAA nonpower men's basketball conferences in Division I and how *SportsCenter*'s coverage has changed requires a model that examines coverage and frames from 2010, 2011, and 2014.

Following two specific approaches by Entman (2004), this research asked whether there is a content bias in *SportsCenter*'s coverage of the NCAA Tournament bubble. To examine this issue, the researcher examined whether *SportsCenter* used the same approach to frame midlevel schools from the power conferences in the same way that it frames top-level schools from nonpower conferences in discussions about the NCAA Tournament's bubble; whether *SportsCenter* omits teams from nonpower conferences (or frames them in a negative light) in discussions about the NCAA Tournament's bubble; and whether *SportsCenter* presented weaker teams from power conferences in a positive light in discussions about the NCAA Tournament bubble. Finally, the research examined *SportsCenter*'s approach to covering the NCAA bubble over time.

## METHODOLOGY

To obtain sufficient data for this study, a single episode of *SportsCenter* was recorded each morning in the three weeks leading up to the day the NCAA Division I men's basketball tournament field was selected in 2010, 2011, and 2014. The three weeks before the tournament constitute the period when the NCAA Tournament bubble is discussed the most. This accounted for 63 *SportsCenter* presentations, or 21 presentations per year. Shows were recorded during the morning cycle of *SportsCenter* because that gave producers of the show time to update information from the previous night.

During each show, all mentions of NCAA men's college basketball (as they pertained to the upcoming NCAA Tournament) were coded. Mentions included these terms: (a) game stories; (b) graphics that mentioned a particular team; (c) commentary from ESPN analysts about a team's chances for qualifying for the tournament; (d) graphics that mentioned the team as one of the last four in or first four out of the tournament, according to ESPN's so-called Bracketologist Joe Lunardi; and (e) previews that stated the importance of a team winning an upcoming game to solidify their chances for qualifying as an at-large team.

In all, *SportsCenter* ran clips on 157 college basketball games in the 2010 season, 132 game clips from the 2011 season, and 134 clips in 2014. Comments about the NCAA Tournament by basketball hosts and analysts, including Lunardi, Doug Gottlieb, Jay Bilas, Dick Vitale, Hannah Storm, Hubert Davis, Digger Phelps, and Rece Davis, were recorded and transcribed. Conversations between pundits discussing the possibilities of certain teams qualifying for the tournament were transcribed, as well as the graphics the show used to differentiate teams on the television screen. Terms like *RPI* (Ratings Percentage Index) were examined in connection with mentions of conferences and conference affiliation, examining how ESPN concentrated on those terms. Other terms examined included mentions of wins against the RPI top 50 and losses against the RPI top 50 and the importance analysts placed on those attributes. Other terms examined included *the eye test* and *bid thief.* To check intercoder reliability, two coders examined 10% of the recorded *SportsCenter*s and using Holsti's intercoder reliability method, the results came back at .93.

## RESULTS

After examining the data for patterns in its coverage of the NCAA Tournament bubble before the 2010 and 2011 tournaments, four frames became evident. First, and most evident, was that teams competing for one of the final at-large bids from the power conferences became the dominant narrative of *SportsCenter*'s NCAA Tournament bubble conversation. Teams from the top six conferences were mentioned more often and served as the dominant frame. Second, narratives describing teams from the nonpower conferences were inconsistent, negative, or absent and frames were used to describe these teams as inferior to schools from the power conferences. Third, though the conference that teams played in was not supposed to be a factor to the NCAA selection committee, ESPN's *SportsCenter* coverage appeared to place importance on such affiliations, particularly in 2010 and 2011. The importance of conferences diminished in the 2014 round of *SportsCenter*s. Finally, *SportsCenter* analysts saw teams from nonpower conferences that lost in their conference tournaments as bid thieves.

## The 2010 and 2011 Tournaments

The first frame dealt with establishing the viability of mediocre or middle-of-the-pack teams from the power conferences as superior to top teams from the nonpower conferences. This frame serves as the dominant frame when examining *SportsCenter*'s coverage of the NCAA men's basketball bubble.

This frame is presented in numerous ways. One method is repeated coverage of teams from these 6 power conferences compared to the other 25 conferences. In 2010, of 157 game clips examined, 71.3% were about teams from the top 6 conferences. In 2011, of the 132 game clips covered, 106 of them, or 78.5%, were from the 6 major conferences. In 2014, 61% of the 134 game clips covered were from the power conferences. The fact that these teams are mentioned so often establishes a specific narrative when *SportsCenter* covers college basketball. That narrative concentrates on the teams from the power conferences and not just on teams ranked in the top 25. When specific teams were identified as bubble teams, *SportsCenter* concentrated its coverage on teams from the top six conferences. During the period of study during the 2010 season, the University of Illinois received 27 mentions in *SportsCenter*, including coverage of all of its games. The University of Minnesota, another Big Ten team, also received plenty of coverage, finishing with 24 mentions on *SportsCenter*. The number of times these teams were mentioned established them as viable bubble teams.

On February 24, 2010, *SportsCenter* ran a preview of the game between Illinois and Michigan: "The bubble this year is really gigantic as we head to March. Sitting squarely atop that, Demitri McCamey and his Fighting Illini, facing Michigan." The University of Illinois won 51–44, and anchor Hannah Storm remarked:

> So, with 10 losses on the year, but they do have 10 wins in conference play. Is this going to be enough to get Illinois to the Dance? They've got an RPI (Ratings Percentage Index) and a strength of schedule outside the top 50, a couple of no-nos there, however, they do have wins over Vanderbilt, at Wisconsin and Michigan State at home, three very impressive wins to help their chances at home.

As Storm delivered her commentary, a graphic popped up with Illinois' résumé. The graphic included the team's RPI of 65, strength of schedule of 68, and its record against teams from the RPI top 50. On March 3, Illinois lost to Ohio State University 73–57. Analyst Doug Gottlieb said this about Illinois: "They were swept by Ohio State; more troubling is the home loss instead of the loss at Ohio State. Look at the inside RPI number, 73, hanging on by just a thread, but I believe Illinois has played itself out, losing four of its last five." The graphic showed Illinois with an 18–12 record and an RPI that had dropped from 65 to 72. On March 8, *SportsCenter* reported on Illinois' loss to the University of Wisconsin. After the game, the graphic showed Illinois with an 18–13 record, an RPI of 72 and a note that said, "(Joe) Lunardi says: IN." The frame was established by repetition. The importance of this coverage relied less on Illinois's credentials to be in the tournament than on the constant discussion of the Illini's chances of making the tournament. The frame placed the University of Illinois on the bubble and considered the school as a legitimate bubble team.

*SportsCenter* framed Minnesota the same way. On February 25, 2010, Minnesota lost to Purdue. The announcers turned their focus to the Golden Gophers. Gottlieb had this to say about the University of Minnesota:

> Minnesota is out. They have a schedule they could win out, and if they do win out, including at Illinois this weekend, you could see them hopping back on the bubble. As we go through the litany of games last night where teams needed to win, they simply lost. The bubble has expanded. It will contract again later at some point, but right now it's expanding. Minnesota is out right now, but they could play themselves back in later.

After defeating Illinois, Minnesota started getting daily mentions as one of the first four teams out in Lunardi's Bracketology segment. This happened for three days until, on March 3, Minnesota lost to Michigan 83–55. Gottlieb, after saying that he believed Illinois was out of the tournament, said this about Minnesota: "I'm not even going to bring up their résumé. They're no longer under consideration. Even if they made a late run to the Big Ten Championship game, I don't think they'd make it."

Illinois and Minnesota were mentioned together. The teams reside in the same conference, and this became important because the show consistently presented the two as a tandem, playing for one spot in the NCAA Tournament. This followed an established narrative. The teams were from the same conference (Big Ten). This is important because conference affiliation is not supposed to play a role in selection for the tournament (Coleman, DuMond, & Lynch, 2010).

Illinois was reported as a candidate for the NCAA Tournament until selection day. The team had an RPI in the 70s and 14 losses (including 6 of its final 7 games) but was mentioned 27 times on ESPN as a viable tournament candidate. Minnesota had an RPI of 60, 12 losses, and was 9–9 in conference play. These two teams were prototypical middling major basketball teams. Combined, they received 51 mentions as possible NCAA Tournament teams. The narrative centered on these teams as ones viewers should consider as viable NCAA squads. Negative mentions with pundits declaring their chances in a negative light served a purpose of keeping the teams in the conversation. *SportsCenter* analysts framed both squads as prototypical bubble teams.

The same frame was prevalent during the 2011 run of *SportsCenter*s examined. The teams that received the most coverage from *SportsCenter* in the weeks leading up to the NCAA Tournament were the University of Colorado (16 mentions in either game stories, résumés, pundit discussions, or mentions as one of the final four in or first four teams out of the tournament), Virginia Tech University (14 mentions), the University of Alabama (16 mentions), and the University of Georgia (12 mentions). The emphasis was on teams from the six major conferences that had questionable résumés. The fates of these schools, and their viability as NCAA Tournament teams, became the dominant frame when reporting on the tournament bubble.

Simultaneously, *SportsCenter* framed schools from outside of the top six conferences as inferior or ignored them. The 2011 coverage of St. Mary's University, a West Coast Conference school that lost its tournament championship game to Gonzaga on March 7, provides an example. On March 8, ESPN's Lunardi reported that St. Mary's was going to make the NCAA Tournament as an at-large team. But after the March 8 story, St. Mary's was mentioned once as an at-large possibility: On March 13, the day of the tournament selection, Lunardi said it would qualify as an at-large bid again that day. St. Mary's did not make the tournament as an at-large bid. No pundits made a case for or against St. Mary's in those five days. St. Mary's did not receive the constant attention that Colorado or Virginia Tech received. St. Mary's, a top team from a nonpower conference, was not mentioned as a viable option. At the same time, teams such as Colorado and Virginia Tech remained in the public's eye. Omission is an important part of framing salience. Leaving St. Mary's out of the discussion kept a viable team from outside of the top six conferences outside of the at-large conversation.

*SportsCenter* concentrated on Colorado during the lead-up to the selection of the 2011 NCAA men's basketball tournament field. Colorado defeated Kansas State three times during the season. Pundits pointed to those wins as proof that Colorado deserved to be in the tournament. On March 9, 2011, Gottlieb compared Villanova, a team from the Big East Conference that fell from 15th in the nation to out of the Associated Press rankings after losing 10 of its past 15 games, to Colorado.

> Villanova, on the numbers, you would be hard to put them in versus, say, a Colorado right now. The logical reason is, with the exception of the loss to VCU, they were stellar. Strength

of schedule was good; they played a decent non-conference schedule. They didn't play a lot of road games outside of Philly—actually, they didn't play one. They've lost 10 of their last 15 games…. Look at Colorado. On pure empirical data, their numbers are far weaker. But 5–6 against RPI top 50, plus they have a road win at K-State. If Colorado were to win two more times, which means another big win against K-State, I would switch to them over Villanova.

Both of these schools had negatives that could have turned committee members against them. Gottlieb concentrated on the aspects that could get them into the tournament. These teams were deemed as natural candidates for selection into the tournament. Compare this to the treatment of the Missouri Valley Conference's University of Northern Iowa before the 2010 tournament. Northern Iowa was ranked 22nd in the nation in late February, when it lost a road game at Evansville. The loss was Northern Iowa's fourth of the season. Said ESPN anchor Storm:

> Northern Iowa has had a fine season at 24–4, 14–3 in the Missouri Valley. They won the regular season in the Valley. One would think, though, that they would have to win the (Missouri Valley Conference) tournament. They have wins over Boston College, Sienna and Iowa, but they do have some bad losses—not only this one against Evansville, but also against DePaul.

Northern Iowa was seemingly being held to a higher standard than Villanova or Colorado. The consistent narrative when discussing the tournament bubble was to emphasize the positive in the six power conferences while mentioning the negatives. At the same time, *SportsCenter* emphasized the negative in teams from the other 25 non-power conferences and mentioned the positive.

In the 2010–2011 season, the University of Rhode Island of the Atlantic 10 conference finished the regular season with a record of 23–9 and an RPI of 40, the lowest RPI ranking of any team that did not make the tournament. Rhode Island was listed as one of the first four in or last four out for nearly the entire three weeks before the tournament, and it had 21 mentions on *SportsCenter*, but few were in the form of discussions. Most mentions came in the form of the "Last Four In, First Four Out" graphics that played daily on the show. When Rhode Island was discussed, the conversation was negative.

This difference in how teams were covered and framed by *SportsCenter* became clearer when examining how *SportsCenter* covered the final four teams in the 2010 and 2011 NCAA Tournament. The final four teams selected into the 2011 NCAA Tournament were the University of Alabama–Birmingham, Virginia Commonwealth University, the University of Southern California, and Clemson University. This is known because the 2011 NCAA Tournament went from 65 to 68 teams and the final four at-large selections played in an opening round game, with the winners advancing as 11 seeds or 12 seeds. Teams left out of the tournament that had an argument for being in the tournament were St. Mary's, Colorado, Virginia Tech, and Harvard.

Alabama–Birmingham ended the season 22–8 and with an RPI of 31. The team was the regular-season champion of Conference USA but was not mentioned as a possible at-large bid on *SportsCenter* in the three weeks preceding the selection of NCAA Tournament field. *SportsCenter* pundits ignored the team until it was selected. The same can be said for Virginia Commonwealth, which entered the NCAA Tournament with a 23–11 record and an RPI of 49. This team was mentioned on *SportsCenter*, but the mentions came from the point of view of Old Dominion University. On March 7, the day of Virginia Commonwealth's game with Old Dominion in the Colonial Athletic Association's tournament championship game, *SportsCenter*'s Lunardi said this about Virginia Commonwealth: "The real game with bubble implications is VCU versus Old Dominion in the Colonial championship game. A win by VCU could give the CAA three bids for the first time in its history."

A day later, after Old Dominion University won, the comment before the game clip was: "Lots of teams around the land are big fans of Old Dominion. If Virginia Commonwealth got a win, a lot of people thinking that could shrink the bubble."

Southern California was 19–14, with an RPI of 66, and Clemson was 21–11, with an RPI of 57. The coverage of Southern California was particularly interesting. On March 7, Lunardi mentioned the team in his "in or out" section, declaring it out but making the comment that the team was "an interesting team sneaking into the conversation." On March 11, the day Southern California played the University of Arizona, Southern California was mentioned again on Lunardi's "First Four Out" list. The next day, after a 67–62 loss to the University of Arizona, Lunardi had the University of Southern California marked as "in," with an RPI of 65. The commentator remarked: "USC is in despite losing to Arizona in the Pac-10 semis." Later in the show, Lunardi justified his switch by saying:

> Schedule strength and quality wins are why Southern Cal is right here, plus the fact they suffered some of their early season losses without starting point guard Jio Fontan—so I think the Trojans are in the tournament.

Both Clemson and Southern California received plenty of coverage and were framed as deserving of invitations to the NCAA Tournament. Even after losses, the teams were portrayed as bubble contenders. Viewers of *SportsCenter* knew they were in the discussion and were the type of teams that were deserving of one of the final four selections into the NCAA Tournament. Virginia Commonwealth and Alabama–Birmingham were ignored. After the two schools from outside of the top six power conferences were selected, *SportsCenter* analysts argued that neither school was in the discussion and that both schools were unworthy of selection into the tournament while schools such as Colorado and Virginia Tech were mistreated by the selection committee.

The term *bid thief* deserves special attention. The term is used to describe a team that has amassed a stellar record over the course of the year and is deserving of an NCAA at-large bid. This team is expected to win its conference tournament and automatically earn that bid. When the team loses, pundits report that this team has fallen into the at-large pool and knocked out another team; therefore, it becomes a bid thief. Bid thieves almost always come from conferences outside of the six conferences.

On March 8, 2011, ESPN's Lunardi said that the Horizon League championship game between Butler University and the University of Milwaukee would be a game with tournament bubble implications:

> You know, Butler is a team that, if you go by the brand, you are obviously going to select them should they need an at-large bid. They've had a very uneven season this year. What happens if they lose to Milwaukee for the third time, this one at Milwaukee for a championship? If Butler gets an at-large bid and Milwaukee gets the automatic, then there is going to be a bid stolen and somebody is going to be left out on Selection Sunday.

Butler, a team that played in the NCAA Tournament championship game the year before, was called a potential bid thief if it lost its tournament championship game. Not only that, but also the team was mentioned as an NCAA Tournament possibility only because of its brand. This maintained the frame against schools from the nonpower conferences. Analysts on this segment framed Butler as a midmajor and therefore inferior to more deserving teams from the six conferences. Butler would go on in 2011 to play again in the Division I finals against Connecticut.

The same frame was used in the 2010 season with St. Mary's. The team won the West Coast Conference final over Gonzaga to earn an automatic bid to the NCAA tournament. Despite the win, pundits framed them as a questionable team.

> It didn't change the bracket map, because we already had St. Mary's in the field. But if St. Mary's had lost, someone could have slipped in. I think I would have kept St. Mary's in, but if you look at the last four in, you have a group that was clearly rooting for Gonzaga. We're not going to put the Gaels in the category of "bid thief," but we do know that at least it would have raised a question for some of these teams, and now it doesn't.

## THE 2014 TOURNAMENT

Research found that *SportsCenter* changed its approach to coverage of the NCAA Tournament bubble in 2014. Most of the conversation about the bubble was gone in 2014. Gone in particular were instances where pundits placed one team from a power conference up against a team from another conference and compared the two teams together. Also, the show no longer compared teams from conferences together as an either/or proposition in terms of the NCAA Tournament. This was emphasized during the March 16, 2014, *SportsCenter* when pundit Jay Bilas made the following comment while talking about possible number one seeds:

> I think the NCAA's logic has some flaws. Wichita State has three wins against teams from the top 50. I think they're a number one seed and among the best teams in college basketball but there is no metric that has them in the top four. I agree that they deserve a number one seed but how do we logically go and pick the next team by counting quality wins.... I think Michigan is really good but I think they're in the same pile as Kansas and Syracuse and some other teams. So, you look at Michigan and look at how they did in the Big Ten but they all tell us that everyone is an independent so the Big Ten shouldn't matter, it's all about the number of quality wins.

Bilas's argument about picking a number one seed reflected a change from previous research. The 2014 bubble coverage did not fit with that of 2010 and 2011. The narrative stayed away from conference affiliation. The teams most often mentioned were teams from traditional power conferences (assuming that the Big East was still treated like a power conference). Two teams from a nonpower conference were mentioned, the University of Dayton and St. Joseph's University, as possible bubble teams in *SportsCenter* mentions of the NCAA bubble. Most talk about the bubble was relegated to an examination of ESPN's Joe Lunardi's bracket predictions, concentrating on the last four teams to qualify and the first four teams out. In 2010 and 2011, pundits discussed these possibilities more often and in more depth.

Two more examples from the 2014 run of *SportsCenters* demonstrated the change in how the tournament bubble was discussed:

> And here's Lunardi's field as we get closer to selection Sunday. The biggest win of the night belongs to Providence. The Friars are now in according to Joey Brackets at the expense of Minnesota. The Gophers join Florida State, Nebraska and Missouri on the outside right now looking in.

The clip, from March 5, showed Providence winning in double overtime and the announcer said afterwards that the win appeared to move into the bracket according to Lunardi. The next clip, from March 6, highlighted Dayton:

> The Dayton Flyers making a case that they deserve to be in after that win against 17th-ranked St. Louis. That win propelled them into Lunardi's last four in. Cal has taken a few steps back after losing three straight. The Golden Bears face Colorado on Sunday to end the season.

No mention was made of conference affiliation or the strength of specific conferences. Still, some major events went unnoticed. On Monday, March 10, the University of Wisconsin–Green Bay lost to Wisconsin–Milwaukee in the Horizon League semifinals. Many online sites, including Jerry Palm and CBS.com, mentioned the importance of the loss and questioned whether Wisconsin–Green Bay would be able to qualify as an at-large, ESPN never mentioned the loss in *SportsCenter* and didn't run a segment on last four in and first four out that day (Palm, 2014).

Finally, the term *bid thief* was only used to describe Providence, a bubble team that won the Big East Tournament to qualify for the tournament. Providence was the most often mentioned team in bubble discussions during the 2014 season. The Friars were mentioned 15 times as a bubble contender.

## CONCLUSION

From this study, it appears *SportsCenter*'s coverage of the NCAA Tournament bubble concentrates on universities from power conferences and the narrative is based on the assumption that mediocre or middling teams from power conferences are the obvious choice to play in the NCAA Tournament. *SportsCenter* also frames teams from non-power conferences differently from teams from power conferences. The emphasis is always placed on the quality of power conferences. This preeminent frame has not changed over the years. *SportsCenter* concentrates its coverage on the power conferences and relegates teams from nonpower conferences as inferior to teams from the top conferences. In many instances, teams from non-power conferences are "othered" or treated as different from the normal. This was evident in coverage of the bubble in 2010 and 2011 and also in its coverage of undefeated Wichita State in consideration for a number-one seed in 2014.

Much of this narrative could be attributed to ESPN's financial obligations to specific conferences. ESPN has multimillion-dollar deals with the five power conferences and had a major deal with the Big East conference through 2013. In comparison, ESPN signed a deal with the Missouri Valley Conference in 2010 for $210,000. The high dollars lead to high visibility and exposure. ESPN promotes teams and conferences connected to ESPN's brand. ESPN has also played a role in conference realignment, prompting former Boston College athletics director Gene DeFilippo to explain Syracuse and Pittsburgh moving to the Atlantic Coast Conference from the Big East in the following way to Boston.com reporter Mark Blaudschun in 2011: "We always keep our television partners close to us," he said. "You don't get extra money for basketball. It's 85 percent football money. TV— ESPN—is the one who told us what to do. This was football; it had nothing to do with basketball" (Blaudschun, 2011, para. 18). DeFilippo later apologized for the remark. Although DeFilippo's comment concentrated on football and specifically said that basketball was a nonfactor, the power of the statement was that ESPN had leverage over the power conferences. Basketball may be the second factor in ESPN's NCAA deliberations, but the network has the ability to determine realignment and, once concluded, a financial responsibility to promote teams in those conferences, in both football and basketball.

One change noticed was the reduction of conversation about the bubble and, in particular, a reduction in conversation about the bubble related to power and nonpower conferences in 2014. This could be because of the trend of success of teams from outside of the power conferences from 2010 to 2013. It could also be because ESPN is uncertain where leagues like the reorganized Big East and American Athletic Conference stand in terms of power conferences. What is certain is that the narrative in 2014 was different from the narrative of 2010 and 2011.

*SportsCenter*'s use of terms like *bid thief* and *eye test* did not change. Both terms remain as a means of promoting or demoting a team without merit. The eye test is most often used as a term that middling majors pass, while strong teams from non-power conferences fail. *Bid thief* was also constantly used as a term for nonpower conference schools until the 2014 example of Providence from the Big East conference. The question remains as to how will ESPN will treat the Big East in upcoming years, considering the network no longer has television rights to its games. Will Big East teams be treated like teams from nonpower conferences or will the network consider the league a power conference?

As the dynamic of change continues during tumultuous times for the NCAA and television networks that cover the NCAA, *SportsCenter*'s coverage may continue to change to reflect those changes. More study is necessary to see whether these trends, particularly in the time of conference realignment, will continue.

# CHAPTER FOURTEEN

# Lipsyte, the League, and the "Leader"

## An Ombudsman's Tale

DAVID STATON

In late August 2013, sports news and entertainment giant ESPN formally dropped its association with PBS's stalwart, public affairs series *Frontline* on a documentary concerning players' brain injuries in the National Football League (NFL). The media entities had collaborated extensively for 15 months. The work of two seasoned investigative ESPN reporters, brothers Mark Fainaru-Wada and Steve Fainaru (a Pulitzer Prize winner), provided the nucleus of the news gathering team. Their reporting included a series of investigative stories, *NFL at a Crossroads: Investigating a Health Crisis*, which aired on the ESPN franchise *Outside the Lines* in the months preceding the *Frontline* documentary. *League of Denial* was slated to debut in early October.

In the wake of its abandonment of the project, ESPN found itself issuing denials, defenses, and decisions. In the United States, ESPN's eponymously titled flagship cable network (it has seven domestic cable channels) reaches 98.5 million households and approaches 3 million viewers each day with its primetime slate of sporting events, news reports, and talk/entertainment programming. So when the announcement of the split with PBS became known via a *Frontline* press release, many news and information outlets used the opportunity to question the sports industry leader's commitment to journalism. However, a thorough review of the press coverage surrounding the event finds few who spoke out or wrote in a public forum of its faithfulness to ethics, journalistic or otherwise. Rather, the tone generally sounded something like this:

> So what's more damaging to a corporate image: to be considered sloppy, naive or compromised? Or all three? You get to pick in the wake of ESPN's announcement Thursday that it was removing its brand from an upcoming two-part documentary by PBS's *Frontline* that "reveals the hidden story of the NFL and brain injuries." (Lipsyte, 2013a, para. 1)

That's how ESPN's ombudsman Robert Lipsyte led off his column titled "Was ESPN Sloppy, Naive, or Compromised?" published on espn.go.com three days after the network pulled its name from the *Frontline* documentary. The network appoints ombudsman for 18-month stints to monitor its television, radio, print, and digital offerings (it has a vast and heavily trafficked website) on behalf of the public, acting as a sort of reader/viewer advocate. A respected, long-time sports journalist in print and broadcast, Lipsyte began his ESPN ombudsman stint two months prior to the PBS controversy. The pointed assessment in his August 25, 2013, article was among the first columns he wrote in the ombudsman's capacity. As things played out, it wouldn't be the last time he tackled the topic.

At the heart of the *League of Denial*'s reporting is the linking of NFL players' experiences with severe medical consequences from game-related concussions to the League's awareness and denials that such a causal relationship existed. In short, the reporting compellingly ties chronic traumatic encephalopathy (CTE) to in-game play and shows the NFL as knowingly callous in its disregard for player welfare. CTE is a brain disease, previously called dementia pugilistica, which produces aggression, anger, depression, and dementia-like symptoms. Breakthrough research early in 2013 saw UCLA medical researchers able to diagnose CTE in living players. Previously, however, the disease was only diagnosed postmortem, and evidence garnered from those autopsies fuels *League of Denial*. As Fainaru and Fainaru-Wada reported, in 49 of 50 postmortem brain studies of NFL player's brains, chronic brain damage was present. Further, *League of Denial* contended the League had ongoing awareness of the issue and actively set out to discount the science behind the football-concussion-disease nexus. The reporting does not shy away from suggestions implicit and explicit that the League knew it had a health crisis on its hands and, in defense of its empire, concocted and crafted junk science, misdirection, character assassination, and steadfast denials to protect its brand.

With so much at stake, it is fair to consider why the press were not more vocal in condemning ESPN's actions. And why was Lipsyte, in his capacity of ombudsman or a "reader's agent," not fully invested in explaining the decision at length to the readership he is called upon to serve? Was he caught between duty to readership and duty to management?

## CODES AND CONFLICT

Ettema and Glasser (1985) claim "investigative reporting is unabashedly moralistic" (p. 203) and performed by the best journalists doing the best journalism (p. 184). Kovach and Rosenstiel, in their touchstone book, *The Elements of Journalism* (2001), echo that notion: "Every journalist—from the newsroom to the boardroom—must have a personal sense of ethics and responsibility—a moral compass. What's more, they have a responsibility to voice their personal conscience out loud and allow for others around them to do so as well" (p. 181). A code literally and figuratively, professional and personal, binds such efforts. In this case, because "The Worldwide Leader in Sports" operates on a number of media platforms, more than one code of ethics may have applied. However, the two most germane to that of the ombudsman role are the Society for Professional Journalists (SPJ) and the Public Relations Society of America (PRSA). Although Lipsyte was a sports journalist since 1957, the ESPN hiring marked his initial foray into the working world of the ombudsman, a position that often requires blending hard-nosed journalism with the wordsmithing skills of public relations. Early on in his tenure, he would bristle at the notion of his job being compared to that of a public relations professional, but seminal literature in the study of ombudsmen (Ettema & James, 1987) demonstrates ombudsmen routinely deal with the thorny distinction between public accountability and public relations. SPJ and PRSA are professional media organizations, employing a code of ethics, and specific language in each speaks to being honest, accurate, fair, and accountable to the public. Part of the SPJ code, for instance, insists on accountability as well: "Journalists are accountable to their readers, listeners, viewers and each other" (Society for Professional Journalists, 1996, para. 5). And, too, the public relations field has an emphasis on open communication and accountability: "Protect and advance the free flow of accurate and truthful information" and "Foster informed decision making through open communication" is part of the language in its code (Public Relations Society of America, 2000). Clearly, accountability is a valued principle with these associations and its practitioners. As to defining accountability, Christians (1985) puts a fine point on it:

> To say that agents are accountable for their behavior means that they can be called to judgment in respect of their obligations. That is, one can legitimately raise questions or even lay charges if necessary, and expect reasonable answers…. within the sociopolitical frameworks in which this notion operates, vis-a-vis the media, we must consider it in three different senses: the media are accountable to the government, to themselves as professionals, and to the public. (p. 3)

ESPN is no stranger to hot-button or controversial coverage having been held accountable and, by turns, criticized and praised for such high-profile sports stories as the Penn State sexual abuse scandal, its extensive coverage of steroids and performance-enhancing drugs in professional and collegiate sports, and the made-for-television spectacle of *The Decision*, in which National Basketball Association (NBA) player LeBron James, at the time a coveted free agent, announced his decision to sign with the Miami Heat. In this regard, network executives surely knew its reporters were narrating a potentially tendentious story (and had been for well more than a year) in which professional football players were demonstrated to have suffered grievous injury. At the same time, the network by virtue of its reportorial discovery had knowledge that the *prima facie* duty by NFL to protect its laborers was being ignored. It also held forth a promise to the audience to report the story. It had an obligation to operate within a set of understood conventions that govern behavior (Elliot-Boyle, 1985). One is obligated to fulfill promises, Ross (1951) contends: "ease of performance is no necessary or even unusual characteristic of that which is our duty" (p. 109). In this case, the sports network's duty was to do what was right and what was good, though it may not have been easy.

## RIGHT AND GOOD

In 1930, Ross's *The Right and the Good* was published by Oxford University Press. In this influential work, the Scottish philosopher sought to "examine the nature, relations, and implications of three conceptions which appear to be fundamental in ethics—those of 'right,' 'good' in general, and 'morally good'" (p. 1). Right and good are not a hand-in-glove fit, Ross contends. Maximizing good is a concern, but not the only concern underscoring duty; a right decision may not have a good outcome. What makes actions right is that they produce more good than could have been produced by making another choice (p. 16). Ross puts it this way: "An act is not right because it, being one thing, produces good results different from itself; it is right because it is itself the production of a certain state of affairs. Such production is right in itself, apart from any consequence" (p. 46). Such a position has been called "a universalist contextualism: universal in abstract *prima facie* duty, contextual in actual duty" (Meyers, 2003, p. 93). By his measure, Ross placed himself somewhere between Aristotle's virtues (his longtime subject of study) and Kant's categorical imperative.

A significant part of Ross's philosophy holds there are a variety of relationships that are morally significant including potential benefactor-potential beneficiary and promiser-promisee. This relationship of promiser and promisee would describe a duty between the representatives of a media outlet (the reporters and ombudsman alike at ESPN) and audience. These relationships are characterized by *prima facie* (or conditional) duties: "Unlike the duty to promote the good, the duties of fidelity, reparation and gratitude rest on personal relations with others, which generate special rather than general duties" (Skelton, 2012, FE 76, 186).

In determining these special duties, Ross points out there is no strict ranking among the *prima facie* duties that apply equally across every situation. However, the one which is "more incumbent" becomes one's actual moral duty. Ross provides a list of these duties, though he notes it is not a comprehensive list. This list of *prima facie* duties include (a) fidelity as a duty to fulfill; (b) reparation as a duty to make up for previous wrongful acts; (c) gratitude as duty to repay others for past favors; (d) justice as a duty to prevent or correct a mismatch; (e) beneficence as a duty to improve the conditions of others; (f) self-improvement as a duty to improve one's own condition; and (g) nonmaleficence as a duty not to injure others. The debt to Aristotle is evident here and where Ross does not specifically mention "the mean" in decision making, he again offers echoes of the Greek philosopher. With both Ross and Aristotle, personal judgment enters the picture. In *The Right and the Good*, Ross (1930) borrows from Aristotle's *Nichomachean Ethics* directly, writing "the decision rests with perception" (p. 42). As a result, "where ethical intuitions are concerned, what we intuit are *prima facie* obligations to act dutifully, duties which can be overridden by stronger duties, as the situation dictates" (Cameron, n.d., para. 3). In other words, Ross posits a pluralistic deontological view with something of a hierarchy; the duty of beneficence, for instance, trumps that of self-improvement. In this way, the rigidity of Kantian absolute power of moral authority and act utilitarianism (Ross calls that philosophic strain hedonistic) is ultimately rejected in favor of considered decision based on moral intuition or perception.

Moral intuition may seem a bit squishy, but Ross believes that moral maturity points toward clarity when two duties appear to conflict. Ross in fact compares intuition or self-evidence as to the principles of mathematics; they cannot be deduced from anything else we know, yet we know they are true (Carson, 2005, p. 141). The decision is evident for those who have "reached sufficient mental maturity and have given sufficient action to the proposition" (Ross, 1930, p. 20). And, following that determination whatever that actual duty is, one is morally obliged. By abandoning the *League of Denial* documentary, ESPN and its ombudsman abdicated their duty in numerous ways, leaving an unfulfilled promise to its audience and its core mission. To be sure, there were several bad actors in this scenario, however, for ombudsman Lipsyte acts as sort of a "point man" for the organization and, in a sense, its public face. It is this role and how Lipsyte enacted it that I wish to interrogate. However, a bit of a back story of some of the other players in this scenario, their investment, and the stakes of the enterprise are worth a brief consideration.

## THE LEAGUE AND THE "LEADER"

The NFL is the world's most lucrative professional sports league, collectively valued at more than $37 billion (Ozanian, 2012). It grossed more than $9 billion in 2013 (Burke, 2013). "The Worldwide Leader in Sports" (ESPN's self-styled slogan) adds nearly $2 billion each year to the League's coffers. In exchange for that consideration, the sports TV powerhouse is allowed to broadcast one game a week for the length of the NFL regular season. That game, *Monday Night Football*, is ESPN's number-one-rated show by a wide margin.

With such sums at stake and in an effort to sustain the ratings juggernaut, the potential for conflicts or compromise of journalistic standards abounds. ESPN holds itself forth as a news and entertainment organization and in any amount of publicity materials it fully stresses the caliber of its journalists, many of whom have distinguished, traditional news backgrounds in print and broadcast. The network's president, John Skipper, says a line is drawn between news and programming (entertainment) functions:

> We have a programming group, whose job it is to acquire rights, to work with the leagues, to be their partners in presenting their games on our air—and then we have the news and information group, whose job it is to do enterprise journalism.... And the programming guys cannot interfere with the journalism. The single thing that irritates me most is the assumption that we have some sort of unmanageable conflict.... We employ hundreds of writers and journalists, and I don't think you'll find a single instance of somebody saying they were asked to pull off of a story. (Guthrie, 2013, para. 13)

Nonetheless, news and entertainment can be an uneasy marriage and a sage referee may be required to keep one from subsuming the other. This official might best balance the needs of one or the other by embracing ethical guidelines and best practices intrinsic to each. At the same time, this person could offer to act as a go between for the public and the press and to offer a degree of transparency; viewers would know what role (entertainment or news) according to particular rules of order. With regards to the news role, this is why the position of ombudsman was created. And this, ostensibly, is why ESPN appointed Lipsyte as its latest ombudsman.

## WATCHING THE WATCHERS

When the Hutchins Commission published its findings, *A Free and Responsible Press*, in 1947, it accorded tremendous power to the press and tremendous protections, going so far as to assert those safeguards "as a moral right because it has an aspect of duty about it" (Commission on the Freedom of the Press, 1947,

p. 8). It also issued a warning: "If modern society requires great agencies of mass communication, if these concentrations become so powerful that they are a threat to democracy… then those agencies must control themselves or be controlled by government" (p. 5). Toward monitoring themselves, the report suggested turning the watchdog into the watched:

> If the shortcomings of the American press can best be overcome by the efforts of the press itself, the abandonment of the practice of refraining from mutual comment and the adoption instead of a resolute policy of criticism of the press by the press are indicated. (Commission on the Freedom of the Press, p. 66)

This, needless to say, was not well received by its intended audience. The outspoken press critic Walter Lippmann offered this observation, "I may say that I have tried (such criticism) and have had it tried on me, and my conclusion is the hard feelings it causes are out of all proportion to the public benefit it causes" (Nemeth, 2003, p. 6).

To great extent, the Commission's recommendations lay dormant for some 20 years, but in 1967, those same concerns were given new voice, this time by *New York Times* labor writer and editor A. H. Raskin. Unabashed and unafraid to take on an unpopular position, Raskin "took to task what he saw as the 'unshatterable smugness' of most publishers, editors and the 'self righteous, self-satisfaction and self-congratulation' that characterized so much of the American press" (Ettema & Glasser, 1987, p. 3). What was needed was a department of internal criticism and the head of this department "ought to be given enough independence in the paper to serve as an ombudsman for the reader" (p. 4). This assertion and the ideas and ideals of the ombudsman fits neatly within Ross's ethical framework. An appropriate obligation by members of the press would have its members follow several of his outlined duties, including fidelity (to its readers), justice (in its role as the Fourth Estate), and beneficence (to improve the condition of others).

The same year as Raskin's call to arms, the *Louisville Courier-Journal* became the first newspaper in the United States to appoint an ombudsman. Three years later, the *Washington Post* followed suit. And, in 1971, Ben Bagdikian, a celebrated media critic with a lengthy career as a journalist, was hired for that slot with the *Post*. It didn't last long. Bagdikian, citing a conflict with management over where his loyalties lay, left the job in less than a year (Nemeth, 2000). "I was told that I was disloyal to management," Bagdikian recounted, "and I said, 'Well, as ombudsman I don't regard my loyalty as being to the management, but to the readers'" (Nemeth, 2003, p. 51). This clearly speaks to a particular and practical issue for the ombudsman; the watchdog who is supposed to guard the integrity of the discipline and the publication must also not bite the hand that feeds. But, to do so, a strong likelihood exists that the ombudsman's role moves from that of public accountability to one of public relations. Ettema and Glasser (1987) performed seminal research in this area. Among their findings,

> That newspaper ombudsmen in the United States generally do not have the authority to protect reader interests, except perhaps in the most token sense, lends credence to the second reason editors cite for not creating such a position: Because ombudsmen are really answerable to newspaper management, not to the newspaper's readers, an ombudsman can only widen the gap between a newspaper and its readers. (Ettema & Glasser, 1987, p. 5)

It is a tricky business, as Ettema and Glasser (1987) noted, placing the ombudsman on the horns of a two-pronged dilemma; publishers don't want a strong advocate that might cripple morale, but they also don't want a weak individual in that spot who would parrot institutional decisions. And, as is made evident in the previous passage, editors look for reasons not to hire an ombudsman. Ben Bradlee, the *Washington Post's* longtime leader, quipped, when you hire an ombudsman, "you're buying a little trouble" (Nemeth, 2003, p. 146). The groundbreaking study by Ettema and Glasser in 1987, "Public Accountability or Public Relations? Newspaper Ombudsmen Define Their Role," sought to interview each of the ombudsmen in North America. Of the more than 1,600 newspapers being published in the United States at that time, the researchers found that 33 had ombudsmen. Among the significant findings from the 32 who responded to their survey instrument:

- Ombudsmen, overwhelmingly White and male and selected to the position from within the news organization, rated as their strongest obligations to "give readers a sense that the newspaper cares about them; to sensitize reporters and editors to readers' concerns; to sensitize management to readers' concerns."
- On the average, several public relations activities are much more important to the ombudsmen's conceptions of their role than are several press criticism activities.
- The ombudsmen most strongly endorse the idea that in the "final analysis," their loyalty is to readers and least strongly endorsed the idea that "in the final analysis" their loyalty is to the newspaper.

These results appeared in *Journalism Quarterly* and its editor at the time, Guido H. Stempel III, heard from a number of displeased ombudsmen. They were not happy with the indication they were aligned with public relations. "Stempel believed the reaction was a result of the tendency among newspeople to associate the term 'public relations' with the stereotype of corporate communications specialists who would do anything to avoid revealing information harmful to their organizations" (Nemeth, 2000, p. 62).

In 1999, Nemeth replicated the Ettema and Glasser study. Salaries had changed and some women were serving in ombudsmen capacity, but little else significant had changed. Each of the major data points was quite similar. "As in the 1985 study, the ombudsmen in 1999 rated their public relations activities consistently ahead of their public criticism activities" (Nemeth, 2003, p. 36). Less support for press criticism roles was also noted. In a succinct summation of the findings, Nemeth noted.

> Because handling complaints unavoidably requires dealing with the public, the ombudsman who successfully handles complaints and solves problems provides a public relations benefit to the news organization.... While it is clear that ombudsmen have a public relations function, it is less clear that they act as agents of media accountability. Media accountability can be defined as "the process by which news organizations or journalists are obliged to render an account of their activities to recognized constituencies such as audience members, news sources, advertisers, professional colleagues, or government regulatory bodies." (Nemeth, 2000, p. 63)

The lead is buried above, but the takeaway is evident—whether acting in a public relations roles or the capacity of a journalist, there exists an obligation to provide an accounting to the public. Lipsyte's is one voice in a large company, but it is a significant one. And ESPN must have thought the role of ombudsman was significant, having retained someone (or in the case of Poynter Review Project a small group) to oversee and explain its goings on since it hired its first in 2005. For the ESPN ombudsman, there is much to be accountable for and many to be accountable to. Kovach and Rosenstiel (2014) are direct on this point: "The primary purpose of journalism is to provide the information citizens need to be self governing." (p. 9)

## OVERSIZED OVERSIGHT

ESPN is a big, fast-moving operation valued at more than $50 billion; the market value of the *New York Times*, by comparison, is $1.3 billion. The fact sheet for the "Worldwide Leader in Sports" details a dizzying array of figures aside from the viewership data previously mentioned: it presents 9,000 hours of radio programming a week to 24 million listeners; its website, espn.go.com, generates hundreds of millions of hits monthly with an average viewing audience of 77,000 each minute; that same website posts about 800 items each day.

"They're just so freaking huge, that it's almost impossible now to talk about values across the entire organization," the Poynter Institute's ethicist Kelly McBride told a reporter (Deggans, 2013a, para. 11). McBride was the lead writer for the Poynter Review Project, a small group of writers from the institute that served in the capacity of ESPN ombudsman immediately prior to Lipsyte's appointment. "As you go from product to product," McBride continued, "it's not the same consistent set of values because they all serve different communities. The biggest challenge for them when it comes to ethics is identifying on a really large scale what their core values are" (para. 13). McBride also noted that, from her perspective, ESPN's interest in identifying its values ebbs and flows.

That uneasy tension noted in the 1985 Ettema and Glasser study lurks here: Are ombudsmen loyal to readers or to their publications? And what of those values? How and in what way are they expressed and how does that intersect with the role of ombudsman? Do these values align with an ethical code of SPJ or of PRSA? Regardless, Lipsyte, who in the case of the *League of Denial* was straddling multimedia worlds by writing a response on a website about a filmic journalistic effort, might have turned to a professional code of ethics for either of those disciplines to guide his actions. It is the duty of the ombudsman to act as advocate or agent for the viewer or reader; he or she is, in effect, policing policy and adherence to standards.

Lipsyte also may have looked for guidance or suggestion from something more particular to his ESPN job—the Organization of News Ombudsmen (ONO). In its 10-point mission statement, ONO (n.d.) spells out its commitment to, among other things, "protecting and enhancing the quality of journalism by encouraging respectful and truthful discourse about journalism's practices and purposes" (n.d. para. 20) and "the news ombudsman's primary objective is to promote transparency within his / her news organization." (n.d. para 21). These objectives are similar to those of SPJ and PRSA and they echo the reasons top leaders of "The Worldwide Leader in Sports" cite(d) when hiring its ombudsmen. John Walsh, ESPN's executive vice president and executive editor, noted on its website upon the appointment of the Poynter Review Project: "Our goal is to improve our content through increased accountability, transparency and timeliness" (ESPN MediaZone, 2011, para. 2). And, when Lipsyte succeeded that group and assumed the ombudsman position, his endorsement and abilities were similarly heralded: "We struck gold with Mr. Lipsyte…. he's a legend in the field" (Deggans, 2013b, para. 8). Stiegman told a Poynter Institute staffer:

> He was provocative, was mindful of what ESPN's business goals were, mindful of ESPN's goals as a journalistic entity and he challenged us. He offered a tremendous analogy: He sees the role as being a window washer for ESPN. It's about transparency; his job is to keep those windows clean. (para. 8)

In this assessment, the upper echelon of ESPN is invoking, however pragmatically articulated, an ethical obligation of transparency. Or, "The Worldwide Leader" is effectively making a promise to its vast audience and heeding the advice of the outgoing ombudsman, the Poynter Review Project, which in its last column cautioned:

> Whether the story is child sexual abuse, head injuries, the proper role of college athletics, performance-enhancing drugs, public funding of stadiums or the advancement of women,

we need journalists such as ESPN's—and they, in turn, need standards and practices that are clearly and wisely defined, and faithfully followed. (McBride & Fry, 2012, para. 39)

For his part, Lipsyte shared his vision and understanding of the position during a live chat on the espn.go.com website:

I'm not a PR entity in the sense that I represent you and anybody who is listening to, watching or reading ESPN. I'm not doing PR for ESPN. I'm trying to make ESPN more transparent for you, and let you know why they do certain things and their motivations. Sometimes I think they are dead wrong, and I'll say that too. That is not PR. (ESPN Sportsnation, 2013)

## NETWORK OF DENIAL?

The events leading up to Lipsyte's Internet chat had occurred several weeks prior. Following the lead of a *New York Times* article on August 22, many news outlets began to report of a hastily called meeting that took place at a Manhattan eatery between the top brass of the NFL, Commissioner Roger Goodell and ESPN's John Skipper. "The meeting was combative," the *Times* reported. "Leagues know that broadcasters like ESPN are both journalistic and entertainment entities, and they are adept at exploiting the divisions between them" (Miller & Belson, 2013, para. 7). In response to the *Times* article, both the NFL and ESPN issued denials that the "combative" meeting had led to the sports network dropping its backing of the *Frontline* project. On its behalf, ESPN declared it was unhappy with the lack of editorial control it was able to exert on the documentary. To be precise, Skipper strongly objected to a trailer promoting *League of Denial*, dubbing the commercial teaser over the top and overly sensationalized. The two-minute promotional ad serves up a sequence of 35 jarring hits drawn from NFL contests, *Frontline* narrator Will Lyman sonorously intoning "*Frontline* investigates what the NFL knew and when they knew it," and an insistent soundtrack featuring Jay Z and Rihanna. Moving forward, ESPN would not lend its name or brand to the project.

Without regard to underlying reasons, what was clear is that ESPN pulled its name from the project one week after the meeting. The timing is, at best, odd. A scant three weeks prior, ESPN's senior coordinating producer attending a Television Critics Association Panel "described the collaboration as a 'conscious decision' to 'literally get in bed with *Frontline*.'" He explained that the NFL "'is going to have to understand that'" (Hayden, 2013, para. 2). The top producer also recognized *Frontline* as the gold standard in long form investigative journalism. When the announcement broke, the NFL preseason was in full swing, with regular season games (and *Monday Night Football*) a couple of weeks away. Scores of media outlets seized the opportunity to question the timing of the "break up" and the sports network's commitment to investigative journalism. And though the efficacy and effects of ESPN's withdrawal were discussed, ethics have largely gone unmentioned or have been soft-pedaled.

On October 15, following the broadcast of *League of Denial*, Lipsyte weighed in on the public withdrawal by his employer of its association with the PBS *Frontline* exposé. The nearly two-hour program was forthright in linking a debilitating illness to injuries sustained by NFL players in the line of duty. He led off the column, titled "Winning Ugly: ESPN journalism prevails," with this opening salvo, "By the end of the show, after all the questioning, the carping and the confusion over credits, it was clear that serious journalism had won. ESPN could be proud of its contributions to the PBS *Frontline* documentary *League of Denial: The NFL's Concussion Crisis*" (Lipsyte, 2013b, para. 1). With this column, Lipsyte's goal to "keep those windows clean" carelessly left some visible smudges on ESPN's reputation.

Ombudsman Lipsyte, in his postmortem column, followed the "'atta boy!'" that serious journalism had won, with a few questions surrounding integrity and morale. However, on balance, he illuminated several points in defense of the "triumphant and bittersweet moment" of the decision to drop its affiliation and the subsequent airing of the program: much of the reporting had appeared in shorter forms previously on ESPN because Fainaru and Fainaru-Wada had been staffers; the agreement between PBS and ESPN's Fainaru and Fainaru-Wada was "seat of the pants" (para. 36); viewers might be suffering from "concussion fatigue" (para. 29); *League of Denial* was a ratings success for PBS. Lipsyte concludes the column: "Despite what at times seemed like sloppiness or *naïveté* or compromise, ESPN journalism won. It may have won ugly, but it won" (para. 41). Curiously, however, in Lipsyte's penultimate paragraph he writes, "There is no end of stories out there, not least the ramifications of the settlement and the sequestered information that the ESPN audience needs as parents, players and fans, to make their emotional, physical and moral choices."

The invocation of morals is curious in a column that, though acknowledging some culpability, speaks to or, even worse, rationalizes the abrogation of that duty. That there were other bad actors in this scenario is beside the point. Lipsyte, in any capacity, was the public's eyes and ears. His staunch denials that his role of ombudsman equated with public relations does not get him off the hook for not acting in a conscious manner to the benefit of his audience. His duty, which is by definition tied to his role as ombudsman, is to offer transparency and understanding to the editorial decisions of his employer. The duty, in this case, seen through the prism of Ross's *prima facie* obligations, would include fidelity in the keeping of promises or agreements—the promise to uphold journalistic tenets, or those of the ombudsman or those of public relations or those of ONO, the professional ombudsman association. And, if his decision seemed to conflict with other duties, either personal or professional, he may have performed a sort of mental balance sheet to arrive at the "right" action. Finally, moral intuition also could have guided his decision.

By clamping down on the spreading of significant information, in a compelling and insidious sense, ESPN and the NFL did not have their feet held to the fire for their lack of compliance to the duties of beneficence and malfeasance. They are, arguably, culpable in withholding information that could prevent brain injury and the moral decision regarding that simply cannot present any conflicting duty. Lipsyte, to a certain degree, appears complicit in not clearly revealing the story behind the story; big money shaped this decision, of that there can be little doubt. The moral obligation here is clear and does not present conflicting charges of duty: a core value, either by definition of the public relations code or the professional journalists' code, insists on transparency. From the perspective of Ross, Lipsyte's duties of fidelity are clear-cut and to ignore them is an abrogation of his responsibilities. Lipsyte should have done what was right and what was good. But something else got in the way of his moral duty—an observance of the rights and the furtherance of others was not observed. "As soon as a man does an action because he thinks he will promote his own interests thereby, he is acting not from a sense of its rightness but from self-interest" (Ross, p. 16). Lipsyte likely did not act solely in his self-interest; rather, he selectively reported to his audience and likely placated his ESPN bosses. In so doing, he did not follow moral intuition, adhere to professional codes of ethics, or properly act on moral duty.

## CONCLUSION

On April 2, 2014, the Peabody Awards, honoring excellence in quality programming for TV and radio, announced its winners. *League of Denial* and PBS received an award (the Peabody does not specify category) for the *Frontline* investigation. Similarly, ESPN's *Outside the Lines* franchise received a Peabody for its concussion reporting, *NFL at a Crossroads: Investigating a Health Crisis.* To each organization's credit, both likely contributed to the growing dialogue surrounding the issues of concussions and CTE in the NFL. But it's worth noting that Peabody Award judges considered the most compelling aspect of ESPN's reporting to be the evidence of questionable advice given by a league-sanctioned physician, who painted concussions as minor injuries and wielded much influence in shaping league medical policies. The jurors for the PBS documentary, however, noted the film's "dogged pursuit of evidence, meticulous argumentation, and willingness to take on the most powerful organization in professional sports" (n.d. para. 1).

Appearances matter in an inherently visual medium and ESPN has knowingly and masterfully crafted an internationally successful look and brand built largely on image and outsize, on-air personalities. It *is* the Worldwide Leader in Sport broadcasting according to *Forbes* magazine (2012) and its position is staunchly guarded and protected by Skipper and the network. In its official announcement regarding the subject (released August 22, 2013, little more than six weeks before *League of Denial* was slated for broadcast), the network emphasized there would be no co-branding on the project in its press release to other media outlets. Additionally, it followed that release—and the attendant attention it garnered—with a pointed denial that its relationship with the NFL had shaped its decision: "'The decision to remove our branding was not a result of concerns about our separate business relationship with the NFL.' said ESPN in an emailed statement" (Tracy, 2013, para. 2). The network's emphasis on branding and business rather than notions of truth or integrity is telling and clearly at odds with Kovach and Rosenstiel's statement regarding journalism's primary purpose. In his remarks on the subject, ombudsman Lipsyte also falls short of the ideals and primary objective set forth in ONO's guidelines to promote transparency of the news organization. In his column reflecting on the announcement of the de-branding, "Was ESPN Sloppy, Naive, or Compromised," Lipsyte (2013a) notes:

> Commissioners are always trying to strong-arm or sweet-talk ESPN executives, especially Skipper. How well they succeed is a matter of constant speculation, both among Ombuddies and from some inside ESPN. Right or wrong, there is a perception that the company's decisions—both long-term and moment-by-moment—are often made to promote, or at least not provoke, important partners. (para. 15)

At this juncture, Lipsyte might have defused this "perception" with an honest account, taking the opportunity to address previous instances in which the NFL used its influence with the network, namely its cancellation of ESPN's one-time hit series *Playmakers*, a fictional account of a professional football team. Instead, two paragraphs later, readers encountered this quote from Lipsyte's boss, Skipper: "I am the only one at ESPN who has to balance the conflict between journalism and programming" (para. 17). That sounds like an explanation—and an expectation—an ombudsman would investigate. It does not sound typical of the separation that exists in most broadcast network structures between newsrooms and programming or in journalistic print media between advertising and editorial departments. It also creates the appearance of a blurring between editorial and entertainment. In the case of *League of Denial*, that is a compromise the powerful institution does not seem to mind making nor, apparently, did its ombudsman.

# CHAPTER FIFTEEN

# Power Through the People

## ESPN and the Impact of User-Circulated Emotional Value on News Efficacy

SAMUEL M. JAY

On September 10, 2013, *Sports Illustrated* (*SI*) published the first part of "The Dirty Game," a five-part investigative report that chronicled years of violations the Oklahoma State University football program committed (*SI* Staff, 2013). In the days that followed, the Oklahoma State football team, which was entering the third week of the season undefeated and ranked 11th and 12th in the *USA Today* and *Associated Press* Division I college football polls, respectively, became a major topic of discussion in sports news. The Cowboys' success only strengthened the circulation of the story, which eventually transcended both *SI* and sports media coverage as *SI*'s rivals ESPN (Trotter, 2013), *Bleacher Report* (Chiari, 2013), and *USA Today* (Myerberg, 2013) ran news of the allegations along with non-sports outlets *Business Insider* (Manfred, 2013a), *Forbes* (Smith, 2013), and *The Christian Science Monitor* (Murphy, 2013).

    *SI*'s five-part series was broken down into individual reports ("The Overview," "The Money," "The Academics," "The Drugs," and "The Sex") that documented the "juiciest allegations" (Manfred, 2013b, para. 1) surrounding the Oklahoma State program, including players being paid for on-field performances, grade manipulation and other academic misconduct, the use and selling of drugs, and that members of a hostess program (Orange Pride) were having sex with Oklahoma State recruits (*SI* Staff, 2013). The story was made more sensational with testimony from former Oklahoma State players who told George Dohrmann and Thayer Evans, the *SI* reporters who wrote the articles, that the coaching staffs of both former head coach Les Miles and current head coach Mike Gundy knew of the violations and took part in the establishment and continuation of the rule breaking (*SI* Staff, 2013).

The event would evolve into a full-blown "scandal" (Manfred, 2013a, para. 1; 2013b, para. 1), a term used to describe only the worst instances of wrongdoing and rule breaking in sports such as the performance-enhancing drug use by the New York Yankees' Alex Rodriguez, which was referred to as a "doping scandal" (Corcoran, 2014, para. 3) and the New Orleans Saints' payments to National Football League (NFL) players for on-field performances, which was known as the "'Bountygate' scandal" (Reed, 2012, para. 2). The severity of such allegations triggered a level of intrigue not found in the daily coverage of sports and when those sports are "amateur" attraction increases exponentially.

When the Oklahoma State scandal surfaced, media intrigue was bolstered because the program had both a track record of previous violations—Oklahoma State had been placed on probation twice before by the NCAA (1978–1981 and 1989–1992)—and had only recently reentered the upper echelon of the college football hierarchy, two characteristics that help fuel the coverage of scandals in college sports (Branch, 2011; Fleisher, Shughart, Tollison, & Goff, 1988). Consider the story of the Southern Methodist University football program: During the 1980s the Mustangs went from a program defined by decades of losing to the most successful Division I football team in the country. However, along its path to the top, SMU committed several recruiting violations, which spurred mentions of scandal during coverage of the National Collegiate Athletic Association's (NCAA) death penalty judgment in 1987 to the point that even now SMU serves as the poster child of wrongdoing in college sports (Matula, 2010). The Southern Methodist story was referenced again when the Oklahoma State report broke (Tramel, 2013), a rhetorical choice colored by Oklahoma State's checkered past and uncharacteristic success, and a journalistic reference that affirmed the immorality of the Cowboys' latest infractions.

Still, as incriminating as the report had been, within days the focus shifted from the allegations to the extra-textual details surrounding *SI*'s coverage. On September 12, ESPN.com's Brett McMurphy (2013) uncovered inconsistencies between academic information about former Oklahoma State players referenced in the report and documents acquired from the university. Other news outlets, from inside (Yoder, 2013) and outside (Manfred, 2013b) the sports sphere poked holes in the allegations, making claims of "shenanigans" (Yoder, 2013, para. 6) and "bullshit" (Cosentino, 2013, para. 1) and calling one of the *SI* reports "a hack who can't write" (Whitlock, as cited in Augustine, 2013, para. 9).

As a result, by the time the Oklahoma State Cowboys played Saturday, September 14, much of the focus had shifted toward either the reporting practices of *SI*'s Dohrmann and Evans or the fact that "nobody cares about this kind of college football 'corruption' anymore" (Leitch, 2013, para. 5). Once the 2013 college football season hit its stride in the weeks of late November and early December, the Oklahoma State story, which months before carried such value *all* news sources needed to at least mention it, had escaped public memory.

At the time, the Oklahoma State case was the "latest college scandal" (Wetzel, 2013, para. 1) in a string of stories with similar narratives, from Texas A&M's Johnny Manziel possibly being paid for signing autographs to Alabama defensive end Luther Davis reportedly taking money while playing. "Nothing. Or at least not much," came from those stories as athletes, coaches, administrators, journalists, and fans moved on (Wetzel, 2013, para. 3–4). However, it can be argued that something other than shoddy reporting and/or apathy was at work. The aim of this chapter is to delve more deeply into the event to lay bare how and why coverage shifted away from the Oklahoma State scandal itself toward criticism of *SI*'s coverage.

It is important in this analysis to look at the role of ESPN, the self-proclaimed "Worldwide Leader in Sports," and its discourse in ordering the sports news sphere. However, rather than viewing ESPN as the monolith of sports news, it is important to recognize the role of its multiplatform reach (across TV, radio, and digital content). As will be highlighted, it is through both the consumption of mass mediated content across various outlets and the recirculation of that content by autonomous individuals via digitally mediated communicative acts (e.g., Twitter "tweets") that ESPN-reported stories attain the emotional value needed to make them compelling.

The following critical examination supports this argument and is founded on four principles:

1. ESPN-generated content reaches more people than its competitors through a multiplatform approach that includes print, television, radio, and online coverage ("ESPN Fact Sheet," n.d.).
2. Through this multiplatform approach, ESPN users are offered more opportunities to form emotional connections to content.
3. Due to these emotional ties, users are more apt to circulate ESPN content beyond ESPN-specific outlets.
4. Through this user-enabled circulation, ESPN content is afforded more opportunity to gain the rhetorical value needed to remain in the sports news stream for extended periods of time.

This chapter begins by unpacking the rhetoric of a sports scandal through an understanding of the scandal process as one that creates a scapegoat meant to purify an affected public (Burke, 1969). Next, the researcher discusses how ESPN's proliferation across multiple media outlets creates a hypermediated text (Bolter

& Grusin, 2000) that enables users to more effectively apply the scapegoat frame. The chapter then turns to premediation (Grusin, 2010), a theory that highlights the ability of media technologies to transmit emotion-laden rhetoric and order an environment in which users experience emotions and then explains how rhetorical circulation functions as a process through which users give rhetoric the emotional value needed for prolonged efficacy (Chaput, 2010).

Before concluding with an analysis of the consequences for ESPN and ESPN users, there is a return to the Oklahoma State fallout and a critical look into the proliferation of ESPN-produced criticism of the *SI* story through user-generated and recirculated content via Twitter, a social media site that has become "a core component of the global communication system" (Honan, 2014, para. 2) and a barometer of relevancy for news consumers, news producers, and academics (Meraz & Papacharissi, 2013). This analysis of related Twitter content shows how users worked to circulate the ESPN content and made the extra-textual components of the *SI* story—rather than the story itself—the more compelling narrative.

## THE SCANDAL AND THE SCAPEGOAT

According to *MediaZone* (ESPN, Inc., 2014), an ESPN-produced resource summarizing the corporation's media presence, ESPN has seven domestic cable networks, 350 radio stations carrying full-time ESPN Radio programming making it the largest sports talk radio network in the country, multiple national and market-specific websites, a magazine, a "digital and content-driven business" aimed at women, and two of the top five free sports-related applications available for the Apple iPhone, the most popular mobile phone in the United States (StatCounter, 2014, para. 42).

In 2012, ESPN produced nearly 30,000 hours of television content and 8,500 hours of radio content. *ESPN The Magazine* was the leading publication within the 18–34 male demographic and ESPN's *SportsCenter* averaged up to 115 million viewers per month (ESPN, Inc., 2014). The amount of content needed to sustain this traditional media foothold (TV, radio, and print) has facilitated ESPN's agenda setting of the sports news sphere. However, though this reality has been critically examined in the past (e.g., Bissel & Zhou, 2004, Clavio & Pedersen, 2007), more attention needs to be placed on the entirety of ESPN's media presence, especially its expansion into digital media—Web and mobile Web, social media, and mobile phone apps—where ESPN's multiplatform approach has fully taken hold.

Consider these statistics: In 2013, ESPN accounted for 31% of the world's digital sports consumption (more than the second ranked [Yahoo! Sports/NBC

Sports] and third ranked [NFL Internet Group] sources combined), with more users (56.3 million) and time spent (5.6 billion minutes) with ESPN digital content than any other sports related digital entity. ESPN was also the top sports news outlet for mobile users, accounting for 2.4 billion minutes of content consumption that year (ESPN, Inc., 2014). In the United States specifically, ESPN's digital properties were the top source for sports news and held a massive lead over the closest competitor, Yahoo! Sports/NBC Sports (Bibel, 2013). ESPN has not so much opened up the dissemination of addition sports perspectives, but rather become a media entity whose perspective reaches more users with more speed because of its expansion during the modern communication age, an occurrence that is characteristic of many news organizations during the rise of digital technologies (Harsin, 2008).

ESPN's ubiquity is particularly important during moments when a significant event interrupts the flow of the daily sports news stream. For example, during the summer of 2012, in the middle of the Major League Baseball (MLB) season, ESPN personnel were stationed at the New York Jets training facilities to cover the preseason workouts of then quarterback Tim Tebow, a personality who had drawn millions of viewers to ESPN during the previous NFL seasons (Yoder, 2012). This was a big story throughout most sports outlets, but ESPN was unique because of the quantity of its ongoing coverage of Tebow, a phenomenon that began when Tebow was the quarterback for the Denver Broncos and evidenced in the dozens (and often hundreds) of daily references he garnered across ESPN-produced content throughout his time in the NFL (Burke, 2012). Thus, ESPN framed much of the coverage and while some went elsewhere for their Tebow news, millions of users still looked to ESPN for information.

Although the Tebow story was significant because it broke up the monotony of summer sports news—similar to a blockbuster trade in the NFL, NBA, or MLB—the sports scandal is a different animal. Instead, the scandal is a negative event that draws attention because it is disgraceful, morally offensive, and/ or causes damage to the reputation of the object of focus (OED Online, 2014). Unlike a positive event like the Tebow coverage, the scandal is traumatic.

In rhetorical terms, Burke (1969) claims such trauma arises because linguistic hierarchies have been disrupted and the natural binaries that form across the often-mysterious landscape of language usage fail to adequately define the in-between spaces of daily life or the fluid interconnectedness between language-users. The scandal is one of these rhetorical moments and is experienced as traumatic because the established hierarchy and the place of those within it lose validity within these interconnected relations.

With the Oklahoma State story, there were two scandals whose rhetoric two media entities circulated: The scandal related to the Cowboy football program *SI* created and circulated, and the scandal related to the journalistic integrity of the

*SI* writers, Dohrmann and Evans, which ESPN created and circulated and then ESPN users recirculated. In the first event, trauma was felt because the place of Oklahoma State in the college football hierarchy was called into question, which in turn shined light on the integrity (or lack thereof) of college sports (Branch, 2011; Wetzel, 2013); Oklahoma State had become a top-tier program and the scandal problematized its position. In the latter, the prestige of *SI*, a credible and respected voice in sports media for decades, was thrown into doubt. In both situations, the introduction of a scandal meant the order of the sports world and the identities of entities within it were thrown into doubt.

In response to traumas such as these, news media outlets encourage purification and closure by providing the "symbolic medicine" needed to move past a scandal (Brummett, 1985, p. 247). By ordering the traumatic event, news provides the sensemaking tools for individuals to move themselves toward structured understandings that reestablish the legitimacy of the affected hierarchy (Ott & Aoki, 2002). The scapegoat is one of these discursive frames and functions best during traumatic events that trigger a shared sense of guilt in response to the language chasms (Burke, 1969). Those who rely on the validity of a hierarchy to define their social relations feel guilt when that hierarchy is called into question and to make sense of such a situation a "chosen vessel" is selected into which the shared guilt can be purged (Burke, 1969, p. 406). Once this guilt is alleviated, the legitimacy of the hierarchy is reestablished.

Oklahoma State was the chosen vessel *SI* established during the fall of 2013, a time when several scandalous stories pocked the college football landscape and affected those invested in its established order, including fans, schools, coaches, and media outlets. Football schools with storied histories, namely Texas A&M and Alabama, were under the watchful eye of the NCAA for violations within their programs, and Oklahoma State allowed the affected others to believe their actions paled in comparison. Similar moments of guilt and purification are commonplace in the world of sports (Butterworth, 2008). Consider, for example, the A-Rod and New Orleans Saints cases mentioned above. In the coverage of both, these objects disposed the negative attention surrounding rampant performance-enhancing drug use and excessive violence, respectively.

However, the Oklahoma State story took on an added level of complexity when ESPN reframed the narrative of the scandal and shifted attention away from Oklahoma State toward *SI*, making the story one about a lack of journalistic integrity. ESPN then provided the explanatory "equipment for living" (Burke, 1971, p. 293) needed to solve the problem it created. ESPN spun a scandal out of a scandal, made the story one about journalistic practice, and to reestablish the legitimacy of sports journalism, transformed *SI* and the Oklahoma State story's two writers, Dohrmann and Evans, into the scapegoats needed to collect shared guilt.

## HYPERMEDIACY AND PREMEDIATION

ESPN's replacement of one scandal for another was not a novel act of journalism. One news source exposing the invalidities of another's coverage is a relatively common practice (Hollander, 2010). What made ESPN's reaction to the *SI* story exceptional was that ESPN was able to drown out the original scandal with a scapegoating of the *SI* writers that was disseminated across ESPN's traditional and digital outlets. Therefore, though *SI* may reach a "collective audience of more than 30 million" through its website, mobile application, and print magazine (Time, Inc., 2014, para. 2), this pales in comparison to ESPN's multiplatform approach, which gives ESPN's perspective the potential to trump all others.

Such activity becomes more problematic when taking into account the efficacy afforded through ESPN's digital media presence. According to Bolter and Grusin (2000), digital media has altered what users believe to be a "real" or "true" experience of the world to the point that rather than having the medium itself hidden as a means of reaching a "feeling of fullness," digital media offers a "hypermediated" experience to users who achieve "an authentic experience" through the consumption of information provided across multiple media technologies (Bolter & Grusin, 2000, p. 53).

In terms of news, the Web page is the ideal example of hypermediated immediacy because it offered a holistic view of current events not by removing the medium, but by making the medium obvious to the user (Bolter & Grusin, 2000). ESPN offers many examples of such media with the collage-like ESPN.com and the omnipresent graphics found on the "Bottom Line" and sidebars of its television broadcast(s) (Bolter & Grusin, 2000, p. 191). *ESPN The Magazine* has taken up this same hypermediated aesthetic to give users all the information desired without veiling the presence of mediation.

This was also found in McMurphy's (2013) initial report for ESPN.com on the questionable journalistic practices of *SI*'s Dohrmann and Evans. When accessing McMurphy's story, users were not only given the text of the report but also provided with a *SportsCenter* video that documented the inconsistencies of the *SI*'s coverage and several links to additional stories that included rebuttals to the Oklahoma State scandal. In sum, ESPN provided visitors with a holistic account of the Oklahoma State case, including the allegations, but problems with *SI*'s coverage as well. A feeling of complete transparency was meant to help users reach a more complete, compelling, and hypermediated understanding of the whole story and, in turn, made ESPN's framing more convincing.

The hypermediated approach is also meant to trigger an "authentic emotional response" (Bolter & Grusin, 2000, p. 53). By immersing oneself in both the discursive and non-discursive (i.e., emotional) information, the user forms a complete awareness of the situation. However, this information is rarely neutral and thus, digital technologies function to "affectively attune" the audience through the consumption of both "discursive and biopolitical formations" (Grusin, 2010, p. 5). In turn, the relationships between users and media products with which they interact are capable of solidifying both an individual and collective emotional response that is dependent upon a rhetorical frame and its dissemination.

The development of more interactive and co-creative digital technologies such as mobile phones and social media have affected communication, including the transfer of emotional information (Vincent, 2010) alongside the transmission of discursive content. This is what makes ESPN's multiplatform approach unique, especially its digital presence as ESPN offers users more opportunities to interact with hypermediated texts and the emotionally laden discourse they present. Thus, though ESPN was the original source of criticism about *SI*'s Oklahoma State coverage, consumers could access this information that was spread far and wide via media channels not capitalized upon as effectively by competitors such as *SI*. Users felt compelled to recirculate one particular rhetorical frame over another and kept ESPN's perspective on the Oklahoma State story in the news stream.

## RHETORICAL CIRCULATION

The advancement of communication, especially through digital technology, has changed how rhetorical agency is understood (Chaput, 2010; Greene, 2004). Rather than rhetorical agency being measured according to whether one's rhetoric effectively solves the problems of a rhetorical situation, agency involves any act of communication that adds and circulates emotional value (Chaput, 2010). Emotion is what holds discourse together and what fuels the "communicative practices that inspire behavior" (Chaput, 2010, p. 8). Thus, anytime a language user circulates content, he or she is both reaffirming and building upon the emotional value of that discourse. In turn, he or she is practicing rhetorical agency by adding to the discourse the emotional value needed for it to be rhetorically effective.

Emotional value and rhetorical value are further intertwined since emotion is what compels language users to circulate and consume discourse and to add to its rhetorical effectiveness (Chaput, 2010). Thus, each time affected users desire to put the "symbolic medicine" (Brummett, 1985, p. 246) to work emotional value and rhetorical value is added. For example, the *SI* story was compelling because it created a scapegoat into which emotional energy (guilt) could be purged. Users practiced agency by adding to the rhetorical effectiveness of the Oklahoma State story through the addition and circulation of their own emotional energy.

When turning to ESPN's criticism of the story, it becomes clear how a savvy news source like ESPN and user agency work in unison to give more rhetorical value to certain discourse, especially with the application of digital technologies.

For instance, when ESPN.com's McMurphy uncovered questionable journalism by *SI*'s Dohrmann and Evans, that rhetorical framing of the Oklahoma State scandal was more compelling because users had been faced with ESPN's hypermediated coverage, which made them feel as if the ESPN perspective was a more complete and "authentic" one (Bolter & Grusin, 2000, p. 53). In turn, these users, having consumed the rhetorical and emotional value of the mediated story, were orientated or "attuned" (Grusin, 2010, p. 81) to understand the Oklahoma State scandal through a specific emotional and rhetorical framework, which compelled them to act as agents by recirculating the story, thus giving it more value and efficacy.

To further explicate this program of sports news production, it is important to look at the dissemination of the *SI* and ESPN stories and show that one framing of the Oklahoma State situation came to trump the other due to the user-generated production of emotional and rhetorical value and not necessarily the validity of one story over another. More precisely, this was a process enabled more by ESPN's multiplatform approach than by any issues of journalistic integrity surrounding *SI*'s coverage; it was not that *SI*'s story was wrong, but rather that the sheer reach of the ESPN perspective enabled emotional orientations to that story, which was then given additional value via users' recirculation.

## TRACKING TWITTER

As a social networking site, Twitter allows users to read and post tweets of up to 140 words through website, SMS, and mobile phone interfaces. As of July 2014, there were 271 million monthly active users who send an average of 500 million tweets per day (Twitter, Inc., 2014). As prolific as this presence might sound, "Twitter users are only 18% of Internet users and 14% of the overall adult population" (Rainie & Smith, 2014, para. 4) compared to the 71% of Internet users active on Facebook (Duggan & Smith, 2013). However, in relation to news, Twitter has become a revered source, and especially since the events surrounding the Arab Spring uprisings, it has been viewed as a valid instrument for understanding processes of consumption and production used by news professionals and academics alike (Meraz & Papacharissi, 2013).

Twitter has become a news source "that says something meaningful about how engaged users discuss topics, find each other, and share information" (Rainie & Smith, 2014, para. 13). Thus, when it comes to understanding how ESPN is able to trump the perspective of its competitors through the access to and use of user agency enabled by a multiplatform approach that includes social and mobile media, Twitter provides the ideal object of study, a claim that is reaffirmed by the fact that the social media site is used by 76% of its users through mobile technologies (Twitter, Inc., 2014).

Topsy, a search engine software that indexes and ranks Twitter activity according to the popularity of key words and links and the social influence (the number of Twitter followers and average re-Tweets) of Twitter users, was used to track the dissemination of the *SI* coverage Dohrmann and Evans wrote and ESPN's criticism of the coverage McMurphy first published on ESPN.com (Topsy Labs, 2014).

To produce a data set that would provide the most accurate reading of the difference between *SI* and ESPN's influence and show how ESPN's advantage is linked to the company's reach across platforms, Topsy was used to search the original links of the six *SI* stories Dohrmann and Evans wrote and McMurphy's ESPN.com story, the first to criticize the *SI* pieces. Subsequently, the Topsy data were evaluated according to the number of times the stories were tweeted, the level of Twitter influence held by those who sent the tweets, and the amount of times a tweet by a *Highly Influential* twitter user (100,000+ followers) was re-tweeted (Topsy Labs, 2014).

*SI*'s "Overview" (Dohrmann & Evans, 2013a) received 195 tweets from Twitter users, including 11 by *Highly Influential* users, that is, a category of Twitter users—their specific characteristics undefined by Topsy Labs—that account for only 0.5% of the total number of users on Twitter (Topsy Labs, 2014). These users included Bonnie Bernstein (@bonniebernstein), the sportscaster and journalist who previously worked for ESPN and CBS. Bernstein has more than 100,000 Twitter followers, 12 of whom re-tweeted her tweet on the *SI* story. Richard Deitsch (@richarddeitsch), a writer for *SI*, was another *Highly Influential* user who tweeted about the *SI* column.

The second part of the *SI* coverage, "The Money" (Dohrmann & Evans, 2013b), received 2,300 tweets, 187 by *Influential* Twitter users (1,000+ followers), including Peter King, a writer for *SI* with 1.2 million followers, 52 of whom re-tweeted his post. ESPN personalities and *Highly Influential* users Jay Bilas (@JayBilas) and Andy Katz (@ESPNAndyKatz) also tweeted the story and had their posts re-tweeted a combined 187 times. The third installment, "The Academics" (Dohrmann & Evans, 2013c), elicited 576 tweets, 68 by *Influential* tweeters, including Dohrmann (@georgedohrmann) and Evans (@thayerevanssi), who combined to account for roughly 20,000 followers, 37 of whom re-tweeted the journalists' story.

The fourth part, "The Drugs" (Dohrmann & Evans, 2013d), received 578 tweets, 68 by *Influential* users, including Dohrmann and Evans again who then elicited 72 re-tweets. The fifth story in the Oklahoma State coverage, "The Sex" (Dohrmann & Evans, 2013e), received 306 tweets, 30 by *Influential* Twitter users, including Doug Gottlieb (@gottliebshow), a former ESPN commentator with 161,000 followers, three of whom retweeted the post. The final installment, "The Fallout" (Dohrmann & Evans, 2013f), received 242 tweets, 25 by *Influential* tweeters, including Dohrman and Evans, who received 20 retweets, and Dan Wetzel (@danwetzel), a columnist for Yahoo! Sports whose tweet was a critique of the Dohrmann and Evans story.

There are some interesting characteristics of the Twitter circulation of the *SI* stories that need to be clarified. First, the number of tweets declined from the first story to the last. Perhaps this was due to apathy as Wetzel (2013) has asserted or the awareness of weak journalism triggered users to turn away from *SI*'s coverage. Either one may be correct, but in relation to the argument of this chapter, it is possible that ESPN's critique of the coverage, which came online soon after the first installment, played a part in turning users away from *SI*. Second, the most re-tweeted post from throughout the *SI* coverage came from Bilas (145 re-tweets), an ESPN analyst. Thus, it appeared that ESPN helped add value to the perspective of its competitor, even more so than *SI* commentators who were tweeting about the Oklahoma State coverage.

Circulation of McMurphy's story for ESPN.com, which received 1,300 tweets, 83 from *Influential* users, further reaffirmed ESPN's dominance. However, while these numbers do not differ much from the most popular of the *SI* stories, the second level of dissemination—the re-tweeting—reasserts the reach of ESPN. For example, Bilas tweeted McMurphy's story and then had it retweeted 58 times. Dick Vitale (@DickieV), another ESPN personality, tweeted the story to his 615,000 followers and had it retweeted 52 times. Outside of the Twitter universe, other major sports news outlets, including *SB Nation* (Kirk, 2013) and *Sports on Earth* (Leitch, 2013), covered the ESPN story only to have it tweeted by users. In addition, other ESPN entities, including ESPN Radio and *SportsCenter*, covered the McMurphy report, further broadcasting the *SI* critique to users who could then circulate that information to others.

In sum, this analysis showed that the existence of user circulation was present in response to the *SI* coverage and ESPN's critique of that coverage. In both cases, the additional emotional value and, in turn, the increase of rhetorical effectiveness was involved. However, as recognized in the decrease of tweets on the *SI* coverage as the days waned and the increase in tweets regarding the ESPN critique, users became less interested in the scandal surrounding the Oklahoma State program and more interested in the scandal surrounding *SI* and the coverage's authors, Dohrmann and Evans. It can be argued that this was due to the reach of ESPN. Through digital media, ESPN was able to get more content to more users and increase the opportunity for these users to create and circulate emotional value and give the ESPN critique more rhetorical efficacy.

## CONCLUSION

By looking at one case study, the coverage of the scandal surrounding the Oklahoma State football program in September 2013, it is clear that ESPN has transmitted its rhetoric more effectively than its competitors. In this case, *SI* broke a story that offered the college football landscape an ideal scapegoat into which it could purge guilt suffered in response to seedy activity at some of its most recognizable schools. However, as powerful as that rhetorical framing was, ESPN's creation of its scandal trumped its competitor and offered up a new scapegoat that helped reaffirm the order of college football in a different way. In the latter case, attention was diverted away from Oklahoma State toward questionable journalism, a move that helped add stability to amateur athletics but also reasserted ESPN's dominance at the top of the sports media hierarchy.

ESPN provided a hypermediated representation of the *SI* story, an approach that left users with a more holistic understanding of the event. It then extended the reach of this hypermediacy across digital platforms and increased the opportunities for users to consume the emotional rhetoric of the McMurphy story while adding value and rhetorical effectiveness through their own circulation of the coverage. Users had an emotional connection to the story and felt compelled to spread that emotional energy. In turn, they added to the staying power of this new rhetorical frame, which took negative attention away from Oklahoma State and focused it on ESPN's competitor, further enabling the "slow death by a thousand pinpricks" suffered by the *SI* coverage (Yoder, 2013, para. 11).

Although Twitter is a viable source for tracking news relevance, this chapter would have benefited from the analysis of additional social media coverage of both the *SI* and ESPN stories. For example, examining the dissemination of this content through Facebook could have provided a more complete understanding of both ESPN's and users' influence. Future scholarship that attempts a related analysis could acquire the funding needed to access this additional data (Facebook and other analytic tools are not free as was the case with Topsy) and paint a more thorough picture. Also, qualitative inquiry into the motivation of Twitter users could offer a better understanding of the emotional connection users had with *SI* and ESPN content.

However, it is clear that ESPN has a major influence over what sports news is covered and how that information is disseminated. Although ESPN may not consciously set a news agenda, its reach, through traditional and digital media, is so vast that the company's perspective reaches farther and wider than its competitors. When users who experience the dissemination of this content as a positive emotional experience farther fuel that process, it is clear that ESPN's pull will continue, at least until its competitors are able to access and use technology with the same effectiveness.

Editor's Note: The NCAA's investigation of Oklahoma State's football program, based on *Sports Illustrated*'s 2013 series of reports, found the school had committed two violations. Penalties handed down in April 2015 included one year's probation for the football program.

# CHAPTER SIXTEEN

# North of the Border

## The Influence of ESPN on TSN and Sportsnet in Canada

MICHAEL L. NARAINE AND GASHAW Z. ABEZA

Starting with one network in 1979, ESPN has experienced a rapid expansion with additions such as ESPN2, ESPNNews, ESPNU, in addition to an array of networks worldwide (Goff & Ashwell, 2009; Wood & Benigni, 2006). Perhaps one of the more remarkable aspects of ESPN's ascension as the quintessential sports programming entity in the world is the operation and co-ownership of properties outside of the United States. In 1996, ESPN's parent company, Disney Corporation, entered into an inter-industry joint venture with Fox Sports' parent company, News Corporation, to disseminate content across Southeast Asia (Law, Harvey, & Kemp, 2002). The agreement allowed ESPN to gain knowledge access to resources and infrastructure to broadcast in the region. This particular example demonstrates that ESPN has been continually finding "ways to expand its presence" (Vogan, 2012, p. 137), even if said expansion requires working with direct competitors. Moreover, it also exemplifies the transformation that ESPN has undergone since its inception; the focus has shifted from a niche channel servicing the U.S. market to a sport media empire that operates in and influences other broadcasters in other countries.

Canada serves as an interesting and relevant case for examining ESPN's global influence. Although ESPN has solely owned and operated broadcast properties in other countries (e.g., Brazil, Australia), given the unique circumstances regarding telecommunication policy, foreign ownership regulations, and the presence of intra-national conglomerates, using Canada as a case study of ESPN's international influence is warranted.

With the evolution of Canadian telecommunications policies to protect domestic and cultural interests, substantial foreign ownership over domestic broadcasters (including sports) has been effectively restricted (Harvey & Law, 2005). The result of these policies has led to a mass media landscape in Canada dominated by two major empires: Bell Canada Enterprises (BCE) and Rogers Communications (Scherer & Harvey, 2013; Scherer & Whitson, 2009). Their dominance in the Canadian media landscape has also extended to sports broadcasting, with the operation of The Sports Network (TSN) by BCE and Sportsnet (RSN) by Rogers. Given these dynamics, foreign broadcasters like ESPN have had to choose alternative means by which to scale its content for the Canadian market.

The aim of this chapter is to examine the effect ESPN has on an international scale by identifying the Canadian (sport) media oligopoly and any similarities that exist between the oligopoly and ESPN. Although ESPN as it exists in the United States is not present in Canada, it does wield influence over TSN and RSN, whether directly (i.e., minority ownership) or indirectly (i.e., best practices). Though ESPN has persisted as a salient topic among sport communication scholars (as evidenced by this book; Freeman, 2001), there has been a notable absence of literature to address its potential influence abroad, particularly from the perspective of its presentation and practices. As such, this chapter addresses this information gap and stimulates research that adds to the previous examinations of ESPN such as its coverage of female athletes (e.g., Kian, Mondello, & Vincent, 2009; Tuggle, 1997), the hiring of women and minorities (e.g., Coventry, 2004), and representation of body images (e.g., Bissell & Zhou, 2004).

## CANADIAN SPORTS BROADCASTING

A discussion of the influence of ESPN on Canadian sports broadcasters would be incomplete without first documenting how there came to be two major all-sports networks in Canada. Though this section is not primarily focused on ESPN, it is meant to provide context to the research situation, especially for those unfamiliar with the trajectory of Canadian telecommunication and the development of TSN and RSN. This section begins with examining TSN, Canada's first 24-hour sports network, followed by the emergence of RSN.

## TSN

Five years after ESPN started broadcasting in the United States, TSN was launched in Canada (Sparks, 1992). The Canadian Radio-Television Commission (CRTC)—the regulatory body developed to safeguard Canadian content and restrict foreign ownership of the broadcast system (Dewing, 2012)—had issued a broadcast licence to the Labatt Brewing Company in 1984 for an all-sports speciality channel on cable systems. Owning TSN was a valuable circuit of promotion for Labatt (Whitson, 1998); the alcoholic beverage company could promote its brand and products on the network in addition to airing telecasts of the Toronto Blue Jays, also (then) owned by Labatt. Under Labatt's ownership, TSN received significant increases in subscribers, growing from approximately 380,000 in February 1985 to approximately 5.3 million in the fall of 1989 (Sparks, 1992). The popularity of a Canadian all-sports network also led Labatt to gain a licence for TSN sister network, Réseau des Sports (RDS) in 1987 (Scherer & Harvey, 2013). Where the trajectory of TSN's development takes an unexpected turn occurred two decades after its arrival.

In 1995, a Belgian beer company, Interbrew, acquired Labatt and its holdings. Under Canadian law, Interbrew could operate Labatt's facilities, but the CRTC restricted majority ownership of broadcast companies and broadcast licences by a foreign entity (Grant & Wood, 2004)—an issue that other American sport media empires operating in Canada faced previously (Valentine, 1997). Thus, TSN would have to pursue an alternative ownership arrangement. Initially, TSN divided its majority interest into three Canadian investment groups and added ESPN as a fourth partner who would hold a 20% stake (Grant & Wood, 2004). Although the arrangement seemed to position TSN to blend domestic and global sport programming (Silk, 1999), the deal, which the CRTC approved in 1996, did not last.

The Canadian investments groups did not want to maintain their interest in TSN much longer, which left ESPN without a Canadian partner and continual CRTC approval. This was problematic for ESPN, which used TSN for content distribution. After some internal disputes with prospective partners, ESPN convinced the investment groups to support the acquisition of TSN and RDS by CTV Inc., a national broadcaster that "happily agreed to take up all the Canadian shares" (Grant & Wood, 2004, p. 244). CTV Inc. was familiar with sports broadcasting with forays into Olympic broadcasting (MacNeil, 1996) and having forged content partnerships with ABC's *Wide World of Sports* (Cavanaugh, 1992). The CRTC agreed to the transfer, dependent upon CTV Inc. selling its interest in another all-sports channel that it had (i.e., what will later become RSN). Nevertheless, the acquisition, which occurred in 2000, was followed by the purchase of CTV Inc. and its various networks (e.g., TSN) by BCE, a large Canadian media conglomerate working to converge content and platforms (Scherer & Harvey, 2013). In the aftermath of these sales, TSN and RDS maintained their joint venture status with ESPN. Under the agreement approved by the CRTC, ESPN would have a program licencing deal with the two channels where it retained a 20% stake (Grant & Wood, 2004). By adding CTV Inc. (including TSN), BCE became a dominant player in the Canadian broadcast market (Neverson,

2010), leading to the CRTC granting applications to the conglomerate for multiple feeds and specialty sport channels. ESPN Classic Canada, Leafs TV, NHL Network, and Raptors NBA TV were speciality channels approved by the CRTC under BCE control, and led to the creation of TSN2 and RDS2 (Neverson, 2010; Scherer & Harvey, 2013).

In the decade after BCE's convergence of properties, including the majority control of TSN, TSN2, RDS, and RDS2, the all-sports channels have been able to leverage their parent companies' large cash reserves to acquire coveted content. For instance, TSN and RDS secured the exclusive broadcast rights for the Canadian Football League (CFL) in 2005 for approximately $16 million per year (Scherer & Whitson, 2009). Two years later, they secured the rights to air the National Hockey League's (NHL) Montréal Canadiens in 2007 (Scherer & Harvey, 2013). These two examples are just an illustration of how TSN, under the ownership of BCE, has sustained itself in the digital era. But as indicated previously, TSN's success created the circumstance for another all-sports channel to be developed and then purchased by a conglomerate looking to consolidate its holdings. And, as it turned out, that conglomerate would be BCE's primary rival and, ironically, a vital partner.

## RSN

The trajectory of RSN is similar to TSN's in that the 24-hour all-sports channel experienced a partnership deal with an American broadcaster for content and an ownership change that eventually led to its control by a large media conglomerate (i.e., Rogers). In 1998, CTV Inc. launched a regional sports broadcasting network that consisted of four feeds whose focus was the "coverage of local teams" (Scherer & Harvey, 2013, p. 71) across Canada. However, CTV Inc. only owned 40% by 2000. Similar to the TSN ownership structure in its early years, RSN (then known as CTV Sportsnet) had investors like Molson (a Canadian brewer that rivals Labatt) and one of ESPN's major rivals, Fox Sports (Grant & Wood, 2004). Rogers also held a small stake in CTV Sportsnet initially, and saw the potential in sports broadcasting to diversify its holdings.

Initially, the CRTC balked at allowing Rogers to increase its ownership stake in CTV Sportsnet (Townsend, 1999). However, this changed when CTV Inc. indicated its interest in the then more-lucrative TSN. Rogers was able to purchase CTV Inc.'s divested interest, in addition to the stake held by Molson, and subsequently rebranded the network to become RSN (i.e., Rogers Sportsnet; Grant & Wood, 2004). At the time of the acquisition, Fox Sports retained its stake (Kruse, 2009) and scaled its content north through a program licencing agreement similar to the relationship between ESPN and TSN (Grant & Wood, 2004). But what allowed RSN to consolidate its regional feeds and compete against TSN was its integration with other Rogers holdings, particularly the Toronto Blue Jays.

After acquiring RSN and one of Toronto's all-sports radio stations, Rogers purchased the Toronto Blue Jays in 2000 with the intention of securing content for its sports broadcasting properties (Field, 2006). RSN was not the only network in North America to have exclusive rights to a team owned by a parent company (see Genovese, 2013), but it certainly aided in garnering more viewership. Indeed, through its parent company, RSN has had regular broadcast access to the Toronto Blue Jays and Major League Baseball rights (Bellamy & Whitson, 2009).

RSN operates its regional feeds (i.e., Sportsnet Pacific, Sportsnet West, Sportsnet Ontario, and Sportsnet East) to showcase local, professional sports franchises (e.g., Edmonton Oilers, Calgary Flames, and Ottawa Senators) but also broadcasts national content (e.g., Canadian interuniversity athletics and major junior hockey) that airs simultaneously on two or more feeds and their newer national channels (e.g., Sportsnet One and Sportsnet 360). Although the network is young (relative to TSN), it has become quite the adversary given that its parent company, Rogers, competes directly against BCE. For instance, Rogers acquired the national rights starting in 2014 to all NHL games, including all playoff games, on all platforms (e.g., television and online/digital) for 12 years at $5.2 billion Canadian dollars (Rush, 2013). Thus, despite the minority ownership of ESPN on TSN, RSN has succeeded in becoming a viable sports broadcaster in Canada.

Although they rival each other for viewership and advertising, RSN's and TSN's parent companies have also worked together in the past to secure sports content. TSN and RSN have been involved as corporate partners with Maple Leaf Sports and Entertainment (MLSE), the multibillion-dollar organization that owns and operates professional franchises, facilities, and real estate in the city of Toronto (O'Reilly, 2013). That relationship drastically changed in 2011 when BCE and Rogers teamed up to purchase 75% equity in MLSE that was equally divided between the competing conglomerates (Scherer & Harvey, 2013). As partners, BCE and Rogers have leveraged their ownership of MLSE to gain access to broadcast rights for TSN and RSN and restrict any potential competitors (e.g., Canadian Broadcasting Corporation, Shaw Communications, and Quebecor Media). Their foray into professional sport franchise ownership may have been unprecedented, but they worked together previously to secure content away from the competition. As a consortium, BCE and Rogers partnered to secure the broadcasting rights to the 2010 and 2012 Olympic Games at a price of $153 million (Scherer & Harvey, 2013). Both media conglomerates made use of their properties with BCE airing coverage on TSN, TSN2, RDS, RDS2, and CTV, while Rogers aired coverage on all of their regional RSN feeds, including the nationally available Sportsnet One. These agreements speak to BCE and Rogers wanting to control the marketplace with the existing (sport) media oligopoly.

Although they sometimes work together, TSN and RSN (and their spinoffs) compete for the same viewership and sponsorship dollars. As such, both parent companies have opposed additional all-sports channels before (Killingsworth, 2005), fearing an oversaturation of networks. Indeed, in this race to achieve better ratings and increase viewership, it is the four letter all-sports network in the United States that puts forth innovative programming and "all best practices out there for the copying" (Peddie, 2013, p. 96) by many sportscasts, including the two Canadian all-sports networks.

## ESPN *SPORTSCENTER*

Part of the reason for ESPN's success has been its ability to captivate its viewership. Given that "more than a third of young Americans watch ESPN regularly" (Mindich, 2009, p. 25), the network has fared well with high target demographics (e.g., 18–24-year-old males) by producing content that is both informative and entertaining. One particular show that has become a staple for the network and embodies those characteristics that keep viewers tuned in is *SportsCenter*.

ESPN's *SportsCenter* is a television sports news program that airs game highlights, interviews, interest stories, and other segments in a package designed to engage its viewers. The program has been considered to be "clearly the most watched and most quoted of all sportscasts" (Eastman & Billings, 2000, p. 196) and reaches millions of homes in the United States (Eitzen & Sage, 2008). Alhough it is often seen as a nightly recap show, the program airs across the three major points in a daily schedule: morning, evening, and night (Brown & Bryant, 2006). Frequency aside, the program is much more than the actual content that it airs; one of the key characteristics of *SportsCenter* is the package/delivery system that is employed to present sports information to the audience.

The presentation of *SportsCenter* can be separated into two unique characteristics: the anchor and production capabilities. The anchor is one of the fundamental aspects for presenting information to the audience. Anchors have had a tremendous impact on news content (e.g., interviews) but have also shaped the overall presentation and format of their broadcasts (see Fensch, 2001). This sentiment extends to anchors of sports news programs as well. However, sports news audiences are increasingly disengaged with repetitive content (Sandomir, 2004b), which has led ESPN's anchors to balance a formal dissemination of information with satire, humour, and informal behavior. As Farred (2000) noted, ESPN's anchors are "self-consciously offbeat and wacky, yet still able to provide serious commentary" (p. 110). In this vein, anchors make reference to popular culture, societal issues, and engage in witty banter within their structured format thereby transcending the potentially mundane updates of sports scores and information (see Brown &

Bryant, 2006; Miller & Shales, 2011). This combination of "shtick" and reporting is often cited to the chemistry between co-anchors Dan Patrick and Keith
Olbermann (Freeman, 2001). This particular duo would offer terms and phrases
like "en fuego" (Patrick's coined term for a consistently dominant performing athlete), but they were also supported by a cast of other anchors following suit. There
have been a range of anchors on *SportsCenter* who have become renowned for
their abilities such as Chris Berman's punctuated voice and Stuart Scott's urbane
mannerisms including using nicknames for players (Farred, 2000). Although the
sports highlights program has been maligned for its coverage of women (Adams &
Tuggle, 2004; Messner, Duncan, & Cooky, 2003; Tuggle, 1997), Freeman (2001)
contended that ESPN made a concerted effort to hire more female anchors (and
reporters, in general) including Robin Roberts, Linda Cohn, Andrea Kremer, and
Suzy Kolber and incorporate them into the model of banter and shtick.

The second characteristic of *SportsCenter* can be conceptualized as production
capabilities. This umbrella term refers to all the nuances not related to human resources (e.g., anchor talent) such as graphics, backdrop, and format (e.g., segments)
that are intricate to the production of the program. In reference to *SportsCenter*,
Allen (2008) characterized its production value to include:

> Twirling circles of an animated zoom lens disassembling itself then flying back together
> again, cascading dissolves, burst wipes, a meteor blazing across the screen, whose force flips
> the picture over like a mirror, from football on one side to baseball on the other. (p. 424)

Much of this description of *SportCenter*'s production capabilities underscores the inclusion of graphics that simulate automation and industrialization, a sentiment akin to
the sport as industrialized labour (Trujillo, 1995) and the sport/war metaphor (Jansen
& Sabo, 1994). However, the production capabilities of *SportsCenter* extend beyond
just transition graphics. In research on fantasy sport participation, Ruihley and Hardin
(2013) explicitly identified a respondent who referred to "the stat ticker" (p. 65) on
ESPN. The ticker, known as "the bottom line," is a graphic strip usually found on the
bottom of the *SportsCenter* broadcast that features previous and live scores, updates,
and other news without the visual highlights of the game or circumstance. In essence,
the ticker allows viewers to get updated on a score quicker, especially if they missed
the highlight package containing the game or story they were interested in viewing.
Indeed, alongside anchors, the production capabilities of *SportsCenter* have enabled
the broadcaster to amass a large audience base (Brown & Bryant, 2006).

This literature review has revealed the historical trajectory of the two major
all-sports networks in Canada (i.e., TSN and RSN), its parent companies, and the
flagship program of ESPN (i.e., *SportsCenter*). In doing so, there is an established
basis to then understand the similarities (if any) that TSN and RSN have with
ESPN. As such, the following methodology is used to assist in an understanding
of the impact ESPN has had in Canada.

## Method

This study examined the potential effect ESPN has had on the Canadian sport media oligopoly, and any (dis)similarities that exist in terms of the manifest content, format, and presentation of all-sports networks. The appropriate approach to achieve the stated purpose was to perform a textual analysis. Textual analyses have long been used by communication researchers interested in systematically describing and interpreting the characteristics of a recorded or visual message (Frey, Botan, & Kreps, 1999). It is an unobtrusive and nonreactive tool used to study a text that is explicitly stated (Potter, 1996). The method has been adopted in a number of sport communication studies (e.g., Antunovic & Hardin, 2012; Barnett & Hardin, 2011; Billings, MacArthur, Licen, & Wu, 2009; Chang, Crossman, Taylor, & Walker, 2011; Corrigan, Paton, Holt, & Hardin, 2010; Eliopulos & Johnson, 2012; Sanderson, 2010), and is considered an appropriate method for this study because it provides the researchers a systematic and objective way to assess how Canadian sports broadcasters are (dis)similar to ESPN in terms of text that is explicitly stated (i.e., the manifest content, format, and presentation).

The study analyzed 15 hours of programming from the three all-sports networks collected over a delineated time frame of days (n = 5). The period chosen for the analysis was randomly selected from a 365-day sampling frame. The sampling frame itself was established from a one-year period of daily broadcast transmissions. As a sample case, the following newscasts were selected for analysis: *SportsCenter* from ESPN, *Sportsnet Connected* from RSN, and *SportsCentre* from TSN. These newscasts were chosen because they conform to the typical programming features (e.g., highlights, scores, exclusive interviews) covered on all the three broadcasting channels. The three programs selected air at various points throughout the broadcast day, which required the development of a recording scheme that enabled data collection from morning, evening, and late night broadcasts. All TSN and RSN content was recorded on a Personal Video Recorder (PVR) and later digitally uploaded to an external hard drive. Because ESPN is not available in Canada due to CRTC licencing controls, a paid virtual private network (VPN) was used to view and record ESPN content. All ESPN content was recorded using a tablet (e.g., personal computing device) and later uploaded to that same external hard drive that stored the TSN and RSN data.

Given the lack of an established textual analysis coding scheme, a coding strategy was devised that was intended to identify a list of specific items (i.e., create a coding sheet) underlying the (dis)similarities between the shows. The coding sheet was initially developed through a pilot study of three hours of programming from the three shows, one hour from each. These mutually inclusive classification items are identifiable mark, sports ticker, anchor-to-anchor banter, popular culture references, special segments, and transitions (see Table 16.1). The identifiable mark classification referred to presentation of the broadcaster's logo (not the logo of the program) on screen that was visible to the audience. The sports ticker category referred to a particular graphic during sports news broadcasts that presented scores, news updates, and additional information (e.g., injuries, player transactions, and upcoming broadcasts) as well as upcoming events and items to be featured on air. The anchor-to-anchor banter classification consolidated instances where anchors moved away from reporting the news to the audience, but engaging in conversation (often times with increased levels of wit and humour) with their co-anchor (or sport analyst in cases where two anchors were not present). Popular culture references are instances where anchors made explicit reference to a popular culture item (e.g., politicians, movies, music, and fashion models) as they reported the sports news. The penultimate category, special segments, were those occurrences in the broadcasts where traditional highlight packages (i.e., specific details pertaining to a match or event) were not shown and instead were replaced by a segment with a compilation or montage of highlights (e.g., Top 10, the worst play of the day, and the highlight of the night) or feature pieces/human interest stories. The final category that appeared on the coding sheet was labelled transitions, referencing to graphics that separate highlight packages from one another, introducing a segment or block of highlight packages, or opening/closing the broadcast. All of these items were analyzed in terms of either frequency (i.e., number of appearances) or duration (i.e., length of time).

Table 16.1 Coding sheet for textual analysis.

| Categories | Measurement Units |
| --- | --- |
| *Identifiable mark* | duration of time |
| *Sports ticker* | duration of time |
| *Anchor-to-anchor banter* | frequency of occurrence |
| *Popular culture references* | number of mentions |
| *Special segments* | frequency of appearance |
| *Transitions* | frequency of appearance |

Two independent coders were used in this study. The reliability of the coding sheet had been tested through the pilot study where the coders conducted a separate textual analysis of three hours of programming. As Riffe, Lacy, and Fico (2005) noted, conducting a pilot test analysis is useful to assess the accuracy and reliability of the coders as well as to identify unclear categories between the coders. Inter-coder reliability was calculated post data collection to evaluate the degree to which the two coders tended to carry exactly the same assessment on each classification item (Kolbe & Burnett, 1991; Neuendorf, 2002). Any differences between the coders' understanding were adjusted and the coding process was adapted accordingly. The interobserver agreement (IOA) is often used by investigators in event recording and time sampling (Thomas, Nelson, & Silverman, 2010), and thus was utilized in this instance. The initial IOA from the pilot was 60% and demonstrated a particularly high variance in the coding of logo presence (e.g., which logos were being documented). Upon review, coders adjusted for the variance, which rendered an IOA of 80%, sufficient to continue to the next phase of the methodology. Following testing for inter-coder reliability, the two coders met upon completion of the data collection phase to parse through the information. In addition to marking down the frequency or duration of classification items, the coders agreed to identify additional elements of the sports news presentations (e.g., placement of graphics, logos, and tickers, camera angles, vernacular, and anchor positioning/presentation) as they observed them and to indicate some of these occurrences in their field notes.

## Results and Discussion

After reviewing the data, results were organized and consolidated into one table similar to the coding sheet. Table 16.2 represents the results of the investigation by indicating mean scores for the sample period. For the first classification item (i.e., logo) and the second classification item (i.e., sports ticker), the percentage of time that the item appeared during the broadcast was calculated by actual on-screen time (rounded to nearest minute) in relation to the program in its entirety. For example, if RSN had their logo visible on-screen for 60 minutes of the broadcast, it would be represented as 100.0% for that day and then averaged out of the specified time frame. The values for the remaining classification items were expressed as mean values for frequency of occurrences during the time period.

With respect to logos and identifiable marks, to maintain consistency, broadcaster logos (i.e., ESPN, TSN, or RSN) were noted when they appeared alongside the sports ticker, usually in the bottom left or bottom right of the screen. Although there were various instances where the network's logo appeared on the anchor's desk and in the background, television channels often display their logos embossed in a corner of the screen and thus the "bottom ticker logo" was selected. Across the three networks, there were interesting results yielded regarding the logo. ESPN kept its logo on screen for the majority of the broadcast, even during conventional commercial advertising breaks. This was not the case with TSN and RSN who removed their logos for the conventional commercial breaks. However, a common thread among the three networks was supplanting of the broadcaster's logo from the ticker with a sponsor logo (e.g., Advil, Tim Horton's, Subway, and Hotels. com). Sponsor presence as the identifiable mark tended to last 12–18 seconds and then would revert back to the network's logo. Yet, despite this practice, ESPN kept its logo visible and paired with its ticker for a large proportion of the *SportsCenter* broadcast.

Ticker visibility also had similar results to that of the identifiable mark classification. The ESPN ticker was rarely removed from the broadcast, even with special segments or conventional commercial advertising breaks. In the instances it was removed, they were one-minute intervals and it was an advertisement specific to the cable/satellite provider. In TSN's and RSN's circumstance, ticker visibility was not nearly as great as ESPN's, but still demonstrated a long on-screen presence. The common thread among the three broadcasters here is that ticker visibility was all greater (or equal to) the presence of the identifiable mark, a notion supported by the earlier statement regarding sponsorship in lieu of the broadcaster's logo.

Table 16.2 Textual analysis results for ESPN, TSN, and RSN sports news programming.

| Categories | ESPN | TSN | RSN |
| --- | --- | --- | --- |
| *Identifiable mark* | 93.9% | 69.5% | 72.5% |
| *Sports ticker* | 97.3% | 73.1% | 72.5% |
| *Anchor-to-anchor banter* | 10.8 | 4.3 | 6.0 |
| *Popular culture references* | 4.6 | 0.6 | 5.2 |
| *Special segments* | 3.4 | 5.3 | 5.0 |
| *Transitions* | 66.2 | 81.0 | 67.0 |

The four remaining classification items (i.e., those that were assigned a value based on frequency, not duration) also yielded similarities and differences among the three networks. Anchor-to-anchor banter was quite prevalent on ESPN *SportsCenter* (n = 10.8) relative to TSN's and RSN's offerings. It was initially thought that TSN would have less banter than ESPN, but more than RSN, yet the data indicated that *Sportsnet Connected* had 1.7 more banter moments per show than *SportsCentre*. The popular culture references item revealed that RSN's *Sportsnet Connected* yielded 5.2 references per show, greater than ESPN (n = 4.6) and TSN (n = 0.6). TSN had longer highlight packages and focused on explaining the circumstance of the content, not necessarily invoking the use of popular references to perpetuate "coolness." TSN and RSN boasted more special segments per show than ESPN (n = 5.3 and n = 5.0, respectively), which was explained through a more vested interest in showing highlights of U.S. collegiate athletics and airing content from sports not in season (i.e., the National Football League), whereas the Canadian broadcasters delineated their highlights to in-season sports (i.e., professional hockey and basketball). The (graphic) transitions item yielded a large number across the three broadcasters. Highlights from a particular sporting match would often be segregated by a short on-screen graphic (e.g., 4th quarter, 2nd period, overtime, and shootout), allowing the viewer to follow along with the chronological sequence of events. Transitions were also yielded from instances such as the "coming up" segments (i.e., moments before the program would move to a commercial break), where a graphic would segment tidbits of highlight packages.

In addition to the inclusively mutual classification items, key attributes of the three sports news shows were identified. The presentation of all three broadcasts featured graphics and designs that depicted various machinery, continuous tracks, rotors, blades, and other mechanical parts, with TSN and ESPN sharing near identical color schemes, typefaces, and graphics. Another common practice on all three broadcasts was the use of informal vernacular. ESPN was noted as a leader in this respect with phrases such as "brick-o-licious," "melancholy on melancholy," "unreal," and "saucy," while all three networks commonly used the terms "on fire" and "ice cold." A common practice within the three broadcasts included moving the anchor(s) away from their traditional position behind a desk. Although the majority of on-screen time was spent reporting from behind a desk, there were several instances on ESPN, TSN, and RSN where the anchor(s) would be standing off to the side. Along this vein, anchors on ESPN's *SportsCenter* were identified as informal, often speaking to each other and not making eye contact with or walking away from the camera, a stark contrast from *SportsCentre* and *Sportsnet Connected* where anchors were more likely to be formal and constantly engaged with the camera even when bantering with their co-anchor. Lastly, while gender issues were not a focus of this chapter, TSN was the only broadcaster to have a female anchor on every night (including one instance where both anchors were female), while ESPN did not have a female anchor present.

The results depict much of what scholarship has examined with respect to ESPN *SportsCenter*, in addition to demonstrating (dis)similarities found on TSN and RSN. Much of what was observed on ESPN vis-à-vis anchors and its production value was in line with Allen's (2008) and Farred's (2000) characterizations. However, the results here suggest these depictions are not solely relegated to just ESPN but are also applicable to the major Canadian all-sport broadcast networks as well. Both TSN and RSN featured anchors who were witty and engaged in banter, graphic tickers, and broadcasted their sports news show in a similar manner to that of ESPN. Where TSN and RSN were dissimilar to ESPN was in the intensity of the presentation/format. That is to say, the degree to which ESPN used its graphic ticker (i.e., on-screen throughout the majority of commercial advertising) differed from that of TSN and RSN. ESPN also had a higher number of anchor-to-anchor banter moments on average, suggesting that TSN and RSN may have adopted ESPN practices, but have not refined them.

## CONCLUSION

This chapter serves to generate an appreciation for the Canadian all-sports network landscape in addition to revealing (dis)similarities with ESPN in the United States. The chapter has highlighted Peddie's (2013) assertion that Canadian sport media empires look to ESPN for best practices and revealed this perception to be true through the similarities existent within the presentation of sports news. Thus, aside from their minority interest in TSN, ESPN's effect in Canada can be attributed to the adoption of similar presentation styles and format. Looking ahead, as BCE and Rogers continue to consolidate their respective empires, there is much TSN and RSN can learn from ESPN such as the graphic ticker affixed with a sponsor logo during commercial advertising breaks. As such, future research should continue to look at how TSN and RSN modify their presentation and format, relative to ESPN; a longitudinal study that is coupled with a multiple method approach (e.g., interviews with anchors and executives) could yield a greater appreciation for ESPN's impact on TSN and RSN. Alas, while ESPN may never be licenced to air content within Canadian borders, its practices and presentation are quite visible to Canadian audiences.

# The ESPN Effect
# and Its Audience

# CHAPTER SEVENTEEN

# ESPN and the Fantasy Sport Experience

BRODY J. RUIHLEY, ROBIN HARDIN, AND ANDREW C. BILLINGS

ESPN was approaching giddiness. It had hired Matthew Berry (aka the Talented Mr. Roto), embraced fantasy games, and was reaping the benefits. Virtually all forms of fantasy games were successes for the multimedia conglomerate. It added daily games, most notably *Streak for the Cash*, and bolstered its presence in the burgeoning fantasy community even more. When John Diver, ESPN Senior Director for Product Development, discovered that the World Curling Championships were taking place, he figured a daily game for curling would be broadening and ridiculous because the American audience had no knowledge of curling stars nor did the majority even understand the rules of the game. The result? "We literally crashed the servers on all major curling websites" (J. Kosner, personal communication, January 17, 2014), said ESPN Executive Vice President John Kosner. He continued: "I got correspondence from them saying, 'What are you doing to us?' Well, what we'd done to them was create a curling fantasy game within *Streak for the Cash*. Fantasy lunatics were googling curling websites and blew them up" (J. Kosner, personal communication, January 17, 2014).

This chapter is not about fantasy curling, but the story does underscore two main postulates within the chapter: (1) the power of ESPN's full-fledged adoption of fantasy gaming, and (2) the depth and fervency of the people who participate in fantasy sport games. Without question, fantasy sport has taken hold of the culture in North America as nearly 33.5 million Americans and 3.1 million Canadians participate in fantasy sport ("Industry Demographics," 2014). One of the primary drivers of this increased surge in participation is accessibility to the Internet. The Pew Internet and American Life Project estimates 87% of U.S. adults are online and using the Internet (Pew Research Center, 2014). This, in turn, has made sport communication entities develop and maintain a strong Web presence. This is a best-case scenario for fantasy sport because the activity is developed, controlled, and consumed primarily online and uses Web-based programs created by companies to host games and league-style competitions (Ruihley & Hardin, 2013). Fantasy sport uses statistics from actual competition in events from Major League Baseball (MLB), National Football League (NFL), NASCAR, National Basketball Association (NBA), and many other sport organizations. It is a natural fit for sport media companies providing this type of information to expand into the business of fantasy sport.

After initial reluctance, ESPN expanded into this market in such a powerful manner that it has become an industry leader in providing fantasy sport games and expertise for consumers within its dedicated internal website *Fantasy and Games*. This site is typical of any sport media entity Web portal providing information concerning baseball, football, basketball, hockey—and a plethora of other sports—with the difference being all content is focused on fantasy sport. Enacted sport and fantasy sport coverage should be considered siblings without being twins; each may focus on how a given game unfolded, but while enacted sport may deal with more relevance of a team win or loss along with color commentary about the manner in which the game unfolded, fantasy sport predominantly focuses in cold, hard facts pertaining almost exclusively to individual player performance.

This chapter focuses on ESPN and the fantasy sport experience. Covered topics will include the evolution of ESPN and fantasy sport, ESPN and fantasy journalism, ESPN's place in the fantasy marketplace, and ESPN's vision for fantasy sport. Aiding in the discussion of these topics are in-depth interview responses from three ESPN employees critical to the creation and advancement of ESPN's fantasy sport products. The interviewed professionals are (alphabetically) as follows:

- **Matthew Berry**, Senior Fantasy Analyst for ESPN. Although he has only one title, Berry is active in the ESPN fantasy sport experience. He writes for ESPN.com, hosts *Fantasy Focus* (a daily podcast), co-hosts *Fantasy Football Now* (Sunday television program), and makes regular appearances on ESPN television and radio programs. Berry is an Emmy Award Winner (*Fantasy Football Now*) and a Hall of Famer representing the Fantasy Sport Writers Association and Fantasy Sport Trade Association.
- **John Diver**, Senior Director of Product Development for ESPN. Diver started at ESPN in 1996 and his first responsibility was to write the rules for fantasy baseball. His other responsibilities include managing the more

than 40 fantasy and game products, managing prize budgets, design processes, and testing products. In 2004, Diver left ESPN and joined Yahoo! for a short-stint before returning to ESPN.
- **John Kosner**, Executive Vice President of Digital and Print Media at ESPN. As of 2014, Kosner had been with ESPN for 17 years, 10 of those overseeing ESPN Digital Media. Kosner generally oversees ESPN.com, ESPN Mobile, applications, Grantland.com, ESPNW, and *ESPN The Magazine*. In addition, Kosner manages content development for social media including partnerships with Facebook and Twitter. Kosner is credited as "pioneering online video" (ESPN MediaZone, 2014) including ESPN Motion, ESPN3, and the WatchESPN application, as well as assisting in the development of ESPN Insider (ESPN paid subscription service).

Using in-depth interviews with each of these three people who occupy distinctly different aspects of ESPN's fantasy sport presence, insight can be gleaned pertaining to the overall effect ESPN's endorsement of fantasy has had on the activity and the communication that surrounds it.

## EVOLUTION OF ESPN AND FANTASY SPORT

The year was 1995 and ideas about digitalizing the activity of fantasy sport started coming to fruition. While coining fantasy sport as the original sports social network, Kosner states that ESPN has been involved with the activity since "Starwave started ESPN.com in April of 1995" (J. Kosner, personal communication, January 17, 2014). This is where Diver enters the ESPN picture:

> I met an engineer… with this Paul Allen company called StarWave…. And they said we can automate the whole process. We can get live stats out of stadiums, we can get nightly loads, we can automate the process between people making real time roster moves. I sat there and… had this, what I call my Bugsy moment. You have ESPN as a brand, the Internet for connection, and fantasy games…. I quit my job that day, and right then I started working. (J. Diver, personal communication, January 16, 2012)

He notes that the first fantasy program written for ESPN was fantasy football in 1995, followed by fantasy baseball in 1996, much later than many other Internet startups related to fantasy sport (Fanball, Yahoo!, etc.). Initially, ESPN had 2,000 signups for $20 per team. It was not until the early 2000s that ESPN adopted its current free play model. Notes Diver: "We totally changed our shift in business and we went for just trying to get as many people as possible" (J. Diver, personal communication, January 16, 2012). This became the status quo for ESPN until 2006. This is when Berry joined ESPN full-time. As Kosner explains, prior to

Berry, one aspect of ESPN's fantasy reputation was that "it was kind of a dull place to play and [ESPN] really didn't have a sensibility of a fantasy player" (J. Kosner, personal communication, January 17, 2014). Kosner adds, "When Matthew arrived, in terms of his column, his persona, his podcasts, his segments on TV—that all began to change [throughout ESPN's various platforms]" (J. Kosner, personal communication, January 17, 2014). Along with the work of so many, Berry began to tackle the issue of how to promote the activity of fantasy sport to ESPN management and its consumers. Berry claims that one of the biggest failures was not recognizing "how passionate and how large the fan base was of fantasy players" (M. Berry, personal communication, January 16, 2012). To combat the notion that fantasy sport is just a "niche, it's a small little thing" (M. Berry, personal communication, January 16, 2012), Berry would have to persuade ESPN producers and executives with numbers and figures of the consumer base. For instance, ESPN internal research indicated that though the average nonfantasy playing sports fan consumed seven hours of ESPN media per week, the average fantasy-playing sports fan consumed more than triple that amount: 22 hours per week (ESPN Department of Integrated Media Research, 2010). When comparing to other sports, Berry stated:

> The message that I basically gave... consistently was that based on the amount of fan interest, the amount of revenue it generates for the company, and the importance of fantasy sports, not just to our fans interests, but also to the bottom line and future growth of ESPN. I don't think our coverage is commensurate with what that level is.... I didn't feel we did enough on television or radio or maybe even the magazine, on some level, that was equal to the amount of interest that our fans had. (M. Berry, personal communication, January 16, 2012)

When administration would agree with Berry, their next question usually was, "How do we do fantasy on television?" Berry stated that with all the entities and sport outlets under the ESPN umbrella, everyone wants his or her 30 seconds on *SportsCenter*, noting that the clutter "gets challenging" (M. Berry, personal communication, January 16, 2012). Accepting the challenge of promoting fantasy sport, ESPN introduced several new fantasy content aspects to their brand. ESPN has expanded, now offering the same type of items and services for fantasy sport as it does for traditional content such as mobile Web applications and breaking news alerts. ESPN has on-air programming dedicated to the activity, along with game highlights during *SportsCenter*, often including information pertaining strictly to fantasy sport. Game previews also have given attention to the fantasy-minded, including statistic predictions as part of the pregame notes. One of the most visible and notable programming is the hit NFL pregame show, *Fantasy Football Now*, possessing the highest ratings of any series on ESPN2 (as of 2012). Diver believes that this show was a significant driver in the advancement of fantasy sport at

ESPN because the TV-side now believed that "fantasy is a viable play for content, and just not going around the horn talking about the weather and if the defensive lineman has a hurt foot" (J. Diver, personal communication, January 16, 2012).

Using the reach and media platforms of ESPN is something that has affected the positive growth for ESPN's fantasy sport experience. Kosner states,

> I think the beautiful thing is that [the outlets] all come together. That was really critical in our move this summer to displace Yahoo! as number one in fantasy football.... It's best online, but that experience is changing. The key breakthrough for us was a great fantasy football application. More and more of this is being done online. And you can... draft players, change alerts, just do all that stuff from your phone standing in line at Starbucks. That's fantastic. (J. Kosner, personal communication, January 17, 2014)

With the combination of innovative ideas, new business models, key hires, and the most powerful brand in sport media, fantasy has thrived at ESPN. Although complete user numbers are not available for ESPN fantasy sport participation (because of proprietary reasons) it is well known that fantasy sport is prospering at ESPN (K. Ota, personal communication, March 17, 2014). What *is* known is that ESPN surpassed Yahoo! in total users for fantasy football in 2013 with 6,276,790 fantasy football participants (Duffy, 2013), roughly 20% of the North American fantasy sport-playing public. ESPN's total fantasy football growth rate has been extraordinary, having grown at a faster rate than Yahoo! from 2003 to 2013. ESPN started that period with 74,136 users versus Yahoo!'s 2,747,060 users (Duffy, 2013); in 2003, for every user ESPN had playing fantasy, Yahoo! had 37 users. In addition, total registered participants for ESPN fantasy sports increased by 15% in 2013, and unique users for ESPN Fantasy Football increased by 23% from the 2012 season to the 2013 season. The average audience on the fantasy sport website during the fantasy football regular season in 2013 was 223,000 per minute across all platforms on NFL Sundays, a 9% increase from 2012. Fantasy basketball had a 5% increase from 2012 to 2013, and fantasy hockey participation saw a 10% increase during the same time period (Duffy, 2013). For those anticipating a ceiling for fantasy sport consumption, that plateau has yet to be discovered.

The evolution of fantasy sport with and through the outlets of ESPN is extraordinary and rapid. From the humble beginnings of 2,000 football participants in 1995 to more than six million in 2013 is proof that ESPN has quickly become a fantasy sport powerhouse. ESPN offers the traditional fantasy experiences with the sports of baseball, football, basketball, and hockey but also offers the opportunity to participate in a variety of other sports. ESPN is reaching out to fans of sports and wants to involve them in the fantasy sport experience. A user does not have to have an interest in the four major spectator sports in the United States to participate in fantasy sport via an ESPN platform. Fantasy NASCAR, golf, soccer, cricket, and even fishing are also offered by ESPN. There is something for everyone who has an interest in participating in this activity. Fantasy participants can also determine the length of their participation by taking part in one-time-only events or season-long events. A person may choose only to become involved with fantasy golf during the four major tournaments because of a particular affinity for those events. He or she can participate in a league created for a group of friends or can join a larger event composed of hundreds or thousands of other participants. ESPN offers something for everyone. All that is needed is a desire to be involved in fantasy sport.

## Fantasy Sport Journalism

The proliferation of fantasy sport participation and the demand for fantasy-relevant information has led to a new type of sport communication professional: the fantasy sport journalist and the fantasy sport expert (Ruihley & Hardin, 2013). With the quick ability to enter the fantasy sport marketplace as a fantasy sport writer, the result was the need to ensure that ESPN was hiring the best people who were following appropriate journalistic practices. Some writers were doing tremendous, sophisticated work, yet the majority of the work offered as fantasy sport journalism was lacking appropriate source attribution (see Loop & Parkhurst, 2010). The advent of social media platforms such as Twitter has more recently exacerbated this problem (Loop, 2013).

The need to separate quality from clutter resulted in the Fantasy Sports Writers Association awards, but also led to major entities focusing on vetting candidates to secure the most journalistically equipped talent. ESPN realized this and has hired experts to provide information and content regarding fantasy sport. Berry anchors the fantasy sport team for ESPN. In addition to Berry, Christopher Harris, Erik Karabell, and Stephania Bell provide news and commentary across all of ESPN's platforms. Each has a particular area of expertise, such as Bell's analysis in regards to how injuries will affect fantasy performance for particular athletes. In discussing the journalistic side of fantasy sport, Kosner states,

> You have to make your content interesting and relevant. You notice at ESPN, we've gone so far to hire a woman named Stephania Bell, who is an injury expert. So, she really got her start doing injuries, as related to fantasy. It wasn't long before ESPN as a whole said, "Wow, Stephania has a great point of view on injuries... and that's [interesting] information... even if I didn't play fantasy." (J. Kosner, personal communication, January 17, 2014)

A typical fantasy sport article appearing on ESPN.com in March, for example, analyzes players for MLB fantasy teams or how the free agent movement in the NFL may influence the upcoming fantasy NFL season. Fantasy content on the site includes written commentary, performance projections, podcasts, blogs, video highlights, and video news-type features. Basically, it is the information that would be found on any other type of news outlet, only all of the content is focused on providing information to the fantasy sport user.

Berry's attitude on his role as a fantasy journalist can be summed up in six words: "You can't out-info the Internet" (M. Berry, personal communication, January 16, 2012). He elaborates:

> I believe and I certainly attribute a great deal of my success whatever that may be to the fact that I try to make fantasy fun, that I don't try to get bogged down in tons and tons of numbers. I mean, I do my research, but I'm not going to out-stat somebody else. I'm not going to out-scout someone else. I think the people that are fans of mine enjoy it because I take that analysis and make it succinct and in an entertaining, fun, interesting, funny way. (M. Berry, personal communication, January 16, 2012)

This content has proliferated across all of ESPN's platforms as well. Traditional print journalists write content for newspapers and also have to be prepared for television interviews, podcasts, radio interviews, and be ready to place self-created videos online. This is no different for the fantasy sport experts and news anchors at ESPN. The fantasy sport experts at ESPN have to provide content across multimedia platforms and be able to provide commentary on breaking news as well. An NFL analyst has to appear on *SportsCenter* to provide insight on the impact a player trade may have on each team. A fantasy sport analyst likewise has to be prepared to provide insight into the impact the trade will have on the fantasy sport performance of the player. *SportsCenter* anchors and hosts of other news-oriented programming had to expand their knowledge base so they could provide information about fantasy sport during the broadcasts of their programming. Fantasy sport not only created the position of a fantasy sport expert but also altered the content of traditional news shows, providing a new type of information about sports.

## ESPN and the Fantasy Marketplace: Present And Future

As seen with the rise to the top of fantasy football providers, ESPN's place in the fantasy marketplace is strong, even in the midst of heavy competition. From the major fantasy hosts such as Yahoo!, CBS Sports, or any league office, to information outlets such as Rotoworld or Rotowire, ESPN is in a daily fight for the attention of fantasy-minded consumers. When asked about competing in this young marketplace, Berry and Diver mentioned marketing professionals and administrators suggesting ways to get more users. Berry states,

> One of the things we talked about was [that we] wanted to get more users, and... there were basically two ways to do it. One, was to try to go after Yahoo! and CBS and places where there were other [participants] and try to convince them to switch.... We certainly

did that and we went... fully free.... Yahoo! followed a few years later giving up their paid live scoring. (M. Berry, personal communication, January 16, 2012)

Berry also elaborated on how ESPN decided it was easier to grow the fantasy sport industry rather than cannibalize it:

> Frankly, an easier path would be a path of more opportunity.... Instead of trying to convince people that played to switch, we thought it would be easier just to grow the pie.... Because of the reach of ESPN... we thought it might be easier... to convince people, that were already prone to liking sports that just haven't played fantasy.... So, that was one of the things we did and one of the ways we attempted that was to try to make it cool. That fantasy football had sort of been pigeon-holed as this kind of nerdy enterprise as kind of a geeky pastime, and so, what we wanted to do was to make it... not geeky, it's not nerdy, it's just something that everyone does. You know? What do guys like? Guys like movies where stuff blows up, they like fast cars, they like attractive women, they like cigars, and playing craps at the table in Vegas, and they play fantasy sports. (M. Berry, personal communication, January 16, 2012)

Diver adds to the idea of growing the pie, justifying the approach in simply stating that "It's really hard to get people to switch" (J. Diver, personal communication, January 16, 2012). Diver discussed the idea that people get used to their fantasy provider, the design of the site, and the fact that participants become loyal to their site. He states,

> I think any kind of design is learned behavior. We do all kinds of surveys. It's something that we have a central survey group at ESPN. I interface with them a lot to sort of target market these and then I'm good at reading the numbers and the CBS guys are very loyal to CBS. They love their interface.... Because they're used to it. And that's why any kind of re-design that we try to do, whether it [is] on the sports side or the fantasy side... 90% hate it. And, then six months later, if we went back to the old way, they'd say, "I hate the old way." So, the design part of it is part of it. (J. Diver, personal communication, January 16, 2012)

Diver focused on a more specific demographic, while Berry's focus was more on taking the geek stereotype out of the activity.

> We've focused more... on trying to get that 18 year old who's going to college. He's got nine buddies. We get them to sign up and play fantasy football with us, and we have them for the next 40 years. So, we've been shifting our target marketing to younger people as opposed to this pipe dream that people think that you can make people switch, which is not the case. (M. Berry, personal communication, January 16, 2012)

In discussing competition and the driving force of attracting new consumers, Diver offers:

> I think that part of our job... is to create habits. We want people to have bookmarks, go check their fantasy basketball page, go look at tomorrow's lineup, make sure they don't have any bench players, make sure no one's hurt, pick [their] *Streak for the Cash*, go look at [their]

English Premier Soccer League team. So, in that case, I think that I like to get into the psyche of the user and think, OK what is this person doing? If someone has 45 minutes a day that they sit in front of their computer or on their cellphone clicking around and looking at things, we want to try to get a percentage of that. (J. Diver, personal communication, January 16, 2012)

Such habit formation appears to be paramount to the entire construction of the ESPN fantasy sport media empire. If ESPN wants to continue being known as "one-stop shopping" for the sports fan, it needs to be central to virtually all aspects of the fantasy sport experience.

The vision for ESPN and the future of fantasy sport is one that is abundant and expanding. ESPN offers some unique features for its football and baseball fantasy sport consumers. Fantasy football features the Commissioner's Toolkit, allowing simulated press conferences with *SportsCenter* anchors, which can be shared via social media. Video messages from players accepting or rejecting trades as well as messages providing reminders to set lineups for upcoming games are part of the toolkit. Draft report cards and scheduling tools are also available. Features for fantasy baseball include mock drafts, draft kits including player rankings, FantasyCasts for real-time fantasy scoring, and interactive features such as message boards and chats.

Discussing the evolution of the mock draft feature, Kosner expressed surprise at the popularity. He states,

One of our engineers said, "Well, what if we provided a mechanism where people could use the draft engine to practice for their fantasy draft?" This sounded to me like the craziest thing ever. Are people really going to practice for their fantasy draft? But we did use the feature about five to six years ago called the *Mock Draft Lobby*.... Every day on ESPN.com, from June through the start of the season, you have 50 rooms of about 10 players each practicing for their fantasy draft. Basically, people enter mock drafts with total strangers, with a purpose of practicing for the draft. And so, this is activity that really isn't counted under [a] daily game. These are just people in there practicing. (J. Kosner, personal communication, January 17, 2014)

Additionally, Kosner identifies three areas that need to be considered in future growth. The first is a concern that there is a long way to go in terms of alerts and recommendations for more information. He argues that "nobody has really done a brilliant job... in terms of harnessing third-party social networks like Facebook and Twitter around fantasy games" (J. Kosner, personal communication, January 17, 2014). The second area Kosner mentioned was the idea that ESPN will have "more of a multicultural effort with fantasy games in the next few years" (J. Kosner, personal communication, January 17, 2014). This is in response to soccer gaining more fantasy attention. And lastly, Kosner believes there will be "growth in new, easy-to-play, daily fantasy games, especially those that have components that lend themselves to a sort of social sharing" (J. Kosner, personal communication, January 17, 2014). As Diver notes, "The challenges... in our case, on a year-to-year basis, are renewing the sponsorships... [and] how do we deal with the advertisers." (J. Diver, personal communication, January 16, 2012)

## CONCLUSION

To tie all of this information back to foundational tenets of communication theory, ESPN's strategy is perhaps best embedded (and, hence, summarized) within the joint lenses of agenda setting and framing theories. Beyond the basic notion founded in agenda setting that postulates that media does not tell us what to think but can be quite effective at telling us what to think about (McCombs & Shaw, 1972), sports scholars (see Billings & Eastman, 2003) have focused much effort into how media conglomerates can frame conversations in dramatically different fashions (see Goffman, 1974). Entman (1993) claimed that "to frame is to select some aspects of a perceived reality and make them more salient in a communicating text" (p. 52). Such possibilities seem exceedingly pertinent to a multi-platform multimedia entity purporting to be the "Worldwide Leader in Sports," as ESPN possessed all of the mechanisms to mainstream fantasy play as well as the "street cred" to shift its image away from initial connotations of connections to fantasy games such as *Dungeons and Dragons.*

Tankard (2001) argued that framing can be viewed in a variety of manners, including the lenses of selection, emphasis, and exclusion. Each is a useful heuristic for understanding the power and influence of ESPN media as it related to fantasy sport play. First, in relation to selection, simply acknowledging that fantasy sport was a part of being a sport fan was an immense breakthrough for the fantasy industry. ESPN claimed that its hiring of Berry represented a "tipping point" moment, and this was likely because of the role selection plays within overall framing mechanisms. Even if Berry (or any other fantasy-related content) was only receiving a modicum of seconds on ESPN's airwaves, the fact that fantasy was anywhere in the conversation of being a modern sports fan advanced the fantasy industry. In essence, the moment ESPN added a fantasy element to each of its seemingly myriad platforms, the conglomerate was making the claim that being a fan and being a fantasy sport player involved some level of overlap between the two circles.

Second, Tankard (2001) noted the power of emphasis within media framing. This also became part of the ESPN equation related to fantasy sport. As fantasy discussions percolated on homepages (rather than being several Web clicks away) and fantasy sport discussions at least somewhat migrated to flagship programming such as *SportsCenter*, the message was seemingly clear: Fantasy is not just a potential part of being a contemporary sports fan, it is possibly an essential element to modern fandom.

Finally, Tankard (2001) noted the frame of exclusion and the cognitions that can arise from it. If fantasy had continued to be excluded from mainstream ESPN programming, fantasy would likely have a much more niche status in later years. Moreover, ESPN does exercise some level of exclusion at least within programming and non-Web content as football and baseball receive some level of mainstream coverage (and magazine special issues, etc.) but other forms of fantasy (NASCAR, daily games) are relegated to Web presences only, negating any sense of mainstream impact of these secondary fantasy sport game formats.

ESPN has certainly recognized the potential for fantasy sport and the demand for participation in it. The opportunity to have a fantasy experience in virtually every sport is offered by ESPN, and substantial resources have been devoted to the endeavor. These resources are websites, media platforms, employees, and airtime for information in regards to fantasy sport. This devotion of resources has in turn created more attention to fantasy sport and increased fantasy sport awareness; it is a symbiotic relationship. Fantasy sport has grown due to ESPN's commitment to it, and participation via ESPN platforms has increased due to this increased interest. ESPN's decision to embrace fantasy sport has been a positive business decision not only for ESPN but also for the entire fantasy sport industry.

# CHAPTER EIGHTEEN

# Missed Opportunity

## The Decline of Athletics on ESPN and America's Passive Culture

JEFFERY GENTRY AND GARRET CASTLEBERRY

A frenetic Bud Palmer of NBC Sports yelled out the final laps of the men's 10,000-meter run for American viewers at the 1964 Summer Olympics in Tokyo, assisted by Dick Bank. For the first time, satellite technology permitted live Olympic coverage from halfway around the world. Seventy-five thousand spectators roared their approval at the breakneck speed of the athletes after six miles of racing. Palmer continued:

> And here we go on the final lap for the gold medal in the 10,000 meters. And up front is Bill Mills. He's pressing Ron Clarke, the world champion.... But [Mohammed] Gammoudi goes out ahead. It's Gammoudi right now leading in the 10,000 meters.... He's out ahead of Ron Clarke.... CAN RON CLARKE CATCH GAMMOUDI!? They're going through the field. He's coming up. He's passing Gammoudi. (Yamaha, 2010; dialogue transcribed by the authors)

In the chaos of runners being lapped in the home stretch, Palmer was oblivious to what was taking place behind the two leaders. As retold by Mohammed Gammoudi (Duffy, 2012), American Billy Mills looked like an arrow shot from a bow, in what can arguably be described as a supernatural act caught on film. Bank, who was supposed to be merely filling the role of spotter for Palmer, could no longer contain himself: "Look at—LOOK AT MILLS!! LOOK AT MILLS!!" Palmer finally noticed the American and called his sprint finish for first place, all while Bank screamed, laughed, and invoked the name of his creator.

Bank's excitement reflected America's passion for athletic excellence. Unlike today's prepackaged and tape-delayed track broadcasts, viewers in the United States watched the race live even though it aired late at night. Decades later, readers of *Track and Field News* (2012) watched Mills's closing lap online and gushed: "It is the greatest athletic feat ever. It is the most dramatic ending on video since *Ben Hur*. It is the most surprising victory since Agincourt 1415. No matter how many times you watch it, it only gets better with age.... It is soul-stirring, it is cosmic!!" (para. 1, 3).

Televised track and field spectacles continued to mesmerize American TV audiences for another decade. Major competitions were hyped in the print media as well, including many *Sports Illustrated* cover stories in non-Olympic years. One example was the "Dream Mile" showdown between Americans Jim Ryun and Marty Liquori in Philadelphia in 1971, live and in prime time. According to *New York Times* columnist Tom Connelly (2011), "Like Ali-Frazier, Liquori-Ryun lived up to its hype," with Liquori taking the world-record holder by a stride (p. D5). Such television spectacles, including Frank Shorter's Olympic gold in the marathon a year later, prompted an explosion in amateur running participation across America.

The running boom was in full swing in 1979 when ESPN began cablecasting. Soon everything changed. By Connelly's (2011) reckoning, "Forty years on, it's hard to imagine the average American giving a second thought to any track rivalry, never mind debating it on sports radio" (p. D5). This chapter does not claim that ESPN decimated televised running and track and field (known around the world as "athletics"), only that its 35-year history reflects and reinforces changes in American culture that left these sports behind.

## METHODS

This study synthesizes two independent qualitative methods. First we provide historical-comparative research in the style of Putnam (1995). According to Yuginovich (2000), historical-comparative research provides a tool to explain why certain social practices developed as they did in a particular culture. Neither strictly positivist nor interpretive, "it combines a sensitivity to historic or cultural contexts with theoretical generalization" to analyze and theorize about the relationships of social phenomena (p. 71). Putnam's (1995) "bowling alone" research identifies social change based on a combination of facts and inductive reasoning. Unlike critical theory, this part of our analysis grants ESPN its motives as a profit-seeking agent with legitimate ownership of its worldview. The question is whether the network's programming choices produce societal benefits versus deficits.

Putnam (1995) investigated the trend of Americans bypassing civic engagement in favor of a "widespread tendency toward *passive* reliance on the state" in recent generations (p. 65; emphasis added). He observed deteriorating participation in community organizations that provide services for others, as well as a decline in social activities that promote mutual belonging. The author's use of the word *passive* is noteworthy. Although he described how passive pursuits like television per se eclipse active groups, equally salient is how media *content* may influence change. In other words, some media content may be more civically engaging than other content. Thus an increasingly passive or lethargic society may trade active content for passive. Does a passive society eschew sports programming that could motivate them toward a fitness activity? For example, a televised road race may inspire viewers to head out the door for a walk or run. Passive programs such as televised poker may instead motivate viewers to spin their chairs around and play Internet poker. New research can extend Putnam's *passive reliance* concept to media content on networks such as ESPN.

Putnam (2000) defined social capital as "networks, norms, and social trust that facilitate coordination and cooperation for mutual benefit" (p. 67). Social capital amplifies reputations and reduces incentives for individual opportunism. According to Putnam, social capital is powerful, raising all boats in the community via improved incomes, reduced crime, and healthier lives. In contrast, virtual escapes such as television have made community involvement shallower, with individuals spending more time alone with electronic media than with other people. This transformation can lead to social isolation, placing a wedge between individual interests and collective interests. Putnam's concern here is the drastic increase in media consumption in recent generations. However, *within* the media landscape, we can analyze whether ESPN's programming choices support community values or detract from them. Do its programs emphasize mutual benefit, amplify reputations, and discourage opportunism? Do ESPN's programming choices value collective interests over individual interests, thus serving to strengthen American community rather than diminish its social capital?

In answering the key questions that Putnam prompts, it is also beneficial to analyze ESPN critically, in conjunction with the influence it assumes from corporate parent and synergistic enabler Disney. We use terminology from critical theory that exposes ESPN's corporate priorities that undermine social capital. These observations add theoretical depth to the issues under investigation. Overlaying some of critical theory's robust vocabulary helps differentiate the two oppositional courses of social capital and media hegemony. Thus we draw upon the language of critical theory (e.g., Williamson, 1967) to reveal how ESPN's corporate-casting model minimizes sports such as track and field in favor of homogenized programming blocks and hyper-masculine ambiance that privileges both in-studio content and sports spectacle. This analysis recognizes scholars who lend credence to the cultural effects of sports spectacle on audiences (Grove, Dorsch, & Hopkins, 2012; Rose & Friedman, 1994), as well as filmmakers who brazenly welcome controversy and debate (Picker & Sun, 2002) when critiquing ESPN's corporate parent.

## Facts on the Ground: Then and Now

ESPN's programming schedule has changed dramatically over the years. In the early 1990s it aired five hours of morning fitness programs on its flagship channel, such as *Body Shaping, Bodies in Motion*, and *Kiana's Flex Appeal* with Kiana Tom (Rodriguez, 1993). The network also offered *Running and Racing* (1988–2002), which Toni Reavis and later 1971 dream miler Liquori hosted. ESPN and ESPN2 covered track and field extensively in those days, including more international meetings and collegiate competitions than can be found on ESPN's networks today. The network put no capital resources or promotional efforts into these programs, relying on the shows' production companies to do any heavy lifting (Rodriguez, 1993). Basically, ESPN sold its airtime similar to the outright infomercials aired on its lesser channels today (A. Burfoot, personal communication, July 29, 2014). In the case of *Running and Racing*, the result was a lackluster monthly program on major road races around the country. By the time each episode aired, the races were several weeks old. Production values were minimal, with the host narrating b-roll footage and summarizing results. Former syndication models of production had allowed networks more economic stability so long as the content generated appropriate audience levels that translated into ad revenue. Deregulation laws throughout the past 25 years helped chip away such traditional production outlets toward ESPN's inward brand-focused models in the 2010s (Mullen, 2008; Williams, 1974).

ESPN and ESPN2, the two most widely distributed ESPN-branded channels, reveal a trend toward homogenization in their programming today. For example, on the non-randomly selected summer day in 2014, ESPN and ESPN2 aired the programs shown in Table 18.1 (sorted by genre, hours, and percent of total).

Table 18.1. Example day's program share: ESPN and ESPN2 by Genre—Wednesday, July 23, 2014.

| Program Genre | Hours | Share of Total |
| --- | --- | --- |
| *SportsCenter* | 16.5 | 34% |
| General chat/talk | 15.5 | 32% |
| Baseball chat/talk | 2 | 4% |
| Football chat/talk | 4 | 8% |
| Baseball game coverage | 7.5 | 16% |
| Soccer game coverage | 2 | 4% |
| Investigative journalism | .5 | 1% |
| Total | 48 | 100% |

Table 18.1 reveals ESPN's programming day was dominated by men in suit jackets talking about sports (79%). Chat/talk shows included *NFL Live, Baseball Tonight, ESPN First Take,* and 12 others. Nothing like *Body Shaping* or *Running and Racing* exists on ESPN/ESPN2 today. However, ESPN and ESPN2 do provide limited coverage of the *Reebok CrossFit Games,* a summer miniseries involving impromptu calisthenics, weightlifting, and endurance exercises (McIntyre, 2014).

ESPN, ESPN2, and ESPNU provide occasional coverage of track and field meetings with little or no promotion. Yet poker tournaments are now broadcast regularly. ESPN's involvement began in 2003 with the World Series of Poker. According to Duncan (2014), this attention helped create today's boom in poker participation. The year before poker's television debut, *Running and Racing* left ESPN before disappearing altogether.

As ESPN replaced athletics and fitness programs with chat shows and poker, several noteworthy trends in American culture coincided. Based on agreed-upon data, Putnam (2000) observed rising body-mass indexes (BMI), the disappearance of walking, and the rise of gambling. He found that sports participation among adults fell drastically at the same time *watching* sports increased. This shift reflected the "changing balance between active participation and passive spectatorship" (p. 113). Putnam was careful not to imply causality, only observing that these shifts occurred together. The trend of "observing up, doing down" permeates all spheres of American life (p. 114).

New evidence demonstrates that America has become passive. Lethargy has become the national pastime, and overweight is the new normal. In 1980, one in seven American adults was obese. Today the number is more than one in three, with a projected rate of 50% by 2030 (Begley, 2012). The average American is 25 pounds overweight. The problem is not overeating, as caloric intake remains flat since 1994 (Sifferlin, 2014). The dramatic decline in exercise is to blame. For ESPN's largely male demographic, the ratio reporting zero physical activity skyrocketed from 11.4% in 1994 to 43.5% in 2010.

Players in all the major sports ESPN covered have grown heavier. Although today's players are no less athletic than their predecessors, Weir (2010) notes an unpublished study by Harvard's Eric Ding reporting that an all-time high of 55% of MLB players are overweight, with significantly higher mortality rates than their thinner teammates. Neporent (2013) noted statistics from ESPN indicating that NFL linemen are more than 50 pounds heavier than their predecessors in 1979. Larger players mean more force when they collide, resulting in higher concussion rates. Neporent cites research on the rise in chronic traumatic encephalopathy (CTE), the degenerative brain disease linked to a spate of suicides by former NFL players.

A final salient trend coinciding with ESPN's rise is the disappearance of physical education (PE) in America, with varsity sports dominating in the nation's public schools. The elder author of this chapter enjoyed 10 years of required physical education—through the sophomore year of high school. As schools have dropped PE, today's youth are 15% slower and heavier than their parents at the same age (Marchione, 2013). Many schools that cut support for PE have built large stadiums and state-of-the-art training facilities for varsity athletes. For example, Allen, Texas, built a palatial $60 million football stadium in 2012—now closed due to structural flaws (Prisbell, 2014). That same year Texas reduced its high school physical education requirement to one credit, and PE teachers were among the first layoffs when the state slashed education funding (Meyers, 2012). Allen High School is among the many schools requiring only one PE credit (Stafford, 2014). The vast majority of students are left in the seats to watch the few celebrated elites in action.

In contemporary America, even some varsity athletes have lost cultural resonance. The glory belongs not to the cross-country, track and field, or soccer teams. These students, though fitter and healthier than the anointed athletes, are relegated to comparative anonymity. Instead the glory goes to the largest, heaviest players—those in football, basketball, and to a lesser extent baseball. These high school/college "revenue sports" receive the lion's share of funding and are hyped by public relations offices. At the college/professional level they receive copious attention on ESPN's sports chat shows. All the trends noted here, from ESPN's program schedule, to declining activity at all ages, to elitist physical education, corroborate the passive culture.

## ANALYSIS

We see above that ESPN's programming is consistent with an increasingly sedentary U.S. society. This process is twice enabled due to a media culture whose economic incentives (i.e., corporate ideology) encourage further media consumption that begets traditional media criticisms like increased audience passivity and isolation. In this section we consider the value implications of these choices, extending Putnam's notion of social capital to the literal, physical level. The following observations identify social ills related to the passive culture, as well as noting how ESPN could have been different.

### Observation 1: ESPN Reinforces the Passive Society

Television is inherently a leisure pursuit. But now ESPN's content has become leisurely. Despite a smattering of CrossFit and track and field, ESPN emphasizes sports chat over game action, and airs so-called sports such as poker instead of athletics and fitness-instruction. Thirty years ago it was unheard of to broadcast men sitting around a table playing cards. Now it can be seen in prime time on the "Worldwide Leader in Sports." ESPN features little content related to dynamic sports. Instead, viewers see hours of studio chat on the major sports of football, baseball, and basketball. Players and viewers have grown larger over ESPN's history: a majority of both groups are overweight and many are clinically obese (Neporent, 2012). Perhaps viewers can better relate to these players as opposed to identifying with track runners, whose BMIs usually fall in the normal range.

As more Americans defer sports participation in favor of watching elites (Putnam, 2000), personally knowing an athlete becomes rare. According to Hollander (2010), elite runners are "almost alien" (para. 4) whereas amateur runners "are not *athletes*" (para. 5; emphasis in original). This dismissal is common despite evidence that humans are the best-adapted long-distance-running species on the planet, and owe our evolutionary survival to just this talent (e.g., McDougall, 2011). Non-athletes likewise perpetuate the myth that running is somehow hard on people's knees and joints, despite empirical evidence showing otherwise (Logan, 2013).

Sports chat and poker are not the only physically passive enterprises broadcast on ESPN. Despite its athletic and brutal nature, we argue that even football qualifies as a leisure sport. Practically no one older than 22 plays the game, and women are unrepresented at all ages. Compare this absence to long-distance running, in which millions of adults participate every week and compete regularly (Running USA, 2014). Football fans are a leisure class who, from the comfort of couch or stadium, watch a gladiatorial sport for amusement. Likewise, few ESPN viewers regularly played baseball or basketball after college. According to the Physical Activity Council (2014), fewer than 20% of adults participate in team sports, compared to more than 60% participation in fitness sports. ESPN viewers' only personal involvement in these sports often involves fantasy leagues that are no more dynamic than poker. For adults, these are beer and gambling sports, not participatory sports. ESPN emphasizes sports that are alien to their viewers' dynamic experience.

ESPN's choices not only reinforce the passive society, they indirectly promote serious social problems. The high salaries of football players are derived largely by TV revenue, some from ESPN's *Monday Night Football*. The pursuit of economic security via sports has long represented a hallmark goal for many underprivileged families. Arguably, star athletes' salaries feed viewer fantasies to encourage children into youth football, which can result in injuries such as concussions. The new awareness of concussions in football is a nationwide crisis and NFL scandal, leaving observers such as journalist Rick Reilly (2013) reevaluating their love of the game. Yet until recently, ESPN hosts celebrated devastating hits with, "You just got... jacked up!"

ESPN's prime viewing audience consists of young adult men. This group further reflects America's descent into passivity, as sliding educational attainment and underemployment bedevil this group today. According to Roberts (2011),

America has produced a generation of young men who often lack ambition, drop out of college, and live in their parents' basements. They even lack ambition sexually, delaying marriage and turning to pornography rather than pursuing actual mates. Once married, today's men have fewer children than ever. The moribund birth rate has produced a rapidly aging population and unsustainable dependency ratios (Gentry, 2013).

## Observation 2: ESPN Diminishes Social Capital

Putnam's (1995) notion of social capital values human interactions that create cooperation, mutual benefit, and amplify reputations. Can sports participation and even sports broadcasting support these values? ESPN's anointed sports are football, basketball, and baseball. Others receive strong support depending on the season, and still others receive no attention at all. They share elements that distinguish them from sports such as running and track and field. We suggest that these differences impact social capital, with zero-sum games contrasted with positive-sum games (see Table 18.2). Classically, a zero-sum game is one in which any gains made by one side are offset by losses on the other. We apply this metaphor to sports, with zero-sum games producing negative social impacts equal to or greater than beneficial impacts, and positive-sum games offering net-benefits to participants. Zero-sum games are associated with immediate and long-term health problems, such as the football and baseball examples noted previously. They feature dramatic confrontations such as a power-pitcher striking out a feared slugger to end a scoring threat, or the high-flying forward dunking over his opponent. Referees are intrusive and integral to most zero-sum games, providing fodder to ESPN's pundits to debate their controversial calls. Finally, they give dramatic emphasis to winners and humiliated losers, "who's hot/who's not," and who got "posterized." The second-best team in the league is branded losers for choking in the big game: *They'll dwell on this loss all summer. Can they ever recover?* This is the dominion of ESPN.

Table 18.2. Differences in social capital among sport genres.

| Genre | Health | Confrontation | Referees | Humiliation |
|---|---|---|---|---|
| Zero-sum Game | Negative | High | Intrusive | More |
| Positive-sum Game | Positive | Low | Peripheral | Less |

Zero-sum games: Football, basketball, baseball, boxing, poker, et al.
Positive-sum games: Running, track and field, bicycle racing, swimming, et al.

Positive-sum games involve competition, certainly, but yield positive synergies for all. Running and track and field provide net health advantages to their amateur and professional participants, not concussions and early heart disease. Even among opponents, camaraderie is high and confrontation low. As Gentry (1995) whimsically noted, track and field is covered less on U.S. television because "not enough fights break out between opposing high jumpers" (p. D2).

Officials are unnoticed in most meetings of these sports. Rarely are they called upon to scrutinize a photo finish or disqualify a runner for going outside his or her lane. Humiliation is likewise uncommon except when self-inflicted, such as a hurdler tumbling to the track. The athletes do not make excuses or work the referees the way zero-sum-game players/coaches do. Whoever is in the best shape and executes wins. Second-place athletes usually congratulate the winners immediately and sincerely. Placing second in the 2013 New York City Marathon could not have been too devastating for Ethiopia's Tsegaye Kebede when 50,264 racers finished behind him.

Positive-sum games are more equitable in gender performance. For example, the women's marathon world best is within 10% of the men's. Zero-sum games, which dominate ESPN, feature male supremacy. Tuggle (1997) reported that ESPN devoted only 5% of *SportsCenter* airtime to female competitors. Female participation is drastically lower in zero-sum games, perhaps due to their diminished social capital. Cooperation, mutual benefit, and enhanced reputations are served in positive-sum games. This is not to say they should dominate the airwaves, only that they provide greater social capital than their counterparts.

## Observation 3: ESPN Projects Corporate Media Hegemony

ESPN's corporate media strategy communicates several distinctions on a macro level. ESPN exhaustively simulcasts its radio talk shows over its multichannel television tiers. This redundant synergy model signals on one hand an attempt at synthesizing broadcast mediums while on the other hand a failed execution at creative brand and audience extension. Whereas alternative channels might legitimize positive-sum games such as marathons, the ESPN cable block effectively reduces itself into an echo chamber closer in execution to "CNN Headline News" as opposed to NBC's billion-dollar multilingual, multicultural, cross-gender biannual prestige spectacles in the Summer and Winter Olympics. In comparison, ESPN encourages mass consumption via sound bite ad infinitum, and NBC broadcasts strike greater balance between an ambiance of tradition and inspiration that equalize contemporary sports' reliance on high definition and overproduced spectacle. NBC's Olympic model, which marginalizes athletics three out of every four years, contrasts ESPN's rock'em sock'em and even wrasslin'-esque turns that bring into question the media brand's journalistic integrity as well as its self-congratulatory kingship atop the sports hegemony throne (Adams & Tuggle, 2004; Kian, Mondello, & Vincent, 2009; Messner, Duncan, & Williams, 2006).

Although a claim could be made that NBC/Universal and Fox Sports/News Corp. are expanding the number of channels they operate and audience reach, these calculated financial gambles are necessitated because of ESPN's direct financial dominance and synergistic media hegemony. ESPN charges cable companies upward of $5.54 per month per subscriber, a number that inflates regularly despite ESPN constituting a fraction of the cable viewing audience (Parramore, 2013; Sandomir, Miller, & Eder, 2013; Scheckner & Peers, 2011; Thompson, 2012). Simultaneous hyperinflation of player salaries, sports stadium mega-palaces, and ballooning cable costs regardless of channel viewership communicates the hegemonic encroachment that ESPN inoculates, aggrandizes, and thereby encourages via imitation among its competitors. The financial ramifications play at such an exaggerated level that competing costs like these threaten to destabilize the structures of cable TV altogether and not necessarily to the benefit of consumers (Sandomir et al., 2013).

The corporate model ESPN produces can also be identified at the personal/personnel or micro level. The full-bodied suits that studio commentators adorn couples with overtly *visualize style*, class distinction, and legitimacy over viewers, while the same boardroom apparel covertly communicates authority, control, and corporatization or corporate legitimacy (see Brummett, 2009). Dressed more like politicians than community leaders, talking heads (usually former players and coaches) refer to sports like the NFL as a business, which reflects the mentality on the minds of hosts, producers, and (now) audiences. With business priorities surfacing at each tier of ESPN's hierarchy, this transmedia model has transformed from an outdoor focus to an indoor one.

In striking contrast to athletics coverage that may inspire viewers to hit the asphalt, a good businessperson knows there is no recess during work hours. The studio production design embraces high definition in the most spectacular sense (Winslow, 2014), privileging interiority over exteriority to draw viewers into the studio ambiance like the contemporary post-production mise-en-scene of expensive summer blockbusters. The similar strategic studio set designs posit a diametrically discouraging motivation that, over time, opposes active engagement (and by extension Putnam's social capital). Instead, the lurid lenses detail pinstripe suits and polka dot ties in ways that invite theatrics through ambiance. Continual lavish upgrades in studio presence and presentation recall emerging trends toward what Debord (1983) guardedly identifies as a society of "the spectacle" (pp. 3, 5, 44, 49). Semiotician Judith Williamson (1967) might also ward off seductive technological entrapments like high definition and its propensity to elicit "desire" (p. 65) while hailing viewers—a process of "appellation" (p. 44)—toward increased televisual consumption.

We could argue secondarily that ESPN's primary production shifts, from outdoor athletic events toward indoor climate-controlled and corporately stylized programming blocks, denote a substitution from outdoor exteriority. Williamson

(1967) would call this kind of corporate ideology "The Natural," in which her quotation marks ironically denote a pseudo-natural state. The author goes on to theorize that "culture" produces "science" that "reveals" a false nature identified as "The Natural" (p. 135). Thus in permeating "The Natural" through in-studio spectacle, ESPN converts the *active* nature of sports into a *passive* commodity for consumers. Following this informed deduction and compounded by the habitual urgency in keeping up with 24-hour information cycles, the net result produces media consumption that mitigates leisure culture due to the temporal urgency that live sports/news is predicated upon.

## Observation 4: ESPN Could Increase Social Capital and Remain Profitable

Missed opportunities befall the business world daily. When consumers complain that a product lacks a preferred feature, the salesperson may say, "Not enough people would want that." When that same company goes bankrupt months later, a top executive may lament, "If only we had added that [same] feature." The point is that corporations make mistakes all the time. To assume that ESPN would go broke if it put modest resources into athletics is just that: an assumption. We do not know because they have not tried. They have never invested in athletics the way they have soccer, the X-Games, or even poker.

The 2014 FIFA World Cup was highly profitable for ESPN, with higher ratings than the most recent World Series and NBA Finals (Velasco, 2014). This success countered the assumption that Americans are apathetic about soccer. The World Cup was successful because ESPN (and ABC) marketed it heavily and invested high production values. ESPN likewise pays millions for Major League Soccer despite the league's second-tier status. ESPN President John Skipper hailed the MLS deal for 2015–2022 as a futures investment: "We're buying pork bellies. We think they'll become more valuable over time.... We reach 115 million fans every week. It's a question of where we turn on the promotional fire hose" (p. B16). Clearly, investment and hype can build a market for entertainment programming that did not exist previously.

Why did ESPN not invest in athletics during the running boom when the channel was launched in 1979? It would have been far cheaper in real dollars than the new MLS deal. MLS is a minor league and the United States is a minor factor in the World Cup. But Team USA is the number-one track and field power in the world and has been for all of modern history. Even during the height of the Soviet and East German doping programs, America won the initial 1983 World Championships in Helsinki. Nothing has changed since. At the 2014 World Relays, the United States scored 60 points, with Jamaica second with 41 and Kenya third with 35. America's distance runners are resurgent, featuring Galen Rupp's and Jenny Simpson's major victories, and Meb Keflezighi's victory in the 2014 Boston Marathon.

Although running in America began to dip in the latter 1980s, the second running boom is in full force. *Running USA* (2014) reports more than 19 million Americans ran a certified road race in 2013, including 541,000 marathon finishers. Both are all-time records and three times greater than 1980. Women account for 57% of all road racers today, and more than half of today's runners are in a coveted TV age range (adults 25–44). They comprise a massive, underserved sports market.

Although ESPN ignores track and field and running, the social mediascape runs rampant with popular technologies that synergize global positioning systems (GPS) with social media. Examples include Nike+Running, MapMyRun, and Garmin Connect. Arguably, the *Track and Field News* sentiments on Mills's historic run, noted above, highlight levels of passion and celebration that constitute a key tenant of *fandom*. Scholars of fan studies would collectively agree that if a passionate group of fans excite a large enough base, then these outlier voices suddenly legitimize an authentic audience niche with untapped market potential (Deuze, 2007; Gray, Sandvass, & Harrington, 2007; Johnson, 2013). Fast-forward to the 2010s and niche cultural markets signal chief demographic interest among media producers, relaying the potential for track and field's return to the national consciousness. However, as sports technologies increase, so too must the presentation of sports spectacle if a marginalized sport like running is to reenter the limelight.

The new CrossFit Games would seem to be a successor to athletics coverage on ESPN. Although ESPN and ESPN2 provide only a few hours of coverage per year, CrossFit may provide net disadvantages to social capital. CrossFit's mascot is named Pukey the Clown, suggesting that the sport is more about reality-TV spectacle than fitness. According to Basso (2013), injuries plague CrossFit athletes because they have to perform power exercises such as weightlifting after being freshly exhausted from aerobics. He concludes that CrossFit is a business bubble that will burst, to be overtaken by traditional, proven sports. The corporation CrossFit also has a tendency to sue its critics (Fainaru-Wada, 2014), which would seem to undermine rather than amplify reputations as envisioned by Putnam (2000).

When television ventures into track and field and running outside the Olympics, ratings are modest. But who is to blame? Professional runner David Torrence (2013) provides a decisive opinion:

> TV has done the absolute WORST job of promoting our sport and our elite athletes, and to put it simply: make us look cool… Track and Road Races are broadcasted the EXACT same way they have been broadcasted for DECADES. There has been very little innovation, very little creativity, very little drive to try and make it more entertaining on the screen. (para. 1, emphasis in original)

Torrence is correct about the lackluster TV ethos and production values afforded these sports, which appear randomly and without promotion. Even in the Olympics, track is unnecessarily tape-delayed and underproduced.

## CONCLUSION

Neither Skipper nor any other network chief has turned on the promotional fire hose for athletics on television. This leaves individuals such as Torrence (2013) languishing in obscurity despite making a good living as a runner. With 19 million certified road racers in the country and countless other unofficial joggers, the ratings haul for well-produced coverage could be substantial. But we will never know as long as television chooses pseudo-sports like the *World Series of Poker* (ESPN) and *American Ninja Warrior* (NBC) instead. Thrilling athletic performances occur all summer at venues across America and around the world. Long ago more of these spectacles found their way to broadcast, ironically when we had far fewer channels (A. Burfoot, personal communication, July 29, 2014). If ESPN were as invested in the participatory cultural prospects of its audience as it is in maintaining market-share media hegemony, then the cable network might actually live up to its self-described status as the "Worldwide Leader in Sports." Until U.S. broadcasters invest synergetic creative output that *encourages* dynamic sports, these (re) emerging niche markets will retain only a cult TV following in America.

This chapter has extended Putnam's construct of social capital to account for media content, not simply media use per se. Content itself can be dynamic or passive, and in recent years ESPN has traded the former for the latter. We also developed a model to compare zero-sum games to positive-sum games—sports with a greater potential to create social capital and beneficial impacts. Future research could compare ESPN's focus on zero-sum games against lesser competitors such as NBC's Universal Sports.

Consider the potential social capital obtainable by increased media attention on athletics. If television prompted more Americans to join the millions of runners on the roads, our staggering health-care costs and related suffering could diminish. Today's obesity epidemic cannot be blamed on overeating, but on a lack of physical activity. ESPN and its competitors need not serve the interests of passivity and social decline described by Putnam (2000). Instead they could lead a renewal of personal health and increased social capital. Despite the mythos of the solitary long-distance runner, athletics brings people together face-to-face for training runs, competitions, and social events. This phenomenon was once integral to the human species. As marathon legend Bill Rodgers stated (Beech, 1998), "I believe in living an active life—using your body and your muscles. We're all meant to move. We're all meant to be athletes" (p. 13).

# The Future of the ESPN Effect

# CHAPTER NINETEEN

# Facilitating Conversations Through Sport

## An Interview with Chris LaPlaca, ESPN Senior Vice President

ANDREW C. BILLINGS

In March 2014, Chris LaPlaca, ESPN's senior vice president for corporate communications, sat with me to look back on the 35-year history of ESPN, specifically with an eye toward the impact ESPN has had on society. LaPlaca was named ESPN, Inc.'s senior vice president, corporate communications in June 2008. He is responsible for the company's worldwide internal, public, and media relations strategies, including oversight of consumer, corporate, and employee communications for ESPN's 50 business units. He also oversees the company's day-to-day working relationship with The Walt Disney Company's corporate communications and investor relations groups.

AB:     You've been here 34 years. Are you surprised at how ESPN has evolved?

CL:     The honest answer is yes. If you were walking around here in 1980, there's no possible way you could have thought our campus would look like it is today— that we would be involved in all the kind of things that we're involved in, that we would be a global company, that there would even be such a thing as social media, for example. We were just hoping to do a single cable television network. Cable was not the dominant medium then, so the answer has to be yes. Now, 34 years later, I don't believe anyone is surprised when we succeed. Our stated mission is to serve sports fans, so taking on challenges that seem unclear and then succeeding? That's who we are. So, I don't think we're surprised when we do something like a World Cup Soccer tournament and it goes well, even though most Americans didn't grow up understanding Brazilian soccer. It's in our DNA.

**AB:** Some people were surprised a single channel dedicated to sports could work, but, even among the believers, would you say even they underestimated the ceiling?

**CL:** Absolutely underestimated the ceiling. Nobody could've predicted the growth of cable TV as a medium. Not just ESPN—CNN, MTV, all of those folks who were there in the beginning did more than you could imagine. We were just hoping to make an imprint. The one thing we did have back then was we were all sports fans. We *were* our audience. We didn't have audience research back then. We looked around and said, "We like this and we're just like the people we're trying to serve, so let's keep going."

**AB:** You were your own focus group?

**CL:** We were. I think the early seeds of the culture were formed when so many people outside of Bristol did not believe. They said: "This is nonsense, this will never work. What? Cable TV? 24-hour sports? Who's going to watch 24 hours a day?" But we liked what we were doing. We thought that once people found us, they'd like it too. We didn't worry too much about the criticism back then. Brick by brick, look what happened: We became who we are and now we are at the top of the mountain. We have a lot of challenges, a lot of competition emerging everywhere. We're not dismissive of any of it. That said, we're not walking around all day looking behind us trying to see what's going on, to check on what "they" are doing. We're looking ahead. But we're paying attention because we know what happened when people didn't pay attention to us.

**AB:** When it's called ESPN, that seemed to be partly acknowledging that perhaps you couldn't program 24 hours of sports. That's why there's the "E" for "entertainment" here. Just in case you can't program all sports all the time, you haven't painted yourselves in a corner. You can say: "We're *entertainment and* sports."

**CL:** True. Back then, we didn't have enough content, we were programming day-to-day. "You got a hockey game? Yes. Can you send us the tape? Yes. OK, we'll air it tomorrow." That's what we did.

**AB:** Has ESPN gotten too big? Do you have too much power?

**CL:** Look, I understand the notion of big needing inspection. We understand that other people do perceive us that way and we're all right with it. We welcome the inspection, we welcome the focus; it's what leaders should become accustomed to. But, that thought process ignores two things. First, it ignores the tremendous amount of competition; sports are an exploding genre. You have distributors who now have sports networks. You have content partners—NFL, MLB, NBA, tennis, golf—with their own channels, websites, and platforms. We used to have the only 24-hour sports channels. Now, there's FOX Sports 1... and NBC... and CBS. Everyone has one. We operate in an extremely competitive environment. Second—and for me this has gone from frustration to amusement—is how people ignore the notion of "How did we get there and how do we stay?" Some rich uncle didn't die and leave us this business; we built it. We did it in full view of everybody. Anyone could've done what we did. It was all there for the taking if you had enough courage, vision, ingenuity, determination, and patience. We're the ones who did it, so we don't feel like we need to make any apologies for that. Once you get past that, how do we stay where we are? How do we wear the crown? I would say to you that everybody who works with the 7,000 of us every day feels like they want to be a little bit better than they were yesterday. We're not going to be complacent; the biggest thing that we worry about is complacency, because once you feel like you've got it all figured out, that's when you start to go south, and that has not entered our culture in 34 years. I think that should be celebrated. The arc of most truly successful companies is usually 10–15 years before they start to get bumpy. We're in year 34 and there's no sign of that. We take pride in that.

AB: So is it fair to say that ESPN's size is a consequence of success and the desire to stay on top?

CL: Yes. We're very open and transparent. We've hired smart people to criticize us on our website; we're the only major sports media company out there with an ombudsman. We engage with consumers. We listen. To dismiss us with the two words "too big" is missing the broader picture.

AB: One common argument for that line of reasoning is the share of the cable bill that goes to ESPN, which is far more than any other network. Is that speaking to the value people place on sports in this country? Is it simply a matter of leverage?

CL: There's no easy answer to that question. The desire for sports has always been there. George Bodenheimer, our executive chairman, tells a great story. It's 1981. He's in Texas. He's going to cable distributors trying to sell ESPN. Every time he went to Texas, Oklahoma, and that region... every time he sat down, the local cable operator would say: "Well George, you've come to the right place because this here is a sports town." It's only in recent years that you could make the argument that it is the most popular entertainment genre around for a variety of reasons because one, it rallies people, and two, you have to watch sports live. You have to. You don't have to watch *Scandal* live, you don't have to watch *Modern Family* live. But, you *have* to watch sports live. One more thing here: a focus on costs alone ignores the flip side, which is the tremendous value we bring to fans and our business partners. The scope and quality of what we provide is unparalleled.

AB: What is your response to the call for a la carte programming options? Some think it's only fair, particularly in the case of ESPN's cost to nonsports fans, while others see people getting less for the same price. If The History Channel only has 10% of people who would pay for it, then that 10% has to pay ten times as much to make up for the 90% who opt out. If half the people opted out of ESPN, would it then cost twice as much for the other half?

CL: You would pay more and get less in an a la carte world. Everybody would. Let's say you put two stacks of studies on a table. One stack is: "Here's why a la carte makes sense," and the other stack is "Here's why people would pay more and get less." The one arguing it makes sense would be about an inch high. The one arguing it makes no sense would be about three feet high. No economist really thinks that it's a smart model. But, the conversation persists because it's a great headline.

AB: Complete the sentence: "ESPN is…"

CL: I'm not going to say ESPN is the worldwide leader in sports because that's too cliché. I would say ESPN is a global, multimedia, sports entertainment company that's laser-focused on fulfilling its mission of serving its sports fans in every way imaginable. It sounds cliché, but everybody comes to work thinking that way.

AB: Are there platforms that you feel are underutilized right now for ESPN?

CL: We could do more with every platform. That's the attitude we have. We don't ever think we've got it all figured out. Some people look at our core linear television business as being mature; we don't think that's true. I just showed you a new Digital Center 2, which is massive. It's going to reinvent the way we do *SportsCenter*. When there's an emerging technology, we've got people who know that's coming. If we think there's an application that will serve sports fans better than we serve them today, we'll figure that out. If there's an apparent immediate business model—great. If not, we're still going to consider it. That way, if one emerges we'll be ready.

AB: ESPN sometimes will make a technology decision that will influence the entire media adoption choices, such as high definition. Can you talk about the decision to go to HD?

CL: I was in that meeting. It was a very serious discussion; HD was coming. Smart people had been experimenting with it, and, in the meeting, I remember our head of technology saying: "It looks great. It's going to be terrific. Games will look better for fans, so fans will love it. We should do it for that reason." Was there a business model there? We didn't know. But [then President] George Bodenheimer simply said "OK, I'll call Bob"—meaning [Disney leader] Bob Iger. Next thing we know, we're going to go HD. Gary Shapiro, who's the president of the Consumer of Electronics Association, said that when ESPN got into the HD game, it did more to sell HD sets than any other single occurrence. We jumped in early, only because it served the mission, not because we were certain there was a business there already.

AB: How about 3D television?

CL: We did the same thing with 3D and that didn't quite work as well. People weren't ready. But, no one knows more about how to produce games in 3D than we do. We're not going to sit here and say that was a failure because of the knowledge we gained going through that process.

AB: Let's talk a little bit about what gets programmed. It used to be you really thought your bread and butter had to be live sports programming. All of these new non-ESPN sports channels have some element of live sports, which increases the cost of that inventory. It seems an ESPN process has been to focus a little bit more on talking about sports and discussing them whether it's *Pardon the Interruption* or other shows throughout the day where those are easier or cheaper to produce. At what point did ESPN decide to invest more during the day in not playing replays from the night before but instead facilitating a sports talk culture?

CL: Debating about sports has happened in bars, in living rooms, at family gatherings, since they began playing games. Sports talk radio was a big deal before we launched ESPN Radio. I understand where you're coming from. Make no mistake, live sports are still our core, it drives the most customers; it still attracts the biggest audience. It is mostly what people talk about the next day if they're lucky to see that game. However, there's a saying at ESPN we have called "game around the game." We don't have the Super Bowl, but we have the "game around the game" and provide a lot of content. People want it. Some people are a little concerned about how much debate is added into our conversation, but it is just one way we serve sports fans. If you like debate, you'll watch *First Take*; if you just want the news of the day, here's what you have to do: Turn the channel. It's not hard to do.

AB: Do you have guidelines that govern commentary?

CL: Yes. We're not going to let people just say what they want to say without being able to back it up. "Just say whatever you want" is not how we play. But the other part of that is that most of those programs are still live. Why? Well, the way we did it before, we had to rush someone to the studio and break in to say, "We interrupt this taped game to tell you so and so just got traded." That didn't feel right. We shoot it live because the immediacy was intoxicating for fans. It also added another level of energy to the campus. Live is always better than tape, so we're looking for live every chance we get.

AB: You've added more channels, you've got more platforms. The presumption for many was that if you have more platforms, you can show a wider variety of sports; you can highlight different things. Yet, a recent study found that *SportsCenter* is at an all-time high (72%) with the percentage of coverage devoted to the main three sports of men's basketball, baseball, and football. Everything else moves to the periphery. Do you see that as a problem?

CL: What bothers us the most is the theme of our being monolithic to a degree. We don't have a 7 a.m. meeting every day to say, "Here's our story line, everyone will follow it and this is what we're going to do all day long." Instead, you have a bunch of meetings like that for every website, every television show, every radio show. If the content falls a certain way, it's because everyone made that decision in the best interest of their corner of this big brand that is ESPN. While it would stand to reason that more popular sports get more attention, we cover a wide variety of stories and sports throughout the day.

AB: There's no direct competitor for ESPN. Coke has Pepsi, Nike has Adidas, but ESPN basically is one side and all others, combined, represent the competition.

CL: But, everyone's trying to look like us now. Are we leading in that? Yes. Will that last forever? Well, if we play our cards right, it's going to last a really long time. When Fox Sports 1 launched, everybody around our campus started walking a little faster. A little more swing to your step to stay on top. Most who work here played sports so they know: we're on a team, we work together, and we win together. But, only if we work hard.

AB: How would you respond to claims that your relationships with other leagues and athletes compromise your journalistic abilities?

CL: It could not be further from the truth. This is one of [ESPN President] John Skipper's biggest pet peeves. Things like the PBS *Frontline* situation [where ESPN pulled out of a film collaboration about football and concussions/CTE issues] might give people reason to think: "Wait a minute—what's going on behind the curtain?" We understand that. But that's a superficial look; in reality, we recently won Peabody and duPont awards for our coverage of concussions in football. It is a fine line from outside looking in. But, our programming people, the ones who manage relations with the leagues? They're not even in the same building with the journalists. The folks who do journalism might make the people who do programming aware of something and say: "Look, we're going with a tough story, we've asked so and so for comments, here's what they've told us, so we don't want you to be surprised we're running this." But, they don't ask permission, it's just an awareness call. Church and state are alive and well here. Show me a competitor who has done more on concussions or PEDs or labor issues or race issues or what have you in sports.

AB: Are there features ESPN has done that you're particularly proud of?

CL: A few years ago, we did a piece from Barrow, Alaska. It was a high school football story. Kids were dropping out, there was drug use, suicide—and their football field was gravel. We did a piece on it and donations came in. They built an artificial football field because of the piece *SportsCenter* did. Also, Michael Sam recently talked to us and the *New York Times*. Why did he do that? Because he felt like we're a place that he could go to come out and we would handle that responsibly. To look at *SportsCenter* or other news products just through the prism of highlights or just core sports misses the broader picture.

AB: Some of your newer projects such as Grantland and Nate Silver's 538 still have sports at their core, but are more about everything from entertainment culture to politics.

CL: All of those things—538 included as the most recent expansion—are meant to keep us moving forward. To keep innovating and trying new things. If you don't keep moving forward, you go backward, and we don't want to go backward. The business community is littered with companies who once owned their space and now are no longer relevant. We don't want to be that company, so what's the best way to go about it? Actively think about it. Consider how can we get better. 538 is the latest example of that, and if it takes us some different places, that's OK, because sports is not only the subset of society, it is a big part of our society. If you ask someone on this campus a question about current events, they'll give you a smart answer because we know more than just who won the game. But we won't stray too far from our core.

AB: With Nate Silver, was it just the mindset of: "We're going to hire someone smart with a proven track record, even though we're not sure what the end result is going to be?"

CL: Exactly. With Nate, we knew what he was about [data-driven analyses, becoming famous largely through prognosticating political elections], but he wanted to expand it and we were OK with that because he started in sports.

AB: Most studies find women's sports are covered at an all-time low proportion: one to one and a half percent on *SportsCenter*. Most other women's programming is featured via platforms other than the main ESPN channel. Has ESPN neglected women's sports?

CL: No one does more women's coverage of sports than ESPN. No one covers more social issues in sports related to women than ESPN. We do a tremendous amount of feature work that goes well beyond what most studies look at. You'll get WNBA highlights, women's tennis highlights, women's college basketball highlights... we do a lot of women's sports. We feel like we're covering the vast gamut of the sporting environment very, very well, and we're proud of some of the stuff we do beyond the core.

AB: Let's talk about espnW. There was a lot of confusion when it launched as some thought it was a TV channel when it's actually a website. Some thought it would be all women's sports, but it's branded as sports content for women. What caused that decision to create espnW and what are you hoping to achieve for women's sports?

CL: espnW is sports done by women for women. At any given moment, 30–40% of our audience is women. We did not create espnW so they could have their little place over here. We embrace women in everything we do. Name a company that does more coverage of women's sports in all of our platforms than ESPN? You can't... nobody does more than us. We did a women's golf tournament our second or third day of existence in 1979. We've done women's sports from the very beginning and we don't do it because we think it's a moral obligation; we do it because women are in our audience and they're sports fans, too. We want to cater to them. That said, what we're trying to do with espnW is embrace women's sports fans in different ways. It's working. It's a very solid, valuable business for us. It's becoming more multidimensional than the digital side of the house. The ESPN Films *Nine for IX* series were tremendous films; we're going to do more. There's things we're doing behind the scenes with espnW that no one sees. We have an initiative with the U.S. State Department where we're bringing women from other parts of the world, where women and girls don't have the opportunities they have here, to help improve their lives. I had lunch with a woman from Pakistan who wants to go back and teach little girls about the value of sport and how can she promote it and market it in her country, and she was here for several weeks because of espnW. We do quarterly reports updating initiatives launched at our annual espnW conference. We're committed to it in ways not readily apparent, so I would say that folks who think we're diminishing women are really not paying attention.

AB: One area that you have done noticeably better than the rest of the sports industry is in hiring practices. Studies have found that women populate about 10% of the sports newsrooms outside of ESPN. Your percentage is noticeably higher. Minority hires as well are higher than the rest of American sports media. It's not where it could be or should be, but certainly leading compared to some others. Is part of being the worldwide leader in sports being a leader on social issues and equity as well?

CL: Yes—that's part of who we are. We did a show on the "N" word the other day, which was a smart conversation, because that word keeps coming up in sports. We could not ignore it... we needed to cover it in a smart way. Because sports are not separate from society, we do take a responsibility to cover them appropriately with sensitivity, intelligence, and sophistication. To do that, you have to have the right kind of people in the room, to have the right kind of conversations and who think about it brightly and smartly. We're very invested in making sure that we have the right kind of people, because diversity is measured in a variety of ways. We do things no one sees. We have eight employee resource groups on our campus and one of them is an LGBT group; I am an ally and was their executive champion for their first three years. Many support different races and ethnicities. When something related to these groups arises and it enters into the sports conversation, we'll go to them and ask them to help us think about it. You don't see them, you probably don't even know they exist, but they're influencing *SportsCenter* and other programs.

AB: You have an overall brand, but you've got offshoots of it that I think handle those things differently than others, including the film series, *30 for 30*, as well as *SportsCentury* before that. Those are seemingly different from some elements of storytelling with other aspects of ESPN. How do you decide what are the best platforms for a given story?

CL: Sometimes it's just organic. An editor on one of our websites might have an idea and share it. We can launch anywhere. There's a lot of collaboration even though we have separate distinct platforms. If something is big enough, good enough, and smart enough, it'll originate on.com or *ESPN The Magazine*, but it'll travel everywhere. That's the beauty of our company in many respects because we have the infrastructure to do that. We feel an obligation to do those things where warranted. The one constant is we try to do it with much sensitivity and sophistication, to give it as thorough a view as we can. We're not going to do it unless we can do it the right way.

AB: With some of these produced features or things like *30 for 30* and other original programming, the question becomes your degree of editorial control. Ten years ago, you had a successful show, *Playmakers*, but the NFL didn't like it, so it was canceled after one year; some *30 for 30* films are even league produced, making some feel they could be more promotional than they should, glossing over certain edges of some of these stories. How much editorial control does ESPN exhibit on those types of cases?

CL:  It's a collaborative process, but we have final say. If you become dictatorial in working with smart, creative people, you won't get to work with them much longer. We're not going to air anything that we don't feel passes muster, that we don't feel is well told, that we don't feel is factually correct, or fairly presented. We work with a variety of voices and we think *30 for 30* is some of the best content we've ever produced. But make no mistake: our standard is high. For example, we had a filmmaker, I won't say who and I won't say which film, who was doing a documentary. Some highlights were taken out of context and put in the narrative to tell the story, and it didn't actually happen that way in that order. We have enough people who went back and researched it, and we made the filmmaker fix it. We didn't make a grand pronouncement; it would embarrass the filmmaker. No one sees that, but we think that kind of thing keeps our films responsible. We're all about great storytelling in everything we do but if it's not right, you're not going to see it on ESPN.

AB:  Take me through the process for matching content to formats.

CL:  We have this concept called "best available screen." If you want to watch a game, your best available screen is likely your TV in your family room. Now, you might not be able to do it. So, maybe the next best available screen is your iPad, so we have WatchESPN. We try to make the experience you have—whatever screen you're using—of similar great quality. Mobile and social are two platforms in which we are all involved and have done a lot of creative interesting new things, but that have a lot of growth potential. Sports are at the intersection of mobile and social. What does that mean? Well, you go to your phone to get a score, you go to your phone to check Twitter, next thing you know, you're texting with your cousins. Maybe you're going to your phone to watch the game and then doing all of what I just said. Social and mobile are two platforms that are emerging; we're very heavily invested.

AB:  When you talk about that concept of "best available screen," is that the reason why most studies find that threat of cord-cutting is overblown? People say they can get everything they need on the Internet, but the bottom line is that very few people are saying that they want to watch sports on their phone instead of watching them on their living room TV.

CL:  You're absolutely right. I'll tell you a story: I'm at the Super Bowl three years ago, and I'm there with a friend; he's a journalist—Maryland grad. We're inside of this crowded restaurant in an alcove, you wouldn't get a great signal. He's got his iPhone up against his water glass... he's watching a Maryland basketball game, on WatchESPN. Not ideal, but that was the best available screen for him. Picture was crystal clear; it was awesome. If the best you can do at the time is your little iPhone, we're going to make that experience as great as we can make it with existing technology or anything we can bring to it. Sports are the antidote to the cord-cutters.

AB: Let's enter fantasy sport into the equation. What was the moment that you realize that fantasy is a platform ESPN needed to embrace?

CL: I don't know if there's a singular moment... the hiring of Matthew Berry in 2007 was a key, but it started before that. You don't just all of a sudden say: "Let's get into fantasy and hire Matthew on Thursday." You build to that, so I'm not sure when it started. It's just another example of "we are our audience." I joined a bunch of colleagues who played fantasy baseball and it made me a better fan. You see it now integrated into everything we do.

AB: Does it influence how you report on sports? Four out of 10 NFL fans, if given a choice, would take a win from their fantasy team over a win from their NFL team. Usually they're hoping for both. Still, if the fundamental assumption years ago was that people tune into sports to see who wins—and some of these people are saying I don't necessarily care who wins the game I care about who scores and who doesn't score—does that change the way you report it?

CL: No, it does not, but it does change how you package it. We didn't used to put up top running back stats, but now we do. When we do a highlight, we're going to tell you what happened in that game and why it happened. It doesn't change the way we tell the story. It'll just change the way we package certain information to make it a little bit easier for fantasy players to obtain.

AB: What about the argument that ESPN has the power to change what we value in sport? For instance, if basketball players are more likely to go for a slam dunk over a 15-foot jump shot because that's going to make *SportsCenter*?

CL: I guess I understand the criticism, but I would argue vehemently that *SportsCenter* reflects what's happening in sports, it doesn't create what happens in sports. I did a little research on this a while ago. Remember [NFL wide receiver] Billy "White Shoes" Johnson? One of the best wide receivers ever. Noted not just for wearing white shoes but also his end zone dances. You know the first time he did his end zone dance? 1974. *SportsCenter* hadn't been invented yet. We had no influence over Billy "White Shoes" Johnson; ESPN wasn't even born yet. The guy who's credited with popularizing the dunk is Bob Kurland. He was a seven-foot center for Oklahoma State and dunked a lot. No one else did it because they thought it was a form of showboating. That was 1945, so *SportsCenter* wasn't born for another 34 years. They're going to do it regardless because they did it before we were even here. I wonder why nobody asks what parents teach their kids and what coaches teach their teams, vs. what *SportsCenter* teaches kids as well as why nobody ever credits us for what *SportsCenter* staples like the *Make A Wish* series can teach.

AB: Can ESPN make a sport more or less popular? ESPN created the X-Games and made it a brand, sold it well, and people bought in, especially the young demographic. On the opposite side, there's the argument that if you don't have the NASCAR contract, you don't show NASCAR as much, or if you don't have the Olympic contract, you lessen your focus.

CL: Let's get into that. With X-Games, those sports were already happening, they just weren't under one umbrella. There's highlight restrictions on the Olympics; we do as much as we can. I don't know what people want us to do. Until someone tells us we can show more, there's no easy answer. But, overall, it's a logistical fact that if we're in your arena to cover the game, we already have someone there who can do a cut into *SportsCenter*. People say, "Oh, there's no hockey on ESPN." We disagree. But, when we were in the arenas every night, we could do a cut-in. We do the best we can, but for some things we're not there every night. We lost the NASCAR deal a few years ago and they wouldn't let us in the track. We still did coverage—a mile away in a parking lot—but, we still did it. What do people want us to do? Some of it is just logistics and not attitude. There's only so much you can do.

AB: Can ESPN create an interest that we didn't even know we had, such as the addition of televised poker?

CL: Poker was an interesting phenomenon. We probably did have something to do with that. The interest in poker was already there, but, through being able to show a face-down card combined with percentage chances of winning a hand, people saw it in a new way. We have the brand and the platforms that can help things resonate, but the interest has to already be there. We can't make it or break it, we can only give it exposure.

AB: Picture ESPN 10 to 20 years out. How does ESPN look different? Does it need to have a more international footprint?

CL: We're global now. If you go and visit us in Latin America, we look there like we look here…it is amazing.

AB: But I know when trying to transplant ESPN into China, that didn't go as well. It seemed to be a culture fit.

CL: True. We look different in Europe and Asia than we do in Latin America. In Australia, we look kind of like we look here. What we're trying to do internationally is take our brand—not export our sports, but export our brand—and be locally authentic as best we can. We're pretty international now. As for the future, we're already thinking about that. For instance, right now, if we wanted to, we could watch a game on ESPN, hit a button, and there's another screen, you can watch *Modern Family* alongside the ESPN game. You see an ad that you like for a car you're thinking about buying, click on it, and there's all the specs on that car and where you can go to buy it. We could do that two years ago, but just because you can do it with technology doesn't mean people want it. Personalization and immediacy are buzzwords now. The one constant, though, is that if it's something that we think sports fans will like, we will not wait for the model to emerge. We will get there, we will go first, and we will figure it out so we're ready.

AB: Last question. What has the overall effect of ESPN been on society?

CL: I would say overall, it's been very positive and beneficial. I fully recognize that we are not perfect and that we make mistakes like anybody does or any company does. We have celebrated sports and the many wonderful stories within sports. We've created the ability for other sports to emerge. In many respects, we have created an industry that is vibrant. The sports media industry is big now, but it wasn't in 1979. There are more jobs in sports now. All of that is good. We think we do a lot of things every day that lead to positive outcomes and we're proud of that. But, that's not really what we think our mission is; our mission is to serve sports fans better than anybody through every imaginable vehicle we can. In so doing, much good happens. We are creating conversations that weren't always there. We used to call *SportsCenter* the "national gathering place for sports fans." In 2014, there are a lot of places people can gather but, still, sports are number one because, with the work we've done and the leadership we've provided, it's never been a better time to be a sports fan than now. You have many choices, many outlets, many opportunities, many devices, many everything. It all started back in September of 1979 and we couldn't be more proud of that.

# CHAPTER TWENTY

# Afterword

## Challenging the Worldwide Leader in Sports

ADAM C. EARNHEARDT

When host Lee Leonard introduced the world to ESPN on September 7, 1979, few people would have bet on the network surviving one year, let alone becoming one of the dominant forces in global sports in the early twenty-first century (Greenfeld, 2012). The network has gone beyond its original goal of being a 24-hour channel for sports programming to a cultural and social institution in the United States and beyond. "When ESPN put its full-page twenty-fifth anniversary ad in the *New York Times* on September 7, 2004, it was calling attention to the impact the organization has had on changing the nature of the sports media game" (Smith & Hollihan, 2009, p. xiii).

While ESPN recognizes its prominence on the world media stage, it continues to test the boundaries with new content, media forms, and celebrities. ESPN's studio hosts are both celebrated and panned. Color analysts such as Dick Vitale have become entertainers and pitchmen, and the coffers of sports leagues are flush with revenue because of the network's insatiable need for popular content. In November 2012, Forbes recognized ESPN as one of the world's most valuable media properties at $50 billion (Badenhausen, 2014). The network has influenced professional sports leagues that have been around for more than a century as well as created new sports franchises such as the X-Games.

As the network celebrated its 35th anniversary in September 2014, my coeditors and I thought it was appropriate to consider the effect and affect that ESPN, and its sister networks around the world, have had on sport media. Quite frankly, when we started to shop this proposal to potential publishers, we were surprised a book with this focus—a collection of scholarly articles aimed at understanding and dissecting ESPN and its content—didn't already exist.

The final product was better than we could have imagined, thanks to the wonderful contributions from some of the leading and emerging scholars in the field of sports media and communication. The chapters in this book represent a unique cross-section of research aimed at understanding the rise and prominence of one of the leading sports media companies in the world. These studies challenge the notion of ESPN's worldwide supremacy, expose issues regarding gender and ethnicity in ESPN's varying mediated forms, and examine carriage fees and issues regarding the exportation of ESPN content. These chapters represent only the tip of the iceberg when examining the uses and effects of ESPN, its expansive cultural artifacts, and the institution that has dominated sports media content for more than 35 years. As many of the authors in this book suggest, there is much more to discover about the rise and future of ESPN.

## FUTURE DIRECTIONS

While this book attempted to provide answers to several questions surrounding ESPN's rise to universal prominence, and reviewed components of ESPN's empire, it leaves many questions unanswered. For example, sports media scholars might consider how sports fans contributed to the rise of ESPN, and how social media—controlled by fans, players, sports organizations, and media outlets—work in concert to develop and maintain the global ESPN brand. Additionally, it is important to continue to explore and understand the challenges the network faces as it moves into new regions of the world. Of interest to media critics is the expansion of ESPN content produced in the United States and proliferation of its global footprint.

All explorations should be rooted in this one observation: ESPN is not the worldwide leader in sports. They are, however, one of many worldwide leaders in sports media entertainment, primarily in the realms of production and distribution. This is not meant to delegitimize ESPN's power and influence in sports media. This is not meant to lessen ESPN's standing on the global media landscape. It is simply meant to challenge the perception of ESPN's global prominence. Billings (2011) argued that "ESPN is truly a widespread media giant, offering content in virtually every conceivable domain" (p. 5). But even Billings stopped short of claiming worldwide supremacy for ESPN.

Anointing a worldwide leader in sports, or anything, is a dubious task open to criticism and condemnation. Furthermore, their pursuit of worldwide dominance is ongoing, with strategies to examine and outcomes to review. ESPN is certainly available as an international sports media platform and its content is available, in electronic and print media, in more than 200 countries (Smith & Hollihan, 2009). However, the moniker "Worldwide Leader in Sports" deftly positions ESPN's media empire as a target for media critics who see cultural imperialism in the form of U.S. media imprints in other countries.

For example, ESPN has used other, less culturally imperialistic network slogans including "The Total Sports Network," "The Number One Sports Network," and "American's Number One Sports Network." ESPN senior vice president Chris LaPlaca said (see Chapter 19, this volume) that ESPN's moniker—worldwide leader in sports—is cliché, although he went on to describe a multibillion-dollar company that has, in many ways, set the global tone for sports media consumption. That ESPN is viewed by some as a cultural and media imperialist is not surprising considering that the United States, home base to ESPN, is widely seen as "the chief agent of neo-imperialism" (Wagg, Brick, Wheaton, & Caudwell, 2009, p. 134).

Classifying ESPN as a sports media empire is a safe and accurate descriptor when comparing their brand expansion to that of other television-based networks. For example, the ESPN family of channels includes the primary channel, ESPN, as well as ESPN2, ESPN3, ESPNU, ESPN Classic, ESPNNews, and ESPN Deportes. More recently, ESPN became the distribution partner of SEC Network and the Longhorn Network. At present, no U.S.-based cable network (and few international networks), regardless of content or genre, can compete with this kind of expansive branding, production, and export.

This branding is developed through more than just televised media that represent the largest piece of the ESPN conglomerate. ESPN has made great inroads in the publishing arena and with Web-based content. How the company expands its footprint beyond its current holdings will essentially rely on two intertwined variables: fans and social media.

## ESPN, Fans, and Social Media

Thanks in part to social media, the fan is now a worldwide leader in sports. According to a 2013 sports engagement study, fans who use social media to follow sports are doing so while they watch favorite teams compete (Broughton, 2013). Furthermore, sports fans now produce large amounts of sport-thematic chatter on prominent social media platforms such as Facebook and Twitter. For example, during the Brazil-Germany 2014 Word Cup match, fans set a record for most tweets about a single sporting event with more than 35 million posts (De Menezes, 2014). However, without the tools and information provided by ESPN and other networks, fans would have far less reach and limited information to share with others.

Fans want to engage other fans and are using social media as the new forum in which to connect with others to talk about sports. ESPN provides forums in various social media platforms for fans to engage others, including other fans, athletes and teams, coaches and owners, and commentators and hosts. Understanding who these fans are, what motivates them, and how to reach them is paramount in ESPN's marketing and research agenda. For example, an ESPN-sponsored study found that male teens, more than females and any other age group, have the greatest desire for sports (Hoffarth, 2009). They spend a considerable amount of time talking about sports and consider their knowledge of sports to be a form of social currency. It appears as though ESPN is acting on these results through the development of pervasive social media campaigns targeted at these demographics (DeCastro, 2013).

Like most prominent media outlets, ESPN relies heavily on social media to promote its brand and content. According to a 2011 internal policy, ESPN considers social media as "important venues for content distribution, user engagement, news gathering, transparency, and the amplification of talent voices" ("Social Networking," 2011). It would seem ESPN has found a way to harness the power of social media. For example, as of August 2014, @espn has more than 10.7 million Twitter followers, ranking it 80th worldwide among the most followed Twitter addresses. In comparison, no other sports media company is in the top 100, and, in terms of news agencies, only BBC Breaking News (@bbcbreaking), CNN (@cnn) and CNN Breaking News (@cnnbrk), and the *New York Times* (@nytimes) have more followers.

ESPN encourages its hosts and other talent to engage in responsible social media use ("Social Networking," 2011). This was not always the case. In 2009, a policy was issued forbidding reporters and other ESPN talent from posting sports-related information on social media (Hall, 2009). However, a revised 2011 policy promotes social media content creation and distribution, fan engagement, and branding. This new policy appears to encourage ESPN talent to engage others on social media.

As of August 2014, ESPN boasts two of the most followed accounts on Twitter with @ESPN and @SportsCenter (8.9 million followers; ranked 115th). Beyond the top two company Twitter accounts, @ESPN and @SportsCenter, the only other ESPN-related accounts in the top 1000 most followed accounts are owned by Adam Schefter (NFL analyst, @AdamSchefter, 3.0 million followers, ranked 676th) and Bill Simmons (ESPN analyst, Grantland.com curator, @BillSimmons, 2.8 million follower, ranked 762th).

The closest sports networks with active social media platforms, based outside the United States, and ranked in the top 1000 on Twitter (in terms of followers and rank) include (as of August 2014):

- @ntvspor—3.6 million followers, ranked 501st (sports network based in İstanbul, Turkey)

- @TwitterSports—3.5 million followers, 502th (sports-related news and information)
- @SkySportsNewsHQ—3.0 million followers, 685th
- @BBCSport—2.6 million followers, 811th

To some extent, this suggests ESPN has a strong grasp of sports-related Twitter content. It appears that ESPN is keenly aware of its ever-evolving audience and the power sports fandom plays in its ability to stay ahead of competing media outlets. To manage this online presence, ESPN appointed multiple directors to manage social media content. In an attempt to bring fans, athletes, and ESPN talent closer together, Katie Richman, ESPN's director of social media strategy and social products, noted that their social media presence started as an organic endeavor among a few employees:

> Very quickly, we established more property-specific accounts—primarily on Facebook, then Twitter. Our on-air commentators and analysts were some of the early advocates and content creators on Twitter. (DeCastro, 2013)

Although Samuel Jay and Brody Ruihley and his colleagues began to unravel some questions concerning the functions of ESPN's multiple mediated platforms (such as fantasy sports), there are many questions about the fan experience left unanswered. For example, some questions revolve around the use of social media by ESPN and their employees, and how their social media presence fosters connections with fans, athletes, teams and organizations, and others. Understanding how fans use and interact with ESPN produced content in the social mediated environment, including ESPN's use of fan-produced content (akin to CNN's iReport) and sharing of ESPN-produced content with others, will provide more insight into motivations, uses, and effects of ESPN and sports media. Furthermore, expanding these studies to explore the use of ESPN-produced content outside the United States and multiple formats will provide useful information for expanding the ESPN brand in other regions.

## ESPN, Journalism, and Global Reach

Other areas ripe for investigation include ESPN's journalistic abilities and its ability to reach beyond the U.S. border with meaningful sports stories. ESPN journalists and hosts currently provide basic information about outcomes of contests, analysis, and forecasts (Miller & Shales, 2011). However, paramount to ESPN's success are their endeavors to provide other enterprise and investigative sports news while competing with other hard sports-news-producing outlets such as Yahoo! Sports and Fox Sports. For example, some scholars have challenged ESPN's quality of sports journalism and believe that much more needs to be done in establishing standards of professionalism (Oates & Pauly, 2007) to prevent sports journalists from becoming public relations bullhorns.

ESPN's expansion into investigative news has created importance for stories on the international stage such as fan looting and rioting, international issues involving the Olympics and the World Cup, and other scandals involving athletes, coaches, and others. Couple these issues with ESPN's (and other sports broadcasters) coverage of those events, and the importance for such a text grows tenfold. These stories are important, as sports offer one of the mirrors of society, a mirror in which we sometimes refuse to look.

According to executives, ESPN has every intention of growing the international brand and extended its global reach (Miller & Shales, 2011; Smith & Hollihan, 2009). Aside from outlets in Australia, Canada, Mexico and Central American countries, and Brazil, little is known about the impact of ESPN on other countries and cultures. Future studies might focus on content provided to these international outlets, whether the content is produced in the United States or in the home country, and how the home audience receives that content.

ESPN must be cautious of content produced in the United States for distribution in other countries. As stated earlier, content produced in the United States and exported to other countries may lead some critics to levy accusations of cultural imperialism. For those in other countries who embrace the moniker "worldwide leader in sports," ESPN would be king among the imperialists. Global sports media, it would seem, have largely been immune from the absorption of other U.S. media exports. LaPlaca argued that ESPN has been focused not on exporting U.S. sports but on exporting the ESPN brand—with sensitivity paid to the adoption of brands and cultural expectations in other countries and regions of the world.

Naraine and Abeza's review of ESPN and Canadian sports media (see Chapter 16) offers some support for this argument. We also know that primary sports media outlets in other countries, although likely influenced by ESPN, are not part of the "mothership" (a name commonly used for ESPN by Dan Patrick, host of the Dan Patrick Show on NBC Sports and former ESPN *SportsCenter* anchor).

ESPN International boasts an impressive line-up of channels in other countries including ESPN Australia, ESPN Brasil, ESPN Caribbean, ESPN Pacific Rim, and various channels in Latin America. More recently, however, ESPN dropped more than a dozen channels in Asia including ESPN China and ESPN India after selling its majority share on those affiliates. ESPN ceased operations in Israel, North Africa, and the Middle East, although they maintain some online offerings in those regions.

The ESPN audience is available in these other countries. But little is known about how the ESPN-generated content might be received in other countries. Furthermore, little is known beyond some general demographic data about how fans with varied ethnic and racial backgrounds might embrace ESPN content. A review of an ESPN fan study suggests little is still known about how to produce content for appropriate demographic angles (Hoffarth, 2009). For example, ESPN must continue to address issues related to content aimed at Hispanic viewers and female viewers.

## CONCLUSION

Answering these questions will help to more fully explain the prominence of ESPN on the global sports media stage. ESPN has changed the way people around the globe consume sports, the way we talk about sports, and influenced the way we think about the people who play these games. At a time when global sports consumption is growing, it is important to understand ESPN's role in sports media and culture. We wanted this book to provide an opportunity to have philosophical discussions about the place of sports in the world, and the impact of ESPN on sports consumption, management, marketing, and communication.

What does the future hold for ESPN and the world of sports media? When we started this process, we left open paths that lead to the broadest possible areas of examination. But there is still so much to uncover. For example, future ESPN researchers might consider taking McChesney's (1989) *media-sport complex* view to ESPN's origination of events, partnerships with leagues, etc. (that ESPN has become the epitome of what McChesney talked about 25 years ago).

Regardless of what paths future scholars take, it is important to recognize that this is likely the first in an anthology of studies examining one of the greatest media triumphs. To that end, and like this book, future studies of ESPN are better served by a mixture of new and emerging sports scholars, rather than running out the same stable of authors in sports media research books. My coeditors and I encourage new sports media scholars to consider new avenues for examining ESPN, and we challenge our fellow seasoned scholars to help us set the course for understanding ESPN's position as a worldwide leader in sports.

# References

Aaker, D. A. (1996). *Building strong brands.* New York: Free Press.

Aaker, D. A., & Joachimsthaler, E. (2000). *Brand leadership.* New York: Free Press.

ABC, ESPN pen CFA football deals. (1985, March 11). *Broadcasting, 108,* 66–67.

Acosta-Alzuru, C. (2003). "I'm not a feminist... I only defend women as human beings": The production, representation, and consumption in a telenovela. *Critical Studies in Media Communication, 20*(3), 269–294. doi:10.1080/07393180302775

Acosta, R. V., & Carpenter, L. J. (2012). *Women in intercollegiate sport. A longitudinal, national study, thirty-five year update. 1977–2012.* Retrieved from http://acostacarpenter.org/AcostaCarpenter2012.pdf

Adams, N, Schmitke, A., & Franklin, A. (2005). Tomboys, dykes, and girly girls: Interrogating the subjectivities of adolescent female athletes. *Women's Studies Quarterly, 33*(1/2), 17–34.

Adams, T., & Tuggle, C. A. (2004). ESPN's *SportsCenter* and coverage of women's athletics: "It's a boys' club." *Mass Communication & Society, 7*(2), 237–248. doi:10.1207/s15327825mcs0702_6

Adande, J. A. (2012, February 22). Jeremy Lin, race and lessons learned. *ESPN.* Retrieved from http://espn.go.com/nba/story/_/id/7595841/nba-jeremy-lin-race-lessons-learned

Alfano, P. (1983, May 24). ESPN struggling, but making an impact. *New York Times,* p. B12.

Allen, E. (2008). Chesting, or: The Little League bounce can be stopped. *Anitoch Review, 66*(3), 421–433.

Anderson, D. (2012). *The New York Times story of the Yankees: 382 Articles, profiles and essays from 1903 to present.* New York: New York Times Publishing.

Anderson, E. (2005). *In the game: Gay athletes and the cult of masculinity.* New York: State University of New York Press.

Anderson, E., & Kian, E. M. (2012). Examining media contestation of masculinity and head trauma in the National Football League. *Men and Masculinities, 15*(2), 152–173. doi:10.1177/1097184X11430127

Anstine, D. B. (2004). The impact of the regulation of the cable television industry: The effect on quality-adjusted cable television prices. *Applied Economics, 36*(8), 793–802. doi:10.1080/0003684042000229523

Antunovic, D., & Hardin, M. (2012). Activism in women's sports blogs: Fandom and feminist potential. *International Journal of Sport Communication, 5*(3), 305–322.

Arnason, B. (2013, June 26). Copper based broadband decline is accelerating, sort of. *Telecompetitor.* Retrieved from http://www.telecompetitor.com/copper-based-broadband-decline-is-accelerating-sort-of/

Arnovitz, K. (2010, October 22). LeBron James: Sticking it to ownership. *ESPN.com.* Retrieved from http://espn.go.com/blog/truehoop/miamiheat/post/_/id/257/lebron-james-sticking-it-to-ownership

Arritt, D., Thomas, P., & Abrams, J. (2005, August 5). X Games report; Trick is in scoring, but Stenberg wins gold. *Los Angeles Times*, p. D4.

Augustine, B. (2013, September 12). *ESPN* calls Jason Whitlock's comments on *Sports Illustrated's* Oklahoma State reporting "not appropriate." *New York Daily News.* Retrieved from http://www.nydailynews.com/sports/college/espn-tells-whitlock-pipe-si-criticism-article-1.1453939

Axon, R. (2013, September 11). Tim Montgomery, former fastest man, up and running. *USA Today.* Retrieved from http://www.usatoday.com/story/sports/olympics/2013/09/10/tim-montgomery-100-meter-world-record-prison/2795863/

Badenhausen, K. (2013, November 9). Why ESPN is worth $40 billion as the world's most valuable media property. *Forbes.* Retrieved from http://www.forbes.com/sites/kurtbadenhausen/2012/11/09/why-espn-is-the-worlds-most-valuable-media-property-and-worth-40-billion/

Badenhausen, K. (2014, April 24). The value of ESPN surpasses $50 billion. *Forbes.* Retrieved from http://www.forbes.com/sites/kurtbadenhausen/2014/04/29/the-value-of-espn-surpasses-50-billion/

Barnett, B., & Hardin, M. (2011). Advocacy from the liberal feminist playbook: The framing of Title IX and women's sports in news releases from the Women's Sports Foundation. *International Journal of Sport Communication, 4*(2), 178–197.

Barrett, L. C. (2006, July 7). Jemele Hill on being black, female, young—and on the sports page. *Columbia Journalism Review.* Retrieved from http://www.cjr.org/behind_the_news/jemele_hill_on_being_black_fem.php?page=all

Barthes, R. (1972). *Mythologies.* (A. Lavers, Trans.). Paris: HarperCollins.

Basso, M. (2013, February 12). CrossFit: Have we learned nothing? *Huffington Post.* Retrieved from http://www.huffingtonpost.com/matthew-basso/crossfit_b_2649450.html

Baxter, K. (2010, February 8). World-class soccer prize; ESPN Deportes tracks the drama of earning a place on Mexico's World Cup team. *Los Angeles Times*, p. D3.

Baysinger, T. (2011, September 26). ESPN's Keller wants to break down walls between English, Spanish programming. *Broadcastingandcable.com.* Retrieved from http://www.broadcastingcable.com/news/programming/hispanic-tv-summit-espns-keller-wants-break-down-walls-between-english-and-spanish-programming/38513

Beck, D., & Bosshart, L. (2003). Sports and media. *Communication Research Trends, 22*(4), 1–44.

Beech, M. (1998, August 24). Bill Rodgers, marathoner. *Sports Illustrated, 89*(8), 13.

Begley, S. (2012, September 19). U.S. obesity rates to soar: Report. *The Telegraph Journal*, p. A4.

Bell, B. T., & Dittmar, H. (2011). Does media type matter? The role of identification in adolescent girls' media consumption and the impact of different thin-ideal media on body image. *Sex Roles, 65*(7–8), 478–490. doi:10.1007/s11199-011-9964-x

Bellamy, R. V., Jr. (2006). Sports media: A modern institution. In A. A. Raney & J. Bryant (Eds.), *Handbook of sports and media* (pp. 63–76). Mahwah, NJ: Lawrence Erlbaum.

Bellamy, R., & Whitson, D. (2009). Going south: Professional baseball's contraction in Canada. *NINE: A Journal of Baseball History and Culture, 18*(1), 86–106. doi:10.1353/nin.0.0065

Belson, K. (2012, August 30). Al Jazeera bets heavily on soccer on U.S. TV. *NYTimes.com.* Retrieved from: http://www.nytimes.com/2012/08/31/sports/soccer/al-jazeera-bets-heavily-on-soccer-on-us-tv.html?_r=0

Bercovici, J. (2012, July 18). The next media jackpot: The fight for the $1 trillion Hispanic market. *Forbes.com.* Retrieved from http://www.forbes.com/sites/meghancasserly/2012/07/18/sofia-vergaras-rich-little-secret-a-multi-million-media-empire/

Berman, C. (1999). Foreword. In M. MacCambridge (Ed.), *ESPN SportsCentury* (p. 17). New York: Hyperion.

Bernstein, A. (1997, January 27). That's business. *Sporting Goods Business, 30*(2), 41.

Bernstein, A. & Kian, E. M. (2013). Gender and sexualities in sport media. In P. M. Pedersen (Ed.), *Routledge Handbook of Sport Communication* (pp. 319–327). New York: Routledge.

Bettig, R. V. (1996). *Copyrighting culture: The political economy of intellectual property.* Boulder, CO: Westview Press.

Bibel, S. (2013, November 26). ESPN digital media sets another sports category record in October. *TVbytheNumbers.com.* Retrieved from http://tvbythenumbers.zap2it.com/2013/11/26/espn-digital-media-sets-another-sports-category-record-in-october/218310/

Billings, A. C. (2000). In search of women athletes: ESPN's list of the top 100 athletes of the century. *Journal of Sport and Social Issues, 24*(4), 415–421. doi:10.1177/0193723500244008

Billings, A. C. (2011). Introduction. In A. C. Billings (Ed.), *Sports media: Transformation, integration, consumption* (pp. 1–6). New York: Routledge.

Billings, A. C., Angelini, J. R., & Duke, A. H. (2010). Gendered profiles of Olympic history: Sportscaster dialogue in the 2008 Beijing Olympics. *Journal of Broadcasting & Electronic Media, 54*(1), 9–23. doi:10.1080/08838150903550352

Billings, A. C., Brown, C. L., Crout, J. H., McKenna, K. E., Rice, B. A., Timanus, M. E., & Zeigler, J. (2008). The Games through the NBC lens: Gender, ethnic and national equity in the 2006 Torino Winter Olympics. *Journal of Broadcasting & Electronic Media, 52*(2), 215–230. doi:10.1080/08838150801992003

Billings, A. C., & Eastman, S. T. (2003). Framing identities: Gender, ethnic, and national parity in network announcing of the 2002 Winter Olympics. *Journal of Communication, 53*(4), 569–586. doi:10.1111/j.1460–2466.2003.tb02911.x

Billings, A. C., Halone, K. K., & Denham, B. E. (2002). "Man, that was a pretty shot": An analysis of gendered broadcast commentary surrounding the 2000 men's and women's NCAA Final Four basketball championships. *Mass Communication & Society, 5*(3), 295–315. doi:10.1207/S15327825MCS0503_4

Billings, A. C., MacArthur, P. J., Licen, S., & Wu, D. (2009). Superpowers on the Olympic basketball court: The United States versus China through four nationalistic lenses. *International Journal of Sport Communication, 2*(4), 380–397.

Birrell, S., & McDonald, M. G. (2012). Break points: Narrative interruption in the life of Billie Jean King. *Journal of Sport and Social Issues, 36,* 343–360. doi:10.1177/0193723512442203

Bishop, R. (2003). Missing in action: Feature coverage of women's sports in *Sports Illustrated. Journal of Sport and Social Issues, 27*(2), 184–194.

Bissell, K. L., & Duke, A. M. (2007). Bump, set, spike: An analysis of commentary and camera angles of women's beach volleyball during the 2004 summer Olympics. *Journal of Promotion Management, 13*(1/2), 35–53. doi:10.1300/J057v13n01_04

Bissell, K. L., & Smith, L. R. (2013). Let's (not) talk sex: An analysis of the verbal and visual coverage of women's beach volleyball during the 2008 Olympic Games. *Journal of Sports Media, 8*(2), 1–30. doi:10.1353/jsm.2013.0011

Bissel, K. L., & Zhou, P. (2004). Must-see TV or ESPN: Entertainment and sports media exposure and body-image distortion in college women. *Journal of Communication, 54*(1), 5–21. doi:10.1111/j.1460-2466.2004.tb02610.x

Black, T. R. (1999). *Doing quantitative research in the social sciences: An integrated approach to research design, measurement and statistics.* Thousand Oaks, CA: Sage.

Blaudschun, M. (2011, October 9). Power move by ACC. *Boston.com.* Retrieved from www.boston.com/sports/colleges/articles/2011/10/09/power_move_by_acc/?page=2

Blevins, R. (2014, August 7). Alcorn State signs Hopson to 3-year extension. *The (Jackson) Clarion-Ledger,* Retrieved from http://www.clarionledger.com/story/recruitingreport/2014/08/07/alcorn-state-signs-hopson-to-3-year-extension/13743279/

Bloom, J., & Willard, M. N. (2002). *Sports matters: Race, recreation, and culture.* New York: NYU Press.

Boland, B. (2010, November 10). Why LeBron's "Rise" lowers the value of athlete endorsement. *Advertising Age.* Retrieved from http://adage.com/article/guest-columnists/lebron-s-riselowers-athlete-endorsement/146995/

Bolter, J. D., & Grusin, R. (2000). *Remediation: Understanding new media.* Cambridge, MA: MIT Press.

Boruszkowski, L.A. (2011). Editing subject-filmed documentary: Steve James and the War Tapes. *Journal of Film & Video, 63*(4), 44–52. doi:10/1353/jfv.2011.0027

Branch, T. (2011, October). The shame of college sports. *The Atlantic.* Retrieved from http://www.theatlantic.com/magazine/archive/2011/10/the-shame-of-college%20sports/308643/?single_page=true

Breed, W. (1955). Newspaper "opinion leaders" and processes of standardization. *Journalism & Mass Communication Quarterly, 32*(3), 277–328. doi:10.1177/107769905503200302

*Broadcasting* (1985, March 11). ABC, ESPN pen CFA football deals, *108,* 66.

Brookover, B. (2003, October 3). Lurie says ESPN is irresponsible; The Eagles' owner blasts "Playmakers." *Philadelphia Inquirer.* Retrieved from http://www.philly.com

Brooks, D., & Rada, J. (2002). *Constructing race in Black and Whiteness: Media coverage of public support for President Clinton. Journalism & Communication Monographs 4*(3), 115–156.

Broughton, D. (2013). Fan social media use passes a threshold. *Sports Business Journal.* Retrieved from http://www.sportsbusinessdaily.com/Journal/Issues/2013/09/30/Research-and-Ratings/Catalyst-social-media.aspx

Brown, D. (2012, February 16). Jeremy Lin: Fernando Valenzuela understands Lin-Sanity first hand. Retrieved from http://www.mercurynews.com/ci_19982777

Brown, D., & Bryant, J. (2006). Sports content on U.S. television. In A. A. Raney & J. Bryant (Eds.), *Handbook of sports and media* (pp. 80–110). Mahwah, NJ: Lawrence Erlbaum.

Bruce, T. (2004). Marking the boundaries of the "normal" in televised sports: The play-by-play of race. *Media, Culture, and Society, 26*(6), 861–879. doi:10.1177/0163443704047030

Bruce, T. (2012). Reflections on communication and sport: On women and femininities. *Communication & Sport, 1*(1/2), 125–137. doi:10.1177/2167479512472883

Bruce, T., Hovden, J., & Markula, P. (2010). *Sportswomen at the Olympics: A global content analysis of newspaper coverage.* Rotterdam: Sense.

Bui, Q. (2013, September 27). The most and least expensive basic cable channels in 1 graph. *Planet Money.* Retrieved from http://www.npr.org/blogs/money/2013/09/27/226499294/the-most-and-least-expensive-cable-channels-in-1-graph

Brummett, B. (1985). Electric literature as equipment for living: Haunted house films. *Critical Studies in Mass Communication, 2*(3), 246–261. doi:10.1080/15295038509360084

Brummett, B. (2009). *A rhetoric of style.* Carbondale, IL: Southern Illinois University Press.

Buffington, D., & Fraley, T. (2008). Skill in Black and White: Negotiating media images of race in a sporting context. *Journal of Communication Inquiry, 32*(3), 292–310. doi:10.1177/0196859908316330

Burke, K. (1969). *A grammar of motives* (3rd ed.). Berkeley, CA: University of California Press.

Burke, K. (1971). *The philosophy of literary form* (3rd ed.) Berkeley, CA: University of California Press.

Burke, K. (2001). "Watchful of hermetics to be strong in hermeneutics": Selections from "Poetics, dramatistically considered." In G. Henderson & D. C. Williams (Eds.), *Unending conversations* (pp. 35–80). Carbondale, IL: Southern Illinois University Press.

Burke, M. (2013, August 17). How the National Football League can reach $25 billion in annual revenues. *Forbes.* Retrieved from http://www.forbes.com/sites/monteburke/2013/08/17/how-the-national-football-league-can-reach-25-billion-in-annual-revenues/

Burke, T. (2012, January 12). ESPN broke its own record by making 160 Tim Tebow references in one hour of *SportsCenter.* Here are all of them. *Deadspin.* Retrieved from http://deadspin.com/5875622/espn-broke-its-own-record-by-making-160-tim-tebow-references-in-one-hour-of-sportscenter-here-are-all-of-them

Burns, P. (2012a, February 20). Bristolmetrics: *SportsCenter* said „Lin" more often than „if" or „but" last week. *Deadspin.* Retrieved from http://deadspin.com/5886442/bristolmetricssportscenter-said-lin-more-often-than-if-or-but-last-week

Burns, P. (2012b, February 27). Bristolmetrics: Jeremy Lin's Knicks got more *SportsCenter* coverage last week than all of men's college basketball did. *Deadspin.* Retrieved from http://deadspin.com/5888426/bristolmetrics-jeremy-lins-knicks-got-more-sportscentercoverage-last-week-than-all-of-mens-college-basketball-did

Burt, T. (2004, January 20). ESPN sets up a powerplay for expansion. *Financial Times,* 11.

Butterworth, M. L. (2007). Race in "The Race": Mark McGwire, Sammy Sosa, and heroic constructions of whiteness. *Critical Studies in Media Communication, 24*(3), 228–244. doi:10.1080/07393180701520926

Butterworth, M. (2008). Purifying the body politic: Steroids, Rafael Palmeiro, and the rhetorical cleansing of Major League Baseball. *Western Journal of Communication, 72*(2), 145–161. doi:10.1080/10570310802038713

Buysse, J., & Embser-Herbert, M. S. (2004). Constructions of gender in sport: An analysis of intercollegiate media guide cover photographs. *Gender and Society, 18*(1), 66–81. doi:10.1177/0891243203257914

Buysse, J. A., & Wolter, S. (2013). Gender representation in 2010 NCAA Division I media guides: The battle for equity was temporarily won. *Journal of Issues in Intercollegiate Athletics, 6,* 1–21.

Cable advertising: Growing blip on media radar. (1981, February 19). *Broadcasting, 100*(7), 37–46.

Cafardo, B. (2014, February 19). 2014 Sprint NBA all-star celebrity game on ESPN is most-watched ever. *ESPN MediaZone.* Retrieved from http://espnmediazone.com/us/press-releases/2014/02/2014-sprint-nba-star-celebrity-game-espn-watched-ever/

Cakirozer, U. (2008, June 25). They get their kicks from Euro 2008; European soccer fans gather to watch the tournament at cultural centers, bars and restaurants around the Southland. *Los Angeles Times,* E9. Retrieved from http://search.proquest.com.lib-proxy.fullerton.edu/docview/422229272?accountid=9840

Cameron, J. (n.d.). Retrieved from http://www.giffordlectures.org/lectures/william-david-ross

Campbell, C. P. (1995). *Race, myth and the news.* Thousand Oaks, CA: Sage. doi:10.4135/9781483327211

Capranica, L., & Aversa, F. (2002). Italian television sport coverage during the 2000 Sydney Olympic Games: A gender perspective. *International Review for the Sociology of Sport, 37*(3–4), 337–349. doi:10.1177/101269020203700309

Carson, T. (2005). Ross and utilitarianism on promise keeping and lying; Self-evidence and the data of ethics. *Philosophical Issues, 15,* 140–157. doi:10.1111/j.1533–6077.2005.00058.x

Cart, J. (1989, August 31). There's smoke on Tobacco Road: N.C. State tried to cool Valvano controversy. *Los Angeles Times,* p. 4.

Carty, V. (2005). Textual portrayals of female athletes: Liberation or nuanced forms of patriarchy? *Frontiers, 26,* 132–155. doi:10.1353/fro.2005.0020

Cavanaugh, R. P. (1992). The development of Canadian sports broadcasting 1920–1978. *Canadian Journal of Communication, 17*(3), 301–317.

Ceasar, D. (1989, September 8). ESPN evolution: From a fly to a gorilla in 10 years. *St.Louis Post-Dispatch,* 3D.

Chad, N. (1987, October 18). To TV sports fans, ESPN grows from novelty to necessity. *Washington Post,* B3.

Chad, N. (1988, August 26). Cable TV's infiltration to continue with baseball. *Washington Post,* F3.

Championing the cause of TV deregulation. (1981, June 8). *Broadcasting, 100*(23), 37.

Chang, I. K., Crossman, J., Taylor, J., & Walker, D. (2011). One world, one dream: A qualitative comparison of the newspaper coverage of the 2008 Olympic and Paralympic Games. *International Journal of Sport Communication, 4*(1), 26–49.

Chaput, C. (2010). Rhetorical circulation in late capitalism: Neoliberalism and the overdetermination of affective energy. *Philosophy & Rhetoric, 43*(1), 1–25. doi:10.1353/par.0.0047

Chiari, M. (2013, September 10). Oklahoma State football profiled in *SI's* shocking 5-part investigative report. *Bleacher Report.* Retrieved from http://bleacherreport.com/articles/1768255-oklahoma-state-football-profiled-in-sis-shocking-5-part-investigative-report

Chris, C. (2002). All documentary, all the time? Discovery Communications Inc. and trends in cable television. *Television & New Media, 3*(1), 7–26. doi:10.1177/152747640200300102

Christians, C. (1985). Enforcing media codes. *Journal of Mass Media Ethics, 1*(1), 14–21. doi:10.1080/08900528509358250

Claringbould, I., Knoppers, A., & Elling, A. (2004). Exclusionary practices in sport journalism. *Sex Roles, 51*(11/12), 709–718. doi:10.1007/s11199–004–0720–3

Clarke, S. A. (1991). *Fear of a Black planet: Race, identity politics, and common sense.* In E. N. Gates, *Cultural and literary critiques of the concepts of "race"* (pp. 267–289). New York: Routledge.

Clavio, G., & Eagleman, A. N. (2011). Gender and sexually suggestive images in sports blogs. *Journal of Sport Management, 7,* 295–304.

Clavio, G., & Pedersen, P. M. (2007). Print and broadcast connections of ESPN: An investigation of the alignment of editorial coverage in *ESPN The Magazine* with ESPN's broadcasting rights. *International Journal of Sport Management, 8,* 95–114. Retrieved from http://sportspolitik.com/wp-content/uploads/2011/04/Clavio-and-Pedersen-2007.pdf

Coach Johnny Reb. (1960, November 28). *Time, 70*(23), 36.

Coakley, J. (2009). *Sports in society: Issues & controversies* (10th ed.). New York: McGraw-Hill.

Coche, R. (2013). Is ESPN really the women's sports network? A content analysis of ESPN's internet coverage of the Australian Open. *Electronic News, 7*(2), 72–88. doi:10.1177/1931243113491574

Coleman, B. J., DuMond, J. M., & Lynch, A. K. (2010). Evidence of bias in NCAA Tournament selection and seeding. *Managerial & Decision Economics, 31*(7), 431–452. doi:10.1002/mde.1499

Collins, J. C., & Porras, J. I. (1996). Building your company's vision. *Harvard Business Review, 74*(5), 65–77.

Commission on the Freedom of the Press. (1947). *A free and responsible press: A general report on mass communication.* Chicago: University of Chicago Press.

Connell, R. W. (1987). *Gender and power.* Stanford, CA: Stanford University Press.

Connell, R. W. (1990). An iron man: The body and some contradictions of hegemonic masculinity. In. M. A. Messner & D. F. Sabo (Eds.), *Sport, men, and the gender order: Critical feminist perspectives* (pp. 83–114). Champaign, IL: Human Kinetics.

Connell, R. W. (2005). *Masculinities* (2nd ed.). Los Angeles: University of California Press. doi:10.1177/1097184X03260969

Connelly, T. (2011, May 16). Forty years after a dream mile, a harsh reality for track. *New York Times,* p. D5.

Consoli, J. (2003, January 13). The rookie becomes a player. *MediaWeek, 13*(2), 24–28.

Consoli, J. (2004, July 26). Staying afloat on beer: Without Anheuser-Busch, ESPN might never have made it to 25. *Mediaweek.* Retrieved from http://pdc-connection.ebscohost.com/c/articles/14074586/staying-afloat-beer

Consoli, J. (2013, June 13). FOX Deportes maintaining position as most-watched Spanish-language sports net. *Broadcastingcable.com.* Retrieved from http://www.broadcastingcable.com/news/news-articles/fox-deportes-maintaining-position-most-watched-spanish-language-sports-net/114554

Cooky, C., Messner, M. A., & Hextrum, R. H. (2013). Women play sport, but not on TV: A longitudinal study of televised news media. *Communication & Sport, 1*(3), 203–230. doi:10.1177/2167479513476947

Cooper, J. N., Gwrysiak, J., & Hawkins, B. (2012). Racial perceptions of baseball at historically black colleges and universities. *Journal of Sport & Social Issues, 37*(2), 196–221. doi:10.1177/0193723512455921

Corcoran, C. (2014, February 7). A-Rod drops his lawsuit against baseball bringing possible closure to Biogenesis scandal. *Sports Illustrated: The Strike Zone.* Retrieved from http://mlb.si.com/2014/02/07/alex-rodriguez-drops-lawsuit-biogenesis-mlb/

Cornut, F., Giroux, H., & Langley, A. (2012). The strategic plan as a genre. *Discourse & Communication, 6*(1), 21–54. doi:10.1177/1750481311432521

Corrigan, T. F. (2011, August 10). *Expressed, written consent: The broadcast industry and sports anti-trust legislation, 1953–1961.* Paper presented at the the annual meeting of the Association for Education in Journalism and Mass Communication, St. Louis, MO.

Corrigan, T. F. (2014). The political economy of sports and new media. In A. C. Billings & M. Hardin (Eds.), *Routledge handbook of sport and new media* (pp. 43–54). London: Routledge.

Corrigan, T. F., & Formentin, M. (2011, August 10). *Made by TV: The American Football League and broadcast networks.* Paper presented at the the annual meeting of the Association for Education in Journalism and Mass Communication, St. Louis, MO.

Corrigan, T. F., Paton, J., Holt, E., & Hardin, M. (2010). Discourses of the "too abled": Contested body hierarchies and the Oscar Pistorius case. *International Journal of Sport Communication, 3*(3), 288–307.

Cosentino, D. (2013, September 12). Here's some more bullshit in *SI*'s big Oklahoma State exposé. *Deadspin.* Retrieved from http://deadspin.com/heres-some-more-bullshit-in-sis-big-oklahoma-state-ex-1302372635

Coventry, B. T. (2004). On the sidelines: Sex and racial segregation in television sports broadcasting. *Sociology of Sport Journal, 21*(3), 322–341.

Cranmer, G. A., Brann, M., & Bowman, N. D. (2014). Male athletes, female aesthetics: The continued ambivalence toward female athletes in ESPN's *The Body Issue*. *International Journal of Sport Communication, 7*(2), 145–165. doi:10.1123/IJSC.2014–0021

Crenshaw, K. (1995). *Critical race theory: The key writings that formed the movement*. New York: New Press.

Crolley, L., & Teso, E. (2007). Gendered narratives in Spain. *International Review for the Sociology of Sport, 42*(2), 149–166. doi:10.1177/1012690207084749

Crosset, T. (1995). *Outsiders in the clubhouse: The world of professional women's golf*. Albany, NY: State University of New York Press.

Croteau, D., & Hoynes, W. (2000). *Media/society: Industries, images, and audiences* (2nd ed.). Thousand Oaks, CA: Pine Forge Press.

Cruppi, A., & Bachmann, K. (2010, October 25). Fox, Cablevision: The money game. *adweek.com*. Retrieved from http://login.vnuemedia.com/mw/photos/stylus/155629RtransLO.pdf

Daniels, E. (2009). Sex objects, athletes, and sexy athletes: How media representations of women athletes can impact adolescent girls and college women. *Journal of Adolescent Research, 24*, 399–422. doi:10.1177/0743558409336748

Dart, J. J. (2009). Blogging the 2006 FIFA World Cup finals. *Sociology of Sport Journal, 26*, 106–126.

David Stern says he's never seen anything like Jeremy Lin frenzy. (2012, February 24). *ESPN.com*. Retrieved from http://espn.go.com/newyork/nba/story/_/id/7608874/david-stern-says-never-seen-anything-jeremy-lin-frenzy

Davis, L. R. (1997). *The swimsuit issue and sport: Hegemonic masculinity in* Sports Illustrated. Albany, NY: State University of New York Press.

Day, J. C., & McDonald, S. (2010). Not so fast, my friend: Social capital and the race disparity in promotions among college football coaches. *Sociological Spectrum, 30*(2), 138–158. doi:10.1080/02732170903495937

De Chernatony, L. (2010). *From brand vision to brand evaluation* (3rd ed.). Oxford, England: Butterworth-Heinemann.

De Menezes, J. (2014). Brazil vs Germany sets new record for most tweets about a single sporting event with 35.6m posts on Twitter. *The Independent*. Retrieved from http://www.independent.co.uk/sport/football/international/brazil-vs-germany-world-cup

Debord, G. (1983). *Society of the spectacle*. Detroit: Black & Red.

DeCastro, A. (2013, July 10). Katie Richman helps build ESPN's special blend of social media interaction for espnW, X Games. *Front Row*. Retrieved from http://frontrow.espn.go.com/2013/07/katie-richman-helps-build-espns-special-blend-of-social-media-interaction-for-espnw-x-games/

"Decision" watched by nearly 10 million. (2010, July 11). *ESPN.com*. Retrieved from http://sports.espn.go.com/nba/news/story?id=5371061

Deggans, E. (2013a, March 8). ESPN's ombudsman vacancy emphasizes importance of independent voice in journalism. National Sports Journalism Center. Retrieved from http://sportsjournalism.org/sports-media-news/espns-ombudsman-vacancy-emphasizes-importance-of-independent-objective-voice-in-journalism/

Deggans, E. (2013b, April 25). New ESPN ombud Robert Lipsyte talks about his role. Retrieved from http://www.poynter.org/latest-news/top-stories/211554/espn-ombud-robert-lipsyte-talks-about-his-new-role/

Delgado, R., & Stefancic, J. (2001). *Critical race theory: An introduction*. New York: New York University Press.

Dempsey, J. (2001, March 16). ESPN skeds Spanish-lingo block. *Daily Variety*, p. 35.

Dempsey, J. (2004, February 20). ESPN cuts cabler fee hikes. *Daily Variety*, p. 4.

Deitsch, R. (2006, August 11). ABC Sports to become known as "ESPN on ABC." *SI.com*, Retrieved from http://sportsillustrated.cnn.com/2006/writers/richard_deitsch/08/10/media.circus/

Deitsch, R. (2010, December 20). The stories of their time: ESPN's "30 for 30" fields a rich lineup of documentaries. *Sports Illustrated*. Retrieved from http://www.si.com/vault/article/magazine/MAG1179915/index.htm

Deitsch, R. (2013, March 18). A shot at the champ: Fox promises to come out swinging with a new 24/7 channel, but can FS1 really challenge ESPN? *Sports Illustrated*, *118*(12), 16.

Deitsch, R. (2013, May 20). Media circus: Bad boys hit the screen; ESPN has no plans to lose NBA. SI.com. Retrieved from http://sportsillustrated.cnn.com/more/news/20130520/media-circus-dennis-rodman-espn-nba-epl

Deuze, M. (2007). *Media work: Digital media and society series*. Malden, MA: Polity.

Dewing, M. (2012). Canadian broadcasting policy (Publication No. 2011–39-E). Retrieved from http://www.parl.gc.ca/content/lop/researchpublications/2011–39-e.pdf

Disney brings ESPN to ABC. (2006, August 11). *Financial Wire*, 1.

Dodds, E. (2014, June 9). Quack, quack, quack: An oral history of the *Mighty Ducks* trilogy. *Time* (online). Retrieved from http://time.com/mighty-ducks

Dohrmann, G., & Evans, T. (2013a, September 10). Special report on Oklahoma State football: The overview. *Sports Illustrated*. Retrieved from http://sportsillustrated.cnn.com/college-football/news/20130910/osu-introduction

Dohrmann, G., & Evans, T. (2013b, September 10). Special report on Oklahoma State football: Part 1—The money. *Sports Illustrated*. Retrieved from http://sportsillustrated.cnn.com/college-football/news/20130910/oklahoma-state-part-1-money/

Dohrmann, G., & Evans, T. (2013c, September 10). Special report on Oklahoma State football: Part 2—The academics. *Sports Illustrated*. Retrieved from http://sportsillustrated.cnn.com/college-football/news/20130911/oklahoma-state-part-2-academics

Dohrmann, G., & Evans, T. (2013d, September 10). Special report on Oklahoma State football: Part 3—The drugs. *Sports Illustrated*. Retrieved from http://sportsillustrated.cnn.com/college-football/news/20130912/oklahoma-state-part-3-drugs/

Dohrmann, G., & Evans, T. (2013e, September 10). Special report on Oklahoma State football: Part 4—The sex. *Sports Illustrated*. Retrieved from http://sportsillustrated.cnn.com/college-football/news/20130913/oklahoma-state-part-4-the-sex/

Dohrmann, G., & Evans, T. (2013f, September 10). Special report on Oklahoma State football: Part 5—The fallout. *Sports Illustrated*. Retrieved from http://sportsillustrated.cnn.com/college-football/news/20130916/oklahoma-state-part-5-fallout

Domatob, J. K. (2012, May 31). Jay Hopson is first White ASU, SWAC head football coach. *Jackson Advocate*, pp. 1A, 14A.

Donohue, S. (1998, August 24). Operators rap ESPN for high fees. *Electronic Media*, *17*(35), 16.

Dosh, K. (2010, December 13). espnW: A marketing message gone wrong. Retrieved from http://www.forbes.com/sites/sportsmoney/2010/12/13/espnw-a-marketing-message-gone-wrong/

Doyle, W. (2001). *An American insurrection: The battle of Oxford, Mississippi, 1962*. New York: Doubleday.

Duffy, P. (2012, July 30). Billy Mills' run for glory. *Rapid City Journal*. Retrieved from http://rapidcityjournal.com/news/billy-mills-run-for-glory/article_bf38e6aa-7497-5222-adc4-d39cacbb9a23.html

Duffy, T. (2013). ESPN passed Yahoo! Sports in fantasy football subscribers for first time, according to internal numbers. Retrieved from http://thebiglead.com/2013/09/11/espn-passed-yahoo-in-fantasy-football-subscribers-for-first-time-according-to-internal-numbers/

Duggan, M., & Smith, A. (2013, December 30). Social media update 2013: 42% of online adults use multiple social networking sites, but Facebook remains the platform of choice. *Pew Research Center*. Retrieved from http://www.pewinternet.org/2013/12/30/social-media-update-2013/

Duncan, A. (2014). Reimagining the self-made man: Myth, risk, and the pokerization of America. *Western Journal of Communication, 78*(1), 39–57. doi:10.1080/10570314.2013.807435

Duncan, M. C. (1990). Sports photographs and sexual difference: Images of women and men in the 1984 and 1988 Olympic games. *Sociology of Sport Journal, 7*(1), 22–43.

Duncan, M. C. (2006). Gender warriors in sport: Women and the media. In A. A. Raney & J. Bryant (Eds.), *Handbook of sports and media* (pp. 247–269). Mahwah, NJ: Lawrence Erlbaum.

Duncan, M. C., & Messner, M. A. (1998). The media image of sport and gender. In L. A. Wenner (Ed.), *Mediasport* (pp. 170–185). New York, NY: Routledge.

Dupree, S. (1996, April 1). ABC Sports to go to ESPN. *MediaWeek, 6*(14), 6.

Dusenbery, M. (2012, July 16). Why ESPN's Body Issue could have been great but doesn't quite succeed. *Feministing*. Retrieved from http://feministing.com/2012/07/16/why-espns-body-issue-could-have-been-great-but-doesnt-quite-succeed/

Eagleman, A. N. (2011). Stereotypes of race and nationality: A qualitative analysis of sport magazine coverage of MLB players. *Journal of Sport Management, 25*(2), 156–168.

Eagleman, A. N., Pedersen, P. M., & Wharton, R. (2009). Coverage by gender in *ESPN The Magazine*: An examination of articles and photographs. *International Journal of Sport Management, 10*(2), 226–242.

Eastman, S. T., & Billings, A. C. (2000). Sportscasting and sports reporting: The power of gender bias. *Journal of Sport & Social Issues, 24*(2), 192–213. doi:10.1177/0193723500242006

Eastman, S. T., & Billings, A. C. (2001). Biased voices of sports: Racial and gender stereotyping in college basketball announcing. *The Howard Journal of Communications, 12*, 183–201. doi:10.1080/106461701753287714

Edwards, T. (2012, March 29). Title IX is mine [Video file]. Retrieved from http://espn.go.com/video/clip?id=7752591

Eitzen, D. S., & Sage, G. H. (2008). *Sociology of North American sport* (8th ed.). Boulder, CO: Paradigm Publishers.

Eliopulos, L. M., & Johnson, J. (2012). Inside the vortex of sport celebrification: A textual analysis of Jessica Simpson, Tony Romo, and traditionally constructed gender roles. *International Journal of Sport Communication, 5*(2), 210–230.

Elliot, D. (1985). A conceptual analysis of ethics codes. *Journal of Mass Media Ethics, 1*(1), 22–26. doi:10.1080/08900523.2012.669289

Elueze, R., & Jones, R. L. (1998). A quest for equality: A gender comparison of the BBC's TV coverage of the 1995 World Athletics Championships. *World of Sport & Physical Activity Journal, 7*(1), 45–67.

Engel, M. (2013, March 18). A chat with the author who changed the image of Jim Valvano forever. *The Big Mac blog*. Retrieved from http://sportsblogs.star-telegram.com/mac-engel/2013/03/a-chat-with-the-author-who-changed-the-image-of-jim-valvano-forever.html

Entman, R. M. (1993). Framing: Toward clarification of a fractured paradigm. *Journal of Communication, 43*(4), 51–58. doi:10.1111/j.1460-2466.1993.tb01304.x

Entman, R. M. (2004). *Projections of power: Framing news, public opinion, and U.S. foreign policy*. Chicago: University of Chicago.

ESPN. (2009, Mar. 29). The U: Preview. Retrieved from http://espn.go.com/30for30/film?page=the-u

ESPN. (2013). 2013 ESPN pocket guide. Retrieved from http://espncms.com/ESPNCMS/files/0f/0ff98b46–1db5–4899-bc39-d912b80e4687.pdf

ESPN, ABC Sports to merge advertising sales staffs; Erhardt named to lead combined entity. (1999, September 20). *Business Wire.* Retrieved from http://www.thefreelibrary.com/ESPN,+ABC+Sports+to+Merge+Advertising+Sales+Staffs%3B+Erhardt+Named+to...-a055792925

ESPN becoming "Achilles heel" for Disney, media analyst says: Sports network may have reached plateau in its growth potential, some say. (2004, February 17). *Los Angeles Times*, p. D6.

ESPN Customer Marketing and Sales. (2013). ESPN.com: The interactive center of the sports fan's universe. Retrieved from http://espncms.com/ESPNCMS/files/0f/0ff98b46–1db5–4899-bc39-d912b80e4687.pdf

ESPN Department of Integrated Media Research. (2010, April 15). *ESPN top ten list for sport research.* Paper presented at the Broadcast Education Association Research Symposium, Las Vegas, NV.

ESPN Deportes celebrates 10 years of record-breaking growth reaching more sports fans than any other Spanish-language sports media brand. (2014, January 6). *Business Wire.* Retrieved from http://www.businesswire.com/news/home/20140106006708/en/ESPN-Deportes-Celebrates-10-Years-Record-Breaking-Growth#.VBs4i0v3Cnw

ESPN Deportes debuts TV simulcast of ESPN Deportes Radio's Jorge Ramos y Su Banda. (2009, August 14). *PRNewswire.com.* Retrieved from http://www.prnewswire.com/news-releases/espn-deportes-debuts-tv-simulcast-of-espn-deportes-radios-jorge-ramos-y-su-banda-62231627.html

ESPN Deportes enters 2009–2010 upfront season with record ratings and continued focus on delivering news with the best sportscasters in the Spanish-language media industry. (2009, May 19). *PR Newswire.* Retrieved from http://www.prnewswire.com/news-releases/espn-deportes-enters-2009–2010-upfront-season-with-record-ratings-and-continued-focus-on-delivering-news-with-the-best-sportscasters-in-the-spanish-language-media-industry-61924542.html

ESPN Deportes reloads advertising community with new programming initiative and multiplatform approach. (2008, May 15). *PRNewswire.com.* Retrieved from http://www.prnewswire.com/news-releases/espn-deportes-reloads-advertising-community-with-new-programming-initiative-and-multiplatform-approach-in-its-08-upfront-presentation-57256722.html

ESPN Deportes unveils new initiatives for 2012–2013. (2012, May 16). *PRNewswire.com.* Retrieved from http://www.prnewswire.com/news-releases/espn-deportes-unveils-new-initiatives-for-2012–2013–151770455.html

ESPN fact sheet. (n.d.). *ESPN MediaZone.* Retrieved from http://espnmediazone.com/us/espninc-fact-sheet/

ESPN increases Spanish coverage. (2005, April 24). *Los Angeles Times.* Retrieved from: http://search.proquest.com/docview/422085901?accountid=9840

ESPN MediaZone. (2011, February 24). Poynter panel to act as ombudsman. Retrieved from http://espnmediazone.com/us/press-releases/2011/02/the-poynter-review-project-to-launch-with-espn/

ESPN MediaZone. (2014, March 25). Bios: John Kosner. Retrieved from http://espnmediazone.com/us/bios/kosner_john/

ESPN's Spanish network now on 24 hours but reaches few viewers. (2004, January 9). *Knight Ridder Tribune News Service.* Retrieved from http://search.proquest.com/docview/457158497?accountid=9840

ESPN Sportsnation. (2013, September). Chat with Robert Lipsyte (transcript). *ESPN Sportsnation.* Retrieved from http://espn.go.com/sportsnation/chat/_/id/48530

ESPN's Simmons: A real sportsman (1981, February 2). *Broadcasting, 100*(5), 105.

ESPN statement on offensive Jeremy Lin comments. (2012, February 21). *ESPN.* Retrieved from http://espn.go.com/espn/story/_/id/7591778/espn-statement-offensive-jeremy-lincomments

espnW. (2011a). The Body Issue (Interview with Suzy Hotrod). Retrieved from http://espn.go.com/espnw/body-issue/7053967/suzy-hotrod

espnW. (2011b). The Body Issue (Interview with Hope Solo). Retrieved from http://espn.go.com/espnw/body-issue/6974155/hope-solo

espnW. (n.d.). *espnW...* Retrieved from http://espn.go.com/espnw/about

espnW Women + Sports Summit. (n.d.). *espnW Women + Sports Summit.* Retrieved from http://www.espnwsummit.com/about/

Eskenazi, G. (1989, September 18). ESPN's 10-year journey to the top. *New York Times,* p. D8.

Ettema, J., & Glasser, T. (1985). On the epistemology of investigative journalism. *Communication, 8*(2), 183–206.

Ettema, J., & Glasser, T. (1987, March). Public accountability or public relations? Newspaper ombudsmen define their role. *Journalism Quarterly, 64*(1), 3–12. doi:10.1177/107769908706400101

Evans, A. S. (1979). Differences in the recruitment of Black and White football players at a Big Eight university. *Journal of Sport & Social Issues. 3*(1), 1–10. doi:10.1177/019372357900300201

Everything you always wanted to know. (1999, September 6). *ESPN Press Releases.* Retrieved from http://espn.go.com/espninc/pressreleases/faq.html

Evey, S. (2004). *ESPN: The no-holds-barred story of power, ego, money, and vision that transformed a culture.* Chicago: Triumph Books.

Evey, S., & Broughton, I. (2004). *ESPN: The no-holds-barred story of power, ego, money, and vision that transformed a culture.* Chicago: Triumph Books.

Fabrikant, G. (1987, June 9). It's first and goal for ESPN. *New York Times.* Retrieved from http://www.nytimes.com/1987/06/09/business/it-s-first-and-goal-for-espn.html

Fainaru-Wada, M. (2014, July 27). CrossFit's big growth fuels concerns. *ESPN.go.com.* Retrieved from http://espn.go.com/espn/otl/story/_/id/11262964/crossf-explosive-growth-fuels-safety-concerns

Farred, G. (2000). Cool as the other side of the pillow: How ESPN's *SportsCenter* has changed television sports talk. *Journal of Sport & Social Issues, 24*(2), 96–117. doi:10.1177/0193723500242002

Farrey, T. (2012, June 6). *Too high a price to play.* Retrieved from http://espn.go.com/espnW/title-ix/article/7986414/too-high-price-play

Fatsis, S., & Orwall, B. (2002, September 2). Disney is throwing in the towel on sports-team ownership. *Wall Street Journal,* p. A6.

Fatsis, S., & Pope, K. (1998, January 14). NFL scores nearly $18 billion in TV rights. *Wall Street Journal,* B1.

Fensch, T. C. (Ed.). (2001). *Television news anchors: An anthology of profiles of the major figures and issues in United States network reporting.* The Woodlands, TX: New Century Books.

Field, R. (2006). The ties that bind: A 2003 case study of Toronto's sport elite and the operation of commercial sport. *International Review for the Sociology of Sport, 41*(1), 29–58. doi:10.1177/1012690206073215

Fielding, L. W., & Pitts, B. G. (2002). Historical sketches: The development of the sport business industry. In J. B. Parks & J. Quarterman (Eds.), *Contemporary sport management* (2nd ed.). Champaign, IL: Human Kinetics.

Fink, J. S., & Kensicki, L. J. (2002). An imperceptible difference: Visual and textual constructions of femininity in *Sports Illustrated* and *Sports Illustrated for Women. Mass Communication & Society, 5*(3), 317–339. doi:10.1207/S15327825MCS0503_5

Fisher, E. (2009, March 9). Leagues, media outlets unite to battle online piracy. *Streen & Smith's SportsBusiness Journal*. Retrieved from http://www.sportsbusinessdaily.com/Journal/Issues/2009/03/20090309/SBJ-In-Depth/Leagues-Media-Outlets-Unite-To-Battle-Online-Piracy.aspx?hl=pirate%20streaming&sc=0

Fisher, E. (2014, February 17). SI adding features, pages to 50th Swimsuit. *Street & Smith's SportsBusiness Journal, 16*(42). Retrieved from http://www.sportsbusinessdaily.com/Journal/Issues/2014/02/17/Media/Swimsuit.aspx

Fisher, E. (2014, February 28). ESPN holds top spot in ComScore rankings for fifth straight month, but lead is cut. *Street & Smith's SportsBusiness Daily*. Retrieved from http://www.sportsbusinessdaily.com/Daily/Issues/2014/02/28/Media/Comscores.aspx?hl=comscore%20rankings&sc=0

Fisher, E., & Ourand, J. (2013, April 1–7). MLB clubs look to follow Dodgers: $8B Time Warner deal shakes media landscape. *Street & Smith's Sports Business Journal, 15*(48), 1, 36–37. Retrieved from http://www.sportsbusinessdaily.com/Journal/Issues/2013/04/01.aspx

Fiske, J. (1985). The semiotics of television. *Critical Studies in Mass Communication, 2*, 176–183. doi:10.1080/15295038509360076

Flamm, M. (2011, April 25). Goal, Univision. *Crain's New York Business*. Retrieved from http://search.ebscohost.com.libproxy.fullerton.edu/login.aspx%3fdirect=true%26db=bwh%26AN=65223909%26site=ehost-live%26scope=site

Fleisher, A. A., Shughart II, W. F., Tollison, R. D., & Goff, B. L. (1988). Crime or punishment: Enforcement of the NCAA football cartel. *Journal of Economic Behavior and Organization, 10*, 433–451. doi:10.1016/0167-2681(88)90063-7

Fleming, M. (2013, November 7). AFM: Worldview To Finance Hot Spec Package: Nancy Meyers To Helm 'The Intern'; Robert De Niro, Reese Witherspoon To Star. *Deadline*. Retrieved from http://deadline.com/2013/11/afm-worldview-to-finance-hot-spec-package-nancy-meyers-to-helm-the-intern-robert-de-niro-reese-witherspoon-to-star-629927/.

Flint, J. (2013, January 17). Company town; kicking around a new format for Fox Soccer. *Los Angeles Times*. Retrieved from http://search.proquest.com.libproxy.fullerton.edu/latimes/docview/1269961514/9BBAC40ADD4649CEPQ/5?accountid=9840

Fogel, C. A. (2012). How real were the Cougars? Crime and deviance in the National Football League. *Cross-Cultural Communication, 8*(2), 1–6. doi:10.2968/j.ccc.1923670020120802.1330

Fortunato, J. A. (2001). *The ultimate assist: The relationship and broadcast strategies of the NBA and television networks*. Cresskill, NJ: Hampton Press.

Fortunato, J. A. (2006). *Commissioner: The legacy of Pete Rozelle*. Lanham, MD: Taylor Trade Publishing.

Fortunato, J. A. (2013). Television broadcast rights: Still the golden goose. In P. M. Pedersen (Ed.), *Routledge handbook of sport communication* (pp. 188–196). New York: Routledge.

Foucault, M. (1980). *Language, counter-memory, practice*. Ithaca, NY: Cornell University Press.

Foudy, J. (2012, June 23). *Power of IX: Julie Foudy* [Video file]. Retrieved from http://espn.go.com/video/clip?id=8088693

Fox Sports World and Fox Sports en Español to televise a selection of live matches from Euro 2004. (2004, June 9). *Business Wire*. Retrieved from http://www.thefreelibrary.com/Fox+Sports+World+and+Fox+Sports+en+Espanol+to+Televise+a+Selection+of...-a0117927538

Freeman, M. (2000). *ESPN: The uncensored history*. Dallas, TX: Taylor Publishing.

Freeman, M. (2001). *ESPN: The uncensored history*. Lanham, MD: Taylor Trade Publishing.

Frey, L., Botan, C., & Kreps, G. (1999). *Investigating communication: An introduction to research methods* (2nd ed.). Boston, MA: Allyn & Bacon.

From trade to consumer. (1981, September 28). *Broadcasting, 101*(13), 9.

Fursich, E. (2002). Nation, capitalism, myth: Covering news of economic globalization. *Journalism & Mass Communication Quarterly, 79*(2), 353–373. doi:10.1177/107769900207900207

Fursich, E., & Lester, E. P. (1996). Science journalism under scrutiny: A textual analysis of "Science Times." *Critical Studies in Mass Communication, 13*(1), 24–43. doi:10.1080/15295039609366958

Futterman, M., & Clark, K. (2013, August 30). Deal in concussion suit gives NFL a big victory. *Wall Street Journal*, pp. A1, A5.

Gachman, D. (2014, Jan. 15). ESPN's 'The Price of Gold' takes a closer look at Tonya Harding. *Forbes*. Retrieved from http://www.forbes.com/sites/dinagachman/2014/01/15/espns-the-price-of-gold-takes-a-closer-look-at-tonya-harding/

Gamache, R. (2014). The ESPN assemblage: The political and cultural economy of late sports capitalism. *Journal of Sports Media, 9*(1), 71–93.

Garcia, J. (2009, November 6). ESPN to rule at Disney venue. *Orlando Sentinel*, p. A1.

Gardner, E. (2013, February 19). Dish-ESPN trial offers a rare inside look at TV dealmaking. *Hollywoodreporter.com*. Retrieved from http://www.hollywoodreporter.com/thr-esq/dish-espn-trial-offers-a-422301

Garfield, B. (2012, December 28). The incredible value of live sports. *onthemedia.org*. Retrieved from http://www.onthemedia.org/story/258711-incredible-value-live-sports/transcript/

Gardiner, G. (2003) "Black" bodies—"White" codes: Indigenous footballers, racism and the Australian Football League's racial and religious vilification code. In J. Bale & M. Cronin (Eds.), *Sport and postcolonialism* (pp. 29–43). Oxford: Berg.

Gardner, C. J., Jr. (2012, July 20). ESPN: The Body Issue. blitzweekly.com. Retrieved from http://blitzweekly.com/espn-the-body-issue/

Genovese, J. (2013). "You gotta appease the people who run this place": Corporate ownership and its influence on sports television production. *Electronic News, 7*(3), 141–159. doi:10.1177/1931243113507925

Gentile, L. (2010, October 4). *The espnW retreat: Laura Gentile's opening remarks*. Retrieved from https://www.facebook.com/notes/espnw/the-espnw-retreat-laura-gentiles-opening-remarks/447718508918

Gentry, J. J. (1995, June 22). The top five reasons track and field isn't more popular in the United States. *San Diego Union Tribune*, p. D2.

Gentry, J. J. (2013). The non-crisis in world population. *World geography: Understanding a changing world*. Retrieved from http://worldgeography2.abc-clio.com/

Georgiadis, A. (2010, October 25). Nike tries to rehabilitate LeBron James' image in new 90 second spot. *Advertising Age*. Retrieved from http://adage.com/article/adages/nikerehabilitate-lebron-james-image-90-spot/146690/

Getty's dry hole (1981, June 8). *Broadcasting, 100*(23), 78.

Ghodeswar, B. M. (2008). Building brand identity in competitive markets: A conceptual model. *Journal of Product & Brand Management, 17*(1), 4–12. doi:10.1108/10610420810856468

Gibbons, K. (2009, January 12). Cox adds SiTV in Arizona. *Multichannel News*. Retrieved from http://www.multichannel.com/news/content/cox-adds-si-tv-arizona/364868

Ginn, S. (2006, March 3). Fox aims to draw in Latino fans. *St. Petersburg Times*, p. 9C.

Gitlin, T. (1980). *The whole world is watching: Mass media in the making & unmaking of the new left*. Berkley, CA: University of California.

Glass, A. (2013, October 10). Laura Gentile, espnW imagines the future of women's sports. Retrieved from http://www.forbes.com/sites/alanaglass/2013/10/10/laura-gentile-espnw-imagines-the-future-of-womens-sports/2/

Goff, B., & Ashwell, T. (2009). Sport broadcasting. In L. P. Masteralexis, C. A. Barr, & M. A. Hums (Eds.), *Principles and practice of sport management*. Sudbury, MA: Jones and Bartlett Publishers.

Goffman, E. (1974). *Frame analysis: An essay on the organization of experience*. New York: Harper & Row.

Gonzalez, E. (2013, April 29). From futbol to football: How the NFL and soccer are competing for Hispanic American viewership. *Nielsen.com*. Retrieved from http://www.nielsen.com/us/en/newswire/2013/from-futbol-to-football–how-the-nfl-and-soccer-are-competing-fo.html

Gonzalez, J. (2013, April 4). ESPN Deportes the exclusive presenter of Jungle Fight 50. *espnmediazone*.com. Retrieved from http://espnmediazone.com/us/press-releases/2013/04/espn-deportes-the-exclusive-presenter-of-jungle-fight-50/

Gonzalez, R. (2002, September 24). Spanish expansion for ESPN. *Hartford Courant*, p. C6.

Goodwin, M. (1986, November 11). College pact not in focus. *New York Times*, p. A22.

Goodwin, M. (1987, March 17). Networks save cash, gain a competitor. *New York Times*, p. D30.

Grainger, A., Newman, J. I., & Andrews, D. L. (2006). Sport, the media, and the construction of race. In A. A. Raney & J. Bryant (Eds.) *Handbook of sports and media* (pp. 447–467). Mahwah, NJ: Lawrence Erlbaum Associates.

Gramsci, A. (1971). *Selections from the prison notebooks*. New York: International Publishers.

Granatstein, L., & Schwirtz, M. (1998, March 30). Magazines. *MediaWeek, 8*(13), 32.

Grant, P. S., & Wood, C. (2004). *Blockbusters and trade wars: Popular culture in a globalized world*. Toronto, Canada: Douglas & McIntyre.

Gray, J., Sandvoss, C., & Harrington, C. L. (Eds.). (2007). *Fandom: Identities and communities in a mediated world*. New York: NYU Press.

Greene, R. W. (2004). Rhetoric and capitalism: Rhetorical agency as communicative labor. *Philosophy & Rhetoric, 37*(4), 188–206. doi:10.1353/par.2004.0020

Greenfeld, K. T. (2012, August 30). ESPN: Everywhere sports profit network. *businessweek.com*. Retrieved from http://www.businessweek.com/articles/2012–08–30/espn-everywhere-sports-profit-network

Greer, J. D., Hardin, M., & Homan, C. (2009). "Naturally" less exciting? Visual production of men's and women's track and field coverage during the 2004 Olympics. *Journal of Broadcasting & Electronic Media, 53*(2), 173–189. doi:10.1080/08838150902907595

Gregory, B. L., & Busey, J. C. (1985). Alternative broadcasting arrangements after *NCAA*. *Indiana Law Journal, 61*(1), 65–84. Retrieved from http://www.repository.law.indiana.edu/ilj/vol61/iss1/5/

Gregory, S. (2010, July 8). The LeBron James hour: Is this prime-time overkill? *Time*. Retrieved from http://content.time.com/time/nation/article/0,8599,2002477,00.html

Gremillion, J. (1997, May 12). ESPN takes dead aim at "SI." *MediaWeek, 7*(19), 12.

Griffin, R. A. (2011). The disgrace of commodification and shameful convenience: A critical race critique of the NBA. *Journal of Black Studies*, 1–25.

Gross, J. (2011, August 18). UFC, Fox agree to seven-year deal. *ESPN.com*. Retrieved from http://espn.go.com/mma/story/_/id/6874530/ufc-reaches-seven-year-broadcast-deal-fox-networks

Grotticelli, M. (2013, June 27). "Cord Cutters" turning to online video and OTA antenna. *Broadcastengineering.com*. Retrieved from http://broadcastengineering.com/towersantenna/cord-cutters-turning-online-video-and-ota-antennas

Grove, S. J., Dorsch, M. J., & Hopkins, C. D. (Winter 2012). Assessing the longitudinal robustness of spectators' perceptions of the functions of sport: Implications for sport marketers. *Journal of Marketing Theory and Practice, 20*(1), 23–38. doi:10.2753/MTP1069–6679200102

Grusin, R. (2010). *Premediation: Affect and mediality after 9/11*. New York: Pelgrave Macmillan.

Guthrie, M. (2012, October 18). At 50 years old, how Univision owns the Hispanic Audience. *TheHollywoodReporter.com*. Retrieved from http://www.hollywoodreporter.com/news/univision-how-network-owns-hispanic-379441

Guthrie, M. (2013, June 26). ESPN's John Skipper on sports rights, layoffs and Keith Olbermann: "We don't have a policy here that you can never come back" (Q&A). *The Hollywood Reporter*. Retrieved from http://www.hollywoodreporter.com/news/espn-john-skipper-keith-olbermann-574231?page=2

Gutierrez, P. (2005, April 23). Big Day for ESPN Deportes. *Latimes.com*. Retrieved from http://articles.latimes.com/2005/apr/23/sports/sp-soccertv23

Hale, M. (2012, October 22). A rising star, extinguished, in 1980s Chicago. *New York Times*. Retrieved from http://www.nytimes.com/2012/10/23/arts/television/benji-a-30-for-30-documentary-on-espn.html?pagewanted=print

Hale, M. (2013, July 1). ESPN's "Nine for IX" focuses on women in sports. *New York Times*. Retrieved from http://www.nytimes.com/2013/07/02/arts/television/espns-nine-for-ix-focuses-on-women-in-sports.html?_r=0

Hall, C. (2009, August 5). Twitter ban continues: ESPN bans its reporters from sports-related social media. *Mediaite*. Retrieved from http://www.mediaite.com/online/espn-bans-its-reporters-from-sports-related-twitter-activity/

Hall, P., & Dhar, A. (Producers), & Singleton, J. (Director). (2010). *Marion Jones: Press pause* [Motion Picture]. USA: ESPN Films.

Hall, S. (1981). The whites of their eyes: Racist ideologies and the media. In G. Bridges & R. Brunt (Eds.), *Silver linings: Some strategies for the eighties* (pp. 28–52). London: Lawrence and Wishart.

Hardin, M. (2005). Stopped at the gate: Women's sports, "reader interest," and decision-making by editors. *Journalism & Mass Communication Quarterly, 82*(1), 62–77. doi:10.1177/107769900508200105

Hardin, M. (2011). The power of a fragmented collective: Radical pluralist feminism and technologies of the self in the sports blogosphere. In A. C. Billings (Ed.), *Sports media: Transformation, integration, consumption* (pp. 40–60). New York: Routledge.

Hardin, M., Chance, J., Dodd, J. E., & Hardin, B. (2002). Olympic photo coverage fair to female athletes. *Newspaper Research Journal, 23*(2/3), 64–79.

Hardin, M., & LaVoi, N. M. (2013). Inappropriate behavior and lesbianism: The contrasting falls of two women's college basketball coaches. In L. Wenner (Ed.), *Fallen sports heroes, media, and celebrity culture* (pp. 267–283). New York: Peter Lang.

Hardin, M., Lynn, S., & Walsdorf, K. (2005). Challenge and conformity on "contested terrain": Images of women in four women's sport/fitness magazines. *Sex Roles: A Journal of Research, 53*(1–2), 105–117. doi:10.1007/s11199–005–4285–6

Hardin, M., & Shain, S. (2005). Strength in numbers? The experiences and attitudes of women in sports media careers. *Journalism & Mass Communication Quarterly, 82*(4), 804–819. doi:10.1177/107769900508200404

Hardin, M., Simpson, S., Whiteside, E., & Garris, K. (2007). The gender war in U.S. sport: Winners and losers in news coverage of Title IX. *Mass Communication & Society, 10*(2), 211–233. doi:10.1080/15205430701265737

Hardin, M., & Whiteside, E. (2009). The power of "small stories": Narratives and notions of gender equality in conversations about sport. *Sociology of Sport Journal, 26*, 255–276.

Hardin, M., & Whiteside, E. (2010). Public relations and sports: Work force demographics in the intersection of two gendered industries. *Journal of Sports Media, 5*(1), 21–52. doi:10.1353/jsm.0.0044

Hardin, M., & Whiteside, E. (2012). How do women talk sports? Women sports fans in a blog community. In K. Toffoletti & P. Mewett (Eds.), *Sports and its female fans* (pp. 152–168). New York: Routledge.

Hardin, M., Whiteside, E., & Ash, E. (2014). Ambivalence on the front lines? Attitudes toward Title IX and women's sports among Division I sports information directors. *Sociology of Sport, 49*(1), 42–64.

Hardin, M., Zhong, B., & Corrigan, T. F. (2012). The funhouse mirror: The blogosphere's reflection of women's sports. In T. Dumova & R. Fiordo (Eds.), *Blogging in the global society: Cultural, political and geographical aspects* (pp. 55–71). Hershey, PA: Information Science Reference.

Hardt, H. (1993). Authenticity, communication, and critical theory. *Critical Studies in Mass Communication, 10*, 49–69. doi:10.1080/15295039309366848

Harris, J., & Clayton, B. (2002). Femininity, masculinity, physicality and the English tabloid press: The case of Anna Kournikova. *International Review for the Sociology of Sport, 37*(3–4), 397–413. doi:10.1177/1012690202037004024

Harris, J., & Humberstone, B. (2004). Sport, gender and international relations. In R. Levermore & A. Budd (Eds.), *Sport and international relations: An emerging relationship* (pp. 48–61). New York: Routledge.

Harsin, J. (2008). The rumor bomb: Americans mediate politics as pure war. In M. Ryan & H. Musiol (Eds.), *Cultural studies: An anthology* (pp. 468–482). Malden, MA: Blackwell Publishing.

Harvey, J., & Law, A. (2005). "Resisting" the global media oligopoly? The Canada Inc. response. In M. L. Silk, D. L. Andrews, & C. L. Cole (Eds.), *Sport and corporate nationalisms* (pp. 187–225). New York: Berg.

Hayden, E. (2013, August 23). TCA flashback: When ESPN and Frontline touted concussion doc (Transcript). *The Hollywood Reporter.* Retrieved from http://www.hollywoodreporter.com/live-feed/tca-flashback-espn-frontline-touted-613579

Hechavarria, D. M., Renko, M., & Matthews, C. H. (2012). The nascent entrepreneurship hub. Goals, entrepreneurial self-efficacy and the start-up outcomes. *Small Business Economist, 39*, 685–701. doi:10.1007/s11187-011-9355-2

Heller, M. (1987, April 7). ESPN sports channel now profitable. *The Globe and Mail (Toronto)* [online]. Available from http://lexisnexis.com

Hershey, S. (1982, January 31). Utah-Denver merger denied; NBA signs cable contracts. *The Washington Post*, p. M2.

Hertog, J. K., & McLeod, D. M. (2003). A multiperspectival approach to framing analysis: A field guide. In S. D. Reese, O. H. Gandy, & A. E. Grant (Eds.), *Framing public life* (pp. 139–162). Mahwah, NJ: Lawrence Erlbaum.

Hesketh, P. (1996, June 3). Disney to triple Angels' marketing, target new fans. *Orange County Business Journal*, 1.

Heywood, L. (2007). Producing girls: Empire, sport, and neoliberal body. In J. Hargreaves & P.A. Vertinsky (Eds.), *Physical culture, power, and the body* (pp. 101–120). New York: Routledge.

Hiestand, M. (1997, December 10). Pioneer steers ABC, ESPN to top of game. *USA Today*, p. 1C.

Hiestand, M. (2010, April 28). HBO stakes out documentary turf. *USA Today*, p. C3.

Hiestand, M. (2010, October 1). *ESPN aims for female audience with espnW.* Retrieved from http://usatoday30.usatoday.com/sports/columnist/hiestand-tv/2010-09-30-espnW-baseball-tv-playoffs_N.htm

Hiestand, M. (2012, May 10). $3.6 billion in TV money for ACC a good sign for SEC, Big 12. *USA Today*, p. 1C.

Hiestand, M. (2013, January 30). Mexico's soccer to get more TV exposure in USA. *USAToday.com*. Retrieved from http://www.usatoday.com/story/sports/2013/01/30/espn-univision-soccer-mexican-soccer-team/1877445/

High school sports participation increases for 24th consecutive year (n.d.). Retrieved from http://www.nfhs.org/content.aspx?id=9628

Hispanic upfront: A preview of what's ahead. (2013, May 13). *Cablefax Daily*. Retrieved from http://search.proquest.com/docview/1373773148?accountid=9840

Hoag, A. (2008). Managing media entrepreneurship. *International Journal of Media Management, 10*(2), 74–80. doi:10.1080/14241270802000496

Hoffarth, T. (2009, September 8). The life cycle of a sports fan, according to ESPN research. *Farther Off the Wall*. Retrieved from http://www.insidesocal.com/tomhoffarth/2009/09/08/espn-analysis-o/

Hogarth, P. (2008). Racial ideology and discourse in the NBA: Ron Artest and the construction of black bodies by white America. *Stream: Culture/Politics/Technology, 1*(1), 53–71.

Hollander, B.A. (2010). Persistence in the perception of Barack Obama as a Muslim in the 2008 presidential campaign. *Journal of Media & Religion, 9*(2), 55–66. doi:10.1080/15348421003738769

Hollander, D. (2010, November 4). Are New York marathoners athletes? *Huff Post New York*. Retrieved from http://www.huffingtonpost.com/dave-hollander/are-new-york-marathoners-_b_777238.html

Holmes, L. (2009, October 28). Why even people who hate sports should be watching ESPN's "30 for 30." *NPR.org*. Retrieved from http://www.npr.org/blogs/monkeysee/2009/10/why_even_people_who_hate_sport.html

Holmes, L. (2012, October 2). ESPN's "Broke" looks at the many ways athletes lose their money. Retrieved from http://www.npr.org/blogs/monkeysee/2012/10/02/162162226/espns-broke-looks-at-the-many-ways-athletes-lose-their-money

Honan, M. (2014, March 12). Why Twitter can't keep crashing. *Wired*. Retrieved from http://www.wired.com/gadgetlab/2014/03/twitter-big-fail-whale-now/

Horn, B. (2006, August 12). Welcome to ESPNation. *McClatchy-Tribune Business News*, p. 1.

Horn, J. (1993, September 26). Disney has mighty marketing effort for Mighty Ducks. *Seattle Times*, p. C1.

Hudson, H. E. (1990). *Communication satellites: Their development and impact*. New York: Free Press.

Huff, R. (2011, July 19). ESPN Deportes is scoring historic 1st. *Daily News* (New York), p. 65.

Hughes, G. (2004). Managing Black guys: Representation, corporate culture, and the NBA. *Sociology of Sport Journal, 21*(2), 163–184.

Hundley, H. L. (2004). Keeping the score: The hegemonic everyday practices in golf. *Communication Reports, 17*, 39–48. doi:10.1080/08934210409389372

Hylton, K. (2010). How a turn to critical race theory can contribute to our understanding of "race," racism and anti-racism in sport. *International Review for the Sociology of Sport, 45*(3), 335–354. doi:10.1177/1012690210371045

Ibarra, S. (2008). Nielsen adds ESPN Deportes to Hispanic ratings tracking service. *tvweek.com*. Retrieved from http://www.tvweek.com/news/2008/04/nielsen_adds_espn_deportes_to.php

In Brief. (1979, February 26). *Broadcasting, 96*(9), 38–39.

Industry demographics. (2014). Fantasy Sport Trade Association. Retrieved from http://www.fsta.org/?page=Demographics

Ingle, Z. (2013). *Identity and myth in sports documentaries: Critical essays*. Plymouth, UK: Scarecrow.

Ito, T., & Mallory, M. (1997, May 19). Coming soon: ESPN magazine. *U.S. News & World Report, 122*(19), 54.

Janofsky, M. (1987, March 16). $1.4 billion deal adds cable to N.F.L. picture. *New York Times*, p. A1.

Janowitz, M. (1975). Professional models in journalism: The Gatekeeper and the Advocate. *Journalism Quarterly, 52*(4), 618–626, 662. doi:10.1177/107769907505200402

Jansen, S. C., & Sabo, D. (1994). The sport/war metaphor: Hegemonic masculinity, the Persian Gulf War, and the new world order. *Sociology of Sport Journal, 11*(1), 1–17.

Johnson, D. (2013). *Media franchising: Creative license and collaboration in the culture industries.* New York: New York University.

Johnson, G., & Stewart, L. (2005, September 16). ESPN plans studios next to Staples Center; it expects to produce live shows in facility that will be part of the AEG entertainment complex. *Los Angeles Times.* Retrieved from http://articles.latimes.com/2005/sep/16/sports/sp-espn16

Johnson, J. (1989, January 20). Steinbrenner pardoned by Reagan for '72 election law violations. *New York Times.* Retrieved from http://www.nytimes.com/1989/01/20/us/steinbrenner-pardoned-by-reagan-for-72-election-law-violations.html

Jones, D. (2006). The representation of female athletes in online images of successive Olympic Games. *Pacific Journalism Review, 12*(1), 108–129.

Jones, G. (2003, April 2). Soccer Daily Report; TV deals for leagues. *Los Angeles Times.* Retrieved from http://articles.latimes.com/2003/apr/02/sports/sp-soccer2

Kaestner, R., & Xu, X. (2010). Title IX, girls' sports participation, and adult female physical activity and weight. *Evaluation Review, 34*, 52–78. doi:10.1177/0193841X09353539

Kane, M. J. (1988). Media coverage of the female athlete before, during, and after Title IX: *Sports Illustrated* revisited. *Journal of Sport Management, 2*(2), 87–99.

Kane, M. J. (2011, July 27). Sex sells sex, not women's sports. *Nation.* Retrieved from http://www.thenation.com/article/162390/sex-sells-sex-not-womens-sports

Kane, M. J. (2013). The better sportswomen get, the more the media ignore them. *Communication & Sport, 1*(3), 231–236. doi:10.1177/2167479513484579

Kane, M. J., & Buysse, J. (2005). Intercollegiate media guides as contested terrain: A longitudinal analysis. *Sociology of Sport Journal, 22*, 214–238.

Kane, M. J., LaVoi, N. M., & Fink, J. S. (2013). Exploring elite female athletes' interpretation of sports media images. *Communication & Sport, 1*(3), 269–298. doi:10.1177/2167479512473585.

Kapferer, J. N. (1997). *Strategic brand management: Creating and sustaining brand equity long term* (2nd ed.). London: Kogan Page.

Kaplan, D. (2013, September 9–15). For tax purposes, NFL to have teams make settlement payments. *Street & Smith's Sports Business Journal, 16*(21), 4.

Kaplan, D. (2014, July 21–27). TV money up 20 percent for NFL clubs. *Street & Smith's Sports Business Journal, 17*(14), 3.

Karrfalt, W. (2005, April 4). George Bodenheimer. *Television Week, 24*(14), S6.

Kellner, D. (2003). Cultural studies, multiculturalism and media culture. In G. Dines & J. M. Humez (Eds.), *Gender, race, and class in media: A text-reader* (pp. 9–20). Thousand Oaks, CA: Sage.

Kian, E. M. (2007). Gender in sports writing by the print media: An exploratory examination of writers' experiences and attitudes. *The SMART (Sport Management and Related Topics) Journal, 4*(1), 5–26.

Kian, E. M. (2008). A new era for women's sports? Examining *The New York Times* and *USA Today* coverage of college basketball. *Newspaper Research Journal, 29*(3), 38–49.

Kian, E. M. (2014). Sexuality in the mediation of sport. In J. Hargreaves & E. Anderson (Eds.), *Handbook of sport, gender, and sexuality* (pp. 461–469). London: Routledge.

Kian, E. M., & Anderson, E. (2009). John Amaechi: Changing the way reporters examine gay athletes. *Journal of Homosexuality, 56*(7), 799–818. doi:10.1080/00918360903187788

Kian, E. M., Anderson, E., Vincent, J., & Murray, R. (2013). Sport journalists' views on gay men in sport, society and within sport media. *International Review for the Sociology of Sport*. Advanced online publication. doi:10.1177/1012690213504101

Kian, E. M., & Clavio, G. (2011). A comparison of online media and traditional newspaper coverage of the men's and women's U.S. Open tennis tournaments. *Journal of Sports Media*, *6*(2), 55–84. http://dx.doi.org/10.1353/jsm.2011.0004

Kian, E. M., Fink, J. S., & Hardin, M. (2011). Examining the impact of journalists' gender in online and newspaper tennis articles. *Women in Sport and Physical Activity Journal*, *20*(1), 3–21.

Kian, E. M., & Hardin, M. (2009). Framing of sport coverage based on the sex of sports writers: Female journalists counter the traditional gendering of media content. *International Journal of Sport Communication*, *2*(2), 185–204.

Kian, E. M., Mondello, M. & Vincent, J. (2009). ESPN—The women's sports network? A content analysis of internet coverage of March Madness. *Journal of Broadcasting & Electronic Media*, *53*(3), 477–495. doi:10.1080/08838150903102519

Kian, E. M., & Vincent, J. (2014). Examining gays and lesbians in sport via traditional and new media. In A. C. Billings & M. Hardin (Eds.), *The Routledge handbook of sport and new media* (pp. 342–352). London: Routledge.

Kian, E. M., Vincent, J., & Mondello, M. (2008). Masculine hegemonic hoops: An analysis of media coverage of March Madness. *Sociology of Sport Journal*, *25*(2), 223–242.

Killingsworth, J. (2005). License and poetic license: A critical examination of the complicated relationship between the CRTC and speciality channels. *Canadian Journal of Communication*, *30*(2), 211–232.

Kim, K., Sagas, M., & Walker, N. A. (2011). Replacing athleticism with sexuality: Athlete models in *Sports Illustrated* swimsuit issues. *International Journal of Sport Communication*, *4*(2), 148–162.

King, B. (2014, January 6). ESPN Deportes marks 10th anniversary. *Sportsbusinessdaily.com*. Retrieved from http://www.sportsbusinessdaily.com/Journal/Issues/2014/01/06/Media/ESPN-

Kirk, J. (2013, September 12). Inaccuracies in *SI*'s Oklahoma State story pointed out by ESPN. *SB Nation*. Retrieved from http://www.sbnation.com/college-football/2013/9/12/4723902/oklahoma-state-sports-illustrated-espnDeportes.aspx

Kissell, R. (2013, November 7). FOX Deportes holds off challengers as top Spanish language sports net. *Variety.com*. Retrieved from http://www.dailypress.com/topic/sns-201311071258reedbusi varietyn1200801969-20131107,0,3321283.story

Knight, J. L., & Giuliano, T. A. (2001). He's a Laker; She's a «looker»: The consequences of gender-stereotypical portrayals of male and female athletes by the print media. *Sex Roles*, *45*(3/4), 217–229. doi:10.1023/A:1013553811620

Knight, J. L., & Giuliano, T. A. (2003). Blood, sweat, and jeers: The impact of the media's heterosexist portrayals on perceptions of male and female athletes. *Journal of Sport Behavior*, *26*(3), 272–285.

Koch, J. V., & Vander Hill, C. W. (1988). Is There Discrimination in the Black Man's Game. *Social Science Quarterly*, *69*, 83–94.

Kolbe, R., & Burnett, M. (1991). Content-analysis research: An examination of applications with directives for improving research reliability and objectivity. *Journal of Consumer Research*, *18*(2), 243–250. doi:10.1086/209256

Kondolojy, A. (2014, April 10). Univision Deportes network is number 1 Spanish Language sports network in the first quarter of 2014 in primetime. *Tvbythenumbers.zap2it.com*. Retrieved from http://tvbythenumbers.zap2it.com/2014/04/10/univision-deportes-network-is-number-1-spanish-language-sports-network-in-the-first-quarter-of-2014-in-primetime/252765/

Kovach, B., & Rosenstiel, T. (2001). *The elements of journalism: What newspeople should know and the public should expect.* New York: Three Rivers Press.

Kovach, B., & Rosenstiel, T. (2014). *The elements of journalism: What newspeople should know and the public should expect.* (3rd ed.). New York: Three Rivers Press.

Kreidler, M. (2007, October 5). Hunter was right—Jones got big boost from steroids. *ESPN.com.* Retrieved from http://sports.espn.go.com/oly/trackandfield/columns/story?id=3049868

Kristiansen, E., & Broch, T. B. (2013). Athlete-media communication: A theoretical perspective on how athletes use and understand gendered sport communication. In P. M. Pedersen (Ed.), *Routledge handbook of sport communication* (pp. 84–96). New York: Routledge.

*Kristine Lilly shoots straight.* (2012, March 28). [Video file]. Retrieved from http://espn.go.com/espnW/news-commentary/article/7748489/burns-kristine-lilly-shoots-straight

Kruse, H. (2009). Betting on news corporation: Interactive media, gambling, and global information flows. *Television & New Media, 10*(2), 179–194. doi:10.1177/1527476409332046

Labre, M. P. (2002). Adolescent boys and the muscular male body ideal. *Journal of Adolescent Health, 30*(4), 233–242. doi:10.1016/S1054–139X(01)00413-X

Lapchick, R., Moss II, A., Russell, C., & Scearce, R. (2011). *The 2010–11 Associated Press Sports Editors racial and gender report card.* Retrieved from http://www.tidesport.org/RGRC/2011/2011_APSE_RGRC_FINAL.pdf?page=lapchick/110517

Laskow, S. (2014, February 24). *The Olympics are the closest to coverage parity female athletes get.* Retrieved from http://www.cjr.org/full_court_press/women_olympics_coverage.php?utm_medium=App.net&utm_source=PourOver

LaVoi, N., & Kane, M. J. (2011). Sociological aspects of sport. In P. M. Pedersen, J. Parks, J. Quarterman, & L. Thibault (Eds.), *Contemporary sport management* (pp. 372–391). Champaign, IL: Human Kinetics.

Law, A., Harvey, J., & Kemp, S. (2002). The global sport mass media oligopoly: The three usual suspects and more. *International Review for the Sociology of Sport, 37*(3–4), 279–302. doi:10.1177/1012690202037004025

Lax, L., & Stern Winters, N. (Producers & Directors). (2010). *Unmatched* [Motion Picture]. USA: ESPN Films.

Lazarus, D. (2013, August 23). For some, cable rift spurs cord cutting. *Los Angeles Times.* Retrieved from http://www.latimes.com/search/dispatcher.front?Query=For%20some%2C%20cable%20rift%20spurs%20cord%20cutting&target=all&spell=on

Lazarus, D. (2014, August 1). Company town: A case for a la carte TV. *Los Angeles Times,* p. B1.

Lee, J. W., Sweeney, K., Gregg, E., Kane, J., & Kian, E. M. (2012). *ESPN The Magazine's "body issues": The good, the bad, and the sexy.* Poster presented at the 2012 Sport Marketing Association annual conference. October 23–27, 2012. Orlando, Florida.

Lefton, T. (1996, April 29). Fitting ABC and ESPN into Disney. *Brandweek, 37*(18), 30.

Legge, J., & Hindle, K. (1997). *Entrepreneurship: How innovators create the future.* South Melbourne, AU: Macmillan Education.

Leitch, W. (2013, September 16). Shock and yawn. *Sports on Earth.* Retrieved from http://www.sportsonearth.com/article/60758436

Lemke, T. (2006, September 24). ESPN evolves with new media. *Washington Times,* p. A1.

Lenskyj, H. J. (1998). "Inside sport" or "on the margins"? Australian women and the sport media. *International Review for the Sociology of Sport, 33*(1), 19–32. doi:10.1177/101269098033001002

Lenskyj, H. J. (2013). Reflections on communication and sport: On heteronormativity and gender identities. *Communication & Sport, 1,* 138–150. doi:10.1177/2167479512467327

Leonard, D. J. (2013). Eye candy and sex objects: Race and sport on YouTube. In B. Hutchins & D. Rowe (Eds.), *Digital media sport: Technology, power and culture in the network society* (pp. 124–135). New York: Routledge.

Lester, E. (1994). The "I" of the storm: A textual analysis of U.S. Reporting on Democratic Kampuchea. *Journal of Communication Inquiry, 18*(1), 5–26. doi:10.1177/019685999401800101

Lewis, M. (2009, June 29). FACTBOX—Viewer statistics for U.S. sports networks. *Reuters*. Retrieved from http://www.reuters.com/article/2009/06/29/ussports-networks-idUSN2938763620090629

Lights, camera, accion! Hispanic television in America. (2012, December 15). *The Economist*, 68–69. Retrieved from http://search.proquest.com/docview/1239092863?accountid=9840

Lipsyte, R. (2013a, August). *Was ESPN sloppy, naive or compromised?* Retrieved from http://espn.go.com/blog/ombudsman/archive/_/month/august-2013

Lipsyte, R. (2013b, October 15). *Winning ugly: ESPN journalism prevails*. Retrieved from http://espn.go.com/blog/ombudsman/post/_/id/176/winning-ugly-espn-journalism-prevails

Logan, L. (2013, November 11). The 10 biggest myths about running. *Competitor.com*. Retrieved from http://running.competitor.com/2013/11/photos/the-10-biggest-myths-about-running_40723

Longman, J. (2011, October 21). Fox and Telemundo win U.S. rights to 2018 and 2022 World Cups. *NYTimes.com*. Retrieved from http://www.nytimes.com/2011/10/22/sports/soccer/fox-and-telemundo-win-us-rights-to-2018-and-2022-world-cups.html?_r=0

Loop, M. (2013). Twitter usage in fantasy sports journalism. *International Journal of Sport and Society, 3*(3), 17–29.

Loop, M., & Parkhurst, R. (2010). Attribution scarcity in fantasy sports journalism. *International Journal of Sport and Society, 1*(1), 43–54.

Lopez, H. C. (2013, July 29). What Univision's milestone says about U.S. demographics. *Pewresearch.com*. Retrieved from http://www.pewresearch.org/fact-tank/2013/07/29/what-univisions-milestone-says-about-u-s-demographics/

Lopez, H. C., & Gonzalez-Barrera, A. (2013, September 5). What is the future of Spanish in the United States? *Pewresearch.com*. Retrieved from http://www.pewresearch.org/fact-tank/2013/09/05/what-is-the-future-of-spanish-in-the-united-states/

Lowry, T. (2005, October 17). In the zone. *Business Week, 3995*, 66–78.

Lowry, T., & Grover, R. (2003, November 17). ESPN's face-off over fees. *Business Week*, 66–68.

Lulofs, N. (2013, August 6). Top 25 U.S. consumer magazines for June 2013. *Alliance for Audited Media*. Retrieved from http://www.auditedmedia.com/news/blog/2013/august/the-top-25-us-consumer-magazines-for-june-2013.aspx

Lumpkin, A., & Williams, L. D. (1991). An analysis of *Sports Illustrated* feature articles, 1954–87. *Sociology of Sport Journal, 8*(1), 16–32.

Lynn, M., & Parker, L. (2002). What's race got to do with it? CRT's conflicts with and connections to qualitative research methodology and epistemology. *Qualitative Inquiry, 8*, 7–22.

MacNeil, M. (1996). Networks: Producing Olympic ice hockey for a national television audience. *Sociology of Sport Journal, 13*(2), 103–124.

Maglio, T. (2013, October 23). How FOX Deportes turned it around to dominate Spanish-language sports. *Thewrap.com*. Retrieved from http://www.thewrap.com/fox-deportes-es-numero-uno-big-time/

Mahoney, B. (2012, February 16). Lin has 13 assists, Knicks run win streak to 7. Retrieved from http://sports.yahoo.com/news/lin-13-assists-knicks-run-085346703–spt.html

Manfred, T. (2013a, September 10). This paragraph is the most important thing you'll read about the Oklahoma State football scandal. *Business Insider*. Retrieved from http://www.businessinsider.com/oklahoma-state-football-scandal-most-important-paragraph-2013–9

Manfred, T. (2013b, September 12). The juiciest allegations from *Sports Illustrated's* Oklahoma State football scandal. *Business Insider.* Retrieved from http://www.businessinsider.com/oklahoma-state-football-scandal-juiciest-allegations-2013–9

Marchione, M. (2013, November 24). Kids are less fit than their parents were. *The Capital,* p. D3.

Margulies, W. P. (1977). Make the most of your corporate identity. *Harvard Business Review* 55(4), 61–72.

Martin, A., & McDonald, M. G. (2012). Covering women's sport? An analysis of *Sports Illustrated* covers from 1987–2009 and *ESPN The Magazine* covers from 1998–2009. *Graduate Journal of Sport, Exercise & Physical Education Research, I,* 81–97.

Mastro, D. E., Blecha, E., & Seate, A. A. (2011). Characterizations of criminal athletes: A systematic examination of sports news depictions of race and crime. *Journal of Broadcasting & Electronic Media, 55*(4), 526–542. doi:10.1080/08838151.2011.620664

Matula, T. D. (Director). (2010). *Pony Express* [Television series episode]. Clinkscales, K., et al. (Producers, *30 for 30*). United States: ESPN Films.

Maurer, T. (2012, October 5). Mo' money, mo' problems: ESPN goes "Broke." *Forbes.com.* Retrieved from http://www.forbes.com/sites/timmaurer/2012/10/05/mo-money-mo-problems-espn-goes-broke

Mawson, L. M. (2006). Sportswomanship: The cultural acceptance of sport for women versus the accommodation of cultured women in sport. In L. K. Fuller (Ed.), *Sport, rhetoric, and gender: Historical perspectives and media representations* (pp. 19–20). New York: Palgrave McMillan.

McBride, K., & Fry, J. (2012, November 12) Finale: ESPN's size, power demand scrutiny. *ESPN Poynter Review Project.* Retrieved from http://espn.go.com/blog/poynterreview/post/_/id/522/finale-espns-size-power-demand-scrutiny

McCarthy, D., & Jones, R. L. (1997). Speed, aggression, strength, and tactical naivete. *Journal of Sport & Social Issues, 21,* 348–362. doi:10.1177/019372397021004003

McCarthy, M. (2010, September 30). LeBron blames race for backlash to ESPN's *The Decision. USA Today.* Retrieved from http://content.usatoday.com/communities/gameon/post/2010/09/lebron-james-blamesrace-for-backlash-to-espns-the-decision/1#.UwegBIXqjKc

McChesney, R. (1989). Media made sport: A history of sports coverage. In L. A. Wenner (Ed.), *Media, sports, and society* (pp. 49–69). Newbury Park, CA: Sage.

McChesney, R. W. (2004). *The problem of the media: U.S. communication politics in the twenty-first century.* New York: Monthly Review Press.

McCombs, M., & Shaw, D. (1972). The agenda-setting function of mass media. *The Public Opinion Quarterly, 36*(2), 176–187. doi:10.1086/267990

McConville, J. (1996, April 15). ABC combines sports with ESPN under Bornstein. *Broadcasting & Cable, 126*(16), 18.

McDonald, I. (2007) Situating the sport documentary. *Journal of Sport & Social Issues, 31*(3), 208–225. doi:101177/0193723507304608

McDougall, C. (2011). *Born to run: A hidden tribe, superathletes, and the greatest race the world has never seen.* New York: Knopf Doubleday.

McIntyre, G. (2014, July 20). Crossing into the mainstream: B.C. well represented in CrossFit… a sport that began as a workout regime. *The Vancouver Province,* p. A4.

McKee, A. (2001). A beginner's guide to textual analysis. *Metro Magazine.* Retrieved from http://eprints.qut.edu.au/41993/

McMurphy, B. (2013, September 12). Fath' Carter story questioned. *ESPN.com.* Retrieved from http://espn.go.com/college-football/story/_/id/9665724/documents-undermine-some-oklahoma-state-cowboys-accusers

McNamara, M. (2010, November 2). Television review: ESPN's "Marion Jones: Press pause," the track and field star embraces her fall from grace in the latest "30 for 30" documentary, directed by John Singleton. *Los Angeles Times*. Retrieved from http://articles.latimes.com/2010/nov/02/entertainment/la-et-marion-jones-20101102

McNeal, G. (2012, February 18). ESPN uses "chink in the armor" line twice update- ESPN fires one employee suspends another. Retrieved from http://www.forbes.com/sites/gregorymcneal/2012/02/18/espn-uses-chink-in-the-armor-line-twice-did-linsanity-just-go-racist/

Meân, L. J. (2011). Sport, identity, and consumption: The construction of sport at ESPN.com. In A. C. Billings (Ed.), *Sports Media: Transformation, Integration, Consumption* (pp. 162–180). New York: Routledge.

Meân, L. J., & Halone, K. K. (2010). Sport, language, and culture: Issues and intersections. *Journal of Language and Social Psychology, 29*, 253–260. doi:10.1177/0261927X10368830.

Media Education Foundation. (2005). *Media Education Foundation transcript: Playing unfair: The media image of the female athlete*. Retrieved from http://www.mediaed.org/assets/products/208/transcript_208.pdf

Melewar, T. C., & Karaosmanoglu, E. (2006). Seven dimensions of corporate identity: A categorisation from the practitioners' perspectives. *European Journal of Marketing, 40*(7–8), 846–869. doi:10.1108/03090560610670025

Meraz, S., & Papacharissi, Z. (2013). Networked gatekeeping and networked framing on #Egypt. *The International Journal of Press/Politics, 18*(2), 138–166. http://dx.doi.org/10.1177/1940161212474472

Meredith, J. (1966). *Three years in Mississippi*. Bloomington: Indiana University Press.

Meredith, J. & Doyle, W. (2012). *A mission from God: A memoir and challenge for America*. New York: Atria Books.

Mermigas, D. (2002, October 7). Disney plans new TV model. *Electronic Media, 21*(40), 1.

Messner, M., & Cooky, C. (2010). *Gender in televised sports: News and highlights shows, 1989–2009*. Retrieved from http://www.usc.edu/dept/cfr/html/documents/tvsports.pdf

Messner, M. A., Duncan, M. C., & Cooky, C. (2003). Silence, sports bras, and wrestling porn: Women in televised sports news and highlight shows. *Journal of Sport & Social Issues, 27*(1), 38–51. doi:10.1177/0193732502239583

Messner, M. A., Duncan, M. C., & Williams, N. (2006, Summer). This revolution is not being televised. *Contexts 5*(3), 34–38. doi:10.1525/ctx.2006.5.3.34

Myerberg, P. (2013, September 10). Report: Oklahoma State players received cash from coaches, boosters. *USA Today*. Retrieved from http://www.usatoday.com/story/sports/ncaaf/2013/09/10/oklahoma-state-sports-illustrated-report-part-1-the-money/2791813/

Meyers, C. (2003) Appreciating W. D. Ross: On duties and consequences. *Journal of Mass Media Ethics, 18*(2), 81–97. doi:10.1080/08900523.2011.606009

Meyers, J. (2012, February 19). PE struggles to keep up in Texas classrooms. *Dallas Morning News*. Retrieved from http://www.dallasnews.com/news/education/headlines/20120219-pe-struggles-to-keep-up-in-texas-classrooms.ece

Miller. J., & Belson, K. (2013, August 23). N.F.L. Pressure said to lead ESPN to quit film project. *New York Times*. Retrieved from www.nytimes.com/2013/08/24/sports/football/nfl-pressure-said-to-prompt-espn-to-quit-film-project.html?_r=0

Miller, J. A., Eder, S., & Sandomir, R. (2013, August 25). College football's biggest player? ESPN. *New York Times*, p. A1.

Miller, J. A., & Shales, T. (2011). *Those guys have all the fun: Inside the world of ESPN*. New York: Little, Brown and Company.

Mindich, D. T. Z. (2009). *Tuned out: Why Americans under 40 don't follow the news.* New York: Oxford University Press.

Minow, N. (2003). Television and the public interest. *Federal Communications Law Journal, 55*(3), 395–406. Retrieved from http://www.repository.law.indiana.edu/fclj/vol55/iss3/4

MLS, U.S. Soccer sign landmark TV and media rights partnerships with ESPN, FOX & Univision Deportes. *mlssoccer.com.* Retrieved from http://www.mlssoccer.com/news/article/2014/05/12/mls-us-soccer-sign-landmark-tv-media-rights-partnerships-espn-fox-univision-deportes

Mok, T. A. (1998). Getting the message: Media images and stereotypes and their effect on Asian Americans. *Cultural Diversity and Mental Health, 4*(3), 185–202.

Molden, D. (2013). Embrace the Linsanity: The role of comedy in discussions of "Racism" in the media. Presented at The Asian Conference on Media and Mass Communication, 292–301.

Moore, M. (2012, September 5). Alcorn State University president Brown launches national tour. *Michigan Chronicle*, p. A1. doi:10.1037/1099–9809.4.3.185

Morello, C. (2011, April 5). Demographics among children shifting quickly. *Washington Post*, p. A18.

Morgan, B. (Producer & Director). (2010). *June 17, 1994* [Documentary]. USA: ESPN Films.

Mullen, M. (2008). *Television in the multichannel age: A brief history of cable television.* Malden, MA: Blackwell.

Multi-faceted Title IX 40th anniversary launches today on espnW.com. (2012, March 26). Retrieved from http://espnmediazone.com/us/press-releases/2012/03/multi-faceted-title-ix-40th-anniversary-microsite-launches-today-on-espnW-com/

Multi-screen TV motivators: Part 1: cord cutters and cord shavers. Retrieved from http://tveverywhereirdeto.wordpress.com/2012/07/04/multi-screen-tv-motivators-part-1-cord-cutters-and-cord-shavers/

Murphy, P. (2013, September 10). OSU allegations: Did Oklahoma State pay football players? Retrieved from http://www.csmonitor.com/USA/Sports/2013/0910/OSU-allegations-Did-Oklahoma-State-pay-football-players

Nagle, D. (n.d.). Year in review press releases. *espnmediazone.com.* Retrieved from http://espnmediazone.com/us/press-releases/tag/year-in-review/page/3/

National Asian Pacific American Legal Consortium. (2005). *Asian Pacific Americans in prime time: Lights camera and little action*, 1–13.

Nemeth, N. (2000). A news ombudsman as an agent of accountability. In D. Pritchard (Ed.), *Holding the media accountable: Citizens, ethics, and the law* (pp. 55–67). Bloomington, IN: Indiana University Press.

Nemeth, N. (2003). *News ombudsmen in North America: Assessing an experiment in social responsibility.* Westport, CT: Praeger.

Neporent, L. (2013, January 11). Football head injuries increasing because of bigger, faster players. *Good Morning America.* Retrieved from http://abcnews.go.com/Health/football-head-injuries-increasing-bigger-faster-players/story?id=18183735

Neuendorf, K. (2002). *The content analysis guidebook.* Thousand Oaks, CA: Sage.

Neumark-Sztainer, D., Story, M., Hannan, P. J., Perry, C. L., & Irving, L. M. (2002). Weight-related concerns and behaviors among overweight and non-overweight adolescents: Implications for preventing weight-related disorders. *Archives of Pediatrics & Adolescent Medicine, 156*(2), 171–178. doi:10.1001/archpedi.156.2.171

Neverson, N. (2010). Build it and the women will come? WTSN and the advent of Canadian digital television. *Canadian Journal of Communication, 35*(1), 27–48.

Newell, S. (2012, February 18). ESPN's headline writers join in the Linsanity: "Chink in the armor" edition. *Deadspin*. Retrieved from http://deadspin.com/5886218/espnsheadline-writers-join-in-the-linsanity-chink-in-the-armor-edition

Newman, J. I. (2007). Army of whiteness? Colonel Reb and the sporting South's cultural and corporate symbolic. *Journal of Sport & Social Issues, 31*(4), 315–339. doi:10.1177/0193723507307814

Nielsen-rated sports networks. (2013, November 11–17). *Street & Smith's Sports Business Journal, 16*(30), 18.

Novak, M. (1993). *Joy of sports, revised: Endzones, bases, baskets, balls, and the consecration of the American spirit*. Aurora, ON: Madison Books.

Nunez, G. (2011, May 23). Nacion kicks off in Mexico and beyond. *ESPNFrontrow.com*. Retrieved from http://frontrow.espn.go.com/tag/nacion-espn/

Nunez, G. (2012, July 3). ESPN Deportes: An inside look at E:60 En Español. *ESPNFrontrow.com*. Retrieved from http://frontrow.espn.go.com/2012/07/espn-deportes-an-inside-look-at-e60-en-espanol/

Nunez, G. (2013, May 15). Deportes upfront unveils original programming and road to Brazil 2014; introduces first Spanish-language second screen sports TV companion. *ESPNMediaZone.com*. Retrieved from http://espnmediazone.com/us/press-releases/2013/05/espn-deportes-upfront-unveils-original-programming-and-road-to-brazil-2014-introduces-first-spanish-language-second-screen-sports-tv-companion/

Nylund, D. (2007). *Beer, babes, and balls*. Albany, NY: State University of New York Press.

O'Reilly, N. (2013). Portfolio theory and the management of professional sports clubs: The case of Maple Leaf Sports and Entertainment. In H. Dolles & S. Söderman (Eds.), *Handbook of research on sport and business* (pp. 333–349). Northampton, MA: Edward Elgar Publishing.

Oates, T. P. (2007). The erotic gaze in the NFL draft. *Communication & Critical/Cultural Studies, 4*(1), 74–90. doi:10.1080/14791420601138351

Oates, T. P. (2009). New media and the repackaging of NFL fandom. *Sociology of Sport Journal, 26*, 31–49.

Oates, T. P., & Pauly, J. (2007). Sports journalism as moral and ethical discourse. *Journal of Mass Media Ethics, 22*, 332–347.

OED Online. (2014). Scandal, n. *Oxford English Dictionary*. Retrieved from http://0-www.oed.com.bianca.penlib.du.edu/view/Entry/171874?rskey=UHrEhA&result=1&isAdvanced=false#eid

Ohlmeyer, D. (2010a, July 21). The "Decision" dilemma. *ESPN.com*. Retrieved from http://sports.espn.go.com/espn/columns/story?columnist=ohlmeyer_don&id=5397113

Ohlmeyer, D. (2010b, September 23). Paying a penance. *ESPN.com*. Retrieved from http://sports.espn.go.com/espn/columns/story?columnist=ohlmeyer_don&id=5605956

Ohlmeyer, D. (2010c, October 21). Evolution or devolution? Be it bodies, bias or buzz, ESPN adjusts to an ever-changing media landscape. *ESPN.com*. Retrieved from http://sports.espn.go.com/espn/columns/story?id=5710213

Organization of News Ombudsmen. (n.d.) *About ONO*. Retrieved from http://newsombudsmen.org/about-ono

Ott, B. L., & Aoki, G. (2002). The politics of negotiating public tragedy: Media framing of the Matthew Shepard murder. *Rhetoric & Public Affairs, 5*(3), 483–505. http://dx.doi.org/10.1353/rap.2002.0060

Ourand J. (2010, August 16). Tune in tomorrow? *Street & Smith's Sports Business Journal*. Retrieved from http://m.sportsbusinessdaily.com/Journal/Issues/2010/08/20100816/SBJ-In-Depth/Tune-In-Tomorrow.aspx?hl=Dish+Network&sc=0

Ourand, J. (2011, June 6). How high can rights fees go? More bidders, solid ratings, attractive demos and "TV everywhere" fuel a red hot market, but could the bubble burst? *Street & Smith's Sports Business Journal 14*(8). Retrieved from http://www.sportsbusinessdaily.com/Journal/Issues/2011/06/06/In-Depth/Rights-Fees.aspx

Ourand, J. (2011, July 11–17). How ESPN captured NBC's turf at Wimbledon. *Street & Smith's Sports Business Journal, 14*(12). Retrieved from http://www.sportsbusinessdaily.com/Journal/Issues/2011/07/11/Media/Wimbledon.aspx?hl=How%20ESPN%20captured%20NBC's%20turf%20at%20Wimbledon&sc=0

Ourand, J. (2012, September 24–30). Fox, Turner contribute to $12B rights haul for MLB. *Street and Smith's Sports Business Journal, 15*(23). Retrieved from http://www.sportsbusinessdaily.com/Journal/Issues/2012/09/24/Media/MLB-12B.aspx?hl=Fox%2C%20Turner%20contribute%20to%20%2412B%20rights%20haul%20for%20MLB&sc=0

Ourand, J. (2014a, January 13–19). Tier, placement changes to boost NBCSN numbers. *Street & Smith's Sports Business Journal, 16*(37). Retrieved from http://www.sportsbusinessdaily.com/Journal/Issues/2014/01/13/Media/NBCSN.aspx?hl=Tier%2C%20placement%20changes%20to%20boost%20NBCSN%20numbers&sc=0

Ourand, J. (2014b, July 21–27). World Cup 2018: Fox Sports and Gus Johnson get their turn. *Street & Smith's Sports Business Journal, 17*(14). Retrieved from http://www.sportsbusinessdaily.com/Journal/Issues/2014/07/21/Media/Sports-Media.aspx?hl=World%20Cup%202018%3A%20Fox%20Sports%20and%20Gus%20Johnson%20get%20their%20turn&sc=0

Ourand, J., & Botta, C. (2013, July 1). NHL network on ice. *Street & Smith's Sports Business Journal 16*(12). Retrieved from http://www.sportsbusinessdaily.com/Journal/Issues/2013/07/01/Media/NHL-Network.aspx

Ourand, J., & Karp, A. (2014, April 22). ESPN to broadcast NFL wild card playoff game, NBC to get divisional round matchup. *Street & Smith's Sports Business Daily 20*(154). Retrieved from http://www.sportsbusinessdaily.com/Daily/Issues/2014/04/22/Media/NFL.aspx?hl=ESPN%20NFL%20playoff%20game&sc=0

Ourand, J., & Smith, M. (2012, November 12–18). ESPN homes in on 12-year BCS package: Total for postseason payout put at $7.3 billion. *Street & Smith's Sports Business Journal, 15*(30). Retrieved from http://www.sportsbusinessdaily.com/Journal/Issues/2012/11/12/Media/BCS-ESPN.aspx?hl=ESPN%20homes%20in%20on%2012-year%20BCS%20package&sc=0

Ourand, J., & Smith, M. (2014, July 21–27). SEC Net dodging major battles on distribution. *Street & Smith's Sports Business Journal, 17*(14), 7. Retrieved from http://www.sportsbusinessdaily.com/Journal/Issues/2014/07/21/Media/SEC-Network.aspx?hl=SEC%20Net%20dodging%20major%20battles%20on%20distribution&sc=0

Overman, J. (2003, October 27). Reporter's dram role draws fire. *Hartford Courant.* Retrieved from http://articles.courant.com

Ozanian, M. (2012, August 14). The most valuable NFL teams. *Forbes.* Retrieved from http://www.forbes.com/sites/mikeozanian/2013/08/14/the-most-valuable-nfl-teams/

Palm, J. (2014, March 16). *CBS bubble watch.* Retrieved from www.cbssports.com/collegebasketball/bracketology/bubble-watch

Parker, L., & Lynn, M. (2002). What's race got to do with it? Critical race theory's conflicts with and connections to qualitative research. *Qualitative Inquiry, 8*(1), 7–22.

Parker, S. C., & Belghitar, Y. (2006). What happens to nascent entrepreneurs? An econometric analysis of the PSED. *Small Business Economics, 27*, 81–101. doi:10:1007/s11187–006–9003–4

Parramore, L. S. (2013, February 11). The scams and sexism hidden in your cable bill: Sports channels are increasingly costly to customers, especially women. *AlterNet*. Retrieved from http://www.alternet.org/economy/scams-and-sexism-hidden-your-cable-bill

Parrish, C., & Nauright, J. (2014). *Soccer around the world: A cultural guide to the world's favorite sport*. Santa Barbara, CA: ABC-CLIO.

Parsons, P. R. (2008). *Blue skies: A history of cable television*. Philadelphia: Temple University Press.

Parsons, P. R., & Frieden, R. M. (1998). *The cable and satellite television industries*. Boston, MA: Allyn & Bacon.

Pay-cable world in an uproar as movie firms and Getty make move into the business. (1980, April 20). *Broadcasting, 98*(16), 22.

Pease, E. (1989). Kerner plus 20: Minority news coverage in the Columbus *Dispatch*. *Newspaper Research Journal, 10*(3), 17–38.

Peddie, R. (2013). *Dream job: My wild ride on the corporate side, with the Leafs, the Raptors and TFC*. Toronto, Canada: HarperCollins.

Pedersen, P. M., Whisenant, W. A., & Schneider, R. G. (2003). Using a content analysis to examine the gendering of sports newspaper personnel and their coverage. *Journal of Sport Management, 17*(4), 376–393.

Petek, N., & Ruzzier, M. K. (2013). Brand identity development and the role of marketing communications: Brand experts' view. *Managing Global Transitions, 11*(1), 61–78.

Peterson, D. (2009, April 16). Diversity has no bearing on NBA wins. Retrieved from http://www.livescience.com/3515-diversity-bearing-nba-wins.html

Pew Research Center. (2014). The Web at 25 in the United States. Retrieved from http://www.pewinternet.org/files/2014/02/PIP_25th-anniversary-of-the-Web_0227141.pdf

Peyser, M. (2004). "Playmakers" lands in the end zone. *Newsweek, 143*(7), 54.

Phua, J. J. (2010). Sports fans and media use: Influence on sports fan identification and collective self-esteem. *International Journal of Sport Communication, 3*(2), 190–206. Retrieved from http://www.humankinetics.com/acucustom/sitename/Documents/DocumentItem/18134.pdf

Phua, J. (2012). Use of social networking sites by sports fans: Implications for the creation and maintenance of social capital. *Journal of Sports Media, 7*(1), 109–132. http://dx.doi.org/10.1353/jsm.2012.0006

Physical Activity Council. (2014). 2014 participation report: The Physical Activity Council's annual study tracking sports, fitness and recreation participation in the USA. Retrieved from http://www.physicalactivitycouncil.com/PDFs/current.pdf

Picker, M. (Director), & Sun, C. (Writer). (2002). *Mickey Mouse monopoly*. [Documentary film]. United States: Media Education Foundation.

Pierce, S. D. (2013, September 24). Pierce: RSL-D.C. will be almost impossible to see on TV. *Salt Lake Tribune* Retrieved from http://m.sltrib.com/sltrib/mobile3/56913720–219/goltv-rsl-lake-salt.html.csp

Piñón, J., & Rojas, V. (2011, August). Language and cultural identity in the new configuration of the US Latino TV industry. *Global Media and Communication, 7*(2), 129–147. doi:10.1177/1742766511410220

Plaschke, B. (2014, July 30). Root 66 for Scully: Out of sight, out of their minds if they think we'll buy this. *Los Angeles Times*, p. C1.

Poniatowski, K., & Hardin, M. (2012). "The more things change, the more they…": Commentary during women's ice hockey at the Olympic games. *Mass Communication and Society, 15*, 622–641. doi:10.1080/15205436.2012.677094

Potter, J. (1996). *An analysis of thinking and research about qualitative methods*. Mahwah, NJ: Lawrence Erlbaum.

Prager, R. A. (1992). The effects of deregulating cable television: Evidence from the financial markets. *Journal of Regulatory Economics, 4*(4), 347–363. doi:10.1007/BF00134927

Prentis, R. (2001, June 29). ESPN baseball telecasts getting new dimension. *Atlanta Journal-Constitution*, p. 2F.

Priest, L. (2003). The whole IX yards: The impact of Title IX: The good, the bad, and the ugly. *Women in Sport and Physical Activity Journal, 12*(2), 27–43.

Prieto, B. (2014, January 29). Super Bowl en Español for the first time on FOX Deportes. *The Denver Post*. Retrieved from http://espnfc.com/news/story/_/id/1135765/la-liga,-serie-a-vanish-for-many-u.s.-viewers?cc=5901

Prindiville, M. (2013, April 16). NBC Sports announces Premier League programming plans. *Nbcsports.com*. Retrieved from http://prosoccertalk.nbcsports.com/2013/04/16/nbc-sports-announces-premier-league-programming-plans/

Prisbell, E. (2014, June 10). Blame emerges like cracks in Texas high school stadium. *USA Today*. Retrieved from http://www.usatoday.com/story/sports/highschool/2014/06/09/%20allen-texas-eagle-high-school-football-stadium-cracks-closed/9903781/

Public Relations Society of America. (2000). Public Relations Society of America (PRSA) Member Code of Ethics. Retrieved from http://www.prsa.org/AboutPRSA/Ethics/CodeEnglish/index.html#.UzmVJsdOeiM

Pucin, D. (2011, December 6). Media titans clash in L.A. sports arena: Time Warner has its eye on Fox's most valuable television asset: The Dodgers. *Los Angeles Times*, p. A1.

Putnam, R. D. (1995). Bowling alone: America's declining social capital. *Journal of Democracy, 6*(1), 65–78. doi:10.1353/jod.1995.0002

Putnam, R. D. (2000). *Bowling alone: The collapse and revival of American community*. New York: Simon & Schuster.

Quinlan, T. (2014, August 4). With DirecTV, SEC Network available in 87 million homes. *USA Today*. Retrieved from http://www.usatoday.com/story/sports/ncaaf/sec/2014/08/04/directv-carry-sec-network/13596759/

Rader, B. (1984). *In its own image: How television has transformed sports*. New York: Free Press.

Rader, B. G. (2008). *American sports: From the age of folk games to the age of televised sports* (6th ed.). Upper Saddle River, NJ: Prentice Hall.

Rainie, L., & Smith, M. A. (2014, February 20). Mapping Twitter topic networks: From polarized crowds to community clusters. *Pew Research Center*. Retrieved from http://www.pewinternet.org/2014/02/20/mapping-twitter-topic-networks-from-polarized-crowds-to-community-clusters-2/

Rainville, R., & McCormick, E. (1977). Extent of covert racial prejudice in pro footballers announcers' speech. *Journalism Quarterly, 54*, 20–26. doi:10.1177/107769907705400104

Rashad, A., & Bodo, P. (1988). *Rashad: Vikes, mikes, and something on the backside*. New York: Viking.

Rasmussen, B. (2010). *Sports junkies rejoice! The birth of ESPN*. United States of America: CreateSpace Independent Publishing Platform.

Rasmussen, W. (1983). *Sports junkies rejoice! The birth of ESPN*. Hartsdale, NY: QV Publishing.

Raymond, N., & Baker L. (2013, February 11). Dish Network takes ESPN to trail over licensing deal. *Chicagotribune.com*. Retrieved from http://articles.chicagotribune.com/2013–02–11/business/sns-rt-us-dish-espn-lawsuitbre91b00g-20130211_1_charlie-ergen-dish-network-espn-deportes

Reed, J. (2012, December 11). Reviewing the complete timeline of NFL, Saints Bountygate scandal. *Bleacher Report*. Retrieved from http://bleacherreport.com/articles/1441646-reviewing-the-complete-timeline-of-nfl-saints-bountygate-scandal

Reilly, R. (2013, November 6). Football getting harder to watch. *ESPN.com: NFL*. Retrieved from http://espn.go.com/nfl/story/_/id/9932209/nfl-becoming-guilty-pleasure

Reynolds, M. (2009). *ESPN study cycles through behaviors of sports fans consumption habits differ depending on age, gender*. Retrieved from http://www.csub.edu/~ecarter2/SP11%20490/CH.4%20Profiling%20Sports%20Fans%20&%20Viewers.doc

Reynolds, M. (2013, October 30). Univision Deportes network now Nielsen-rated. *Multichannel News*. Retrieved from http://www.multichannel.com/distribution/univision-deportes-network-now-nielsen-rated/146381

Riebock, A., & Bae, J. (2013). Sexualized representation of female athletes in the media: How does it affect female college athletes' body perceptions? *International Journal of Sport Communication, 6*, 274–287.

Riffe, D., Lacy, S., & Fico, F. (2005). *Analyzing media messages: Using quantitative content analysis in research*. Mahwah, NJ: Lawrence Erlbaum.

Riffe, D., Lacy, S., & Fico, F. (2014). *Analyzing media messages: Using quantitative content analysis in research* (3rd ed.). New York: Routledge.

Roberts, F. (2011, July 5). America's lost boys: Why ARE so many young men failing to grow up? *Daily Mail* (London). Retrieved from http://www.dailymail.co.uk/news/article-2011261/Americas-Lost-Boys-Why-ARE-young-men-failing-grow-up.html

Roberts, G., & Klibanoff, H. (2007). *The race beat: The press, the civil rights struggle, and the awakening of a nation*. New York: Knopf.

Rodriguez, P. (1993, June 30). Are all those exercise shows making anyone fit? *Ft. Worth Star-Telegram*. Retrieved from http://articles.chicagotribune.com/1993-06-30/features/9306300288_1_fitness-pros-fitness-goals-exercise-programs

Roenigk, A. (2009, October 9). For sale by owner: How much should female athletes reveal in the name of self-promotion. *ESPN.com*. Retrieved from http://sports.espn.go.com/espn/news/story?id=4540728

Rogerson, W. P. (2005, February 28). The social cost of retransmission consent regulations. *FCC study commissioned by Advance/Newhouse Communications, Cox Communications, and Insight Communications*. Retrieved from http://apps.fcc.gov/ecfs/document/view;jsessionid=1ZhT-PBsG0Kc2QkSyyLNh9GF2bLV0pvznnlpCk1MdTmxY2hqpf4K6!-321460796!1471562840?id=6517399159

Romano, A. (2003, November 24). Is *Playmakers* off to the showers? *Broadcasting & Cable, 133*(47), 30.

Rose, A., & Friedman, J. (1994). Television sport as mas(s)culine cult of distraction. *Screen, 35*(1), 22–35. doi:10/1093/screen/35.1.22

Rose, L. (2010, June 6). Talking TV with ESPN's "the sports guy." *Forbes.com*. Retrieved from http://www.forbes.com/2010/06/15/espn-30-for-30-business-entertainment-bill-simmons.html

Rosen, C. (2013, October 29). Jimmy Connors isn't there to make friends in "This is what they want." *The Huffington Post*. Retrieved from http://www.huffingtonpost.com/2013/10/29/jimmy-connors-this-is-what-they-want-espn-30-for-30_n_4172230.html

Rosenblatt, R. (2011, October 21). Fox, Telemundo win 2018/2022 World Cup broadcast rights for combined $1 billion. *Sbnation.com*. Retrieved from http://www.sbnation.com/soccer/2011/10/21/2505678/fox-telemundo-2018-22-world-cup-broadcast-rights-fee-espn

Roessner, L. A. (2011). Coloring America's pastime: Sporting Life's coverage of race & the emergency of baseball's color line, 1883–1889. *American Journalism*, *28*(3), 85–114. doi:10.1080/08821127.2011.1067789

Ross, C. (1999, September 20). ESPN/ABC Sports recruits Erhardt. *Advertising Age*, *70*(39), 3.

Ross, W. D. (1930). *The right and the good.* London: Oxford University Press.

Ross, W. D. (1935). *Foundations of Ethics, 1935–1936. Gifford Lectures.* Retrieved from http://www.giffordlectures.org/Browse.asp?PubID=TPFNDE&Volume=0&Issue=0&%20ArticleID=14

Ross, W. D. (1951). *Foundations of ethics.* London: Oxford University Press.

Rovell, D. (2009). *ESPN The Magazine*'s Body Issue: A financial success. *CNBC* online. Retrieved from http://www.cnbc.com/id/34208031/ESPN_The_Magazine_s_Body_Issue_A_Financial_Success

Rovell, D. (2014, January 26). NFL most popular for 30th year in row. Retrieved from http://espn.go.com/nfl/story/_/id/10354114/harris-poll-nfl-most-popular-mlb-2nd

Rowe, D. (2004). *Sport, culture, and the media: The unruly trinity* (2nd ed.). Maidenhead, UK: Open University Press.

Rowe, D. (2011). Sports media: Beyond broadcasting, beyond sports, beyond society. In A. C. Billings (Ed.), *Sports Media: Transformation, integration, consumption* (pp. 94–113). New York: Routledge.

Rowe, D., & Hutchins, B. (2013). Introduction: Sport in the network society and why it matters. In B. Hutchins & D. Rowe (Eds.), *Digital media sport: Technology, power and culture in the network society* (pp. 1–16). New York: Routledge.

Ruihley, B. J., & Hardin, R. (2013). Meeting the information needs of the fantasy sport user. *Journal of Sport Media*, *8*(2), 53–80. doi:10.1353/jsm.2013.0013

Running USA. (2014, July 9). *2014 state of the sport—Part III: U.S. race trends.* Retrieved from http://www.runningusa.org/2014-state-of-the-sport-part-III-us-race-trends

Rush, C. (2013, November 26). NHL signs 12-year TV, Internet deal with Rogers; CBC keeps "Hockey Night in Canada." *Toronto Star.* Retrieved from http://http://www.thestar.com/sports/hockey/2013/11/26/nhl_signs_12year_broadcast_deal_with_rogers_cbc_keeps_hockey_night_in_canada.html

Ryan, E. L. (2010). *Dora the Explorer*: Empowering preschoolers, girls and Latinas. *Journal of Broadcasting & Electronic Media*, *54*(1), 54–68. doi:10.1080/08838150903550394

Sabo, D., & Jansen, S. C. (1992). Images of men in sports media: The social reproduction of gender order. In S. Craig (Ed.), *Men, masculinity and the media* (pp. 169–184). London: Sage.

Salop, S. C., Chipty, T., DeStefano, M., Moresi, S. X., & Woodbury, J. R. (2010). Economic analysis of broadcasters' brinkmanship and bargaining advantages in retransmission consent negotiations. *Study commissioned by Time Warner Cable.* Retrieved from http://97.74.209.146/downloads/broadcaster_brinkmanship.pdf

Sanderson, J. (2010). Framing Tiger's troubles: Comparing traditional and social media. *International Journal of Sport Communication*, *3*(4), 438–453.

Sanderson, J., & Kassing, J. W. (2011). Tweets and blogs: Transformative, adversarial, and integrative developments in sports media. In A. C. Billings (Ed.), *Sports media: Transformation, integration, consumption* (pp. 114–127). New York: Routledge.

Sandomir, R. (1993, June 26). ESPN adding channel and attitude. *New York Times*, p. 35.

Sandomir, R. (2004a, February 5). Pro football; Citing NFL, ESPN cancels "Playmakers." *New York Times.* Retrieved at http://www.nytimes.com/2004/02/05/sports/pro-football-citing-nfl-espn-cancels-playmakers.html

Sandomir, R. (2004b, June 8). ESPN looks back, but not at itself. *New York Times*. Retrieved from http://www.nytimes.com/2004/06/08/sports/08tv.html?ex=1087703656&ei=1&en=831f3e4d708a30f7

Sandomir, R. (2006, August 11). ABC Sports is dead at 45. *New York Times*, p. D2.

Sandomir, R. (2011, August 20). Regional sports networks show the money. *New York Times*, p. D1.

Sandomir, R. (2012, May 15). ESPN doubles up on "30 for 30" documentary series. *New York Times*. Retrieved from http://mediadecoder.blogs.nytimes.com/2012/05/15/espn-doubles-up-on-30-for-30-documentary-series/?_php=true&_type=blogs&_r=0

Sandomir, R. (2013, October 9). Partly by shunning documentary, ESPN lifts it. *New York Times*. Retrieved from http://www.nytimes.com/2013/10/10/sports/football/by-shunning-concussion-documentary-espn-gives-it-a-lift.html?_r=0

Sandomir, R. (2014, May 13). TV networks bank on future of M.L.S. *New York Times*, p. B16.

Sandomir, R., Miller, J. A., & Eder, S. (2013, August 26). To protect its empire, ESPN stays on offense. *New York Times*. Retrieved from http://www.nytimes.com/2013/08/27/sports/ncaafootball/to-defend-its-empire-espn-stays-on-offensive.html?pagewanted=all&_r=0

Schawbel, D. (2012, September 13). How Bill Rasmussen started ESPN and his entrepreneurship advice. *Forbes*. Retrieved from http://www.forbes.com/sites/danschawbel/2012/09/13/%20how-bill-rasmussen-started-espn-and-his-entrepreneurship-advice/

Schechner, S., & Peers, M. (2011, December 6). Cable TV honchos cry foul over soaring cost of ESPN. *Wall Street Journal Online*. Retrieved from http://online.wsj.com/news/articles/SB10001424052970204083204577080793289112260?mg=reno64wsj&url=http%3A%2F%2Fonline.wsj.com%2Farticle%2FSB10001424052970204083204577080793289112260.html

Scherer, J., & Harvey, J. (2013). Televised sport and cultural citizenship in Canada: The "two solitudes" of Canadian public broadcasting. In J. Scherer & D. Rowe (Eds.), *Sport, public broadcasting, and cultural citizenship: Signal lost?* (pp. 48–73). New York: Routledge.

Scherer, J., & Whitson, D. (2009). Public broadcasting, sport, and cultural citizenship: The future of sport on the Canadian Broadcasting Corporation? *International Review for the Sociology of Sport, 44*(2/3), 213–220. doi:10.1177/1012690209104798

Scheufele, D. A. (1999). Framing as a theory of media effects. *Journal of Communication, 49*(1), 103–122. doi:10.1111/j.1460-2466.1999.tb02784.x

Scheufele, D. A., & Tewksbury, D. (2007). Framing, agenda setting, and priming: The evolution of three media effects models. *Journal of Communication, 57*(1), 9–20. doi:10.1111/j.0021-9916.2007.00326.x

Schwirtz, M. (1998, August 24). ESPN expands push in radio. *MediaWeek, 8*(32), 8.

Scully, G. W. (2004). The market structure of sports. In S. R. Rosner & K. L. Shopshire (Eds.), *The business of sports* (pp. 26–33). Sudbury, MA: Jones and Bartlett.

Scully, T. (1985). NCAA v. Board of Regents of the University of Oklahoma: The NCAA's television plan is sacked by the Sherman Act. *Catholic University Law Review, 34*(3), 857–887. Retrieved from http://scholarship.law.edu/cgi/viewcontent.cgi?article=2067&context=lawreview

Seidman, R. (2013, August 23). List of how many homes each cable networks is in: Cable network coverage estimates as of August 2013. *TV by the Numbers*. Retrieved from http://tvbythenumbers.zap2it.com/2013/08/23/list-of-how-many-homes-each-cable-networks-is-in-cable-network-coverage-estimates-as-of-august-2013/199072/

Seven ways you can be an agency hero starting 9/7/79. (1979, September 3). *Broadcasting, 97*(10), 44–45.

Shales, T. (2003, August 26). "Playmakers": On ESPN, A dramatic forward pass. *Washington Post*, C1.

Shaw, R. (1999, August 9). ESPN goes inside. *Electronic Media, 18*(32), 13.

Shea, J. (2000, January/February). How ESPN changes everything. *Columbia Journalism Review, 38*(5), 45–47.

Sheffer, M. L., & Schultz, B. (2007). Double standard: Why women have trouble getting jobs in local televised sports. *Journal of Sports Media, 2*(1), 77–101. doi:10.1353/jsm.0.0005

Sherman, A. (2011, September 29). Cable's ESPN dilemma: Wildly popular—but costly. *Bloomberg Businessweek*. Retrieved from http://www.businessweek.com/magazine/cables-espn-dilemma-wildly-popularbut-costly-09292011.html

Shifman, L., & Thelwall, M. (2009). Assessing global diffusion with Web memetics: The spread and evolution of a popular joke. *Journal of the American Society for Information Science and Technology, 60*(12), 2567–2576. doi:10.1002/asi.21185

Shoemaker, P. J., Eichholz, M., Kim, E., & Wrigley, B. (2001). Individual and routine forces in gatekeeping. *Journalism & Mass Communication Quarterly, 78*(2), 233–246. doi:10.1177/107769900107800202

*SI* Staff. (2013, September 10). Special report on Oklahoma State football: The overview. *Sports Illustrated*. Retrieved from http://sportsillustrated.cnn.com/college-football/news/20130910/osu-introduction/

Siegel, D. (1994). Higher education and the plight of the black male athlete. *Journal of Sport & Social Issues, 18*(3), 207–223. doi:10.1177/019372394018003002

Sifferlin, A. (2014, July 10). It's lack of exercise—not calories—that make us fat, study says. *Time*. Retrieved from http://time.com/2964554/its-lack-of-exercise-not-calories-that-make-us-fat-study-says/

Silk, M. (1999). Local/global flows and altered production practices: Narrative constructions at the 1995 Canada Cup of Soccer. *International Review for the Sociology of Sport, 34*(2), 113–123. doi:10.1177/101269099034002002

Silvestrini, M. (2002, September 24). ESPN announces plans for Spanish-language cable network. *Knight Ridder Tribune Business News*. Retrieved from http://www.highbeam.com/doc/1G1-91949846.html

Silvestrini, M. (2004, January 8). ESPN debuts Spanish-language cable sports network. *Knight Ridder Tribune Business News*. Retrieved from http://www.highbeam.com/doc/1G1-111970703.html

Simmons, B. (2012, May 17). Welcome to another "30 for 30." *Grantland.com*. Retrieved from http://grantland.com/features/another-30-films-subjects-stories-captured-our-attention/

Skelton, A. (2012) William David Ross. *Stanford encyclopedia of philosophy*. Retrieved from http://plato.stanford.edu/entries/william-david-ross/

Smallwood, R., Brown, R. A., & Billings, A. C. (2014). Female bodies on display: Attitudes regarding female athlete photos in *Sports Illustrated*'s Swimsuit Issue and *ESPN The Magazine*'s Body Issue. *Journal of Sports Media, 9*(1), 1–22. doi:10.1353/jsm.2014.0005

Smith, A. F., & Hollihan, K. (2009). *ESPN the company: The story and lessons behind the most fanatical brand in sports*. Hoboken, N.J.: John Wiley & Sons.

Smith, C. (2013, September 11). Billionaire T. Boone Pickens takes issue with *Sports Illustrated*'s Oklahoma State report. Retrieved from http://www.forbes.com/sites/%20chrissmith/2013/09/11/billionaire-t-boone-pickens-takes-issue-with-sports-illustrateds-oklahoma-state-report/

Smith, L. & Bissell, K. (2012). Nice dig! An analysis of the verbal and visual coverage of men's and women's beach volleyball during the 2008 Olympic games. *Communication & Sport, 2*, 1–17. doi:10.1177/2167479512467771

Smith, L. R., & Bissell, K. (2014). Nice dig! An analysis of men's and women's beach volleyball during the 2008 Olympic Games. *Communication & Sport, 2*(1), 48–64. doi:10.1177/2167479512467771

Smith, L. R., Hull, K., & Schmittel, A. (2014). *Form or function? A five-year examination of ESPN The Magazine's "Body Issue."* Paper presented at the 7th Summit of the International Association of Communication and Sport, New York, NY.

Smith, L. R., & Smith, K. (2011, May). *E-Sex-P-N: Athletic Form or Sex Appeal? An Analysis of the 2010 ESPN Magazine Body Issue.* Paper presented at the meeting of International Communication Association, Boston, MA.

Smith, M. (2013, August 12–18). How USGA found a fit with Fox. *Street & Smith's Sports Business Journal, 16*(17). Retrieved from http://www.sportsbusinessdaily.com/Journal/Issues/2013/08/12/Media/USGA-Fox.aspx?hl=How%20USGA%20found%20a%20fit%20with%20Fox&sc=0

Smith, R. (2006). *Sports Illustrated*'s African American athlete series as socially responsible journalism. *American Journalism, 23*(2), 45–68.

Social networking: For talent and reporters. (2011, August). *FrontRow*. Retrieved on June 26, 2014 from http://frontrow.espn.go.com/wp-content/uploads/2011/08/social-networking-v2-2011.pdf

Society for Professional Journalists. (1996). SPJ Code of Ethics. Retrieved from http://www.spj.org/ethicscode.asp

Sparks, R. (1992). "Delivering the male": Sports, Canadian television, and the making of TSN. *Canadian Journal of Communication, 17*(3), 319–342.

Spencer, N. E. (2003). "America's Sweetheart" and "Czech-Mater": A discursive analysis of the Evert-Navratilova rivalry. *Journal of Sport and Social Issues, 27*(1), 18–37. doi:10.1177/0193732502239582

*Sports Business Daily*. (2009, October 30). ESPN's "30 for 30" documentary series drawing rave reviews. *Sports Business Daily*. Retrieved from http://www.sportsbusinessdaily.com/Daily/Issues/2009/10/Issue-35/Sports-Media/Espns-30-For-30-Documentary-Series-Drawing-Rave-Reviews.aspx

Stableford, D. (2012, March 2). Jeremy Lin puns galore: Linterplanetary, Linsurrection and 949 more. *Yahoo! News*. Retrieved from http://news.yahoo.com/blogs/cutline/linterplanetarylinsurrection-950-othergroanworthyjeremy-lin-134919141.html

Stafford, J. (2014). *Academic planning guide: 2014–15.* Allen High School. Retrieved from http://www.allenisd.org/cms/lib/TX01001197/Centricity/Domain/1656/AHS%202014–15%20working%202015–17.pdf

Stand by as ESPN takes over ABC Sports. (2006, August 11). *Orlando Sentinel*, p. D7.

Stansell, C. (1992). White feminists and black realities: The politics of authenticity. In T. Morrison (Ed.), *Race-ing justice, en-gendering power* (pp. 251–268). New York: Pantheon.

Staples, A. (2012, August 6). How television changed college football—and how it will again. *sportsillustrated.cnn.com*. Retrieved from http://www.si.com/college-football/2012/08/06/tv-college-football

StatCounter Global Stats. (2014, February). Top 8 mobile operating systems in the US from Feb 2013 to Feb 2014. *StatCounter*. Retrieved from http://gs.statcounter.com/#mobile_os-US-monthly-201302-201402

Staurowsky, E. (1996). Blaming the victim: Resistance in the battle over gender equity in intercollegiate athletics. *Journal of Sports and Social Issues, 22*(2), 194–210. doi:10.1177/019372396020002006

Staurowsky, E. (1998). Critiquing the language of the gender equity debate. *Journal of Sport and Social Issues, 22*(4), 7–26. doi:10.1177/019372398022001002

Stelter, B. (2012, January 1). In New York and elsewhere, disputes over television fees lead to a few blackouts. Retrieved from http://www.nytimes.com/2012/01/02/business/media/cable-tv-fee-disputes-cause-a-few-blackouts.html?_r=0

Stein, A. (2011). *Why we love Disney: The power of the Disney brand.* New York: Peter Lang.

Stern: Miami's big 3 acted within rights. (2010, July 14). *ESPN.com*. Retrieved from http://sports.espn.go.com/nba/news/story?id=5374799

Stewart, L. (2005a, May 20). L.A.'s A.M. Talk down to Bruno. *Los Angeles Times*. Retrieved from http://search.proquest.com.lib-proxy.fullerton.edu/docview/421982410?accountid=9840

Stewart, L. (2005b, August 5). TV-Radio; Miller's focus now on the recovery of his wife. *Los Angeles Times*. Retrieved from http://search.proquest.com.lib-proxy.fullerton.edu/docview/422076707?accountid=9840

Stewart, L. (2007, June 9). ESPN tries to make accent mark; Spanish-language sports market is growing fast, ESPN Deportes has tapped into it. *Los Angeles Times*. Retrieved from http://search.proquest.com/docview/422159123?accountid=9840

Strachan, A. (2013, November 29). "30 for 30" not just for sports fans. *Ottawa Citizen*, p. C10.

Stroud, M. (1998, March 2). ESPN's "wide world of sports"? *Broadcasting & Cable, 128*(9), 14.

Strudler, K., & Schnurer, M. (2006). Race to the bottom: The representation of race in ESPN's Playmakers. *Ohio Communication Journal, 33*, 125–150.

Sturken, M. (1997). *Tangled memories: The Vietnam War, the AIDS epidemic, and the politics of remembering*. University of California Press: Berkeley, CA.

Suggs, W. (2005). *A place on the team: The triumph and tragedy of Title IX*. Princeton: Princeton University Press.

Suggs, W. (2010). Football, television, and the supreme court: How a decision 20 years ago brought commercialization to the world college sports. In R. E. Washington & D. Karen (Eds.), *Sport, power, and society: Institutions and practices* (pp. 130–134). Boulder, CO: Westview Press.

Sutter, M. (2003a, January 20). A savvy grab for auds. *Variety*, 32.

Sutter, M. (2003b, December 3). Deportes delivers. *Daily Variety*, 41.

Taaffe, W. (1982, March 19). ESPN: The channel that's always there. *Washington Post*, p. D2.

Tankard, J. W. (2001). The empirical approach to the study of media framing. In S. D. Reese, O. H. Gandy, & A. E. Grant (Eds.), *Framing public life* (pp. 95–106). Mahwah, NJ: Lawrence Erlbaum.

Taylor, C. (1994). *The ethics of authenticity*. Cambridge: Harvard University Press.

Telotte, J. P. (2004). *Disney TV*. Detroit, MI: Wayne State University Press.

Texeira, E. (2005, May 2). Study: Asian actors on TV underrepresented. *AZCentral.com*. Retrieved from http://www.azcentral.com/ent/tv/articles/0503asiantv.html

"The Decision" live on 710 ESPN. (2010, July 7). *ESPN.com*. Retrieved from http://sports.espn.go.com/los-angeles/radio/news/story?page=thedecision

The digital consumer. (2014, February 10). *Nielsen*. Retrieved from http://www.nielsen.com/us/en/reports/2014/the-us-digital-consumer-report.html

The season that was: Looking back on some of the business highlights of the 2011–2012 NFL season (2012, January 30–February 5). *Street & Smith's Sports Business Journal, 14*(39), 22–23.

The top 25 U.S. consumer magazines for June 2013 (2013, August 6). Retrieved from http://www.auditedmedia.com/news/blog/2013/august/the-top-25-us-consumer- magazines-for-june-2013.aspx

The untold stories of Black athletes to air on ESPN. (2008, March 6). *DIVERSE Issues in Higher Education, 25*(2), 7.

Thomas, J. R., Nelson, J. K., & Silverman, S. J. (2010). *Research methods in physical activity* (6th ed.). Champaign, IL: Human Kinetics.

Thomaselli, R. (2005, January 24). ESPN takes agnostic tack in ad-sales reorganization. *Advertising Age, 76*(4), 8.

Thompson, D. (2012, December 3). If you don't watch sports, TV is a huge rip-off (So, how do we fix it?). *The Atlantic*. Retrieved from http://www.theatlantic.com/business/archive/2012 /12/ if-you-dont-watch-sports-tv-is-a-huge-rip-off-so-how-do-we-fix-it/265814/

Thompson, D. (2013, June 28). How ESPN makes money—in 1 graph. *theatlantic.com*. Retrieved from http://www.theatlantic.com/business/archive/2013/06/how-espn-makes-money-in-1-graph/277342/

Thompson, T. (2012, March 29). Title IX is mine [Video file]. Retrieved from http://espn.go.com/ video/clip?id=7752591

Tigman, M. (2003). Body image across the lifespan: Stability and change. *Body Image, 1*(1), 29–41. doi:10.1016/S1740–1445(03)00002–0

Time, Inc. (2014). *Sports Illustrated* media kit. Retrieved from http://simediakit.com/

Timex makes every second count with ESPN. (1981, October 30). *New York Times*, p. D1.

Title IX Information. (n.d.). Retrieved from http://www.nacwaa.org/advocacy/title-ix/information

Title IX Primer. (n.d.). Retrieved from http://www.womenssportsfoundation.org/en/home/advocate/ title-ix-and-issues/what-is-title-ix/title-ix-primer

Topsy Labs, Inc. (2014). Topsy social search support. *Topsy*. Retrieved from http://about.topsy.com/ support/search/

Torrence, D. (2013, September 27). Don't blame elite athletes for state of the sport. In T. Reavis (Ed.), *Wandering in a running world*. Retrieved from http://tonireavis.com/2013/09/27/ pro-runner-david-torrence-dont-blame-elite-athletes-for-state-of-the-sport/

Townsend, A. (1999). Cable television 1999: A history of the winding road to competition. *University of New Brunswick Law Journal, 48*(1), 253–264.

*Track and Field News* (2012, October 12). Re: Billy Mills Victory on NPR (User4). Retrieved from http:// trackandfieldnews.com/discussion/showthread.php?138482-Billy-Mills-Victory-on-NPR

Tracy, M. (2013, August 23). The biggest bully: Even ESPN cowers before the NFL. Retrieved from http://www.newrepublic.com/article/114444/nfl-forced-espn-out-frontline-concussions-investigation-report

Tramel, B. (2013, September 10). Oklahoma State football: Former NCAA investigator compares allegations to SMU scandal. *The Oklahoman*. Retrieved from http://newsok.com/oklahoma-state-football-former-ncaa-investigator-compares-allegations-to-smu-scandal/article/3881387

Tran, V. C. (2010). English gain vs. Spanish loss? Language assimilation among second-generation Latinos in young adulthood. *Social Forces, 89* (1), 257–284. doi:10.1353/sof.2010.0107

Trotter, J. (2013, September 10). Report: OK St. players got paid. *ESPN.com*. Retrieved from http:// espn.go.com/college-football/story/_/id/9657658/report-oklahoma-state-cowboys-players-got-paid-les-miles-era

Trujillo, N. (1995). Machines, missiles, and men: Images of the male body on ABC's Monday Night Football. *Sociology of Sport Journal, 12*(4), 403–423.

Tuchman, G. (1978). *Making news: A study in the construction of reality*. New York: Free Press.

Tucker Center for Girls & Women in Sport. (2013). *Media coverage and female athletes*. Retrieved from http://www.mnvideovault.org/index.php?id=25506&select_index=0&popup=yes#0

Tuggle, C. A. (1997). Differences in television sports reporting of men's and women's athletics: ESPN SportsCenter and CNN Sports Tonight. *Journal of Broadcasting & Electronic Media, 41*(1), 14–24. doi:10.1080/08838159709364387

Turner, J. S. (2013). A longitudinal analysis of gender and ethnicity portrayed on ESPN's SportsCenter from 1999 to 2009. *Communication & Sport, 1*, 1–25. doi:10.1177/2167479513496222

Twitter, Inc. (2014). About. *Twitter.com*. Retrieved from https://about.twitter.com/company

Tyree, J. M. (2011). Hope and fear in "The Interrupters." *Film Quarterly, 65*(2), 32–36. doi:10.1525/FQ.2011.65.2.32

United States General Accounting Office. (1990). *Follow-up national survey of cable television rates and services.* Retrieved from http://www.gao.gov/assets/150/149275.pdf

Urquhart, J., & Crossman, J. (1999). The *Globe* and *Mail* coverage of the winter Olympic games: A cold place for women athletes. *Journal of Sport and Social Issues, 23*(2), 193–202. doi:10.1177/0193723599232006

Vagnoni, A. (1996, September). Head games. *Advertising Age's Creativity, 4*(7), 11.

Valentine, J. (1997). Global sport and Canadian content: The *Sports Illustrated* Canada controversy. *Journal of Sport & Social Issues, 21*(3), 239–259. doi:10.1177/019372397021003002

van Riel, C. B. M., & Balmer, J. (1997). Corporate identity: The concept, its measurement and management. *European Journal of Marketing, 31*(5–6), 340–355. doi:10.1108.eb060635

Vascellaro, J. E., & Everson, D. (2011, August 25). TV cash tilts college playing field. *Wall Street Journal*, p. B1.

Velascco, S. (2014, June 24). World Cup: USA-Portugal match sets ratings record. Will fan interest last? *Christian Science Monitor.* Retrieved from http://www.csmonitor.com/%20Business/2014/0624/World-Cup-USA-Portugal-match-sets-ratings-record.-Will-fan-interest-last-video

Video: The Jeremy Lin phenomenon. Watch PBS NewsHour Online. PBS Video. (2012, February 14). *PBS Video.* Retrieved from http://video.pbs.org/video/2196933007

Vincent, J. (2004). Game, sex, and match: The construction of gender in British newspaper coverage of the 2000 Wimbledon Championships. *Sociology of Sport Journal, 21*(4), 435–456.

Vincent, J. (2010) Emotion and the mobile phone. In H. Grieif, L. Hjorth, A. Lasen, & C. Lobet Maris (Eds.), *Cultures of participation: Media practices, politics and literacy* (pp. 95–110). Berlin: Peter Lang.

Vincent, J., Imwold, C., Masemann, V., & Johnson, J. T. (2002). A comparison of selected "serious" and "popular" British, Canadian, and United States newspaper coverage of female and male athletes competing in the Centennial Olympic games. *International Review for the Sociology of Sport, 37*(3–4), 319–335. doi:10.1177/101269020203700312

Vincent, J., Kian, E. M., Pedersen, P. M., Kuntz, A., & Hill, J. S. (2010). England expects: English newspapers' narratives about the English soccer team in the 2006 World Cup. *International Review for the Sociology of Sport, 45*(2), 199–223. doi:10.1177/1012690209360084

Visker, R. (1995). Dropping the "subject" of authenticity. Being in time on disappearing existentials and true friendship with being. *Research in Phenomenology, 24*, 133. doi:10.1163/156916494X00096

Vitale, D. (2012, April 23). Title IX is mine: Dick Vitale [Video file]. Retrieved from http://espn.go.com/video/clip?id=7846914

Vogan, T. (2012). ESPN Films and the construction of prestige in contemporary sports television. *International Journal of Sport Communication, 5*, 137–152.

Vogan, T. (2013). Chronicling sport, branding institutions: The television sports documentary from broadcast to cable. In P. M. Pedersen (Ed.), *Routledge handbook of sport communication* (pp. 128–136). New York: Routledge.

Wagg, S., Brick, C., Wheaton, B., & Caudwell, J. (2009). *Key concepts in sports studies.* Thousand Oaks, CA: Sage.

Walker, J. R., & Bellamy, R. V. (2008). *Center field shot: A history of baseball on television.* Lincoln: University of Nebraska Press.

Wallace, M. (2010, November 1). For LeBron James, hindsight 20/20. *ESPN.com.* Retrieved from http://sports.espn.go.com/nba/truehoop/miamiheat/news/story?id=5749163

Walton, T. A. (2003). Title IX: Forced to wrestle up the backside. *Women in Sport and Physical Activity,* *12*(2), 5–26.

Warner, D. (2013, August 19). ESPN and other cable networks are starting to leak subscribers. *AwfulAnnouncing.com.* Retrieved from http://awfulannouncing.com/2013/espn-and-other-cable-networks-are-starting-to-leak-subscribers.html

Weber, J. D., & Carini, R. M. (2013). Where are the women athletes in *Sports Illustrated?* A content analysis of covers (2000–2011). *International Review for the Sociology of Sport, 48*(2), 196–203. doi:10.1177/1012690211434230

Webster, S. P. (2009). It is a girl thing: Uncovering the stylistic performance of female athleticism. In B. Brummett (Ed.), *Sporting rhetoric: Performance, games, & politics* (pp. 48–64). New York: Peter Lang.

Weir, T. (2010, March 5). Halftime: Baseball has never been fatter. *USA Today.* Retrieved from http://content.usatoday.com/communities/gameon/post/2010/03/halftime-baseball-has-never-been-fatter/1#.U90nj_ldXng

Wenner, L. A. (1989). Media, sports, and society: The research agenda. In L. A. Wenner (Ed.), *Media, sports, and society* (pp. 13–48). Newbury Park: Sage.

Wenner, L. A., & Jackson, S. A. (2009). *Sport, beer, and gender: Promotional cultural and contemporary social life.* New York: Peter Lang.

Wetzel, D. (2013, September 11). Latest college scandals again reveal folly of NCAA rules. *Yahoo! Sports.* Retrieved from http://sports.yahoo.com/news/ncaaf–latest-college-scandals-again-reveal-folly-of-ncaa-rules-210822795.html

Whannel, G. (2002). *Media sport stars: Masculinities and moralities.* London: Routledge.

What you pay for sports. (n.d.). Retrieved from http://www.whatyoupayforsports.com/numbers/

Whiteside, E. (2013). Let them wear towels, an ESPN Nine for IX film. *International Journal of Sport Communication, 6,* 492–493.

Whiteside, E., & Hardin, M. (2011). Women (not) watching women: Leisure time, television, and implications for televised coverage of women's sports. *Communication, Culture & Critique, 4*(2), 122–143. doi:10.1111/j.1753–9137.2011.01098.x

Whitson, D. (1998). Circuits of promotion: Media, marketing, and the globalization of sport. In L. A. Wenner (Ed.), *MediaSport* (pp. 57–72). London: Routledge.

Why does Hilton stay with ESPN? (1981, January 5). *Broadcasting, 100*(1), 79.

Wiggins, D. K. (1988). "The future of college athletics is at stake": Black athletes and racial turmoil on three predominantly White university campuses 1968–1972. *Journal of Sport History, 15*(3), 304–333.

Wiggins, D. K. (1992). "The year of awakening": Black athletes, racial unrest and the Civil Rights Movement of 1968. *The International Journal of the History of Sport, 9*(2), 188–208. doi:10.1080/09523369208713790

Wilbert, C. (2003, November 12). Spanish connection: Hispanic audience catches attention of cable networks. *Atlanta Journal-Constitution,* p. 1F.

Wilkerson, D. B. (2012). Yes deal implies ESPN is worth $66 billion: Analyst. *MarketWatch.* Retrieved from http://www.marketwatch.com/story/yes-deal-implies-espn-is-worth-66b-analyst-2012-11-20

Williams, L. S. (2008). The mission statement: A corporate reporting tool with a past, present and future. *Journal of Business Communication, 45*(2), 94–119. doi:10.1177/0021943607313989

Williams, R. (1974/2003). *Television, Routledge classics edition.* New York: Routledge.

Williamson, J. (1967). *Decoding advertisements: Ideology and meaning in advertising.* New York: Marion Boyers.

Winslow, G. (2008, October 17). More choices for Hispanic viewers. *Broadcasting & Cable, 138*(41). Retrieved from http://www.broadcastingcable.com/news/news-articles/more-choice-hispanic-viewers/85303

Winslow, G. (2013, September 30). Hispanic content is going everywhere. *Broadcasting & Cable*. Retrieved from http://www.broadcastingcable.com/news/news-articles/hispanic-content-going-everywhere/127589

Winslow, G. (2014, May 26). ESPN's new build has eye on tomorrow. *Broadcasting & Cable*, 34. Retrieved from http://www.broadcastingcable.com/news/technology/espn-s-new-build-has-eye-tomorrow/131381

Wolff, A. (1995, June 12). Broken beyond repair. *Sports Illustrated*, p. 22.

Wolter, S. (2013, October 24). A quantitative analysis of photographs and articles on *espnW*: Positive progress for female athletes. *Communication & Sport*. doi:10.1177/2167479513509368

Wood, C., & Benigni, V. (2006). The coverage of sports on cable TV. In A. A. Raney & J. Bryant (Eds.), *Handbook of sports and media* (pp. 157–182). Mahwah, NJ: Lawrence Erlbaum.

Wright, J. (2012, April 27). Title IX is mine: Jay Wright [Video file]. Retrieved from http://espn.go.com/video/clip?id=7863262

Yamaha, M. (2010, February 4). Billy Mills 1964 10,000 meters Olympic gold medal race. Retrieved from http://www.youtube.com/watch?v=VVlKVWFmfhk

Yancy, G. (2005). Whiteness and the return of the black body. *Journal of Speculative Philosophy, 19*(4), 215–241. doi:10.1353/jsp. 2006.0008

Year in sports media report: 2013. (2014, February 4). *Nielsen*. Retrieved from http://www.nielsen.com/us/en/reports/2014/year-in-the-sports-media-report-2013.html

Yin, J., & Miike, Y. (2008). A textual analysis of fortune cookie sayings: How Chinese are they? *The Howard Journal of Communications, 19*, 18–43. doi:10.1080/10646170701801987

Yoder, M. (2012, November 15). ESPN's journalistic integrity coming under close examination. *Awful Announcing*. Retrieved from http://www.awfulannouncing.com/2012-articles/november/espn-s-journalistic-integrity-coming-under-close-examination.html

Yoder, M. (2013, September 13). *Sports Illustrated*'s Oklahoma State investigation is falling apart. *Awful Announcing*. Retrieved from http://www.awfulannouncing.com/2013/september/sports-illustrated-s-oklahoma-state-investigation-is-falling-apart.html

Young, R. (2010). LeBron: "Decision" backlash had "a race factor." *CBSNews.com*. Retrieved from http://www.cbsnews.com/news/lebron-decision-backlash-had-a-race-factor/

Yu, C. C. (2009). A content analysis of news coverage of Asian female Olympic athletes. *International Review for the Sociology of Sport, 44*(2–3), 283–305. doi:10.1177/1012690209104796

Yuginovich, T. (2000). More than time and place: Using historical comparative research as a tool for nursing. *International Journal of Nursing Practice, 6*, 70–75. doi:10.1046/j.1440–172X.2000.00183.x

Zelizer, B. (1992). *Covering the body: The Kennedy assassination, the media, and the shaping of collective memory*. Chicago: University of Chicago Press.

Zelizer, B. (1993). Journalists as interpretive communities. *Critical Studies in Mass Communication, 10*(3), 219–237. doi:10.1080/15295039309366865

Zelizer, B. (2007). On "Having Been There": "Eyewitnessing" as a journalistic key word. *Critical Studies in Media Communication, 24*(5), 408–428. doi:10.1080/07393180701694614

Zhongdang P., & Kosicki, G. M. (1993). Framing analysis: An approach to news discourse. *Political Communication, 10*(1), 55–75. doi:10.1080/10584609.1993.9962963

# About the Editors

**John McGuire** (Ph.D., University of Missouri) is Associate Professor in the School of Media & Strategic Communications at Oklahoma State University. Dr. McGuire has focused his research efforts in the area of sports media, examining professional practices of multimedia sports journalists, image repair of sports figures, sports play-by-play narratives, and sports media network practices. Dr. McGuire's work has been published in *Journal of Sports Media, Communication and Sport, International Journal of Sport Communication,* and the *Journal of Radio and Audio Media.* Dr. McGuire has coauthored chapters in three other edited volumes and was a coauthor of *Campaign 2000: A Functional Analysis of Presidential Campaign Discourse.* In addition to his publishing work, Dr. McGuire is a regular contributor of audio features for Oklahoma Public Radio. Dr. McGuire's work has been honored by Region 6 of the Radio Television Digital News Association and the Oklahoma chapter of the Society of Professional Journalists.

**Greg G. Armfield** (Ph.D., University of Missouri–Columbia, 2004) is Associate Professor in the Department of Communication Studies at New Mexico State University. His research interest explores the role of identity in organizational culture, religion, sports, and fantasy sports. Dr. Armfield has authored or coauthored more than a dozen refereed journal articles and book chapters, which can be found in the *Journal of Communication*, the *Journal of Media and Religion, Speaker and Gavel,* and the *Journal of Communication and Religion.* Dr. Armfield has coedited three volumes of *Human Communication in Action* (Kendall Hunt) with Dr. Eric Morgan. Previously he has served as chair of the division of Communication Studies for the Religious Communication Association and the Applied Communication Division of Southern States Communication Association. Dr. Armfield is a member of the editorial board for the *International Journal of Business Communication* and has reviewed for *Communication Yearbook,* the *Journal of Media and Religion,* the *Journal of Communication and Religion, International Journal of Sport Communication,* and *Communication and Sport.*

**Adam C. Earnheardt** (Ph.D., Kent State University, 2007) is Chair and Associate Professor of Communication Studies in the Department of Communication at Youngstown State University. His research focuses on the intersection of sports fandom and social media, and more recently on the prosocial uses of social media. Dr. Earnheardt has coedited several books on sports fandom including *Sports Fans, Identity, and Socialization: Exploring the Fandemonium* (2012) and *Sports Mania: Essays on Fandom and the Media in the 21st Century* (2008). He authored *Judging Athlete Behaviors: Exploring Possible Predictors of Television Viewer Judgments of Athlete Antisocial Behaviors* (2008) and co-authored *The Modern Communicator: Applications and Strategies for Interpersonal Communication, Group Communication and Public Speaking* (2009). Dr. Earnheardt has served as an expert source on sports fandom in several publications including *Parade Magazine, Psychology Today,* and *Playboy.* He is the former executive director of the Ohio Communication Association and past chair of the National Communication Association's Mass Communication Division. Dr. Earnheardt currently serves as treasurer of the International Association of Communication and Sport.

# About the Contributors

**Gashaw Z. Abeza** is a lecturer and doctoral candidate at the University of Ottawa. His research interest is in sport marketing communication, with specific areas of expertise in social media, relationship marketing, branding, sponsorship, ambush marketing, online broadcast media, and research methods in sport. Gashaw is a member of the Research Centre for Sport in Canadian Society.

**Andrew C. Billings** is Full Professor and Ronald Reagan Chair of Broadcasting at the University of Alabama, also serving as the inaugural director of the Alabama Program in Sports Communication and chair of the Sports Interest Group for the International Communication Association. His research interests lie in the intersection of sport, mass media, consumption habits, and identity-laden content. He is the author and/or editor of nine books, including *Olympic Media: Inside the Biggest Show on Television* (Routledge, 2008), and his writings have been translated into five languages. Additionally, he is also the author of more than 100 refereed journal articles and book chapters in outlets such as *Journal of Communication*, *Journalism & Mass Communication Quarterly*, *Communication & Sport*, *Mass Communication & Society*, and *Journal of Broadcasting & Electronic Media*.

**Kevin B. Blackistone** is a visiting professor at the University of Maryland's Shirley Povich Center for Sports Journalism, an ESPN panelist, and a frequent National Public Radio guest. He was a national sports columnist for AOL from 2007 to 2011 and an award-winning sports columnist for the *Dallas Morning News* from 1990 to 2006. He has covered the Olympics, Wimbledon, World Cup, Tour de France, British Open, pro and college basketball and football championships, Major League Baseball playoffs, championship boxing, Triple Crown races, and other events. His writing interests are at the intersection of sports, society, and race, as indicated by his first journal article, "The Whitening of Sports Media and the Coloring of Black Athletes' Images," published in the *Wake Forest Journal of Law & Policy* in 2012. He also is coauthor of *A Gift for Ron*, retired NFL star Everson Walls's memoir of his kidney donation to teammate Ron Springs, published in 2009.

**Garret Castleberry** (M.A., University of North Texas) is the Director of Forensics and a doctoral candidate for the Department of Communication at the University of Oklahoma. His ongoing research and publications investigate polyvalent critical/cultural themes as well as socioeconomic and mythic narratives embedded within contemporary media texts and popular culture, often with strategic emphasis toward what television studies scholars consider the post-Network televisual landscape. With a diverse background in critical methodologies, Garret's recent publications emphasize combinations of ideological criticism, genre studies, and hierarchies in fandom. Garret runs (privately) and watches ESPN (publicly) but hopes to reverse the social dimension of these two dichotomous hobbies soon.

**Thomas F. Corrigan** is Assistant Professor in the Department of Communication Studies at California State University, San Bernardino. His research examines the intersections of political economy, digital media, and sports media. His peer-reviewed work has been published in *The Political Economy of Communication*, *Journalism: Theory, Practice, & Criticism*, *Cultural Studies <=> Critical Methodologies*, *International Journal of Sport Communication*, and *Journal of Sports Media*.

**George L. Daniels** is the Assistant Dean for Administration in the College of Communication and Information Sciences at The University of Alabama in Tuscaloosa. He serves as the College's diversity officer and handles all matters related to accreditation, awards, and assessment. As an associate professor of journalism, he teaches multimedia reporting classes and media management and applied research methods. His research focuses on issues of new technologies in the newsroom and newsgathering process and diversity in the media workplace. One of the original members of the Alabama Program in Sports Communication, which was created in 2012, Dr. Daniels is a nationally certified master journalism educator as awarded by the Journalism Education Association. Before becoming a full-time faculty member at The University of Alabama, Dr. Daniels worked for eight years as a news producer at television stations in his hometown of Richmond, Virginia, Cincinnati, Ohio, and Atlanta, Georgia. A cum laude graduate of Howard University, Daniels received both his M.A. in journalism/mass communication and his Ph.D. in mass communication from the Grady College of Journalism and Mass Communication at The University of Georgia.

**John A. Fortunato**, Ph.D., is Professor at Fordham University in the Gabelli School of Business, Area of Communication and Media Management. He is also the author of four books, including *Commissioner: The Legacy of Pete Rozelle* and *Sports Sponsorship: Principles and Practices*. He has published articles in *Public Relations Review*, *Journal of Sport Management*, *International Journal of Sport Communication*, *Journal of Sports Media*, *Journal of Brand Strategy*, and multiple law reviews. He serves on the editorial board of four peer-reviewed academic journals, including *International Journal of Sport Communication* and the *Journal of Sports Media*. Dr. Fortunato previously taught at the University of Texas at Austin in the Department of Advertising and Public Relations and he received his Ph.D. from Rutgers University in the School of Communication, Information, and Library Science.

**Jeffery Gentry** (Ph.D., University of Oklahoma) is Professor and Head of the Department of Communications at Rogers State University, Oklahoma. He is a Denver native and die-hard Broncos fan who attended the private launch party introducing ESPN to the state of Montana in 1981. He is also a long-distance runner and three-time qualifier for the Boston Marathon, including the 2015 edition. Gentry studies political rhetoric and has authored two top papers in political communication for the Central States Communication Association. He recently completed a sabbatical leave to New Zealand, where he studied the rhetoric of parliament via quantitative content analysis. He is also trained in rhetorical criticism, survey research, and ethnography. A full-time college faculty member since 1988, he recently published an article over the controversy of human overpopulation for ABC-CLIO/Greenwood Press. Outside of academia, he has also been an athletics contributor to *Oklahoma Runner* magazine and the *San Diego Union-Tribune*.

**Robin Hardin** holds a Ph.D. in communication from the University of Tennessee and is Professor in the Sport Management program at the University of Tennessee. His research interests lie with sport communication and intercollegiate athletics especially in areas of consumer behavior and social media. He has more than 50 refereed publications in the profession's top journals including the *Journal of Applied Sport Management, Journal of Sports Media, International Journal of Sport Management, Journal of Contemporary Athletics, International Journal of Sport Communication, Journal of Intercollegiate Sport, Sport Management Education Journal, Sport Marketing Quarterly*, and *American Journalism*. He also has made more than 100 scholarly presentations. He is also a member of the official statistics crew for Tennessee football, men's basketball, and women's basketball.

**Karen L. Hartman** is Assistant Professor at Idaho State University in Pocatello. She completed her undergraduate work at Furman University in Greenville, South Carolina, where she earned a B.A. in Communication Studies. Her graduate work was done at the University of South Carolina (M.A. in speech communication) and at LSU (Ph.D. in Rhetoric). Karen's research interests include sport, rhetorical criticism, myth, morality, apologia, heroes, and race. She has taught courses such as Introduction to Sport Communication, Sport Public Relations, the Rhetoric of Sport, and Sport Reporting. Her research has been published in the *Journal of Communication Studies, Academic Exchange Quarterly*, and the edited volume *Popular Culture and Mythology*.

**Samuel M. Jay** (Ph.D., University of Denver, 2014) teaches Rhetoric in the Department of Communication Arts and Sciences at Metropolitan State University of Denver. He also works in the sports media and public relations industries. His research interests include the rhetorics of economics, politics, and sports, and their relation to digital media and affect/emotion. In his work he has placed the scholarly concepts of affective rhetoric and digital media into conversation to form a research project focused on evaluating digital technologies/practices through lenses of governmentality, agency, and mediated, emotion-laden communication.

**Edward (Ted) M. Kian** is the Endowed Welch-Bridgewater Chair of Sports Media in the School of Media and Strategic Communications at Oklahoma State University. A former professional sport journalist, Dr. Kian's research focuses primarily on sport communication, specifically examining areas such as portrayals of gender in media content, new media, attitudes and experiences of sport journalists, and marketing of sport to LGBT consumers. He has authored more than 60 journal articles, conference papers, and invited book chapters. Media outlets such as *60 Minutes* and Fox Sports have cited Dr. Kian's research and journalism expertise.

**Scott Lambert** (Ph.D., Southern Illinois Carbondale, 2013) works as Assistant Professor of English/Journalism at Millikin University in Illinois. Lambert spent 13 years as a sports editor in Illinois and has taught journalism at Oklahoma State University, Southern Illinois University, and Millikin University. His research interests focus on media ethics and sports journalism. Lambert has two chapters pending for a Sage project on Media Ethics and Law and a chapter in the upcoming book *A Press Divided: Newspaper Coverage of the Civil War*. Lambert is married and lives in Decatur, Illinois.

**Katherine (Kate) L. Lavelle** (Ph.D., Wayne State University, 2006) is Assistant Professor of Communication Studies at the University of Wisconsin–La Crosse in the Advocacy and Communication Criticism emphasis area. Her research focuses on issues of representation in sports rhetoric, specifically in the areas of race/ethnicity, national identity, and sex/gender. Her sport communication research has appeared in the journals *Howard Journal of Communication, International Journal of Communication and Sport*, as well as the anthologies *Sports Fans, Identity and Socialization; Fallen Sports Heroes, Media, & Celebrity Culture*; and *The Rhetoric of American Exceptionalism*. She is an active member of the International Association of Communication and Sport, where she has served on the board of directors since 2012. Despite living in Wisconsin, she remains loyal to the Cleveland professional sports teams.

**Jason W. Lee,** Ph.D., is Associate Professor and Coordinator of Sport Management at the University of North Florida. Dr. Lee has been published in a wide variety of academic journals including *Sport Marketing Quarterly, Journal of Issues in Intercollegiate Athletics (JIIA), International Journal of Entrepreneurial Venturing, Journal of Sport Management, International Journal of Sport Communication,* and *Journal of Hospitality, Leisure, Sport, and Tourism Education (JoHLSTE)*. Additionally, he has edited two textbooks: *Sport and Criminal Behavior* and *Branded: Branding in Sport Business* (a second edition of this work is nearing completion). Dr. Lee maintains an active research agenda in the areas of sport brand management and visual identity and has written and presented prolifically in this areas, while also serving as an academic and professional resource for various sport and media organizations.

**Michael L. Naraine** is currently attending the University of Ottawa and is a Ph.D. student in the Research Centre for Sport in Canadian Society, under the supervision of Dr. Milena M. Parent. His research interests are concentrated in the areas of strategic management and sport communication, specifically related to new media, networks and systems, stakeholder engagement, and innovation.

**Henry Puente** is Associate Professor of Communications at California State University, Fullerton. His research area currently centers on the marketing and distribution of U.S. Latino/a films and U.S. Latino/a media. Author of *The Promotion and Distribution of U.S. Latino Films*, Henry has extensive entertainment industry experience and is a former film distribution executive.

**Brody J. Ruihley** holds a Ph.D. in sport studies from the University of Tennessee and is an assistant professor in the Sport Administration program at the University of Cincinnati. His research interests primarily lie in fantasy sport motivation, consumption, and other issues related to the activity. A leading researcher of fantasy sport, Ruihley is coauthor of *The Fantasy Sport Industry: Games Within Games* (Routledge, 2014) and has published and presented several research studies on fantasy sport topics including motivation, gender and age differences, media consumption, and message board use.

**Daniel Sipocz** (Ph.D., Southern Mississippi, 2014) started his career in sports reporting and is currently Lecturer of Communication at Indiana State University. He holds two master's degrees from Ball State University in journalism and public relations and a bachelor's in new media journalism from Valparaiso University. Daniel primarily covered female sports for six years as a reporter, which sparked an interest in exploring the ways women and minorities are portrayed to the public by the media. As a qualitative researcher, he continues to investigate issues related to sports media and society. His work regarding the representation of race and minorities in the media has been presented at AEJMC, its regional academic conferences, as well as NCA regional conferences.

**Lauren Reichart Smith** (Ph.D., University of Alabama) is Assistant Professor and the Associate Director of Public Relations at Auburn University. Her main research area lies in the intersection between sports and media, specifically mass media and social media. She currently serves as the Vice Chair for the International Association for Communication and Sport. Lauren's work has been presented at and won top paper awards at SSCA, BEA, IACS, and AEJMC. Her research has been published in *Journalism and Mass Communication Quarterly, Howard Journal of Communication, Communication Research Reports, Electronic News, Journal of Sports Media, International Journal of Sport Communication,* and *Communication & Sport.* Lauren is also a registered member of USA Triathlon and regularly competes in duathlons and triathlons.

**David Staton** is a freelance writer, multimedia producer, and Ph.D. student at the University of Oregon's School of Journalism and Communication. He has an

M.A. in art history from State University of New York Purchase College and a B.A. in journalism from the University of New Mexico. For many years, he was a working journalist for daily newspapers and, later, regional and national magazines. He also worked in the visual arts arena, serving as the director and owner of his own fine art gallery and as the director of a small regional museum. His research area interests include how visual communications inform identity construction, the production of culture, and the digital mediation of cultural and recreational experience.

**Andi Stein** is a professor and graduate program coordinator in the Department of Communications at California State University, Fullerton, where she teaches classes in public relations, journalism, and entertainment studies. She is the author of *Why We Love Disney: The Power of the Disney Brand* (Peter Lang, 2011), and coauthor of *An Introduction to the Entertainment Industry* (Peter Lang, 2009) and *News Writing in a Multimedia World* (Kendall Hunt, 2003). Her article, "When Baseball Players Wore Skirts: The Promotion of the All-American Girls Professional Baseball League," was published in the *Cooperstown Symposium on Baseball and American Culture* (McFarland, 2002). Prior to entering academia, Stein was a journalist and public relations practitioner in the San Francisco Bay Area. She has a B.A. from George Washington University, M.A. from the University of North Carolina at Chapel Hill, and Ph.D. from the University of Oregon.

**Kristi Sweeney,** Ph.D. is Assistant Professor of Sport Management at the University of North Florida (UNF), where she also serves as the chair of the UNF Intercollegiate Athletics Committee and as a member of the University's Title IX Committee. Dr. Sweeney teaches both graduate and undergraduate courses in sport management. Her areas of expertise are sport finance, marketing, gender equity, Title IX, and work life balance in sport. She publishes in the area of sport management and sport marketing.

**Sarah Wolter** is Visiting Assistant Professor at Gustavus Adolphus College in St. Peter, Minnesota. Wolter earned an M.A. in Speech Communication from Minnesota State University, Mankato and a Ph.D. in Critical Media Studies from the University of Minnesota, Twin Cities. Wolter's research interests center on media representations of female athletes and the social, economic, and politically significant aspects of sport. Wolter has published in journals such as *Communication & Sport, Journal of Issues in Intercollegiate Athletics,* the *International Journal of Sport Communication,* and the *Journal of Community Engagement in Higher Education.*

# Index